STRATEGIES OF REMEMBERING IN GREECE UNDER ROME
(100 BC - 100 AD)

Sidestone Press

STRATEGIES OF REMEMBERING IN GREECE UNDER ROME
(100 BC - 100 AD)

EDITED BY
TAMARA M. DIJKSTRA, INGER N.I. KUIN,
MURIEL MOSER & DAVID WEIDGENANNT

PUBLICATIONS OF THE
NETHERLANDS INSTITUTE AT ATHENS VI

© 2017 The individual authors

Published by Sidestone Press, Leiden
www.sidestone.com

Publications of the Netherlands Institute at Athens VI

Co-financed by the SFB 1095 "Discources of Weakness and Resource Regimes" of the Deutsche Forschungsgesellschaft

Imprint: Sidestone Press

Lay-out & cover design: Sidestone Press
Photograph cover: Akropolis, photo: byrefresh(PIX) (stock.adobe.com)

ISBN 978-90-8890-480-6 (softcover)
ISBN 978-90-8890-481-3 (hardcover)
ISBN 978-90-8890-482-0 (PDF e-book)

Contents

Contents	5
About the editors	7
List of contributors	9
Preface: Relaunching the Publications of the Netherlands Institute at Athens Series	11

Introduction   13
*Tamara M. Dijkstra, Inger N.I. Kuin,
Muriel Moser, and David Weidgenannt*

Part I: Building Remembrance

Roman Greece and the 'Mnemonic Turn'. Some Critical Remarks   21
*Dimitris Grigoropoulos, Valentina Di Napoli, Vasilis Evangelidis,
Francesco Camia, Dylan Rogers and Stavros Vlizos*

**Strategies of Remembering in the Creation of a Colonial
Society in Patras**   37
Tamara M. Dijkstra

Contending with the Past in Roman Corinth: The Julian Basilica   49
Catherine de Grazia Vanderpool and Paul D. Scotton

Part II: Competing with the Past

Heritage Societies? Private Associations in Roman Greece   71
Benedikt Eckhardt

**Performing the Past: Salamis, Naval Contests and the
Athenian *Ephebeia***   83
Zahra Newby

**Greek Panhellenic *Agones* in a Roman Colony: Corinth and
the Return of the Isthmian Games**   **97**
    Lavinia del Basso

Part III: Honoring Tradition

**Heroes of Their Times. Intra-Mural Burials in the Urban Memorial
Landscapes of the Roman Peloponnese**   **111**
    Johannes Fouquet

**Public Statues as a Strategy of Remembering in Early Imperial
Messene**   **125**
    Christopher Dickenson

**Shortages, Remembering and the Construction of Time: Aspects
of Greek Honorific Culture (2nd century BC – 1st century AD)**   **143**
    David Weidgenannt

Part IV: History in Athens

Anchoring Political Change in Post-Sullan Athens   **157**
    Inger N.I. Kuin

**Reused Statues for Roman Friends: The Past as a Political Resource
in Roman Athens**   **169**
    Muriel Moser

**Strategies of Remembering in Greece under Rome:
Some Conclusions**   **183**
    Inger N.I. Kuin and Muriel Moser

Index   **187**

About the editors

David Weidgenannt MA

David Weidgenannt works under the supervision of Prof. Dr. Fleur Kemmers at the Goethe University Frankfurt in the project 'KOINON: Common currencies and shared identities. Understanding the structures and daily realities of Greek federal states through an analysis of coin production and coin circulation in the Aetolian and Peloponnesian Koina (5th-1st c. BC)'. He is interested in epigraphy and numismatics. Previously he worked on continuity and change in Roman Epidauros within the project (A 02) 'Vergangenheit als politische Ressource: Erinnern als Strategie im römischen Griechenland' directed by Dr. Muriel Moser as part of DFG-funded SFB 1095 'Discources of Weakness and Resource Regimes'.

Dr. Muriel Moser

Muriel Moser received a PhD from the University of Cambridge. She is a member of the Department of Ancient History at the Goethe University Frankfurt and director of a research project on Roman Greece (A 02) within the interdisciplinary collaborative research group SFB 1095, Discources of Weakness and Resource Regimes, funded by the DFG in Frankfurt. Moser has published on imperial relations to the senators in Rome and Constantinople, as well as on senatorial property and on harbours in the late Roman East. She currently works on social memories in Roman Greece.

Dr. Inger N.I. Kuin

Inger N.I. Kuin received a PhD from New York University. She currently works at Groningen University in the Ancient History Department, studying memory, political change, and crisis recovery in the Roman East during the first century BC for the After the Crisis research project, which is part of the OIKOS Anchoring Innovation research agenda. Kuin has published on religion and humor in antiquity, on race and ethnicity in Lucian of Samosata, on Latin epigraphy, and on Roman Athens.

Tamara M. Dijkstra MA

Tamara M. Dijkstra is in the final stages of her PhD-project at the department of Greek Archaeology of the University of Groningen. She studies social structure and identities in Achaea in the Hellenistic and Roman period, by analysing continuity and change in practices of death, burial, and commemoration. In addition to her PhD-project, she works as an archaeologist in the Halos Archaeological Project in Thessaly.

List of contributors

Lavinia del Basso
Università Ca' Foscari, Venice, Italy, laviniadelbasso@hotmail.it

Francesco Camia
Sapienza University of Rome, Piazzale Aldo Moro 5, 00185 Rome, Italy, francesco.camia@uniroma1.it

Christopher Dickenson
Aarhus University, School of Culture and Society, Centre for Urban Network Evolutions, Jens Chr. Skous Vej 7, 4th floor, 8000, Aarhus, Denmark, christopher.dickenson@cas.au.dk

Tamara M. Dijkstra
Groningen Institute of Archaeology, University of Groningen, Poststraat 6, 9712 ER Groningen, The Netherlands, t.m.dijkstra@rug.nl

Benedikt Eckhardt
Universität Bremen, Institut für Geschichtswissenschaft/FB 08, Postfach 330 440, 28334 Bremen, Germany, benedikt.eckhardt@uni-bremen.de

Vasilis Evangelidis
Hellenic Ministry of Education, Scientific Associate, Athena Research Center, Xanthi Branch, University Campus South Entrance, Kimmeria, P.O Box 159, GR-67100, Greece, v_evangelidis@hotmail.com

Johannes Fouquet
Institute of Classical Archaeology, University of Heidelberg, Marstallhof 4 69117 Heidelberg, Germany, j.fouquet@uni-heidelberg.de

Catherine de Grazia Vanderpool
American School of Classical Studies at Athens, Greece, ced57@caa.columbia.edu

Dimitris Grigoropoulos
Humboldt-Universität zu Berlin, Lehrbereich Klassische Archäologie, Unter den Linden 6, D-10099, Berlin, Germany, dimitris.grigoropoulos@hu-berlin.de

Inger N.I. Kuin
University of Groningen, History Department, Oude Kijk in 't Jatstraat 26, 9712 EK Groningen, The Netherlands, n.i.kuin@rug.nl

Muriel Moser
Goethe Universität Frankfurt, Historisches Seminar, Abteilung für Alte Geschichte, Norbert-Wollheim-Platz 1, 60629 Frankfurt, Germany, m.moser@em.uni-frankfurt.de

Valentina Di Napoli
Swiss School of Archaeology in Greece, Skaramanga 4B, 10433 Athens, Greece, and University of Patras, Department of Theatre Studies, 26500 Patras, Greece, DiNapoli.Valentina@unil.ch, dinapoli@upatras.gr

Zahra Newby
University of Warwick, Coventry, CV4 7AL, UK, z.l.newby@warwick.ac.uk

Dylan Rogers
American School of Classical Studies at Athens, Souidias 54, 106-76 Athens, Greece, dylan.rogers@ascsa.edu.gr

Paul D. Scotton
California State University, Long Beach; Research Associate, Cotsen Institute of Archaeology at UCLA, USA, Paul.Scotton@csulb.edu

Stavros Vlizos
Ionian University, Ioannou Theotoki 72, GR-49100 Corfu, Greece, vlizosst@ionio.gr

David Weidgenannt
Goethe-Universität Frankfurt am Main, Institut für Archäologische Wissenschaften, Archäologie von Münze, Geld und von Wirtschaft in der Antike, Goethe-Universität, Norbert-Wollheim-Platz 1, Fach 27, 60629 Frankfurt am Main, Germany, weidgenannt@em.uni-frankfurt.de

Preface: Relaunching the Publications of the Netherlands Institute at Athens Series

The present volume, *Strategies of Remembering in Greece under Rome*, is the result of a conference organized by Tamara Dijkstra, Inger Kuin, Muriel Moser, and David Weidgenannt. The conference was the first in a new series of conferences at the Netherlands Institute at Athens, the 'early career scholar conferences', where we give scholars at the beginning of their academic careers the opportunity to organise a conference and publish the results. I am proud to have hosted this well-organized and interesting conference, and equally happy to present this collection of papers as the starting point of the re-launch of the *Publications of the Netherlands Institute at Athens*. The aim of this series is to publish the outcomes of research taking place at the NIA, such as archaeological field-work, conferences and individual research, for all fields of scholarship concerning Greece. We wanted to make the renewed series open access, not only because this is a requirement of many funding bodies, but also because we are convinced that scholarly labour is not done for profit and all should be able to benefit from its results. To achieve this aim, we welcome the collaboration with Sidestone Press, who are at the forefront of academic open access publishing. We would like to thank Karsten Wentink and Corné van Woerdekom at Sidestone Press for being such helpful partners in bringing this publication to fruition. We thank the Deutsche Forschungsgemeinschaft for their generous contribution to the funding of this publication through SFB 1095, 'Discourses of Weakness and Resource Regimes'.

Winfred van de Put
director of the Netherlands Institute at Athens

Introduction

Tamara M. Dijkstra, Inger N.I. Kuin,
Muriel Moser, and David Weidgenannt

Already since 146 BC Achaea was under the rule of the Roman governor of Macedonia. The numerous defections of Greek cities during the 1st century BC, however, show that Roman rule was not yet viewed as inevitable at the time. Indeed, at the beginning of the 1st century BC many cities of the Greek mainland were independent, like Athens bound to Rome through some kind of friendship alliance at most. Yet by the end of the 1st century AD, following several decades of war against Rome or amongst Romans on Greek soil, these cities, including Athens, had been incorporated into the Roman province of Achaea. As Athenian independence perished, so did the notion of Greek self-rule. But while the fate of Athens was indeed of great symbolic importance, the large scale changes of the period affected Greek cities and regions in different ways, depending on local circumstances. The experience of Rome's increasing influence in the area we now call 'Roman Greece' was shared but not uniform.

Both ancient and modern narratives of Roman Greece have characterised this period, the 1st century BC and the 1st century AD, as one of economic, political or cultural decline, of crisis or, more generally, weakness.[1] Over the past few decades scholars have started to question this view, pointing to the cultural vitality and the persistence of traditional forms of power and networks of influence that can be observed in the literary, epigraphic and archaeological records.[2] The present volume pursues a similarly revisionist approach. It seeks to show that even though the cities of ancient Greece underwent major political and cultural transformations during this time, it was also a period of great dynamism, innovation, and adaptation. More precisely, the eleven articles assembled in this volume are interested in the ways in which the communities of Roman Greece mobilized their past as a political resource to respond to change. We seek to establish how communities and individuals of Roman Greece used their cultural and historical legacy to engage actively with the increasing presence of Roman rule and its representatives.

Key to our approach is the notion that the Greek past constituted a political resource during the transitionary period that we have chosen to investigate. In this volume we understand 'political' in a broad sense as referring to any form or mode of negotiating one's position in the local community and in the larger context of the Roman Empire. While the focus of the discussion will be on the period between 100 BC and 100 AD, some articles also look at material from earlier or later periods for the sake of comparison or to provide context. During the Roman era Attica and the Peloponnese continued

---

1   E.g. Graindor 1927; Day 1942; Touloumakos 1967; Deininger 1971, esp. 242-261; Bernhardt 1985, 39-49; Hoff 1989, 1997; Spawforth 2012.

2   E.g. Rizakis, Kantirea & Zoumbaki 2001; Zoumbaki 2001; Rizakis, Lepenioti & Zoumbaki 2004; Dally 2008; Stefanidou-Tiveriou 2008; Rizakis & Lepenioti 2010; Dickenson 2016, 2017.

in: Dijkstra, T.M., I.N.I. Kuin, M. Moser & D. Weidgenannt (eds) 2017. *Strategies of Remembering in Greece under Rome (100 BC - 100 AD)*, Leiden (Sidestone Press).

to be special regions because of their legacy as cultural and religious centres of the Mediterranean, thanks also to Roman fascination with Greek history and culture. The epigraphic, literary, numismatic, and archaeological sources furnish numerous examples of how the past was mobilized in order to fashion new individual or local identities, to attract Roman interest and support, or to anchor change. Acts of remembering provided arguments of legitimacy, for instance, in the context of elite competition or during the creation of new associations; they thus functioned both as models for future action and as connections to the past. The legacy of the Greek past defined Greek *and* Roman responses to the changing mutual relationship, even if these responses varied widely. Sulla fashioned himself after the tyrant-slayers Harmodius and Aristogeiton (Kuin *this volume*), while Athenian ephebes evoked the sea-battles of the Persian Wars to fashion their valour (Newby *this volume*). The variety of these strategies attests to the vitality of the region. In times of transition the past cannot be ignored: actors use what came before, in diverse and complex ways, in order to build the present.

The conference on which this volume is based stems from a triple line of inquiry, represented by three research initiatives in which the editors participate. Anchoring Innovation is a research agenda initiated by OIKOS, the national research school for Classical Studies in the Netherlands. The concept of 'anchoring' serves as a metaphor and a heuristic tool for the many different ways in which people connect the new to whatever is already familiar: the old, the known, or the traditional. What is called or considered 'old' or 'new' is not always a matter of objective diagnosis: it is a judgment established through discourse and negotiation (Sluiter 2017). Because the period we have chosen forced significant changes on the affected individuals and societies, the concepts of re-anchoring and anchoring are well suited to promote a better understanding of strategies of remembering in ancient Greece. Secondly, the project 'The past as a political resource: Remembering as a political strategy in Greece under Rome', which is part the SFB 1095 'Discourses of Weakness and Resource Regimes', seeks to scrutinize the manner in which Greek communities in Roman Greece mobilized their past as a political resource under Roman rule, within their own communities and in relation with Rome. Against the discourses of Greek weakness, it seeks to highlight the central role of Greek communities in the use of the past in Roman Greece, and to examine the actors and audiences involved in the acts of remembering as well as the political strategies that were pursued in the process. Finally, the research project 'Civic and Cultural Identity in a Changing World, Analysing the Mortuary Practices of the Post-Classical Peloponnese', funded by the Netherlands Organization for Scientific Research, seeks to understand how the identity of local communities was affected by their incorporation in the Hellenistic kingdoms and the Roman Empire, by exploring tradition and innovation in the way people dealt with their dead. Although this volume originated from these approaches, the following articles, with the exception of the contributions of the editors, have been written independently from the projects; the concepts of anchoring as well as of discourses of weakness and resource regimes, respectively, are presented here merely as possible analytical tools among many other viable options for studying the developments of Roman Greece during the 1st century BC and the 1st century AD.

As is clear from the title of this volume the editors and other contributors are greatly indebted to previous research done using the theoretical frameworks of cultural or communal memory, sometimes subsumed under the moniker 'mnemonic turn'.[3] Nonetheless, we also seek to cast our net wider by looking at uses of the past broadly and by drawing on a variety of theoretical frameworks, yet with a focus on how agents mobilized the past for the specific aim of coping with the present. By bringing together different kinds of methodologies we hope to offer a new and inclusive approach to the evidence, and thereby disclose new insights into the use of the past in Roman Greece. The articles in this volume collectively survey the diversity of strategies of remembering in our period, the many different actors involved, and the various aims and audiences these strategies sought to reach, rather than trying to subsume these phenomena under one, comprehensive form of 'memory' or 'remembrance'. The contributors offer new interpretations of well-known material, highlight less familiar evidence, or establish new connections between different types of sources. Ultimately this volume seeks to serve as a starting point for further inquiry into acts of remembering in early Roman Greece, and beyond.

The eleven articles in this volume trace strategies of remembering in city building, funerary culture, festival and association, honorific practices, and political ideology. They fall into four thematic sections. The first section entitled 'Building Remembrance', which focuses on urban and provincial landscapes, is headed by an overview of the benefits and shortcomings of the so-called 'mnemonic turn' by Dimitris Grigoropoulos, Valentina Di Napoli, Vasilis Evangelidis, Francesco Camia, Dylan Rogers, and Stavros Vlizos, who collaborate in the Athens-based 'Roman Seminar'-initiative. In their article 'Roman Greece and the 'Mnemonic Turn'. Some Critical Remarks' the authors address the role of different agents and audiences

---

3   For general scholarship on the mnemonic turn see Grigoropoulos *et al. this volume*. For antiquity and Greece in particular see *e.g.* Alcock 1997a, 1997b, 2001, 2002; Van Dyke & Alcock 2003; Stein-Hölkeskamp & Hölkeskamp 2010; Dignas & Smith 2012.

in the context of remembrance. Using archaeological examples from different periods and regions they show that concepts of remembrance are not confined to Roman Greece, but occur in other temporal and regional contexts as well. At the same time, they highlight that Achaea is a special case in so far as Roman elites were highly invested in the Greek past and its use in the present, more so than with any other region of the empire. The other two articles in this section examine the construction of memories in two complex cities in Roman Greece, the Roman colonies of Patras and Corinth, to highlight some of the characteristic features of Roman Greece: the interplay of Greek and Roman traditions in these diverse societies. In her article 'Strategies of Remembering in the Creation of a Colonial Society in Patras' Tamara Dijkstra discusses how tomb sites, as *mnemotopes*, were strategically used in Patras during the city's transition from Greek polis to Roman *colonia*. The article addresses the issue from two perspectives: how the tomb of a local hero was used to anchor Augustan rule in the myth-historical narrative of the polis, and, how strategic funerary behaviour was employed in embedding newcomers in the local community. Catherine de Grazia Vanderpool and Paul Scotton in 'Contending with the Past in Roman Corinth: The Julian Basilica' show how in the Roman colony of Corinth the building program was used to engage in a dialogue with the city's Greek heritage. Through its program of statuary and its size, among other things, the Roman basilica competed with the dominating structure of the archaic temple of Apollo.

The second section, 'Competing with the Past', focuses specifically on uses of the past in the context of competitions between groups and associations, and the notion of competing with and comparing oneself to the past. In 'Heritage Societies? Private Associations in Roman Greece' Benedikt Eckhardt compares the private corporate organizations of Roman Greece to associations in Asia Minor and Thrace, using mainly epigraphic evidence, and focusing on their specific structure in Athens. He shows that the associations not only seem to take terminology and concepts from classical literature and mythology, but also engage in mythologizing organizations of the past, consciously reviving older forms of private associations. Zahra Newby's article 'Performing the Past: Salamis, Naval Contests and the Athenian *Ephebeia*' deals with the role of ephebic festivals as conscious re-performances of the past in which young men compete not only with one another, but also with their distant ancestors. She examines the different forms of these ephemeral events by focussing on the relation between the epigraphic and iconographic evidence. Lavinia del Basso's article 'Greek Panhellenic *Agones* in a Roman Colony: Corinth and the Return of the Isthmian Games' analyses the games as a way for both newcomers and natives to engage with the past of their city. Using archaeological, numismatic, and epigraphic material she shows how elements of the traditional games were revived and utilized by the new inhabitants of Corinth.

Section three, entitled 'Honouring Tradition', examines the use of the past as a political resource in the honorific practices of communities in Roman Greece, and how strategies of remembering were employed for elite distinction. Johannes Fouquet's article 'Heroes of Their Times. Intra-Mural Burials in the Urban Memorial Landscapes of the Roman Peloponnese' focuses on the relation between space and social value. Drawing on the concept of *lieu de mémoire* he shows how intra-mural burials interacted with their surrounding space to broadcast social prestige, thereby contributing to the formation of local urban memorial landscapes. Christopher Dickenson's article 'Public Statues as a Strategy of Remembering in Early Imperial Messene' shows how the Messenian 'statue-scape' developed over time, and that the meaning of statues is inextricably linked to their spatial context, especially in relation to other statues from other time periods. David Weidgenannt's article is titled 'Shortages, Remembering and the Construction of Time: Aspects of Greek Honorific Culture (2nd century BC – 1st century AD)'. Using sociological concepts of institutional theory he aims to show how the language of honorific decrees for *euergetai* created the impression of 'eternal benefactors' that included not only one particular person, but also his descendants. Even after death these benefactors were made to serve as models for future actions through their memory.

In the fourth and final part, 'Past and Politics in Athens', the discussion returns to Athens and its relationship with Rome. Inger Kuin's article 'Anchoring Political Change in Post-Sullan Athens' revisits the sources for Sulla's alleged Athenian constitution, a passage in Appian's *Mithridatic Wars* and an inscribed decree from the Athenian agora, from the perspective of political change. This elusive material shows how Greeks *and* Romans adapted to political transformations by anchoring them in (invented) traditions of the past. In 'Reused Statues for Roman Friends: The Past as a Political Resource in Roman Athens' Muriel Moser reconsiders several re-used honorary statue monuments inscribed for members of the Roman elite. She proposes that rather than constituting signs of weakness, these monuments must be located within the relationship of Athens and her Roman benefactors: they constituted a carefully calibrated public strategy of remembering Athens' past in Roman present in order to harness Roman benefactions for the city.

These articles are extended versions of the papers given at the conference 'Strategies of Remembrance in Greece under Rome', which took place at the Netherlands Institute in Athens from the 19th to the 21st of October, 2016. Two papers that were presented at the conference are, at the request of the authors, not included in the volume but will be published at a later stage. The first is the contribution by Athanasios Rizakis and Dimitra Andrianou entitled 'Memories of Thracians on Funerary Monuments from Roman Macedonia and Aegean Thrace', which showed how under Roman rule iconography, epigraphy and onomastic characteristics served to express Thracian identity even after death. Also to be published elsewhere is Panagiotis Doukellis' contribution 'The Time-Space Narration at the Beginnings of the New Era: Strabo as Historian and Geographer of the Empire', which discussed how Strabo's *Geography* used different strategies of remembrance both in the geographical descriptions, but also in the myth-historical information embedded in the text. A report of the conference, including these papers, is available online (Kamphorst and Van Toor 2017).

We would like to thank all of the contributors for the stimulating exchanges during the conference and for their helpful cooperation towards the swift publication of the volume. It is our pleasure also to thank the NIA, the SFB 1095 'Discourses of Weakness and Resource Regimes' as well as the DAI Athen for their generous contributions to the organization of the conference. At the NIA we want to thank in particular Winfred van de Put and Emmy Mestropian-Makri for their help during the conference. We would like to thank Caroline van Toor for compiling the index to the volume. The publication of the volume has been made possible by the NIA and the SFB 1095 'Discourses of Weakness and Resource Regimes'. Last but not least we would like to thank Karsten Wentink and Corné van Woerdekom at Sidestone Press for their efficient and tireless support in seeing this volume into press.

References

Alcock, S.E. 1993. *Graecia Capta. The Landscapes of Roman Greece*, Cambridge.

Alcock, S.E. 1997a. Greece: a landscape of resistance? In: D.J. Mattingly (ed.), *Dialogues in Roman Imperialism. Power, Discourse and Discrepant Experience in the Roman Empire*, Ann Arbor, 103-115.

Alcock, S.E. 1997b. The Heroic Past in a Hellenistic Present. In: P. Cartledge, P. Garnsey & E.S. Gruen (eds), *Hellenistic Constructs. Essays in Culture, History and Historiography*, Berkeley, 20-34.

Alcock, S.E. 2001. The reconfiguration of memory in the eastern Roman empire. In: S. E. Alcock, T.N. D' Altroy, K.D. Morrison & C.M. Sinopoli (eds), *Empires. Perspectives from Archaeology and History*, Cambridge, 323-350.

Alcock, S. E. 2002. *Archaeologies of the Greek Past. Landscape, Monuments, and Memories*, Cambridge.

Bernhardt, R. 1985. *Polis und römische Herrschaft in der späten Republik (149-31 v. Chr.)*, Berlin.

Dally, O. 2008. Athen in der frühen Kaiserzeit – ein Werk des Kaisers Augustus? In: S. Vlizos (ed.), *Η Αθήνα κατά τη ρωμαϊκή εποχή. Πρόσφατες ανακαλύψεις, νέες έρευνες, Αθήνα*, 43-53.

Day, J. 1942. *An Economic History of Athens under Roman Domination*, New York.

Deininger, J. 1971. *Der politische Widerstand gegen Rom in Griechenland, 217-86 v. Chr.*, Berlin.

Dickenson, C.P. 2016. Contested bones – the politics of intraurban burial in Roman Greece. *Ancient Society* 46, 95-163.

Dickenson, C.P. 2017. *On the Agora. The evolution of a Public Space in Hellenistic and Roman Greece (c. 323 BC – 267 AD)*, Leiden.

Dignas, B. & R.R.R. Smith (eds) 2012, *Historical and Religious Memory in the Ancient World*, Oxford.

Graindor, P. 1927. *Athènes sous Auguste*, Le Caire.

Hoff, M.C. 1989. Civil disobedience and unrest in Augustan Athens, *Hesperia* 58.3, 267-276.

Hoff, M.C. 1997. Laceratae Athenae: Sulla's Siege of Athens in 87/6 B.C. and its Aftermath. In: M.C. Hoff & S.E: Rotroff (eds), *The Romanization of Athens. Proceedings of an international conference held at Lincoln, Nebraska (April 1996)*, Oxford, 19-35.

Kamphorst, S.M. & C. van Toor. 2017. H/Soz/Kult Tagungsberichte: Strategies of Remembrance in Greece Under Rome. www.hsozkult.de/conferencereport/id/tagungsberichte-6910, Accessed August 17, 2017.

Rizakis, A., M. Kantirea & S.B. Zoumbaki 2001. *Roman Peloponnese I. Roman Personal Names in their Social Context*, Athens.

Rizakis, A., Cl. Lepenioti & S.B. Zoumbaki 2004. *Roman Peloponnese II. Roman Personal Names in their Social Context*, Athens.

Rizakis, A. & Cl. Lepenioti 2010. *Roman Peloponnese III. Society, Economy and Culture in the Imperial Roman Order: Continuity and Innovation*, Athens.

Spawforth, A.J.S. 2012. *Greece and the Augustan Cultural Revolution*, Cambridge.

Sluiter, I. 2017. Anchoring Innovation: A Classical Research Agenda, *European Review* 25, 20-38.

Stefanidou-Tiveriou, Th. (2008). Tradition and Romanization in the monumental landscape of Athens, in S. Vlizos (ed.), *Athens during the Roman Period. Recent discoveries, new evidence*. Athens, 11-39.

Stein-Hölkeskamp, E. & K.-J. Hölkeskamp (eds) 2010. *Die griechische Welt. Erinnerungsorte der Antike,* München.

Van Dyke, R.M. & S.E. Alcock (eds) 2003. *Archaeologies of Memory,* Malden.

Touloumakos, J. 1967. Der Einfluss Roms auf die Staatsform der griechischen Stadtstaaten des Festlandes und der Inseln im ersten und zweiten Jhdt. v. Chr., Diss. Universität Göttingen.

Zoumbaki, S.B. 2001. *Elis und Olympia in der Kaiserzeit. Das Leben einer Gesellschaft zwischen Stadt und Heiligtum auf prosopographischer Grundlage*, Athen.

PART I

Building Remembrance

Roman Greece and the 'Mnemonic Turn'. Some Critical Remarks

Dimitris Grigoropoulos, Valentina Di Napoli, Vasilis Evangelidis,
Francesco Camia, Dylan Rogers and Stavros Vlizos

Abstract

Since E.L. Bowie's seminal article on the Greeks and their past in the Second Sophistic, the study of Greece in the Roman Empire has been experiencing what has been described in other areas of social sciences and the humanities as a 'mnemonic turn'. The purpose of this article is to rethink the role and scope of these approaches by revisiting some of their assumptions and by posing a series of related questions: was the Roman conquest a catalyst for the emergence of phenomena of mobilization of the past in Greek societies? If such phenomena articulated conscious local responses to the imperial situation, how uniform were these responses across the Greek mainland? Were Greeks unique in this respect compared to other provincial societies across the empire? Did every use and representation of the past always have an ideological significance that can be read from the available textual and material evidence? Can we classify and describe all these phenomena by using the 'language of memory'? By examining these issues, we wish to highlight the complex nature of the evidence and the need to take into account its potential and its limitations when making inferences about remembering as a social and cultural strategy.

Keywords: Roman Greece, memory studies, tradition, Roman provinces

1. Introduction

Several social scientists and cultural historians have observed that since the 1980s the study of culture is undergoing a 'mnemonic turn' or even a 'memory boom' (Huyssen 2000; Klein 2000; Berliner 2005; Kõresaar 2014; Bachmann-Medick 2016, 279). From the rediscovery of the work of Maurice Halbwachs in the 1980s to the explosion of cultural memory studies from the 1990s onwards, this turn has led to the emergence of memory as a category of analysis and as a fundamental concept of culture (Fentress & Wickham 1992; Assmann 2002; Assmann 2008; Hasberg 2004; Olick & Robbins 1998; Klein 2000; Berliner 2005; Radstone 2008). The impact of this broader development has been (and continues to be) strongly felt in the study of mainland Greece and the Aegean following its conquest by Rome; in the last decades, this part of the Roman world has seen an extraordinary amount of work devoted to the power of the past and the role of memory in local provincial societies (e.g. Bowie 1974; Arafat 1996; Alcock 1997a; 2001; 2002). Starting as an attempt to de-construct discourses of nostalgia in Greek literature

in: Dijkstra, T.M., I.N.I. Kuin, M. Moser & D. Weidgenannt (eds) 2017. *Strategies of Remembering in Greece under Rome (100 BC - 100 AD)*, Leiden (Sidestone Press).

of the Imperial period, a wide range of phenomena of uses of the past as well as diverse material and textual evidence have been increasingly examined through this lens (e.g. Alcock *et al.* 2001; Galli & Cordovana 2007; Schmitz & Wiater 2011; *cf.* also Galinsky & Lapatin 2015). A central thesis of most such work has been that these phenomena have much to say not simply about how imperial Greeks viewed and interacted with the past, but also about how they structured their relations with Rome as a subject people. Under the prism of discrepant experience, the Greek past has been viewed as a resource through which local provincial communities could negotiate their status with respect to the Roman authorities, sometimes even as a channel for voicing dissent and as an expression of resistance to the centre (Alcock 1997a, 109-110). The 'turn to memory' marks, therefore, a fundamental shift in how we approach more overarching questions relating to the impact of Roman conquest and the extent of cultural and social change in Roman Greece (Francis 2004, 355).

Here a crucial question arises: is this increased interest a reflection of a shift in modern academic pursuits, related to the broader 'memory boom' as outlined above, or did the phenomena that we study in Roman Greece have the intrinsic significance and magnitude that we wish to ascribe to them? To claim that the one or the other answer alone is right would of course be simplistic and generalizing. After all, terms such as *memoria* and *mneme* were in common use in Rome and Greece during the Imperial period, even if they were not necessarily invested with the same meanings and implications that memory, as defined by modern academics and with its various prefixed adjectives (social, cultural, collective, etc.), has nowadays (Fentress & Wickham 1992; Assmann 2008; Erll 2008; 2011, 101). That said, outside the study of the ancient world the use of (cultural) memory as a conceptual and interpretative tool in historical thinking is coming under increased scrutiny (Kantsteiner 2002; Radstone 2008). Indeed, some of the most vocal critics have branded memory as a post-modern catchword that does not account for the richness of human experiences of, and interaction with, the past (Gedi & Elam 1996; Klein 2000; Berliner 2005; Algazi 2014). More recently, critical voices have also been raised by classical archaeologists working on other periods of the Greek past about the difficulties (and pitfalls) of identifying the workings of memory behind material remains (Morgan 2014).

Even if one does not agree with the above criticisms, the wealth of studies dedicated in one form or another to the role of memory in Roman Greece suggests that the time is ripe for a critical appraisal. The purpose of this article is to rethink the role and scope of these approaches by revisiting some of their assumptions and by posing a series of related questions: was the Roman conquest a catalyst for the emergence of phenomena related to the power of

the past and its mobilization in the present? If such mobilization served to articulate conscious local responses to the imperial situation, how uniform were these responses across the Greek mainland? Were Greeks unique in this respect compared to other provincial societies across the empire? Did every use and representation of the past always have an ideological significance that can be read from the available textual and material evidence? Can we classify and describe all these phenomena by using the 'language of memory' (Algazi 2014, 26)? In what follows, we examine these questions one by one, drawing upon an (both chronologically and geographically) extensive range of archaeological and historical examples and case-studies. Our aim is not to debunk previous work or to downplay the socio-cultural significance of the past in Roman Greece (or any human society, for that matter), but to review the potential and the limits of this discourse and to suggest alternative paths for engaging critically with the evidence.

2. The pre-Roman background

Recourse to the past has been repeatedly described as a phenomenon that characterizes the Imperial period as a consequence of the incorporation of Greece into the Roman Empire, epitomized by the literary and rhetorical production labelled the Second Sophistic (Bowersock 1969; Bowie 1974; Swain 1996; Alcock 1997a; 1997b; 2002; Galli & Cordovana 2007). If it is true, however, that 'the Greeks of the early Roman Empire were magnificently obsessed with their past' and that this phenomenon was 'an active cultural strategy on the part of an unusual subject population' (Alcock 2002, 33), it is likewise true that valorisation and mobilization of the past were not at all unprecedented in earlier Greek self-perception and self-presentation. There is little doubt that long before any experience of foreign conquest the ancient Greeks attempted to locate themselves in the flow of history by narrating and interpreting the past and developing a historical consciousness. Several studies have been devoted to investigating the complexity and variety of these phenomena in ancient Greek cultural and social life. In the following paragraphs, we investigate some examples spanning a large temporal frame of the Greek past, from prehistory down to the early post-conquest Late Hellenistic period, which, as will become evident, have relevance for situating and understanding several practices attested in the Early Imperial period.

Case studies from Greek prehistory speak in favour of the memorialisation of places from very early periods (brief review in Sporn 2015, 71-76). It has been argued, for instance, that the area of the central court in the monumental Middle Minoan IB so-called 'first palace' of Knossos was an 'arena for memory' already during the Early Minoan period, when ceremonial activities involving the consumption of food and beverages took place (Day & Wilson 2002). Also, the so-called 'Building T' at Tiryns, dating to the Late Helladic IIIC period, preserves a clear trace of the destroyed, earlier *megaron*, whose floor and throne were replaced with new ones (Maran 2001; 2011). Speaking explicitly about memory in these early contexts and without supporting textual sources may be risky. These examples, however, at least show that material traces of the past were actively drawn upon as symbols of emerging social and political structures. Similarly, for the Early Iron Age, Carla Antonaccio (1995; see also Morris 1998 and Whitley 1998), in her study of the practice of hero or tomb cult, which reached its peak especially in the 8th century BC, has argued on the basis of archaeological evidence that social and historical motivations can explain this phenomenon. As several other studies have suggested, for the emerging poleis and *ethne* it was extremely important to have control over time even more than over space, and that descent was crucial for determining group membership.[1] Furthermore, studies of oral tradition and the Homeric epic poems have reached the same conclusion, arguing that Greek communities of the Iron Age insisted on kinship and descent as a vital element for defining group identity and orienting collective social memory.[2]

Archaic Greece, which saw the birth of the polis and the attempts of aristocratic families and local communities at legitimizing their power, offers more evocative examples. Scholars agree about the importance of hero cults as core symbols of group identity (Bremmer 2006; Forsdyke 2011), and several communities tried to connect themselves to the heroes of the Greek epics in order to find their place in the Panhellenic cultural landscape. Middle Helladic tombs in the area of Eleusis (Mylonas 1975, vol. 2, 153-154, 262-264, pl. 145), whose original occupants had been forgotten, came to be associated with the fallen leaders of the Seven against Thebes and became the focus of a newly established hero cult. This might have happened in the mid-6thcentury BC, when a *heroon* for the Seven was built at Argos (Pariente 1992), apparently to boost the city's claim to leadership in the Peloponnese (Forsdyke 2011, 151-154). Pausanias (1.39.2) confirms that still in the Roman Imperial period the graves of the Seven leaders were visible on the road from Eleusis to Megara. Both the cult at Eleusis and the one at Argos may

therefore be read in light of a competition between the two poleis, against the general background of inter-city rivalries of the Archaic period.[3] The same phenomenon of competing cities explains the birth of foundation myths, invented by Greek poleis in order to find their place in a wider political landscape, a phenomenon that is well-attested in Roman Imperial times (Leschhorn 1984; MacSweeney 2014; Scherrer 2014, esp. 114-116, on the foundation myth of Ephesus).

Competition for honour and the legitimation of power, however, were not the only purposes for which the past was invoked and manipulated in the Greek polis. Around 500 BC the new-born Athenian democracy decided each year to bury the war dead in a common tomb, the Δημόσιον Σῆμα, thus physically reminding all citizens that it was worth dying for Athens. Shared remembrance in 5th-century Athens was manifest in the creation of collective burials for the war dead and in the elaboration of new spaces and symbols, which strengthened the sense of community and inspired new generations of citizens (Arrington 2015). Likewise inspiring were the ruins of the temples destroyed by the Persians, left to public view in the northern wall of the Acropolis (Ferrari 2002; Kousser 2009); but also, on a less disturbing and traumatic level, public victory monuments scattered on the sacred space of the Acropolis, which celebrated power and pride, or religious festivals, dramatic and rhetorical performances that served as carriers of Athenian social memory in the Classical period in that they were linked to key historical events.[4]

By the time of the Hellenistic kingdoms, civic commemoration had become a deeply ingrained cultural institution that, despite the deep political and social transformations that Greek cities were undergoing in that period, continued to produce new heroes who acted as role models and were added to the long line of local ancestors. This was the case with Eugnotos, for whom around 280 BC a statue was erected in the Boeotian city of Akraiphia, commemorating the battle during which he had lost his life fighting on the side of the Boeotian League. The last two lines of the long epigram inscribed on the statue base urged the Akraiphian young soldiers to bravery: 'But, young men, thus in glory become fighters, thus become

---

1   As argued in Morgan 1991. An example at Geometric Naxos is found in Lambrinoudakis 1988.

2   On Homeric poems, see Grethlein 2010, with bibliography. On Hecataeus and the birth of historiography, see Bertelli 2001. On the use of myth and history in ancient Greece, see Gehrke 2001; 2007. 8th- and 7th-century BC Corinth shows how the Bacchiad and Cypselid dynasties used local epic poems, the arts, and urban landscape in order to control collective social memory; for more see Dubbini 2012.

3   Steinbock 2013, 159-162 affirms that the shift in meaning at Eleusis occurred in the mid-6th century BC. Coldstream 1977, 351, Burkert 1985, 203 and Janko 1992, 163 suggest that this *heroon* was dedicated to the Seven already in the Late Geometric period, when a peribolos wall was built that surrounded the tombs. Bremmer 2006, 15-20, however, is skeptical about the presence of any cult activity at the site. Clarke 2008 shows the vitality of tradition at the time of the formation of the polis.

4   Steinbock 2013 focuses on the use of the past in Athenian public discourse of the 4th century BC. On Athens as 'place of memory', see Hölscher 2010.

brave men, defending the city of your fathers'.[5] One century later, around 180 BC, the same statue was re-inscribed with conscription lists for the Boeotian League, the act of which spurred the young citizens to follow in the footsteps of Eugnotos. Further conscription lists were even added in the 140s BC, at a time when the Boeotian League had been dissolved by the Romans, and when Akraiphia had to call in Megarian arbitrators in a territorial dispute with an unnamed neighbouring city. The statue of Eugnotos thus functioned as a monumental canvas, upon which several important episodes relating to Akraiphia's existence and civic identity were marked over time.

Political integration of cities into the domain of Hellenistic kingdoms, especially in the case of living rulers (and not those of the past, such as was the case before), frequently meant the creation of new forms of commemoration and their integration into existing institutions. When Teos was taken into Seleucid control, around 203 BC, King Antiochos III and Queen Laodike III bestowed on the city many privileges, which are recorded in great detail on two decrees found close to the entrance of the temple of Dionysus.[6] The Teians wished to 'be seen to return appropriate tokens of gratitude, in every occasion, to the king and the queen'.[7] For this purpose, they set up several statues of Antiochos and Laodike in central locations of the city, built a monumental fountain named after the queen in the agora, and instituted a festival in honour of the ruling couple. Civic rituals were addressed to the bronze statue of Antiochos placed in the *bouleuterion*, which included sacrifices offered by the magistrates, the crowning of the statue by the ephebes, and the offering of seasonal agricultural products. The sacrifices are particularly worth mentioning, as the decree states that magistrates and priests should 'perform in the *bouleuterion* a sacrifice upon the common hearth of the city to the king and the Charites and to Memory'.[8] This ritual, which stands out for the explicit presence of the personification of Μνήμη, anticipated many festivals of the Roman Imperial period, such as the procession established by P. Vibius Salutaris in 1st-century AD Ephesos (Rogers 1991).

This concise and, inevitably selective, overview demonstrates that long before the Roman Imperial period Greek communities mobilized and manipulated the past in various ways for legitimating the present and for shaping their sense of belonging. It is important to note that this was not the case just in periods of trauma or great internal stress but an apparently permanent feature of public and civic life; to use Susan Alcock's (2002, 23) words, 'the Hellenes were a memorious people'. In fact, it would appear that it was precisely the physical environment and the political and religious institutions of the polis that from the beginning fostered the development of a 'culture of remembrance' and provided the prime context of memory formation and commemorative practices. The polis was also the context in which the material mechanisms of this culture, such as monumental architecture, sculpture, and the epigraphic habit, were developed. By the Hellenistic period, this culture had been enriched by new commemorative institutions, such as the cult of the rulers, and crystallized into a set of traditions and practices, which were locally specific and contingent upon the political, cultural, and social dynamics of each polis.

3. Non-elite, non-Achaean, non-Greek: Some examples of the heterogeneity of mnemonic audiences in Roman Greece

While the role of the polis as the framework that enabled the formation and reproduction of shared memories cannot be denied for both before and after the Roman conquest of Greece, modern interpretations run the risk of essentializing perceptions of the past in Early Imperial Greece by reducing them to the experiences of elite urban audiences. Indeed, our knowledge of such practices revolves almost exclusively around the behaviours of the members of a specific group (i.e. the political and intellectual local elites) from a specific socio-cultural component of one province (i.e. the cities of Achaea), where such attitudes have been mapped by means of the available textual and archaeological evidence (Zoumbaki 2008). Nevertheless, when speaking about the 'Greek past', we should be aware of the potentially different perceptions by communities with different historical trajectories and status and by individuals with diverse ethnic, social and cultural backgrounds that would have experienced and interpreted the physical remains of the past differently (Alcock 2002, 69).

Tracing the mnemonic behaviours of these diverse audiences is not always an easy task, especially when there is no direct material or textual evidence, as indeed for the majority of the non-elite population, which encompassed a wide range of people from poor farmers to what Mayer (2012) describes as 'middle class', people who were not slaves or very poor, but economically autonomous such as merchants, artisans, and craftsmen (Alcock 2002, 69-70). Depending on their social status, these people may or may not have participated in the culture of public commemoration and institutionalized remembrance in their com-

---

5   ἀλλά, νέοι, γί[ν]εσθε κατὰ κλέος ὧδε μαχηταί, | ὧδ᾽ ἀγαθοί, πατέρων ἄιστεα [ῥ]υόμενοι. Original text is in Perdrizet 1900, 70-73, with extensive commentary and translation in Ma 2005.

6   *SEG* 41.1003, I & II, both commented in Ma 1999.

7   *SEG* 41.1003, I, lines 40-42. Trans. Ma 1999, 310.

8   *SEG* 41.1003, II, lines 33-34. Trans. Ma 1999, 315; see also the discussion by Ma 2009, 251.

munities, but their perceptions were possibly shaped more by local myths, tradition, and oral culture, and their participation in ritual behaviour.[9] Still, Plutarch (*Mor. Prae. ger. reip.* 814c) did not fail to notice, in a rather dismissive tone, that in his time the masses were getting too excited by narrations of the Greek victories at Marathon and Plataea, suggesting that sometimes such stories triggered feelings of unsuitable patriotism or civic pride: '[...] but Marathon, the Eurymedon, Plataea, and all the other examples which make the common folk vainly to swell with pride and kick up their heels, should be left to the schools of the sophists'.[10]

In one case, intellectual tradition and emphasis on Athenian patriotism managed to mobilize the Athenians against the Herulian invasion (Millar 2004, 293-294). At the same time, it is highly unlikely that the classicism and connoisseurship, reflected in the texts of the Second Sophistic and in the lifestyle of the elite, was something shared or understood by the common people.

Still, for Achaea at least, the clichéd image of ordinary people as passive participants in an elite game of self-promotion is not consistent with the role of the demos as a constituent part of a civic system for which the past played an important role (Zuiderhoek 2008, 436; 2014). As explained above, remembering the past was an intrinsic part of the ancient Greek polis, and the urban landscape was laden with commemorative messages through its monuments, statuary, public and sacred spaces (Mylonopoulos 2006, 87) that formed an important part of the everyday life of the people.[11] In this context, elite behaviour, such as donations for repairs of ruined buildings or the revival of ancient rites, cannot simply be explained by a will for self-aggrandizement or as a communication channel with the central authority, but rather has to be viewed as a response to a widespread significance attached to the past in the context of civic life (Millar 2004, 297).

Similarly difficult to discern are behaviours in Greek regions outside Achaea and the traditional commemorative framework of the old city states. In provinces such as Macedonia and Epirus different narratives not only prevailed, but additionally, contrary to southern Greece, physical traces and monuments of the Classical

past were also absent. The large Ionic peripteral temple of the Early Classical period that was reconstructed with the addition of new material sometime during the Early Imperial period in Thessaloniki is a rare example; its reconstruction in the provincial capital arguably represents an engaged intervention that enhanced the potential of the city as a memorial space by showcasing Classical architecture, a practice more on par with Roman metropolitan tastes.[12] Indeed, one may wonder whether such a reference to the Classical past through the reconstruction of iconic architectural forms is sufficient to demonstrate mnemonic behaviour in a region where one would expect that memories of the past were mostly (and inextricably) related to the period of the old Macedonian Kingdom. In the years that followed Pydna (168 BC) control of these memories probably proved essential for the stability of the province, especially when at least three successive uprisings were tied to the legacy of the lost Antigonids (Nigdelis 2007, 53-54). During the Imperial period, the memory of the Hellenistic kingdom and its monuments seems to have gradually been (selectively or forcefully) forgotten or neglected. What probably contributed significantly to this is the gradual decline and disappearance during the Augustan period of the two large power centres of the old Macedonian kingdom, the capitals Pella (Akamatis 2011, 403) and Aigai (Drougou 2009), where such dynastic, patriotic memories could have thrived.

The disjunction between memories of the old Macedonian kingdom and the new reality of Roman Macedonia finds a strong manifestation in the gradual abandonment and looting during the Late Republican to Early Imperial period of many of the great burial mounds that marked the resting place of the land-owning aristocracy of Macedonia (Schmidt-Dounas 2016). This was a phenomenon clearly linked to the disappearance of the old elite after the conquest, but the significance of these imposing monumental landmarks for local societies remains largely unknown. Besides treasure hunting spots, these were sites that could have been used for local rites, for reburials in the tomb itself or along the tumulus as 'tourist' attractions or simply as taboo sites engulfed by mystery (Curta 2016). By way of exception, the 4th-century BC Macedonian Tomb D at Pella (Chrysostomou 1994, 56-59) seems to have been visited frequently after its looting, sometime at the beginning of the 1st century BC, by individuals who left graffiti with obscene language and pederastic content. After the clearance of the main entrance in the late 2nd

---

9   For the perception of past in oral societies, see Assmann 2008, 112, who summarizes the work of the anthropologist Vansina 1985. For the differences between memory and tradition, see Morgan 2014, but also Jones and Russel 2012. For oral tradition and other temporal information in the context of families, see Foxhall 2012.

10   Plut. *Mor. Prae. ger. reip.* 814c: τὸν δὲ Μαραθῶνα καὶ τὸν Εὐρυμέδοντα καὶ τὰς Πλαταιάς, καὶ ὅσα τῶν παραδειγμάτων οἰδεῖν ποιεῖ καὶ φρυάττεσθαι διακενῆς τοὺς πολλούς. Trans. H.N. Fowler.

11   Ma 2009, 251; Price 2012, 16; Steinbock 2013, 48-99. See also Elsner and Squire 2016 about the connection between sight and memory.

12   The identification and exact date of the temple is a matter of debate, see Stefanidou-Tiveriou 2012, 275-276. For the superstructure of the building, older architectural members were used plus supplementary material that was carved in a style so as to imitate the Early Classical style of the older material. For the itinerant temples at the Athenian Agora, see Alcock 2002, 54-58.

century AD, however, the tomb was made more accessible to visitors who added new graffiti to mark their presence. Among them, a dedication to the hero Alexander and to Cassander indicates that the tomb might have been perceived by some as a physical remain from the period of the old Macedonian Kingdom. Interestingly, this coincides with the revival of the interest in the Macedonian kingdom and the commemoration of Alexander the Great that swept the province of Macedonia at the time of the late Antonine and Severan periods.[13]

Varied motives seem to have dictated the mnemonic behaviours of yet another until recently 'obscure' audience: the inhabitants of a number of Roman colonies that were founded on Greek soil during the late 1st century BC as part of a Caesarean and later Augustan grand strategy (Rizakis 1997, 15). The establishment of these colonies over pre-existing cities with a long history and a developed architectural environment inevitably evoked a range of responses towards the local pre-Roman past and its physical remains that go further than what Renato Rosaldo (1989) described as 'imperialist nostalgia'. Practical reasons, especially during the first years after their establishment, led to restoration, reuse, and preservation of pre-existing buildings and monuments (e.g. the Archaic Temple or the South Stoa in Corinth), which only by their presence were *a de facto force of memory*. Religiousness, superstition, and piety also seem to have played a role in the selective preservation of sites and relics (Engels 1990). After all, the foundation of the colony was an act with a deep religious content.[14] Preservation, however, of civic history documents (e.g. the decree of Alexander granting land in Philippi, see Missitzis 1985), remembrance of mythic founders like Patreas in Patras (Paus. 7.20.7 and Dijkstra in this volume), restoration of sacred sites and exhibition of ancient relics as the *xoana* of Dionysus Bakkheios and Lysios at Corinth (Paus. 2.4.7) offered a channel of communication with the broader socio-cultural environment of the province.

Although these colonies were cities with extensive privileges, the link with the past still might have been a central decision for their further success and their ranking in the hierarchy of power. Yet the motives behind the preservation of some monuments are more complex and thus more difficult to be categorized as purely political, religious, or practical. This is the case with the salvage and exhibition at a prominent spot along the main thoroughfare of the Roman colony of Dion of an architectural frieze depicting cuirasses and shields, a frieze that originally belonged to an important pre-Roman public building. The original Hellenistic building from where it was salvaged has been identified as a *bouleuterion* or as a hall that might have sheltered the *apella*, the armed congregation of the Macedonian people. The building seems to have continued to function as one of the main public buildings of the colony over the long period between the 1st century BC and the late 2nd century AD, when the renovation programme began (Christodoulou 2000; 2007). One can only speculate about the motives behind its preservation and public display: was it an attempt to present the Roman basilica as a successor of the old building, a reference (given the characteristic military inspired theme of the frieze) to the Macedonian past, or simply an act of reverence towards a building that was probably an important landmark of the city from the time of its foundation? Both seem possible explanations, which, if nothing else, highlights the complexity of the mnemonic behaviours of the citizens of these cities towards the pre-Roman past.

4. A view from the rest of the Empire

Even if Achaea is often presented as a special case of a society obsessed with its pre-conquest legacy, it was by no means the only part of the Roman world where the past carried significance. The ways in which individuals and communities in the western and eastern provinces interacted with their local pasts is beginning to attract an increasing amount of scholarly attention (Eckardt 2004; Galinsky & Lapatin 2015; Boschung *et al.* 2015). These works, while emphasizing the differences between the two parts of the empire simply relating to the nature of the evidence, also recognize significant contrasts in the responses and processes by which these attitudes were shaped in the post-conquest period. Certainly, the absence of any deep-rooted admiration for local cultural legacies by the Romans (with the possible exception of that of Pharaonic Egypt) and the eventual suppression of (or indifference to) much of whatever persisted in most conquered areas makes a blatant contrast to the situation in Achaea. That said, other Roman provinces were not devoid of material remains and monumental sites of previous times that were no less imposing, which invited provincial populations to interact with them in various ways (Bradley & Williams 1997; Bradley 2002; Díaz-Guardamino *et al.* 2015).

On a first level, comparisons between Achaea and other provincial settings can be drawn on the basis of continuities and shifts in frameworks of official remembrance and the agents that were responsible for sustaining them. For Roman Gaul, Greg Woolf (1996) has emphasized the destruction of traditional frameworks of memory and their gradual replacement with Roman institutions as the

---

13 Gagé 1975; see also Despinis *et al.* 1997, 120, n. 17. For the image of Alexander under the Antonine and Severan dynasties, see Asirvatham 2010, 113 and Chatzinikolaou 2011, 163-165, 337-338, cat.no. 214 (cult of Alexander).

14 Verg. *Aen.* 5.775-6; Tac. *Ann.* 12.24; Briquel 2008.

main reasons behind the apparent indifference towards the pre-conquest past. As already noted in the case of Roman Macedonia, this can perhaps be understood as an effect of the disappearance of the native Late Iron Age elite after the conquest, including the learned classes that would have controlled narratives, modes of representation, and knowledge about the past. In other parts of the Roman world, where a certain degree of continuity in elite structures from the pre- to the post-conquest period is documented, such traditional frameworks seem to have persisted or to have been moulded into new forms of commemorative practice.

A case in point is the commemoration of native rulers in areas that prior to their conquest by Rome were ruled by client kings, as in the region of western North Africa that later became the provinces of Mauretania Tingitana and Caesariensis. During the time of the Numidian kings and under Juba II, at the latest, a Hellenistic-style dynastic ruler cult had been established, while other sources indicate that deification of rulers was also common among Berber populations (Gonzalbes 1981; Coltelloni-Trannoy 1992). The last client king of Mauretania, Ptolemy, was the last in the dynasty, who is said to have set up a cult of his father Juba II (and perhaps also of his grandfather Hiempsal II (Roller 2003, 156; ibid. 27, n. 112). Together with his father, Ptolemy was venerated even after his brutal murder by Caligula and the annexation of the province in AD 40. Statues of both kings were apparently in public display until Late Imperial times, as for instance in the western baths of Iol Caesarea (Cherchel) that were built in the Severan period (Landwehr 1992; Coltelloni-Trannoy 1997, 198-199). Literary sources of the 3rd century AD suggest that by that time Juba II may have been counted amongst the local gods (Roller 2003, 155). At Sala in Mauretania Tingitana, there is evidence for a temple in the forum that was dedicated to the two kings and used down to the 4th century AD (Coltelloni-Trannoy 1997, 198-199).

Another suggestive example is known from the Alpine region between Gallia Narbonensis and Cisalpine Gaul. This was the territory of the Liguri, a tribal kingdom that was ruled by king Donnus at the time of Caesar's campaigns in Gaul and later by his son Cottius (Haeussler 2016, 184). This ruler had retained his kingdom under Augustus as an ally of Rome receiving the title of prefect, a title which he then passed on to his son, Cottius II, until Nero created the province of Alpes Cottiae in AD 60. Ammianus Marcellinus mentions that he saw the tomb of the client king at Segusio and notes that it was venerated devoutly down to his day (Amm. Marc. 15.10.2, 7; Barnes 1998, 98). Segusio was Cottius' royal capital, and excavations in the 19th century have brought to light a temple-like building dating to the Augustan period with a stone urn placed in the cella, which has been interpreted

as the king's tomb (Brecciaroli-Taborelli 1994; Haeussler 2016, 184). The tomb's form and its location suggest that Cottius indeed received special honours from his subjects after his death. Veneration of Cottius continued for generations, certainly under the rule of his son, the last king of the tribal kingdom, and even after the formal provincialization of the kingdom under Nero, until the time of Ammianus.

Similar phenomena can be also observed outside Italy and the Mediterranean, as in the case of the ceremonial complex at Folly Lane in Verulamium (St. Albans) in southeast Britain. Verulamium evolved as an urban centre after around the 60s AD, but its urban origins stretch back to the late 1st century BC, when a series of sub-rectangular enclosures were established (Haselgrove & Millett 1997; Niblett 1999). Sometime after the Claudian invasion of AD 43, and by AD 55 at the latest, the enclosure at Folly Lane received a high-status burial, accompanied by military gear and luxury items. The special care shown in the burial rites and the military accoutrements suggest that this person was an important Briton with close connections to the Romans, possibly a client king of the conquest period or an immediate successor (Niblett 1999). The burial itself became the focus of commemoration in later times. In the Claudian-Neronian period, the Iron Age trackway that had connected the lower enclosure with Folly Lane became the main axis on which the town was laid out. In the Flavian period a temple-shrine was erected on the cremation pyre, while in the mid-2nd century AD a new theatre was connected to Folly Lane by means of a processional way. Folly Lane thus became fully integrated into the landscape of Early Roman Verulamium as a focus of communal remembrance, which involved rituals, performances and votive deposition (Creighton 2006, 128-130).

Although it would be simplistic to generalize, the examples considered above share many common traits. As Ralph Haeussler (2009; 2010) has argued, a common thread seems to be the role that the honorands played in securing the future relationship of their communities with Rome at a turning point in their history. Another common feature is the chronological extent of these practices, lasting several generations. Not least, in none of the above cases was there any attempt by the Romans to suppress or discontinue such practices. Even in the case of the last king of Mauretania, whose memorable tragic end under Caligula may have carried a subversive undertone (Gonzalbes 1981, 158), his commemoration appears to have flourished after the Roman annexation of the old kingdom. These examples show that several societies with different cultural backgrounds and trajectories upon becoming part of the Roman Empire experienced similar pressures, and responded in ways that in many respects can compare to the evidence from Roman Achaea and other areas of the eastern empire (see Fouquet *this volume*; Noreña 2015).

Beyond such cases of official remembrance, people in every part of the Roman world interacted with inherited landscapes and pre-existing material remains. In the last decades, archaeological evidence of Roman-period activity at pre-conquest sites is beginning to emerge from several areas across the eastern and western provinces. From Palaeolithic cave sites (Basch 1956; Alfayé 2010, 195-204; Simón 2013) and megalithic monuments in Iberia (Bradley 2002, 116-118; Sanjuán *et al.* 2007; 2008; Sanjuán & Díaz-Guardamino 2015), Brittany (Vejby 2015) and North Africa (Sanmartí *et al.* 2015), to the Bronze Age megalithic towers, or *nuraghi*, in Sardinia (Blake 1997; 1998), the Iron Age barrow cemeteries in Gallia Belgica (Fontjin 2015) and Hittite rock art in Anatolia (Rojas & Sergueenkova 2014) – the range of sites and landscapes with traces of Roman-period interaction is vast. Such interaction could take various forms and leave various traces (e.g. epigraphy, pictorial representations, material remains), while even within a certain region or type of monument there can be much variation. In Sardinia, for instance, the evidence for Roman reuse of Bronze Age *nuraghi* suggests a wide range of functions, from domestic, to cultic and funerary (Blake 1997; 1998). The chronological span of such later activity is equally wide, with several monuments either being reused for the first time only in the Roman period, or continuing an already established pattern from previous centuries, or showing reuse within one or more phases of the Roman era.

What are we to make of all this? In the absence of literary or other epigraphic information, much of the Roman material recovered from such sites poses several problems regarding its chronology, nature, and interpretation (e.g. Vejby 2015; Fontjin 2015, 195-196). In cases where more source material and finds are available, there are potentially more associations to be established. A case in point is the megalithic tomb known as Petit Mont overlooking the bay of Morbihan in Brittany (LeCornec 1985; 1987; Vejby 2015, 172). This impressive Neolithic chambered cairn has yielded more Iron Age and Roman material than any other such tomb in Brittany, which has one of the largest concentrations of megalithic tombs in Western Europe. Excavation at the entrance also revealed a Latin-inscribed stone mentioning a *votum* by the son of Q. Sabinus (Sanquer 1983, 286-287; LeCornec 1985, 62-64; 1987); the latter is identified as the Roman lieutenant responsible for leading the Roman forces in the final sea battle against the Veneti and their allies during Caesar's campaigns in Gaul. The wider area of the bay was the theatre of this dramatic event described in the *Gallic Wars* (3.11-16), which led to the crushing of the last pocket of local resistance. The altar provides a compelling indication that this megalithic complex, which was already significant for the local Iron Age communities, was appropriated for commemorating this decisive battle (LeCornec 1994, 94; Vejby 2015, 172).

Rather than reflecting native responses, this example is perhaps more indicative of the intentions of the Roman victors who sought to make a statement of domination and control. Other examples, however, have led scholars to interpret evidence for Roman activity at prehistoric monuments as an expression of cultural memory or a form of local resistance to the centre (Blake 1997; Blake 1998; Sanjuán *et al.* 2007; Sanjuán *et al.* 2008; Sanjuán & Díaz-Guardamino 2015). Here it is important to ask if any type of later material attested at pre-existing monuments is adequate for inferring intentional remembering; and, above all, if we concur with Jan Assmann's (2008, 110) definition of cultural memory as something exteriorized and objectified, what was being invoked and remembered? Such experiences were often disjunctive, as noted by Lynn Meskell (2003, 48-52; *cf.* Montserrat & Meskell 1997) for Deir el Medina, a New Kingdom settlement close to the Valley of the Kings in Upper Egypt. In the Ptolemaic and Roman periods this became a pilgrimage site where visitors made *proskynemata*, or written obeisances, to the local gods. Overawed by the dramatic landscape and Pharaonic ruins, these visitors could not understand that what they were venerating were the remains of a village of pyramid builders. These practices, according to Meskell (2003, 50), cannot constitute an expression of social or cultural memory; they were rather 'hybrid forms of commemorative practice' that appropriated the locale without any affective contact to its previous function or meaning.

Given that cultural memory is loosely defined as something which can accommodate diverse representations and practices relating to our relation to the past (Erll 2008; Assmann 2008), it may appear of little consequence to distinguish between them. It is important, nevertheless, whenever possible and if only for analytical reasons, to make a distinction between experiences, in which pre-existing monuments due to their perceived properties fascinated later generations and triggered various responses, and those that involved conscious acts of remembrance and commemoration. Admittedly, it cannot be excluded that visits to ancient sites, or the rediscovery and reuse of material remains enabled speculation about the local past (Alfayé 2010, 196-197), or even the expression of alternative local identities and 'counter-memories' at a personal level. What becomes evident, however, is that both in Achaea and in other provinces formalized remembrance at the level of the community lay primarily in the hands of the local elites and provincial ruling classes, and it is they who ultimately shaped the specific ways in which the local past would (or would not) be remembered and celebrated.

5. Problematizing remembrance

Our remarks aim at opening up a more fundamental discussion, which has important implications for studying memory in the Roman world. It is generally accepted that material remains allow a less elite-centred and more bottom-up approach than written (including epigraphic) sources, but at the same time they are inherently ambiguous: their meanings are not readily apparent or are heavily determined by interpretation. A similar problem has been recently emphasized by Jás Elsner (2017, 266-267) in the context of the archaeological study of pilgrimage. These qualities do not reduce the value of archaeological material as an evidentiary basis from which to infer commemorative behaviours and intentional remembering, but certainly make it more difficult and challenging. If for Petit Mont no epigraphic evidence or historical sources were available and we were left with only the excavated Roman-period finds, how would it be possible to link the archaeologically observed patterns of reuse with intentional commemorative practices?

These problems are no less acute in cases where ample archaeological and textual source material is available, as for instance in the case of the imperial cult in Roman Greece (Kantiréa 2007; Lozano 2010; Camia 2011; 2012). The socio-political motives behind the integration of the imperial cult into the traditional framework of the Greek poleis are straightforward enough. Imperial cult permitted the Greek communities to accommodate the emperor in their own symbolic world. To treat the emperor like a god is a way to negotiate with his autocratic power, so as to experience external authority in a more familiar way and according to Greeks' cultural horizon and tradition.[15] In Greece, new temples or other cult buildings specifically conceived for the emperors were rarely built. With the exception of the *monopteros* of Roma and Augustus on the Athenian Acropolis celebrating Augustus' Parthian campaign of 20 BC (Kantiréa 2007, 125-127; Stefanidou-Tiveriou 2008, 21-23; Dally 2008; Fouquet 2012), in most cases emperor worship was 'hosted' in pre-existing structures, which constituted an integral part of cities' religious and cultural heritage (Camia 2016).

There remains, however, one essential question to be addressed: does the practice of associating Roman emperors and Greek gods always suggest an actual act of remembrance? The choice of pre-existing architectural spaces bears an immediate economic advantage, which becomes more explicit when a collapsed building is used in order to create an independent cult place for the emperors, as happened for example with the re-con-

secration of the *Metroon* in Olympia in the Augustan age (Hitzl 1991; Hupfloher 2006, 240-242; Kantiréa 2007, 147-153; Lo Monaco 2009; Bol 2008). In this context, the use – or reuse – of pre-existing places of worship was difficult to avoid, and regarding each case as a conscious and deliberate evocation of the past can be misleading. The fact that the old *Metroon* was most probably in ruins at the time of the re-consecration and that it was rededicated to Augustus alone, who thus replaced – rather than being associated to – the Megale Meter, warns us against assuming in every case an ideological motivation, although the latter cannot be *a priori* excluded even in those cases when practical advantages seem to be predominant. Needless to say, in some cases both practical and ideological motives will have coexisted (and in the aforementioned case single individuals may still have associated the new temple re-consecrated to Augustus with the old deity). Recognition of such aspects is very important in considering such accommodation as an actual mnemonic act or not.

A well-known evocative example is the altar dedicated to the imperial cult discovered in the Late Helladic tholos tomb at Orchomenos, known as the 'treasury of Minyas' (Antonaccio 1995, 127-130; Alcock 1997b, 28, with further bibliography). This was evidently a deliberate act that reclaimed a local prehistoric funerary monument as a place of emperor worship. Nevertheless, the insertion of the altar seems hardly out of place, since this tomb had already been the focus of cult activity (possibly of local hero Minyas and other gods) already by the Hellenistic period. From a functional point of view, then, this would hardly have created a break with past practice, and indeed this might have been the actual intention, namely to embed the emperor into a web of local pre-existing cult practices. Whether such practices demonstrate the workings of cultural memory, or if we should better call them tradition, or perhaps even an 'invention of tradition' (Hobsbawm & Ranger 1983; *cf.* Busch & Versluys 2015), is better left open to debate. In this case, however, what matters is that it was not so much the presence of an ancient monument *per se* that determined the accommodation of the imperial cult, but the fact that this tomb had already been a focus of local worship and thus was associated with established practices of the Orchomenians.

As Jan Assmann (2008, 113) notes, 'cultural memory reaches back into the past only so far as the past can be reclaimed as 'ours''. He goes on to underline that knowledge about the past in itself does not necessarily signal memory, unless the former is bound to some concept of identity. Developing this point (but from a different perspective) further, Gadi Algazi (2014) emphasizes that remembering is not only just about cognition, but also about recognition: not just knowing about the past but internalizing this knowledge, respecting obliga-

---

15 Beard *et al.* 1998, 158: 'the Greeks employed traditional forms to articulate their position in a new world'. *Cf.* also Price 1984, 52, and for Athens Evans 2011, 90: 'Athenians came to worship Roman emperors by following age-old patterns'.

tions that arise from it and making appropriate gestures. It is thus important, when considering the symbolic or ideological motivations behind patterns of reuse and its evidentiary potential for tracing cultural memory, to take into account of the specific local historical and cultural parameters. Seen from this perspective, cultural memory is not a given, something which is ready to be unlocked in all material remains or sites that exhibit traces of later activity or appropriation. In this context, it is crucial to bear in mind the caveat expressed by Catherine Morgan (2014, 115) that 'there is […] a potentially important distinction between objectified memory (formalized episodes of remembrance and forgetfulness) and the practice of ritual whereby what is inherited (itself an act of selection and definition) is responded to, positively or negatively, in whole or part, consciously or unconsciously. Understanding the function of tradition and memorialisation, recognizing them case by case, requires sensitive examination of the whole fabric, rather than assumptions about ancient perceptions'.

6. Conclusion

In recent years memory has emerged as a central theme that can shed light upon the processes of incorporation of Greece into the Roman Empire. This development invites us to place the paths opening up for this kind of study in a broader historical (diachronic) and comparative (synchronic) perspective. Greek provincial experiences, for all their richness and apparent intensity, were neither unprecedented in Greece itself, nor unique amongst other conquered societies of the empire. By the time of the Roman conquest Greek communities had already developed the frameworks, elements and specific practices through which perceptions of the past were shaped and materialized. In a sense, then, what we are observing is the persistence and reproduction of a set of traditions of commemoration, which, because of the burgeoning importance attached to Greek culture within Roman imperial ideology, acquired

an added significance as cultural capital for Greek provincials. This is what differentiates Achaea from other provincial cultures, and this is where a key difference between the pre-conquest era and the Imperial period lies. In the course of the early empire, control of the past and its representations became a key element in the creation of a provincial socio-political order, a process during which Greek elites progressively aligned themselves with the Roman state and imperial ideology (Spawforth 2012). By celebrating their local civic past and thus learning to appear more 'traditional' and 'canonical', the Achaean ruling classes responded to Roman cultural expectations.

In this sense, there was something opportunistic (or better perhaps, strategic) about showcasing and manipulating local heritage. The crucial question to ask, therefore, is if this kind of behaviour that seems to have been in agreement with (or sometimes even dictated by) the conquering power can be taken to reflect the sum total of cultural memory of the provincial population. Given that much of the source material by default reflects the views of elites and centres on urban experiences, we should be cautious in either assuming that such perceptions were uniform across the Greek mainland or that they were even shared by all social groups and communities within Achaea. It is also important to emphasize that encounters with the past were complex phenomena in Roman Greece and in other provincial societies alike. Even when textual sources exist, interpreting such experiences by reference to cultural memory may not be always so straightforward. Our observations are not meant to debunk the 'mnemonic turn'; far from this, approaches to Greece and the Roman world under this prism are not only legitimate and intellectually challenging but, as the examples discussed above show, have still a lot to offer. Yet, if this 'mnemonic turn' is to become a paradigm, it is important to review the scope of the subject and to revisit the applicability of concepts by examining if and to what extent they help us to better understand the material and textual evidence.

References

Alcock, S.E. 1997a. Greece: a landscape of resistance? In: D.J. Mattingly (ed.), *Dialogues in Roman Imperialism: Power, Discourse and Discrepant Experience in the Roman Empire,* Ann Arbor, 103-115.

Alcock, S.E. 1997b. The Heroic Past in a Hellenistic Present. In: P. Cartledge & P. Garnsey, E.S. Gruen (eds), *Hellenistic Constructs: Essays in Culture, History and Historiography,* Berkeley, 20-34.

Alcock, S.E. 2001. The reconfiguration of memory in the eastern Roman empire. In: S. Alcock et al. (eds) *Empires: Perspectives from Archaeology and History.* Cambridge, 323-350.

Alcock, S.E. 2002. *Archaeologies of the Greek Past. Landscape, Monuments, and Memories,* Cambridge.

Alcock, S.E., J.F. Cherry & J. Elsner (eds) 2001. *Pausanias: Travel and Memory in Roman Greece,* Oxford.

Alfayé, S. 2010. Hacia el lugar de los dioses – aproximación a la peregrinación religiosa en la Hispania indoeuropea. In: F.M. Simón, F.P. Polo & J. Remesal-Rodríguez (eds), *Viajeros, peregrinos y aventureros en el mundo antiguo,* Barcelona, 177-218.

Algazi, G. 2014. Forget Memory: Some Critical Remarks on Memory, Forgetting and History. In: S. Scholz, G. Schwedler & K.-M. Sprenger (eds), *Damnatio in Memoria: Deformation und Gegenkonstruktionen von Geschichte,* Vienna, 25-34.

Alroth, B., C. Scheffer (eds) 2014. *Attitudes towards the Past in Antiquity: Creating Identity,* Stockholm.

Akamatis, I. 2011. Pella. In: R.L. Fox (ed.), *Brill's Companion to Ancient Macedon. Studies in the Archaeology and History of Macedon, 650 BC – 300 AD,* Leiden, 394-408.

Antonaccio, C.M. 1995. *An Archaeology of Ancestors. Tomb Cult and Hero Cult in Early Greece,* London.

Arafat, K.W. 1996. *Pausanias: Ancient Artists and Roman Rulers,* Cambridge.

Arrington, N.T. 2015. *Ashes, Images, and Memories. The Presence of the War Dead in Fifth-Century Athens,* Oxford.

Asirvatham, S.R. 2010. Perspectives on the Macedonians from Greece, Rome, and Beyond. In: J. Roisman & R. Worthington (eds), *A Companion to Ancient Macedonia,* Chichester, 99-124.

Assmann, A. 2002, Gedächtnis als Leitbegriff der Kulturwissenschaften. In: L. Musner & G. Wunberg (eds), *Kulturwissenschaften: Forschung – Praxis – Positionen,* Wien, 27-45.

Assmann, J. 2008. Communicative and Cultural Memory. In: A. Erll & A. Nünning (eds), *Cultural Memory Studies. An International and Interdisciplinary Handbook,* Berlin, 109-118.

Bachmann-Medick, D. 2016. *Cultural Turns: New Orientations in the Study of Culture,* Berlin.

Barnes, T.D. 1998. *Ammianus Marcellinus and the Representation of Historical Reality,* London.

Basch, M.A. 1956. Sobre las inscripciones rupestres del covacho con pinturas de Cogul (Lérida), *Caesaraugusta* 7-8, 67-75.

Beard, M., J. North & S. Price, 1998. *Religions of Rome, I-II,* Cambridge.

Berliner, D. 2005. The Abuses of Memory: Reflections on the 'Memory Boom', *Anthropological Quarterly* 78, 197-211.

Bertelli, L. 2001. Hecataeus: From Genealogy to Historiography. In: N. Luraghi (ed.), *The Historian's Craft in the Age of Herodotus,* Oxford, 67-94.

Blake, E. 1997. Negotiating Nuraghi: Settlement and the Construction of Ethnicity in Roman Sardinia. In: K. Meadows, C. Lemke & J. Heron (eds), *TRAC 96: Proceedings of the Sixth Annual Theoretical Roman Archaeology Conference,* Oxford, 113-119.

Blake, E. 1998. Sardinia's Nuraghi: Four Millennia of Becoming. In: Bradley & Williams 1998, 59-71.

Bol, R. 2008. Augustus – Retter der Hellenen und des gesamten bewohnten Erdkreises – im Zeusheiligtum von Olympia. In: D. Kreikenbom *et al.* (eds), *Augustus – Der Blick von aussen. Die Wahrnehmung des Kaisers in den Provinzen des Reiches und in den Nachbarstaaten. Akten der internationalen Tagung an der Johannes Gutenberg-Universität Mainz vom 12. bis 14. Oktober 2006,* Wiesbaden, 347-363.

Boschung, D., A.W. Busch & M.J. Versluys (eds) 2015. *Reinventing 'The Invention of Tradition?' Indigenous Pasts and the Roman Present,* Paderborn.

Busch, A.W. & M.J. Versluys, 2015. Indigenous Pasts and the Roman Present. In: Boschung, Busch & Versluys 2015, 7-15.

Bowersock, G.W. 1969. *Greek Sophists in the Roman Empire,* Oxford.

Bowie, E.L. 1974. The Greeks and their past in the Second Sophistic. In: M.I. Finley (ed.), *Studies in Ancient Society,* London, 166-209.

Bradley, R. 2002. *The Past in Prehistoric Societies,* London/ New York.

Bradley R. & H. Williams (eds) 1997. *The Past in the Past: The Reuse of Ancient Monuments. World Archaeology* 30, London/ New York.

Brecciaroli-Taborelli, L. 1994. L'heroon di Cozio a Segusio. Un esempio di adesione all' ideologia del principato augusteo, *Athenaeum* 82, 331-339.

Bremmer, J. 2006. The Rise of the Hero Cult and the New Simonides, *ZPE* 158, 15-26.

Briquel, D. 2008. L'espace consacré chez les Étrusques: reflexions sur le rituel étrusco-romain de fondation des cites. In: X. Dupré Raventós, S. Ribichini & S. Verger (eds), *Saturnia Tellus. Definizioni dello spazio consacra-*

to in ambiente etruco, italico, fenicio-punico, iberico e celtico, Rome, 27-47.

Burkert, W. 1985. *Greek Religion: Archaic and Classical*, Oxford.

Camia, F. 2011. *Theoi Sebastoi. Il culto degli imperatori romani in Grecia (provincia Achaia) nel secondo secolo d.C.* Athens.

Camia, F. 2012. Theoi Olympioi e theoi Sebastoi: alcune considerazioni sull'associazione tra culto imperiale e culti tradizionali in Grecia. In: E. Franchi & G. Proietti (eds), *Forme della memoria e dinamiche identitarie nell'antichità greco-romana. Quaderni 2*, Trento, 93-110.

Camia F., 2016. The theoi Sebastoi in the sacred landscape of the *polis*. Cult places for the emperors in the cities of mainland Greece. In: L. Gaitanou & J. Fouquet (eds), *Im Schatten der Alten? Ideal und Lebenswirklichkeit im römischen Griechenland*, Mainz, 9-23.

Chatzinikolaou K., 2011. *Οι λατρείες των θεών και των Ηρώων στην Άνω Μακεδονία κατά την αρχαιότητα (Ελίμεια, Εορδαία, Ορεστίδα, Λυγκηστίδα),* Θεσσαλονίκη.

Christodoulou, P. 2000. *Ελληνιστική ζωφόρος στο Δίον με ανάγλυφες παραστάσεις όπλων: Η θέση της στην βασιλική της Αγοράς και η αρχική μορφή του μνημείου,* PhD Dissertation, Aristotle University of Thessaloniki.

Christodoulou, P. 2007. Δίον: Η ανασκαφή στη βασιλική της Αγοράς το 2007, *AeMTh* 21, 179-84.

Chrysostomou, P. 1994. Ανασκαφικές έρευνες στους τύμβους της Πέλλας κατά το 1994, *AeMTh* 8, 53-73.

Clarke, K. 2008. *Making time for the past. Local history and the polis,* Oxford.

Coldstream, J.N. 1977. *Geometric Greece*, London.

Coltelloni-Trannoy, M. 1992. Le culte royal sous les regnes de Juba II et de Ptolémée de Mauretanie. In: *Histoire et archéologie de l'Afrique du Nord. Actes du Ve colloque international: Spectacles, vie portuaire, religions*, Paris, 69-80.

Coltelloni-Trannoy, M. 1997. *Le royaume de Maurétaniesous Juba II et Ptolémée, 25 av. J.-C. – 40 ap. J.-C.,* Paris.

Creighton, J. 2006. *Britannia: The Creation of a Roman Province*, London.

Curta F. 2016. Burials in Prehistoric Mounds: Reconnecting with the past in early Medieval Greece, *RÉB* 74, 269-285.

Dally, O. 2008. Athen in der frühen Kaiserzeit – ein Werk des Kaisers Augustus? In: S. Vlizos (ed.), *Η Αθήνα κατά τη ρωμαϊκή εποχή. Πρόσφατες ανακαλύψεις, νέες έρευνες,* Αθήνα, 43-53.

Day, P.M. & D.E. Wilson, 2002. Landscapes of Memory, Craft and Power in Prepalatial and Protopalatial Knossos. In: Y. Hamilakis (ed.), *Labyrinth Revisited: Rethinking 'Minoan' Archaeology*, Oxford, 143-166.

Despinis, G., T. Stefanidou Tiveriou & E. Voutiras, 1997. *Κατάλογος γλυπτών μουσείου Θεσσαλονίκης* Ι, Θεσσαλονίκη.

Díaz-Guardamino, M., L. García Sanjuán & D. Wheatley (eds) 2015. *The Lives of Prehistoric Monuments in Iron Age, Roman and Medieval Europe*, Oxford.

Drougou, S. 2009. Βεργίνα. Η εικόνα του τέλους της πόλης των Αιγών, *Εγνατία* 13, 121-132.

Dubbini, R. 2012. I signori di Corinto e l'arte della città. La formazione della polis sotto le dinastie bacchiade e cipselide. In: M. Castiglione & A. Poggio (eds), *Arte – Potere. Forme artistiche, istituzioni, paradigmi interpretativi, Atti del convegno Pisa 2010*, Milano, 57-76.

Eckardt, H. 2004. Remembering and Forgetting in the Roman Provinces. In: H. Eckardt, J. Meade & B. Croxford (eds), *TRAC 2003: Proceedings of the Thirteenth Theoretical Roman Archaeology Conference, Leicester,* Oxford, 36-50.

Elsner J. & M.J. Squire 2016. Sight and Memory: The visual art of Roman mnemonics. In: M.J. Squire (ed.), *Sight and the Ancient Senses,* London, 180-204.

Elsner, J. 2017. Excavating Pilgrimage. In: T. Myrup Kristensen & W. Friese (eds) *Excavating Pilgrimage: Archaeological Approaches to Sacred Travel and Movement in the Ancient World*, London, 265-274.

Engels D. 1990. *Roman Corinth. An Alternative Model for the Classical City,* Chicago.

Erll, A. 2008. Cultural Memory Studies: An Introduction. In: A. Erll & A. Nünning (eds) *Cultural Memory Studies: An International and Interdisciplinary Handbook*, Berlin, 1-15.

Erll, A. 2011. *Memory in Culture,* Basingstoke.

Evans, N. 2011. Embedding Rome in Athens. In: J.Brodd & J.L. Reed (eds), *Rome and religion: a cross-disciplinary dialogue on the imperial cult,* Atlanta, 83-98.

Ferrari, G. 2002. The Ancient Temple on the Acropolis at Athens, *AJA* 106, 11-35.

Fentress J. & C. Wickham, 1992. *Social Memory*, Oxford.

Fontijn, D. 2015. Re-Inventing Tradition in the Roman West? Some Reflections on the Re-Use of Prehistoric Burial Mounds. In: Boschung *et al.* 2015, 189-213.

Forsdyke, S. 2011. Peer-Polity Interaction and Cultural Competition in Sixth-Century Greece. In: N. Fisher & H. van Wees (eds), *Competition in the Ancient World*, Swansea, 147-174.

Foxhall, L. 2012. Family Time: Temporality, Gender and Materiality in Ancient Greece. In: J. Marincola, L. Llewellyn-Jones & C. Maciver (eds), *Greek Notions of the Past in the Archaic and Classical Eras: History without Historians,* Edinburgh, 183-206.

Fouquet, J. 2012. Der Roma-Augustus-Monopteros auf der Athener Akropolis. Herrscherkult und Memoria 'ad Palladis templi vestibulum'?, *Thetis* 19, 47-95.

Francis, J. 2004. Review of Alcock, S.E. 2002. Archaeologies of the Greek Past: Landscapes, Monuments, and Memories, *Phoenix* 58, 354-356.

Gagé, J. 1975. Alexandre le Grand en Macédoine dans la Ière moitié du IIIe siècle ap. J.-C., *Historia* 24, 1-16.

Galinsky, K. & K. Lapatin (eds) 2015. *Cultural Memories in the Roman Empire*, Los Angeles.

Galli M. & O.D. Cordovana (eds) 2007. *Arte e memoria culturale nell'età della Seconda Sofistica*, Catania.

Gedi, N. & Y. Elam 1996. Collective Memory – What is it?, *History and Memory* 8, 30-50.

Gehrke, H.-J. 2001. Myth, History, and Collective Identity: Uses of the Past in Ancient Greece and Beyond. In: N. Luraghi (ed.), *The Historian's Craft in the Age of Herodotus,* Oxford, 286-313.

Gehrke, H.-J. 2007. Marathon: A European Charter Myth?, *Palamedes* 2, 93-108.

Gonzalbes, E. 1981. El culto indígena a los reyes en Mauritania Tingitana: surgimiento y pervivencia. In: *Paganismo y cristianismo en el Occidente del Imperio Romano*, Oviedo, 153-164.

Grethlein, J. 2010. Homer – die Epische Erinnerung an „unvergänglichen Ruhm'. In: E. Stein-Hölkeskamp & K.-J. Hölkeskamp (eds), *Erinnerungsorte der Antike. Die griechische Welt,* München, 386-399.

Haeussler, R. 2009. Ahnen- und Heroenkulte in Britannien und Gallien. Machtlegitimation oder Bewältigung innerer Krisen? In: J. Rüpke & J. Scheid (eds), *Bestattungsrituale und Totenkult in der römischen Kaiserzeit*, Stuttgart, 57-92.

Haeussler, R. 2010. From Tomb to Temple: On the Role of Hero Cults in Local Religions in Gaul and Britain in the Iron Age and Roman Period. In: J.A. Arenas-Esteban (ed.), *Celtic Religion across Space and Time*, Toledo, 201-226.

Haeussler, R. 2016. *Becoming Roman? Diverging Identities and Experiences in Ancient Northwestern Italy*, London.

Hasberg, W. 2004. Erinnerungskultur – Geschichtskultur, Kulturelles Gedächtnis – Geschichtsbewußtsein. Zehn Aphorismen, *Zeitschrift für Geschichtsdidaktik* 3, 198-206.

Haselgrove, C.C. & M. Millett, 1997. Verlamion reconsidered. In: A. Gwilt & C.C. Haselgrove (eds), *Reconstructing Iron Age Societies*, Oxford, 282-296.

Hitzl, K. 1991. *Olympische Forschungen 19: Die kaiserzeitliche Statuenausstattung des Metroon*, Berlin.

Hobsbawm, E. & T. Ranger (eds) 1983. *The Invention of Tradition*, Cambridge.

Hölscher, T. 2010. Athen, die Polis als Raum der Erinnerung. In: E. Stein-Hölkeskamp & K.-J. Hölke-

skamp (eds), *Erinnerungsorte der Antike. Die griechische Welt,* München, 128-149.

Hupfloher, A. 2006. Kaiserkult in einem überregionalen Heiligtum: das Beispiel Olympia. In: K. Freitag, P. Funke & M. Haake (eds), *Kult – Politik – Ethnos. Überregionale Heiligtümer im Spannungsfeld von Kult und Politik, Kolloquium, Münster, 23-24 November 2001*, Stuttgart, 239-263.

Huyssen, A. 2000. Present Pasts: Media, Politics, Amnesia, *Public Culture* 12.1, 21-38.

Janko, R. 1992. *The Iliad: A Commentary. Vol. 4, Books 13-16*, Cambridge.

Jones, S. & L. Russel, 2012. Archaeology, Memory and Oral Tradition: An Introduction, *Journal of Historical Archaeology* 16.2, 267-283.

Kantiréa, M. 2007. *Les dieux et les dieux Augustes. Le culte impérial en Grèce sous les Julio-claudiens et les Flaviens. Études épigraphiques et archéologiques, Meletemata* 50, Athènes.

Kantsteiner, W. 2002. Finding Meaning in Memory: A Methodological Critique of Collective Memory Studies, *History and Theory* 41, 179-197.

Klein, K.W. 2000, On the Emergence of *Memory* in Historical Discourse, *Representations* 69, 127-150.

Kōresaar, E. 2014, Concepts Around Selected Pasts: On 'Mnemonic Turn' in Cultural Research, *Folklore. Electronic Journal of Folklore* 57, 7-28.

Kousser, R. 2009. Destruction and Memory on the Athenian Acropolis, *ArtB* 91, 263-282.

Lambrinoudakis, V.K. 1988. Veneration of Ancestors in Geometric Naxos. In: R. Hägg, N. Marinatos & G.C. Nordquist (eds), *Early Greek Cult Practice, Proceedings of the Symposium Athens 1986,* Stockholm, 235-246.

Landwehr, C. 1992. Juba II. als Diomedes? *JdI* 107, 103-24.

LeCornec, J. 1985. Le complexe megalithique du Petit-Mont à Arzon (Morbihan), *Revue Archéologique de l'Ouest* 2, 47-63.

LeCornec, J. 1987. Le complexe megalithique du Petit-Mont à Arzon (Morbihan), *Revue Archéologique de l'Ouest* 4, 37-56.

LeCornec, J. 1994. *Le Petit Mont, Arzon*, Rennes.

LeCornec, J. 2001. Réutilisation des Monuments Mégalithiques à l'Époque Gallo-Romaine. In: C.T. Le Roux (ed.), *Du monde des chasseurs à celui des métallurgistes. Hommage scientifique à la mémoire de Jean L'Helgouac'het mélanges offerts à J. Briard. Revue archéologique de l'Ouest. Supplément 9*, Rennes, 289-294.

Leschhorn, W. 1984. *Gründer der Stadt. Studien zu einem politisch-religiösen Phänomen der griechischen Geschichte*, Stuttgart.

Lo Monaco, A. 2009. Ospite nelle case degli dei. Il culto di Augusto in Achaia, *RendLinc* ser. 9, vol. 18, 1-42.

Lozano, F. 2010. *Un dios entre los hombres. La adoración a los emperadores romanos en Grecia*, Barcelona.

Ma, J. 1999. *Antiochos III and the Cities of Western Asia Minor*, Oxford.

Ma, J. 2005. The many lives of Eugnotos of Akraiphia, *Studi Ellenistici* 16, 141-191.

Ma, J. 2009. City as Memory. In: G. Boys-Stones, B. Graziosi & P. Vasunia (eds), *The Oxford Handbook of Hellenic Studies*, Oxford, 248-259.

MacSweeney, N. (ed.) 2014. *Foundation Myths in Ancient Societies. Dialogues and Discourses*, Philadelphia.

Maran, J. 2001. Political and Religious Aspects of Architectural Change in the Upper Citadel of Tiryns. The Case of Building T, *Aegeum* 22, 113-122.

Maran, J. 2011. Contested Pasts – The Society of the 12th c. BCE Argolid and the Memory of the Mycenaean Palatial Period. In: W. Gauß *et al.* (eds), *Our Cups are Full: Pottery and Society in the Aegean Bronze Age, Papers Presented to J.R. Rutter*, Oxford, 169-178.

Mayer, E. 2012. *The Ancient Middle Classes: Urban Life and Aesthetics in the Roman Empire 100 BCE-250 CE*, Harvard.

Millar, F. 2004. P. Herennius Dexippus: the Greek world and the third century invasions. In: H.M. Cotton & G.M. Rogers (eds), *Rome, the Greek World, and the East. Vol. 2: Government, Society & Culture in the Roman Empire*, Chapel Hill, 265-297.

Meskell, L. 2003. Memory's Materiality: Ancestral Presence, Commemorative Practice and Disjunctive Locales. In: R.M. Van Dyke & S.E. Alcock (eds), *Archaeologies of Memory*, Malden, 34-55.

Missitzis, M. 1985. A Royal Decree of Alexander the Great on the Land of Philippoi, *Ancient World* 12, 3-14.

Montserrat D. & L.M. Meskell 1997. Mortuary Archaeology and Religious Landscape at Graeco-Roman Deir el Medina, *Journal of Egyptian Archaeology* 84, 179-198.

Morgan, C. 1991. Ethnicity and Early Greek States: Historical and Material Perspectives, *PCPS* 37, 131-163.

Morgan, C. 2014. Archaeology of Memory or Tradition in Practice? In: B. Alroth, C. Scheffer (eds), *Attitudes towards the Past in Antiquity: Creating Identities, Proceedings of an International Conference held at Stockholm University, 15-17 May 2009, Acta Universitatis Stockholmiensis, Stockholm Studies in Classical Archaeology* 14, Stockholm, 173-182.

Morris, I. 1998. Tomb cult and the 'Greek Renaissance': the past in the present in the 8th century BC, *Antiquity* 63, 750-761.

Mylonas, G.E. 1975. *Τὸ δυτικὸν νεκροταφεῖον τῆς Ἐλευσῖνος*, Αθήνα.

Mylonopoulos, I. 2006. Greek Sanctuaries as Places of Communication Through Rituals: An Archaeological Perspective. In: E. Stavrianopoulou (ed.), *Ritual and Communication in the Graeco-Roman World, Kernos supplement* 16, Liège, 69-110.

Niblett, R. 1999. *The Excavation of a Ceremonial Site at Folly Lane, Verulamium*, London.

Nigdelis, P. 2007. Roman Macedonia (168 BC – AD 284). In: I. Koliopoulos (ed.), *The History of Macedonia, Museum of the Macedonian Struggle foundation*, Thessaloniki, 51-86.

Noreña, C. 2015. Ritual and Memory: Hellenistic Ruler Cults in the Roman Empire. In: K. Galinsky & K. Lapatin (eds), *Cultural Memories in the Roman Empire*, Los Angeles, 86-100.

Olick J.K. & J. Robbins 1998. Social Memory Studies: From 'Collective Memory' to the Historical Sociology of Mnemonic Practices, *Annual Review of Sociology* 24, 105-140.

Pariente, A. 1992. Le monument argien des 'Sept contre Thèbes'. In: M. Piérart (ed.), *Polydipsion Argos*, Paris, 195-229.

Perdrizet, P. 1900. Inscriptions d'Acraephiae, *BCH* 24, 70-81.

Price, S.R.F. 1984. *Rituals and Power. The Roman Imperial Cult in Asia Minor*, Cambridge.

Price, S.R.F. 2012. Memory and Ancient Greece. In: B. Dignas, R. R. R. Smith (eds), *Historical and Religious Memory in the Ancient World*, Oxford, 15-36.

Radstone, S. 2008. Memory Studies: For and Against, *Memory Studies* 1.1, 31-39.

Rizakis, A.D. 1997. Roman Colonies in the Province of Achaia: Territories, Land and Population. In: S.E. Alcock (ed.), *The Early Roman Empire in the East, Oxbow Monograph* 95, Oxford, 15-36.

Rogers, G.M. 1991. *The Sacred Identity of Ephesos: Foundation Myths of a Roman City*, London.

Rojas F. & V. Sergueenkova 2014. Traces of Tarhuntas: Greek, Roman, and Byzantine Interaction with Hittite Monuments, *Journal of Mediterranean Archaeology* 27.2, 135-160.

Roller, D.W. 2003. *The World of Juba II and Kleopatra Selene. Royal Scholarship on Rome's African Frontier*, London.

Rosaldo, R. 1989. *Culture and Truth. The Remaking of Social Analysis*, Boston.

Sanjuán, L.G., P.G. González & F.L. Gómez 2007. Las piedras de la memoria (II). El uso en época romana de espacios y monumentos sagrados prehistóricos del Sur de la Península Ibérica, *Complutum* 18, 109-130.

Sanjuán, L.G., P.G. González, F.L. Gómez 2008. The Use of Prehistoric Ritual and Funerary Sites in Roman Spain: Discussing Tradition, Memory and Identity in Roman Society. In: C. Fenwick, M. Wiggins & D. Wythe (eds), *TRAC 2007: Proceedings of the Seventeenth Theoretical Roman Archaeology Conference, London 2007*, Oxford, 1-17.

Sanjuán, L.G. & M. Díaz-Guardamino 2015. The Outstanding Biographies of Prehistoric Monuments in Iron Age, Roman and Medieval Spain. In: Díaz-Guardamino *et al.* 2015, 183-204.

Sanmartí, J. *et al.* 2015. Roman Dolmens? The Megalithic Necropolises of Eastern Maghreb Revisited. In: Díaz-Guardamino *et al.* 2015, 287-304.

Sanquer, R. 1983, Circonscription de Bretagne, *Gallia* 41, 73-298.

Scherrer, P. 2014. Hunting the Boar – The Fiction of a Local Past in Foundation Myths of Hellenistic and Roman Cities. In: Alroth & Scheffer 2014, 113-119.

Sporn, K. 2015. Vergangenheit in der Gegenwart. Spuren-Suche in der griechischen Antike. In: Boschung *et al.* 2015, 69-94.

Schmidt-Dounas, B. 2016. Macedonian Grave Tumuli. In: U. Kelp & O. Henry (eds), *Tumulus as Sema. Space, Politics, Culture and Religion in the First Millenium BC*, Berlin, 101-142.

Schmitz, T.A. & N. Wiater (eds) 2011. *The Struggle for Identity: Greeks and their Past in the First Century BCE*, Stuttgart.

Spawforth, A.J.S. 2012. *Greece and the Augustan Revolution*, Cambridge.

Simón, F.M. 2013. Ritual y espacios de memoria en Hispania antigua, *Acta Palaeohispanica* 11, 137-165.

Stefanidou-Tiveriou, T. 2008. Tradition and romanization in the monumental landscape of Athens. In: S. Vlizos (ed.), *Η Αθήνα κατά τη ρωμαϊκή εποχή. Πρόσφατες ανακαλύψεις, νέες έρευνες*, Αθήνα, 11-40.

Stefanidou-Tiveriou, T. 2012. Τα λατρευτικά αγάλματα του ναού του Διός και της Ρώμης στη Θεσσαλονίκη,

in: T. Stefanidou-Tiveriou, P. Karanastasi & D. Damaskos (eds), *Κλασική παράδοση και νεωτερικά στοιχεά στην πλαστική της ρωμαϊκής Ελλάδας, Πρακτικά Διεθνούς Συνεδρίου, 7-9 Μαΐου 2009*, Θεσσαλονίκη, 273-286.

Steinbock, B. 2013. *Social Memory in Athenian Public Discourse. Uses and Meanings of the Past*, Ann Arbor.

Swain, S. 1996. *Hellenism and Empire: Language, Classicism and Power in the Greek World, AD 50-250*, Oxford.

Vansina, J. 1985. *Oral Tradition as History*, Madison.

Vejby, M. 2015. Enduring Past: Megalithic Tombs of Brittany and the Roman Occupation in Western France. In: Díaz-Guardamino *et al.* 2015, 163-182.

Whitley, J. 1998. Early States and Hero Cults: a Reappraisal, *JHS* 108, 173-182.

Woolf, G. 1996. The Uses of Forgetfulness in Roman Gaul. In: H.J. Gehrke & A. Müller (eds), *Vergangenheit und Lebenswelt: Soziale Kommunikation, Traditionsbildung und historisches Bewußtsein*, Tübingen, 361-381.

Zoumbaki, S. 2008. The Composition of the Peloponnesian Elites in the Roman Period and the Evolution of their Resistance and Approach to the Roman Rulers, *Tekmeria* 9, 25-52.

Zuiderhoek, A. 2008. On the political sociology of the imperial Greek city, *GRBS* 48, 417-445.

Zuiderhoek, A. 2014. Controlling Urban Space in Roman Asia Minor. In: T. Bekker-Nielsen (ed.), *Space, place and identity in Northern Anatolia. Geographica Historica 29*, Stuttgart, 99-108.

Strategies of Remembering in the Creation of a Colonial Society in Patras

Tamara M. Dijkstra

Abstract

This article explores the role of references to and interplay with the local myth-historical past in Patras' transformation from Greek polis to Roman *colonia*, from a political and a social perspective. It addresses how the Roman administration fostered a successful transition by employing the cult of Artemis Laphria as a unifying religious focus for the multi-ethnic and multi-cultural inhabitants of the colony, and by embedding the Augustan re-foundation in the local foundation myths of the polis. In the social domain newcomers to the Patraean colony seem to have employed strategic funerary behaviour to anchor themselves among the local elite in their struggle for social prominence. Although very different in nature, these are instructive examples of how strategies of remembering were instrumental in the development of a colonial society.

Keywords: Patras, Roman colonization, founding myths, tomb architecture

1. Introduction

The colonization of the city of Patras under Augustus was accompanied by a series of radical interventions: the installation of Roman rule, the arrival of thousands of colonists, the introduction of new cults, and the relegation of the original polis population to marginality, causing major disruptions to the local political and social landscape. The inhabitants of the newly founded colony had varied ethnic and cultural backgrounds[1]: they included the original inhabitants, Roman veteran-colonists, Greeks from the surrounding villages summoned to move to Patras, and Roman families from Italy who chose to make a new life in the city (Paus. 7.18.7; Rizakis 1998, 24-28). These social groups had varying political and economic opportunities, legal rights, and social statuses. The reconciliation of these groups was vital to Rome in order for the colony to be successful in its political and economic aims (*cf.* Rizakis 2009; similar in Corinth: Vanderpool & Scotton and Del Basso, *this volume*), but on a social level, the creation of a new social hierarchy was essential for the population of the colony itself as well. It seems that strategies of remembering – of references to and interplay with the local myth-historical past, and of calculated commemorative behaviour – played an important role in this process. These strat-

---

1   But see Cic. *Ad Fam.* 7.2.8; 16.1, 5, 6; *Ad Att.* 5.9; 7.2 and Rizakis 1988 from which it is clear that Patras, prior to colonization, was already home to a multi-ethnic and multi-cultural society.

in: Dijkstra, T.M., I.N.I. Kuin, M. Moser & D. Weidgenannt (eds) 2017. *Strategies of Remembering in Greece under Rome (100 BC - 100 AD)*, Leiden (Sidestone Press).

egies can be interpreted in the framework of 'anchoring innovation', a concept that describes how the acceptance of a new situation – in this case Patras' transformation from polis to *colonia* and its social consequences – is facilitated by connecting it to local traditions and embedding it in existing frameworks (see Sluiter 2017; Kuin *this volume*). This article is divided in two sections. In the first part, it addresses how Augustus promoted a new sense of community between the local and immigrant population of Patras by introducing a regionally revered deity, and it discusses how the Augustan foundation of the colony was connected to the mythical stories surrounding the original foundation of the polis. The second part assesses how members of the immigrant population employed strategic funerary behaviour to anchor their presence in the colony, and to claim a position among the higher echelons of the colonial hierarchy.

2. Anchoring Augustan rule

2.1 The introduction of Artemis Laphria in Patras

Following his victory at the battle of Actium, Augustus founded Nikopolis and the colony at Patras. At the same time the smaller towns in Aitolia, Akarnania, and Achaia were destroyed, and their populations forced to migrate to these two cities, that were to become the major centres of the region (Paus. 7.18.7-9).[2] One of the affected towns was Kalydon. The territory of this town was placed under the control of the colony at Patras, while its population was transported to Nikopolis (Paus. 7.18.8).[3] The chryselephantine cult statue of Artemis Laphria was taken from its temple and was transferred to Patras.[4] Severing the connection between the Kalydonian landscape, the community, and its main deity was an effective display of Roman domination, and can be identified as an example of Augustan religious politics.

As Susan Alcock (1993, 141) observed, the relocation of religious architecture or objects not only served as a demonstration of 'the absolute power of the conqueror'. It had an additional layer of significance: since cult objects

'as sacred things, contained and declared the history and identity of individual civic entities, as well as of the Greeks as a whole' (178), their appropriation should be considered as a form of symbolic violence. As such, cult displacement 'worked effectively to undermine local loyalties, to shatter established relationships of authority and, above all, to weaken any pretense of independence' (179-180).

However, while a direct attack on one of the cornerstones of the Kalydonian community, the relocation of the cult of Artemis had an altogether different effect in Patras, where it was moved. There it was used as a focal point for the creation of a communal identity; if the varied social groups of Patras could come together in her veneration, this would help ensure the success of the colony (*cf.* Rizakis 1998, 37; 2009, 24-27; 2010, 132-133).[5]

Strategies of remembering played an important role in achieving this aim and promoting the adoption of the cult. The choice for Kalydonian Artemis Laphria was significant. Rather than imposing a Roman deity on Patras, a cult was brought in that had a long history of regional veneration. Kalydon, as the site of the myth surrounding Meleager and the boar hunt, was famous throughout the Greek and Roman world (e.g. Diod. Sic. 4.34.2; Ov. *Met.* 8.260-450; Paus. 8.45.6) and Artemis had been revered in Kalydon since Archaic times. Artemis' cult statue was imbued with this local history and meaning, and as such was a reflection of Greek identity. This statue was transported to Patras, and installed on the acropolis, which had long served as its religious centre. Athanasios Rizakis (1998, 36) suggests that the use of the goddess' Latin name by the Roman administration – Artemis became Diana – stimulated the acceptance of the goddess by the Latin-speaking populace. The imperial administration chose to use the image of Diana Laphria on the colonial numismatic iconography, though not until several decades after the colony's foundation: she appears for the first time under Nero (RPC 1, No. 1276, 1277, 1281) and continues to be depicted until the time of Septimius

---

2   For a discussion of the date of Patras' colonization see *e.g.* Rizakis 1998, 24-28. For Pausanias on Augustus see Arafat 1996, 116-138; and 134-138 on Patras and Nikopolis.

3   But see the short preliminary report on the 2016 excavations by the Danish-Greek team under direction of Handberg and Vikatou which briefly mentions the find of a considerable amount of Terra Sigillata pottery dating to the Augustan period, suggesting that the site was not necessarily completely abandoned at this time (http://www.diathens.gr/files/2/6/470/Nyt_fra_4._s_son.pdf, accessed 19 July 2017).

4   Paus. 7.18.8-9; for the relocation of the Kalydonian temple to Patras see Rizakis 2009, 24-27

---

5   For the importance of religion in processes of unification under Augustus, *e.g.* Orlin 2007. See Malkin 1987, esp. chapter 4 on the introduction of gods and sanctuaries in colonies, and chapter 5 on *oikist* cults. Malkin (1983, 203), though speaking of Greek colonies of the Archaic and Classical period, highlights the need for a common colonial identity to ensure the success of a colony, and the crucial role that cults, in his case oikist cults, could play: 'The new *polis* needed and identity (…). The identity of a colony set up as an independent *polis* was a composite matter. The sooner the settlers would have a common, independent tradition to share and the sooner they would have a common hēros as the focus of their worship (and, thus, as their own protector) – the sooner that identity would acquire a life of its own. One should not underestimate symbols; the oikist cult served as a common point of reference for settlers who were themselves not always of the same origin.'

Severus and Caracalla (Grose 1926, No. 6344; SNGCop, No. 202).

The successful adoption of Diana Laphria in the local religious landscape can be inferred from three inscriptions – in Latin – set up by private individuals in her honour.[6] Pausanias (7.18.11-13) further informs us that in his day an annual festival was celebrated in her honour, culminating in the sacrifice of wild animals thrown on a pyre while still alive; if animals managed to escape, he continues, they were recaptured and dragged back into the flames.[7] These festivities brought together the community as a whole, with both the city and private individuals eagerly participating in the offerings (Paus. 7.18.12).[8]

Clearly, the introduction and promotion of the goddess had been effective: over time Diana Laphria, and the cult celebrated in her honour, had proved to be a unifier. The goddess and her cult had become central to the civic and cultural identity of the Patraean community, and were a common source of civic pride for all of the colony's inhabitants.

2.2 Augustus as a modern oikist

The installation of Artemis/Diana Laphria's cult was combined with strategies ensuring local acceptance of Augustan rule in Patras. References to ancient local founding myths were instrumental in this process. The most explicit reference to these foundation myths was the placement of the temple and the altar on either side of the tomb of Eurypylos.[9] Tombs for local heroes and ancestors were an important feature of Greek urban landscapes; they can be seen as a physical manifestation of local history, or *mnemotopes*, and as such, hero tombs served as an important focus for the civic and cultural identity of

the local population.[10] The spatial association of temple and tomb encouraged the local community to associate Eurypylos with Augustus, and to accept Augustus as a modern founding hero.

Eurypylos was venerated as a hero in Patras for putting an end to human sacrifices, which, according to local myth, had been practised there to placate Artemis Triklaria (Paus. 7.19.1-10). In the mythical past, the local population had received an oracle promising them that 'a strange king would come to the land, bringing with him a strange divinity, and this king would put an end to the sacrifice to Triclaria' (Paus. 7.19.6, transl. Jones). When Eurypylos, a Thessalian nobleman, came to Patras (then still known as Aroë) and brought with him a chest containing the cult image of Dionysos Aisymnetes from the spoils of Troy, it was clear to the local population that the oracle had been fulfilled. In Pausanias' time, Eurypylos received annual sacrifices at his tomb site during the festival of Dionysos Aisymnetes (Paus. 7.19.10).

The explicit spatial relation that was created between the temple and altar of Artemis Laphria and the tomb of Eurypylos should be seen as a deliberate attempt to promote the parallels between the myth of Eurypylos and the arrival of Augustus.[11] In much the same way as Eurypylos arrived here in the distant past, Augustus arrived to Patras in the Roman present: as a foreign ruler, bringing with him a deity from the spoils of war, and installing the old cult at its new location.

We may expand the argument to include two other heroes of Patras: Preugenes and his son Patreus. Just as Eurypylos, these two men were regarded as local founding heroes and had tombs in the centre of the city. The tomb of Patreus was located in the agora (Paus. 7.20.5), and that of Preugenes in the grove of Artemis Limnatis opposite the agora (Paus. 7.20.9). We are told that Preugenes and Patreus fled from Sparta and settled in Achaia, where Patreus was responsible for forcing the inhabitants of several small villages to move to one settlement (Paus. 7.6.2). He then named this settlement Patras, after himself. On their flight from Sparta the men had

---

6   Rizakis 1998, Nos. 4-6. It should be noted that no dedications in Greek or by Greek individuals have thus far been documented.

7   For Artemis/Diana Laphria in Patras see Osanna 1996, 70-78; Pirenne-Delforge 2004; 2006 and Goldhill 2010. The latter two discuss the striking character of the celebrations, in which the local and foreign (Roman) character are particularly intertwined. The sacrifice is notably different from normal Greek practice, as living wild animals are being thrown on the pyre, rather than burning a portion of a butchered domesticated animal. It can be seen as an invented ritual which suited the Roman taste for violence and a sense of local antiquity. Pausanias' emphasis on typically local character of the sacrifice, the τρόπος ἐπιχώριος, reinforces the notion of Patras as an exceptional place: the city is very different from the surrounding lands, not only on a political, but also on a cultural level.

8   Paus. 7. 18.12: 'ἐς δὲ τὴν ἐπιοῦσαν τηνικαῦτα ἤδη δρᾶν τὰ ἐς τὴν θυσίαν νομίζουσι, δημοσίᾳ τε ἡ πόλις καὶ οὐχ ἧσσον ἐς τὴν ἑορτὴν οἱ ἰδιῶται φιλοτίμως ἔχουσιν'.

9   Paus. 7.19.1: 'ἔστι δὲ ἐν τῷ μεταξὺ τοῦ ναοῦ τε τῆς Λαφρίας καὶ τοῦ βωμοῦ πεποιημένον μνῆμα Εὐρυπύλου'.

10   For tomb cult and its relation to local identities see *e.g.* Malkin 1983; Alcock 1991; Marantou 2011; Antonaccio 2016. See also n. 4, above.

11   Scholars have noted the poignant similarities between Eurypylos and Augustus before: Rizakis (1998, 37): '(…) comme Eurypylos avait transporté alors le *xoanon* de Dionysos de la côte oppose (Delphes) et introduit son culte à Aroé transformant le chaos initial par l'ordre du synœcisme, de la même façon, Auguste, nouveau fondateur, transporte la statue cultuelle d'Artémis Laphria de Kalydon, l'installe au même endroit (l'ancienne Aroé) et met en œuvre, sous sa protection, un synœcisme plus vaste qui restructure complètement l'espace territorial de la cite.' See also Osanna 1996, 146; Goldhill 2010, 62-63; Papapostolou 2014, 254-255.

taken with them the statue of Artemis Limnatis, and they introduced her cult in the new polis (Paus. 7.20.8).[12]

Again, parallels between the founding heroes and Augustus can be drawn: in the mythological past, Patreus, a foreign ruler, synoecized the villages of the area upon coming to Achaia, named the new settlement after himself, and installed a cult for Artemis. In the Roman present, Augustus, a foreign ruler, synoecized the smaller settlements from the region and forced its inhabitants to live in a colony that he named *Colonia Augusta Achaica Patrensis* after himself – and he, too, installed a cult for Artemis. In many ways, Augustus could be regarded as a modern Patreus.

The three mythical figures central to local history received annual sacrifices at their tomb sites during the festivals for the deities that they had introduced to Patras: Eurypylos during the festival of Dionysos, and Preugenes and Patreus at the festival for Artemis Limnatis (Paus. 7.20.9). If Augustus was seen as the latest in the line of local oikists, we would expect that he was honoured as such, and receive sacrifices during the festival for the goddess that he had brought with him. And indeed there is evidence that Augustus and Artemis received joint veneration: an inscription dated to the 1st century AD informs us that Diana Laphria and Augustus shared a priestess (Rizakis 1998, No. 5; see also Osanna 1996, 76-78), and the Latin legends on the colonial coinage under Nero (RPC I, No. 1276, 1281) and Domitian (RPC II, No. 227) refer to the patron deity as Diana Augusta (Laphria); the epithet Augusta signals the strength of the connection between deity and emperor. The bond between Augustus and Diana, and his reconfiguration as founding hero of Patras, paved the way for the imperial cult.[13]

3. Strategic commemoration: integration and competition in the cemetery

3.1 Burial and commemoration in Patras
The creation of a new community was not only a concern for Augustus. Adaptation to the new status quo was also of essential importance to the inhabitants of the colony, especially since the vast number of newcomers necessitated a rearrangement of the existing social hierarchy. The thousands of colonists and other immigrants who

arrived in Patras had to negotiate their relationship with the local population – who in their turn had to adapt to their new, more marginalised status – and competed among each other for social prominence. This debate was partly played out in the cemetery, where the society of Patras displayed itself by replacing a dead individual with a permanent memorial expressing certain aspects of his or her identity. Death, through funerary ritual and commemorative practices, thus provides the opportunity for self-representation and definition: it allows the expression and shaping of social status and identity. Adherence or divergence from local norms affirms or denies broader communal values and beliefs surrounding death, and it provides the opportunity to assert relationships with local, regional, and supra-regional political or social entities.[14] A study of mortuary practices can help us, therefore, to reconstruct ancient society and its contemporary political, economic, social, and religious concerns. It is, however, important to realize that funerary rituals and commemorative practices do not necessarily reflect reality, but can be used as a distinct form of manipulation: they can misrepresent, disguise or idealise aspects of the buried individual and of society (see esp. Parker Pearson 2009, 83-85). As such, whereas funerary ritual may follow the general rules and norms of a society, every individual burial is carried out in such a way that best befits the specific situation, ideas, beliefs and, which is important for this article, the *aims* of the burying group (Morris 1992, 4; Tarlow 1999, 23-24).

In Patras, three main cemeteries developed along the main thoroughfares of the city (Figure 1).[15] The oldest and largest is the North Cemetery which extends along the road to Aigion and Corinth, and started to be used around 450 BC. The South Cemetery, on the route to Dyme, developed in the later 3rd century BC, and the East Cemetery, along with isolated burial grounds and tombs scattered around the countryside, date to the Roman period. A close examination of continuity and change, of norms and deviations in the archaeological and epigraphic material from these cemeteries, allows the identification of a drastic change in mortuary practices in

---

12 The cult statue of Artemis Limnatis was stolen from its sanctuary by Preugenes and his slaves. In Patras the goddess was honoured in a sacred grove near the agora (Paus. 7.20.7-8), but her statue was placed elsewhere and was brought to the grove by slaves at the yearly festival in a ritual that seems to have been devised to commemorate the foundation of Patras and the original arrival of the goddess.

13 See Rizakis 1989, 184; 1998, 36-37; for the imperial cult in the Peloponnese: Camia & Kantiréa 2010.

14 On the relation between mortuary practices and societies, see most notably Saxe 1970; Binford 1971; Hodder 1981; Parker Pearson 1982; 1993; 2009 [1999]; Morris 1987; 1992. A comprehensive discussion of burials and society in the provincial Roman world: Pearce 2000.

15 The most recent and elaborate overview of the cemeteries at Patras is provided by Dekoulakou (2009), who discusses the wide variety of tomb architecture of the Roman period in Patras. Other general overviews are provided by Petropoulos (1994, 414-415 and σχέδ. 1), Rizakis (1998, 48 and σχέδ. 1), Rizakis & Petropoulos (2006, 16-17, 46 and maps 3 and 4), Flämig (2007, 8-9), Dekoulakou (2009, 163-168 and fig. 1), and Dijkstra (2015).

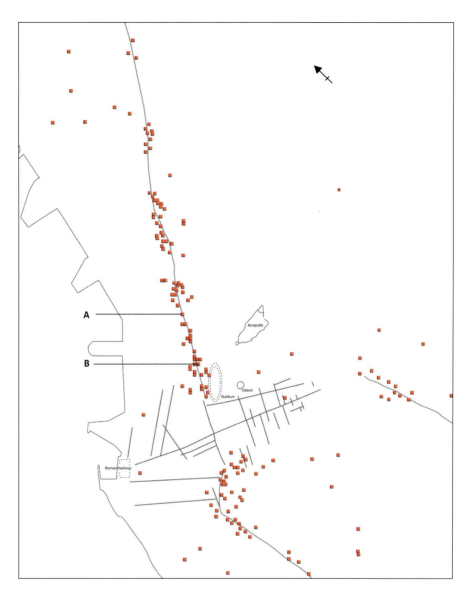

Figure 1. The cemeteries of Patras, and the location of Korinthou 221-223 (A) and the Mausoleum of the Aequani (B).

the early Roman period, and provides instructive examples of how mortuary practices could be strategically employed in the creation of a social hierarchy.[16]

In pre-colonial times, the common practice was inhumation in simple grave types: cist, tile and pit graves.[17] The graves were only rarely marked with stone *stelai*, judging from the limited number that have been preserved. It is possible that markers of perishable material or natural features such as plants or hedges were used to demarcate indivi-

---

16 The bulk of the archaeological material has only been preliminarily published by the Greek Archaeological Service in the Αρχαιολογικά Δελτία. More detailed publications of individual tombs and grave goods include Papapostolou (1977; 1978) on richly furbished Hellenistic graves, and on *polyandria* belonging to a *familia* of gladiators (1989); Dekoulakou (1980) on an early Roman mausoleum and Papapostolou (1983) on the grave goods associated with the tomb (discussed as a case study below), and Petropoulos (2007) on a rural burial site dating to the same period. The publication of grave *stelai* and funerary inscriptions by Papapostolou (1993) and Rizakis (1998; 2008) are invaluable to the study of mortuary practices in Achaia.

17 The map presented here is based on information from preliminary publications by the Greek Archaeological Service in the ArchDelt-series.

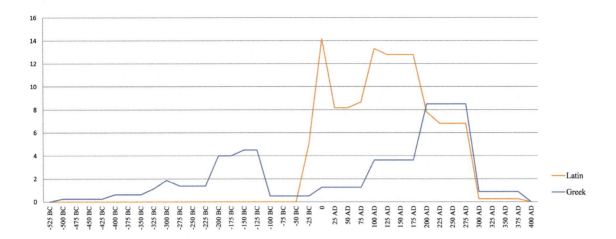

Figure 2. The ratio of Greek and Latin of epitaphs from Patras, balanced average, N=212.

dual graves or burial clusters. Some graves of the Hellenistic period were richly adorned with grave goods, including gold wreaths and various items of jewellery.[18]

After Patras' colonization we note a general decline in the wealth of the grave goods, which is countered by an increased expenditure on tomb construction. Whereas in the Classical and Hellenistic period elaborate tomb architecture was virtually non-existent, soon after the creation of the colony many monumental tombs are erected, such as columbaria, temple tombs, and tomb-altars (see Flämig 2007, Nos. 90-176 and Dekoulakou 2009 for categorization and discussion). Most of the tombs provide spaces for the deposition of cremated remains, the 'Romanus mos' (Tac. Ann. 16.6), though combinations occur (as in the Mausoleum of the Aequani discussed below). Many tombs were meant to include multiple depositions, which signals a stronger emphasis on group identity and continuity. The number of funerary inscriptions, often intended to be attached to the façade of the tombs, rises steeply in the Roman period. The large majority is written in Latin (Figure 2).

The Roman elements displayed in the new mortuary practices (architecture, language, the rite of cremation) and the date of their introduction indicate that they can be attributed to colonists of a Roman cultural background and other newcomers.[19] In the following sections I discuss two case studies from the North Cemetery of Patras which serve as instructive examples of how strategic funerary behaviour could work: Odos Korinthou 221-223 and the Mausoleum of the Aequani, both excavated in 1976 by the local Ephorate of Antiquities (Papapostolou 1976; Dekoulakou 1976). I argue that the owners of these tombs applied different strategies in the deposition of their dead aimed at anchoring themselves and their families in their new surroundings, and to further their socio-political status in the colonial hierarchy.

3.2 Engaging with the pre-colonial elite

The excavation of the plot on Korinthou 221-223 in the North Cemetery of Patras revealed a succession of use spanning from the Hellenistic to the late Roman period (Figure 3).[20] Three well-constructed cist graves made of limestone slabs connected with iron clamps date to the Hellenistic period. The grave goods were noteworthy and include

---

18 See Dimakis 2016, Appendix A 185-189 and Appendix B 224-231 with bibliography.
19 For a comprehensive overview of Greek mortuary practices see Garland 1985, on Roman death and burial: Toynbee 1971; Hope 2009.
20 A preliminary report of the excavation was published by Papapostolou (1976), translated and summarized by Catling (1985, 27). Flämig (2007) described the monumental tombs of the Roman period in her catalogue, Nos. 146-154.

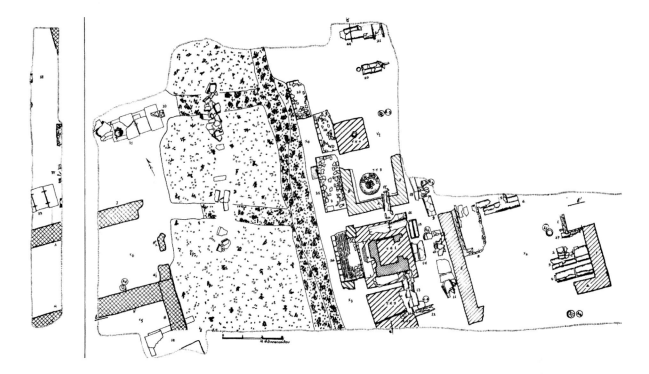

Figure 3. Plan of the excavation of Korinthou 221-223. Source: Papapostolou 1976, 94, plan 3.

several items of gold jewellery, gold thread that probably belonged to a luxurious shroud, gold funerary wreaths, and silver vessels. In one of the graves three bronze coins minted between 146 and 31 BC provide a secure terminus post quem for the grave. Combined, the archaeological and numismatic evidence suggests that this inhumation dates to the transitional phase from polis to colony. Also of Hellenistic date is the material found in the street, consisting of grave *stelai* and architectural blocks, probably the result of a clearing of the area in early Roman times (*stelai*: Papapostolou 1990, no. 12, 15, 17, 28, 29).

Four tombs on the east side of the road belong to the early Roman period. Three of the tombs have a core of *opus caementicium* and had a stone *krepis*. In one of the tombs a *stamnos* was built into the floor, and in another two lead urns were found below the foundation. Another tomb contained a small funerary chamber, with an entrance on its east side. The fourth tomb was a *peribolos*, built in *opus quasi-reticulatum* technique, with the corners in *opus testaceum*. The *peribolos* surrounded a tumulus made of potsherds, measuring ca. 1x0.50 m. It covered a lead ash urn. To the same general period belong three *periboloi*, one of which contained cist and tile graves, the others were badly preserved. Dispersed throughout the plot cremations in clay and lead urns were found, some of which were covered by an inverted pointed amphora.

In the 2nd/3rd century AD three brick built tombs were constructed in front of the early Roman tombs. The tombs had a vaulted chamber that contained several inhumations. Two of these tombs have been identified as belonging to a group of gladiators (Papapostolou 1989, and Rizakis 1984; 1990). The highest level, containing only tile graves, can be dated to the late Roman period, the 5th/6th century AD.

The excavated remains dating to the Hellenistic period are exceptional: whilst in Hellenistic Patras tile graves with simple grave goods were the norm, the graves found here were carefully constructed limestone cists; the wealth of the grave goods and the presence of several decorated stone funerary *stelai* are further indications of significant expenditure on these burials. These graves can be attributed to the social elite of the pre-colonial Patras, and the cluster suggests that this particular area was a prominent section of the Hellenistic cemetery.

Only a short time after the last burial in Hellenistic style occurred, four monumental tombs were constructed here. Whilst in the Hellenistic period the graves were belowground and only topped with a *stele*, the monuments of the Roman period were aboveground and monumental, indicating an increased desire for display. Although no associated epitaphs were recovered, the combination of tomb types, construction methods, and the presence of cremated remains suggests that these tombs belonged to a non-local population group; most likely immigrants from the Italian peninsula.

Despite the expansion of the South Cemetery and the creation of the new East Cemetery in the early Roman period, these early newcomers made a deliberate choice to erect their funerary monuments in the core of the Hellenistic North Cemetery. To understand the motivations behind this, we have to consider the practical and symbolic value of this location.[21] Burial in the North Cemetery was a strategic choice for tomb owners who aimed at status display: as the main land route between Patras and Corinth, the two major Peloponnesian centres, the funerary road of the North Cemetery ensured a sizeable audience for one's tomb.

The close spatial connection with the graves of the pre-colonial elite was motivated by the symbolic value of the place (for similar mechanisms of association see Fouquet and Dickenson *this volume*). Burial sites can be considered as mnemotopes imbued with local history: this is not only true for tombs of mythical ancestors, as discussed above, but the same can be said for the burial places of previous generations of a specific family, or of a society as a whole. I argue that in this case study the burial site of the pre-colonial elite was a mnemotope symbolizing the history of Patras as a Greek polis, and as such, served as a site of local civic identity. It further had an inherent value of elite status. By depositing their dead in this mnemotope, the newcomers could take advantage of its symbolic values. On the one hand, it can be seen as an attempt to engage with and to foster a relationship with the local community, in an effort to anchor themselves and their families in their new surroundings. On the other hand, it was an act of usurpation of an important, meaningful place and it marked the transition from the old to the new reality: in the living society the eminence

of the local, Greek population was relegated to the past, and a new socio-political elite arrived in its place; in the cemetery, the tombs of the newcomers quite literally overshadowed the graves of the polis-elite.[22]

3.3 Competitive Commemoration

The so-called Mausoleum of the Aequani, excavated in 1976 by the local Archaeological Service, is another example of strategic funerary behaviour.[23] The tomb was located in the North Cemetery. Although only the podium and an underground burial chamber have been preserved, the tomb can be categorized as a temple tomb (Figure 4). The podium, measuring ca. 12x8 m and 2.5 m high, was constructed of a solid core of *opus caementicium* which was lined with limestone slabs. In the core of the podium a monolithic sarcophagus was found containing the remains of a young adult male[24] adorned with rich grave goods, including gold leaves (belonging to two wreaths), various items of gold jewellery, a silver rattle, an inscribed rock-crystal dodecahedron, silver *astragaloi*, and a number of ivory objects including a *diptychon*, a relief plaque, and a statuette of a cripple in Alexandrian tradition (see Papapostolou 1983 for a detailed discussion). In a marble box placed at the head of the deceased, outside the sarcophagus, an unspecified number of hen's eggs were found. The display of wealth in the architecture and grave goods allows us to imagine what a spectacle the funerary procession and the burial rites may have been.

---

21 For the importance of *place* in mortuary practices see Parker Pearson 2009[1999], esp. 124-141: 'Where to put the remains of the dead is generally not a matter of functional expediency. The place of the dead in any society will have significant and powerful connotations within people's perceived social geographies. (…) [T]he fixing of the dead in the land is a social and political act which ensures access and rights over natural resources. Placing the dead is one of the most visible activities through which human societies map out and express their relationships to ancestors, land and the living' (141).

22 It is worth noting that at some point in the early Roman period the North Cemetery road was widened, probably to accommodate increased traffic, and that in the process the Hellenistic graves were built over or cleared, and *stelai* were removed from their places; they were used as road fill. Though a practical motivation was certainly present, we may wonder about the symbolism behind these actions, because burial sites, as foci of group identity, often constitute an easy target for symbolic violence. In Patras, the indigenous community may well have considered these graves as representing their past and their identity, and perceived their destruction by the hands of the colonizer as a personal assault.

23 A preliminary report about the mausoleum was published by Dekoulakou soon after the excavation (Dekoulakou 1976), and a more extensive description by her appeared later (Dekoulakou 1980). Papapostolou (1983) published the finds from the inhumation grave found in the podium of the mausoleum. The tomb has received further attention from Catling (1986), Flämig (2003, 2007), Dekoulakou (2009), and Lolos (2016).

24 In the original publication the grave was identified as belonging to a female, based on the grave goods that accompanied the human remains. However, a preliminary study of photographs of the skeleton by anthropologist McGeorge suggests that the individual was more likely to be a young male (Papapostolou 1983, 4, n. 4). If the skeletal remains have been preserved in the storerooms of the Ephoria, modern advances in archaeological science could be applied to inform us about the identity of the individual in much more detail, such as using isotopic analysis to determine provenance.

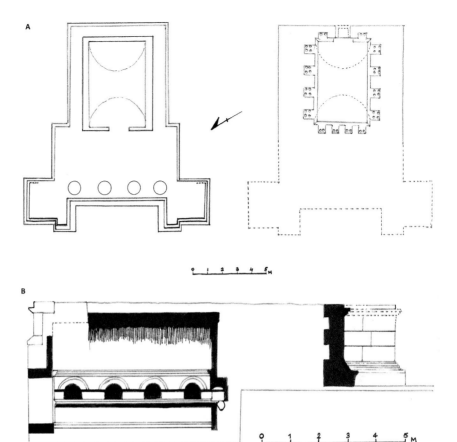

Figure 4. Ermou 80-82, Mausoleum of the Aequani: a. Reconstruction of the burial chamber and the podium; b. Section of the burial chamber and podium (Redrawn after Dekoulakou 1980, 560-561, fig. 2-3, and 572, fig. 8.

The tomb can be dated to the early 1st century AD on the basis of the grave goods (Papapostolou 1983, 31).

The façade of the tomb consisted of an exedra with stone foundations on either side, probably bases for funerary statuary. Above the exedra once rose a temple-like construction with a tetrastyle façade. At the back of the tomb a flight of steps led up to the cella, while a second set of steps led down into an underground chamber. Though it has not been preserved, parallels from other regions indicate that the cella may have housed human remains and funerary statuary; it may also have been used for family gatherings during commemorative rituals (see Von Hesberg 1992, 182-201). The burial chamber, reused in Byzantine times as a church, was a columbarium containing fourteen niches in each of which either two or four cinerary urns were immured.

The reasons for choosing the North Cemetery have already been discussed above, but I again point out that this location provided the largest audience for the monuments. It is noteworthy that the mausoleum is not located in the core of the Hellenistic and early Roman cemetery, but much closer to the urban perimeter. In fact, it seems that it was the only monumental tomb built in this particular area at the time of construction, which means that the Mausoleum of the Aequani dominated the area, and was the first tomb that travellers encountered when leaving the city, and the last one to be seen before entering it. It is likely that because of its size the tomb was not only visible from the funerary road, but also from the acropolis.

The tomb-design displays a blend of cultural influences, combining architectural styles with roots in different parts of the Mediterranean world: the subterranean burial chamber in the form of a columbarium is clearly derived from Italian examples, whereas the upper storey in the form of a tetrastyle temple rather seems to draw from tomb types from the Hellenistic East (Flämig 2003, 567). The decision to use an architectural style usually reserved for religious structures was significant: its innate association with divinity would elicit feelings of reverence and esteem, and may well have worked as a status enhancer (*cf.* Fedak 1990, 66).

A similar mix of cultural influences can be discerned in the mortuary practices: the use of inhumation points to origins in Greece and the wider Eastern world, whereas cremation – for which 44 receptacles were provided in the mausoleum – was the common Roman practice (the overview by Nock (1932), though dated, is still useful). The grave goods associated with the primary inhumation show influences from all over the Mediterranean, including the Italian peninsula, the Greek East, and Egypt.

Compared to other monuments of the early Roman period erected in Patras, the Mausoleum of the Aequani was truly exceptional.[25] Certain aspects of the tomb's construction were deliberately non-conformist: strategic utilization of location, visibility and tomb architecture worked together to maximize the impact the tomb had on its audience. However, rather than engaging with older Greek tombs and establishing a perception of continuity as in our previous case study, this tomb seems to have aimed almost exclusively at social competition – with locals and newcomers alike – to advance the interests of the family that erected it.[26]

Epigraphic evidence found in close connection with the tomb suggests that it belonged to the family of the Aequani.[27] A funerary epigram, in Latin, commemorates the freedman Sextus Aequanus Astius, an Augustalis

(Rizakis 1998, No. 145).[28] An Aequana Musa, daughter of Sextus Aequanus, is known from the local epigraphic record as the priestess of Diana Laphria and Augustus (Rizakis 1998, No. 5). If the connection between the inscriptions and the tomb is correct, this was the mausoleum of a family with Roman citizenship, but whose eclectic mortuary practices reflected a cosmopolitan identity. Their tomb, besides serving as the home for the family dead and reflecting their identity, was instrumental in their ascension to social prominence. In the newly formed colony the immigrants had to vie for their position in the social hierarchy, not merely with the local population, but also among each other. The Aequani, by planting their imposing, non-conformist family mausoleum at a highly strategic location, not only claimed dominance in the cemetery, but also firmly anchored themselves in the living society in the highest echelon of the colonial elite.

4. Conclusions

Strategies of remembering were vital in the refashioning of Patras as a Roman colony, and were employed both by the imperial power and by the new settlers. References to and interplay with the past served to help Patras' inhabitants adapt to the new political and social conditions and to create a new sense of community among them. Augustus' transfer of Artemis Laphria to Patras, and her promotion as the patron deity of the colony, created a religious focus that was acceptable for both the original inhabitants, and the settlers from elsewhere, thus ensuring that the entire community could come together in her veneration. The explicit association of Artemis' temple with the tomb of Eurypylos sought to evoke the similarities between the local foundation myths and Augustus' foundation of the colony. With the connection of Augustus to the Patraean oikists, Augustan rule was anchored in the local historical narrative, thus easing the transition and fostering local acquiescence.

Such strategic action was not limited to the imperial power: the newcomers to Patraean society, too, felt motivated to claim and consolidate their position in the

---

25 But see Lolos (2016) who discusses a tomb documented in 1829 by Blouet in relation to the Mausoleum of the Aequani, which had previously been thought to be one and the same monument. However, despite some clear similarities, Lolos' detailed comparison proves that it cannot in fact be the same tomb. Lolos therefore proposes that a 'twin monument' may have existed in the North Cemetery of Patras, and that these belonged to 'two of the highest officials of the city and their families' (356). It should be noted though that Blouet did not refer to, or drew, a superstructure, and Lolos' reconstruction of the upper storey as a temple tomb is merely a suggestion. Whatever the case may be, as this tomb has not been recovered in the archaeological record, it is impossible to determine its stylistic, temporal or spatial relation to the Mausoleum of the Aequani.

26 Erecting tombs as a means of social competition has been noted for Rome and surroundings by Von Hesberg & Zanker (1987, 12-13) and Heinzelmann (2000, 80). In general see Parker Pearson 2009.

27 Though not in situ, see Dekoulakou 1980, 566-568. The identification is followed by Rizakis (1998), who published the inscriptions (Nos. 145, 208).

28 Dekoulakou (1980, 575) argued that the tomb was commissioned by Sextus Aequanus, the previous owner of Astius. She further suggested, under the assumption that the richly adorned sarcophagus inside the podium of the tomb contained the remains of a female, that Sextus Aequanus erected the tomb for his daughter, Aequana Musa (see Rizakis 1998, No. 5). Papapostolou (1983) does not follow this identification, because the skeletal remains had by then been identified as male. He does not provide a suggestion for the identity of the man, but does argue that the deceased man was a *quindecimvir* of the colony on the basis of the iconography on one of the rings he wears (a tripod). Flämig (2003, 567) suggests that the freedman Astius himself was the commissioner of the tomb.

colonial social hierarchy. Even though, as Roman citizens, the settlers may have had a privileged position in Patraean society, their acceptance as the new local elite may not have been self-evident for every inhabitant of the colony alike. Serving as an arena for the negotiations for social prominence, the cemetery was used for deliberate and calculated strategies of commemoration. In an effort to further their position in the colony, some early settlers chose to erect their tombs in the location where the pre-colonial elite was buried, taking advantage of the symbolism with which this area was imbued, and anchoring themselves to their predecessors. At the same time, these tombs were utilized in social rivalry: the competitive display characterizing early Roman tomb architecture was aimed at enhancing the visibility of its owners on the public stage. The Mausoleum of the Aequani was the epitome of such competitive commemoration: the tomb's domination of the physical landscape of the cemetery mirrored the owners' intentions to dominate the social landscape of the living community.

Acknowledgements
I would like to express my appreciation to Onno van Nijf, Athanasios Rizakis, and Michalis Petropoulos for their valuable suggestions and advice. Thanks are due to Olivia A. Jones for a revision of the English. This research is part of the project 'Civic and cultural identities in a changing world: analysing the mortuary practices of the Post-Classical Peloponnese' funded by the Netherlands Organization for Scientific Research (NWO).

References
Alcock, S.E. 1991. Tomb Cult and the Postclassical Polis. *AJA* 95, 447-467.

Alcock, S.E. 1993. *Graecia capta: the landscapes of Roman Greece*, Cambridge, MA.

Antonaccio, C.M. 2016. Contesting the Past: Hero Cult, Tomb Cult, and Epic in Early Greece. *AJA* 98, 389-410.

Arafat, K.W. 1996. *Pausanias' Greece: Ancient Artists and Roman Rulers*, Cambridge.

Binford, L.R. 1971. Mortuary Practices: Their Study and Their Potential. *Memoirs of the Society for American Archaeology* 25, 6-29.

Camia, F. & M. Kantiréa 2010. The imperial cult in the Peloponnese. In: A.D. Rizakis & C.E. Lepenioti (eds), *Roman Peloponnese III. Society, economy and culture under the Roman Empire: continuity and innovation*. Athens, 375-406.

Catling, H.W. 1985. Archaeology in Greece 1984/85. *AR* 31, 3-69.

Dekoulakou, I. 2009. Monumenti delle necropoli di Patrasso durante il dominio Romano. In: E. Greco (ed.), *Patrasso, Colonia di Augusto e le trasformazioni culturali, politiche ed economiche della provincia di Acaia agli inizi dell'età imperiale romana: Atti del convegno internazionale, Patrasso 23-24 marzo 2006*. Atene, 163-205.

Dekoulakou, I. 1976. Οδός Ερμού 80-82. *ArchDelt* 31(B1), 97-102.

Dekoulakou, I. 1980. Ρωμαϊκό μαυσωλείο στην Πάτρα. In: K. Schefold, J. Pouilloux & Σωματείο φίλων του Νικολάου Κοντολέοντος (eds), Στήλη. Τόμος εις μνήμην Ν. Κοντολέοντος. Athens, 556-575.

Dijkstra, T.M. 2015. Burial and Commemoration in the Roman Colony of Patras. In: S.T. Roselaar (ed.), *Processes of Cultural Change and Integration in the Roman World*. Leiden, 154-174.

Dimakis, N. 2016. *Social Identity and Status in the Classical and Hellenistic Northern Peloponnese: The evidence from burials*, Oxford.

Fedak, J. 1990. *Monumental tombs of the hellenistic age: a study of selected tombs from the pre-classical to the early imperial era*, Toronto.

Flämig, C. 2003. Grabarchitektur als Spiegel der Historischen Prozesse und der Bevölkerungsstruktur im Kaiserzeitlichen Griechenland. In: P. Noelke, F. Naumann-Steckner, & B. Schneider (eds), *Romanisation und Resistenz in Plastik, Architektur und Inschriften der Provinzen des Imperium Romanum*. Mainz, 563-575.

Flämig, C. 2007. *Grabarchitektur der römischen Kaiserzeit in Griechenland*, Rahden/Westf.

Garland, R 1985. *The Greek way of death*, London.

Heinzelmann, M. 2000. *Die Nekropolen von Ostia. Untersuchungen zu den Gräberstrassen vor der Porta Romana und an der Via Laurentina*, München.

von Hesberg, H. & P. Zanker 1987. *Römische Gräberstrassen: Selbstdarstellung, Status, Standard: Kolloquium in München vom 28. bis 30. Oktober 1985*, München.

Hodder, I. 1981. The identification and interpretation of ranking in prehistory: a contextual perspective. In: R. Chapman, I. A. Kinnes, & K. Randsborg (eds), *The Archaeology of Death*. Cambridge, 150-154.

Hope, V.M. 2009. *Roman Death*, Cornwall.

Lolos, Y. 2016. On the Trail of a Large Burial Monument of Patras. In: D. Katsonopoulou & E. Partida (eds), *Philhellene. Essays presented to Stephen Miller*. Athens, 351-360.

Malkin, I. 1987. *Religion and colonization in ancient Greece*, Leiden.

Marantou, E. 2011. Ancestor Worship and Hero Cult. In: H. Cavanagh, W. Cavanagh & J. Roy (eds), *Honouring the Dead in the Peloponnese. Proceedings of the Conference held at Sparta 23-25 April 2009*. Nottingham, 441-458.

Morris, I. 1987. *Burial and ancient society: the rise of the Greek city-state*, Cambridge.

Morris, I. 1992. *Death-ritual and social structure in classical antiquity*, Cambridge.

Nock, A.D. 1932. Cremation and Burial in the Roman Empire. *HTR* 25, 321-359.

Orlin, E.M. 2007. Augustan Religion and the Reshaping of Roman Memory. *Arethusa* 40, 73-92.

Osanna, M. 1996. *Santuari e culti dell'Acaia antica*, Napoli.

Papapostolou, I.A. 1976. Οδός Κορίνθου 221-223. *ArchDelt* 31(B1), 92-95.

Papapostolou, I.A. 1977. Ελληνιστικοί Τάφοι της Πάτρας I. *ArchDelt* 32(A), 281-343.

Papapostolou, I.A. 1978. Ελληνιστικοί Τάφοι της Πάτρας II. *ArchDelt* 33(A), 354-385.

Papapostolou, I.A. 1983. Κτερίσματα ταφής σε ρωμαϊκό μαυσωλείο στην Πάτρα. *ArchEph* 122, 1-34.

Papapostolou, I.A. 1989. Monuments de gladiateurs à Patras. *BCH* 113, 351-401.

Papapostolou, I.A. 1993. *Achaean grave stelai*, Athens.

Papapostolou, I.A. 2014. Νεότερα περί Αχαΐας και Πατρών. *ArchEph* 153, 237-274.

Parker Pearson, M. 1982. Mortuary practices, society and ideology: an ethnoarchaeological study. In: I. Morris (ed.), *Symbolic and Structural Archaeology*. Cambridge, 99-113.

Parker Pearson, M. 1993. The powerful dead: archaeological relationships between the living and the dead. *CAJ*, 3, 203-229.

Parker Pearson, M. 2009. *The archaeology of death and burial*, Stroud [1999].

Pearce, J. 2000. Burial, society and context in the provincial Roman World. In: J. Pearce, M. Millett & M. Struck (eds), *Burial, society and context in the Roman world*, Oxford, 1-12.

Petropoulos, M. 1994. Αγροικίες Πατραϊκής. In: P.N. Doukellis & L.G. Mendoni (eds), *Structures rurales et sociétés antiques. Actes du colloque de Corfu (14-16 mai 1992)*. Paris, 405-424.

Petropoulos, M. 2007. Νικόπολις-Πάτρα μέσω Αιτωλοακαρνανίας. In: K.I. Zachos (ed.), Νικόπολις Β᾽πρακτικά του Δευτέρου Διεθνούς Συμποσίου για τη Νικόπολη (11-15 Σεπτεμβρίου 2002). Preveza, 175-211.

Pirenne-Delforge, V. 2004. La portée du témoignage de Pausanias sur les cultes locaux. In: G. Labarre & M. Drew-Bear (eds), *Les cultes locaux dans les mondes grec et romain. Actes du colloque de Lyon, 7-8 juin 2001*. Lyon, 5-20.

Pirenne-Delforge, V. 2006. Ritual Dynamics in Pausanias: the Laphria. In: E. Stavrianopoulou (ed.), *Ritual and Communication in the Graeco-Roman World*. Liège, 111-129.

Rizakis, A.D. 1984. Munera Gladiatoria à Patras. *BCH* 108, 533-542.

Rizakis, A.D. 1988. Le port de Patras et les communications avec l'Italie sous la République. *CH* 33, 453-472.

Rizakis, A.D. 1989. La colonie Romaine de Patras en Achaie: le témoignage epigraphique. In: S. Walker & A. Cameron (eds), *The Greek renaissance in the Roman empire: papers from the tenth British Museum classical colloquium*. London, 180-186.

Rizakis, A.D. 1990. Munera Gladiatoria à Patras II. *ZPE* 82, 201-208.

Rizakis, A.D. 1995. *Achaïe I. Sources Textuelles et Histoire Regionale*, Athènes.

Rizakis, A.D. 1998. *Achaïe II. La cité de Patras. Épigraphie et Histoire*, Athènes.

Rizakis, A.D. 2008. *Achaïe III. Les cités Achéennes. Épigraphie et histoire*, Athènes.

Rizakis, A.D. 2009. La colonie de Patras en Achaïe dans le cadre de la colonisation Augustéenne. In: E. Greco (ed.), *Patrasso, Colonia di Augusto e le trasformazioni culturali, politiche ed economiche della provincia di Acaia agli inizi dell'età imperiale romana: Atti del convegno internazionale, Patrasso 23-24 marzo 2006*. Atene, 17-38.

Rizakis, A.D. 2010. Colonia Augusta Achaïca Patrensis: réamenagements urbains, constructions édilitaires et la nouvelle identité Patréenne. In: A.D. Rizakis & C.E. Lepenioti (eds), *Roman Peloponnese III. Society, economy and culture under the Roman Empire: continuity and innovation*. Athens, 129-154.

Rizakis, A.D. & M. Petropoulos 2006. Ancient Patras. In: T.E. Sklavenitis & K.S. Staikos (eds), *Patras. From Ancient Times to the Present*. Athens, 4-57.

Saxe, A.A. 1970. *Social dimensions of mortuary practices*. Diss. University of Michigan.

Sluiter, I. 2017. Anchoring Innovation: A Classical Research Agenda. *European Review* 25, 20-38.

Tarlow, S. 1999. *Bereavement and Commemoration, an archaeology of mortality*, Oxford.

Toynbee, J.M.C. 1971. *Death and burial in the Roman world*, London.

Contending with the Past in Roman Corinth: The Julian Basilica

Catherine de Grazia Vanderpool and Paul D. Scotton

Abstract

Lucius Mummius destroyed Hellenic Corinth in 146 BC, yet its remnants endured, perhaps the most prominent being the imposing Archaic Temple of Apollo. When Roman colonizers began work on a new city centre after 44 BC, the temple would still have been a dominant feature in the landscape, a symbol of Corinth's great antiquity and importance. How did the settlers negotiate with this Greek shrine at the new city's heart, along with other traces of the Greek past? We propose that among the earliest solutions was a massive basilica built on the east end of the Forum, an unvarnished statement of Rome, displaying strong links to Vitruvian principles except for its very high podium, which raises the building in an apparent challenge to the Temple of Apollo. The sculptural program within the basilica also grapples with the relationship between conqueror and conquered. Roman content and Greek forms alternate with Greek content and Roman forms: statues of Augustus's sons interpreted as classical Peloponnesian heroes; statues of the imperial family as Hellenistic generals; a statue of an imperial forebear divinized using classical Greek schemata with a Roman twist. Through exploiting topographical position, architecture, and sculpture, the colonizing Romans – many of whom were freedmen probably of Greek origin – acknowledged the power of the Greek past but recast it in Roman terms.

Keywords: Roman Corinth, Roman colony, Augustan architecture, Augustan portrait sculpture, early imperial city planning, early imperial basilicas

1. Introduction

Corinth is a particularly rich source of material for pondering the questions raised by the theme of this volume. Focusing on a key building of early imperial Corinth, we consider the manipulation of city planning, architecture, and art in constructing a Roman city on the remains of a major Greek urban centre. Christened the Julian Basilica by its excavators over 100 years ago, the building dates to the latter part of Augustus's long reign,

in: Dijkstra, T.M., I.N.I. Kuin, M. Moser & D. Weidgenannt (eds) 2017. *Strategies of Remembering in Greece under Rome (100 BC - 100 AD)*, Leiden (Sidestone Press).

most likely between 2 BC and 4/5 AD (Scotton *et al.* 2014).[1] The basilica remained a dominant feature of the city centre until its destruction in the late 4th century AD. A reassessment of the building's architecture, inscriptions and sculpture gives important new information about the central role it played in organizing the colony's nascent forum in terms of space and ideology. How did the building's patrons, planners, architects, and artists deploy their resources and skills to embody Augustus's new order, and how does the structure confront, and negotiate with, Corinth's storied and visible Hellenic past?

The story of Corinth's ancient as well as recent past was contested ground, the nuance depending on the narrator. Shortly before his death in 44 BC, Caesar decreed the establishment of a colony on the site of Greek Corinth, which had been destroyed by L. Mummius in 146 BC. While Caesar founded many colonies, Corinth – and Carthage – were different, the 'most conspicuous,' in Plutarch's telling, their earlier capture and their restoration chancing 'to fall at one and the same time' (Plut. *Caes.* 57: Perrin/Loeb). The relationship between Rome and Corinth carried an unusually heavy, and notorious, burden of history: arguably no other Caesarian or Augustan colony bore quite the same weight as Corinth, with the notable exception of Carthage. The victories over both cities were accompanied by senatorial decrees that apparently dictated the destruction and non-settlement of both (Purcell 1995), although the devastation in Corinth was less than total (Gebhard & Dickie 2003, esp. 266-270 on physical evidence; James 2013). The deliberateness would have added to the impact, the drama, and therefore the strength of memory of these cities' fate. They became symbols of victories over enemies who were depicted as threatening the very being of Rome; the conquests were viewed as pivotal moments in Roman history (Davies 2010).

Rome possessed well-developed strategies for memorialization, as explored extensively in recent scholarship.[2] These helped to embed the memory of Mummius's victory permanently and pervasively in Rome and in Greece even centuries later: Pausanias's vivid description of the sack of Corinth was written more than 300 years after the fact (Paus. 7.16.7-10), as was Dio Cassius's (Cass. Dio 21: Zonar. 9.31). For contemporary dwellers of the city of Rome and for the army Mummius celebrated a three-day triumph which everyone could, and probably did, attend. Such an event would have lived on for generations in the collective memory (Popkin 2016, esp. 6-12). Mummius dedicated a temple and statue to Hercules Victor in Rome, as recorded in an inscription from the Caelian Hill now in the Vatican Museums,[3] and he used booty from Corinth as permanent publicity for his victory, distributing it to cities in Italy as well as in Greece.[4] For both Greeks and Romans the fate of Corinth became subject for historical investigation, debate, philosophic rumination, and poetry beginning soon after the destruction, and persistently thereafter (Purcell 1995; Gebhard & Dickie 2003; Davis 2010). As Gebhard and Dickie have pointed out, Corinth's destruction was a theme that was pressed into service to 'illustrate a variety of points' and judging by the archaeological record, the degree of destruction was overstated.[5]

Corinth's advantages as a colony were clear: it was a prime location for commerce and military purposes, and could provide land for the settlement of veterans (Williams 1993; Walbank 1997; Rizakis 1997; Rizakis 2010). Additionally, for Greeks and Romans alike, the city was fraught with meaning: it was rich in ancient history as

---

1 The basilica was published first by Weinberg 1960. The new study of the architecture was undertaken by P. Scotton, with C. de Grazia Vanderpool examining the sculpture and C. Roncaglia the inscriptions. The results will be published in a forthcoming volume on the Julian Basilica by Scotton and Vanderpool, with a contribution by Roncaglia, in the Corinth Excavation series of the American School of Classical Studies at Athens. A preliminary overview: Scotton *et al.* 2104.

2 E.g. *Memoria Romana: Memory in Roman Civilization*, a project initiated in 2009 under the direction of Prof. Karl Galinksy, http://www.laits.utexas.edu/memoria/ (accessed 9/9/2016). Project participants and contributors include established and emerging scholars in the field of Roman memory studies and present a wide array of approaches as well as extensive references and responses to preceding bibliography. Publications include: Galinsky 2014; Galinsky & Lapatin 2016; Galinsky 2016. See also comprehensive introduction to Roman habits of 'memorialization': collection of papers in Alroth & Scheffer 2014: esp. concluding essay by Edlund-Berry 2014, and theoretical and methodological framework set out in Morgan 2014.

3 *CIL* 1.541 = *CIL* 6.331. It has been suggested that the Temple of Hercules Victor is to be identified with the Round Temple on the Tiber: Ziokowlski 1988; *cf.* summary note Jones 2003, 20, n. 8, 138, n. 16; Popkin 2016, esp. 69-72. The identification has been contested: Pietilä-Castrén 1987, 143-144. On Republican temples celebrating triumphs: Bastien 2008.

4 Graverini 2001; Cadario 2014. Cadario (2014) suggests that leaving artworks behind in Greece not only celebrated victories; the act also displayed piety towards the gods.

5 Gebhard & Dickie 2003, 261-278; Robinson 2011, especially 345-364, with specific reference to Peirene and other waterworks; James 2013.

well as the source of legendary art and wealth; it symbolized the fate of those who chose to resist Rome; and it was a lasting reminder (as well as graveyard) of a powerful opponent's military achievement and ambition.[6] According to the roughly contemporary historian Diodorus Siculus, Caesar, on viewing the site, 'was so moved by compassion…that he set about restoring it' and 'by his clemency made amends' for the harsh treatment meted out by his forebears: for this and other great deeds he deserved the title 'of divus' (32.27.3: tr. Walton/Loeb).[7] The benefits of Roman rule, in Diodorus's narration, would become manifest on this contested site.

2. Corinth's 'past'

The settlement of Corinth probably began just before Caesar's death (Romano 2010). The first Corinthian duovirs, Aeficius Certus and C. Iulius, the former perhaps a client of Caesar's and the latter a freedman (Spawforth 1996, nos. 15 a-d), minted Corinth's earliest *aes* coinage soon afterwards (Amandry 1988, 28-32, pls. 1, 2; RPC I, no. 1116). On the obverse is Caesar, on the reverse Bellerophon on Pegasus, a quintessential Corinthian story with a locus in the heart of the city, since it was at the Fountain of Peirene that the hero captured and tamed the winged horse: perhaps not coincidentally, the Fountain was one of the earliest monuments in central Corinth to experience a major renovation by the first colonists (Robinson 2011, esp. ch. 7). The images summarize the thinking of men who were Caesar's, whether client or freedman; therefore, it is likely that these images reflected Caesar's views as well. The colony was to have two faces, a Roman present and a history that went back to the time of gods and heroes, and they were to be intertwined. The numismatic evidence joins other materials that document the survival, restoration, or co-opting, of myths, buildings and religious practices inherited from the Greek city (Bookidis & Stroud 2004; Bookidis 2005; Robinson 2011; Walbank 2010; Thomas 2010).

Although the Caesarian colony was laid out around 44 BC, from then until the construction of the basilica some forty years later there was limited major building activity in or near the forum, with a few notable exceptions, such as the Fountain of Peirene (Robinson 2011). A similar pattern is evident elsewhere, as at Mérida in the western empire and Patras and Butrint closer to Corinth, where monumental construction was slow to begin until well into the Augustan era if not later, as in the case of Patras (Mérida: Edmunson 2011; Patras: Rizakis 2010; Butrint:

Figures 1 a, b. Corinth aes, Aeficius Certus and C. Iulius, duovirs. obv. Julius Caesar, rev. Bellerophon on Pegasus, 44-43 BC (Photos: M. Hammond and L. Gallimore, Courtesy of the American School of Classical Studies at Athens, Corinth Excavations).

Hernandez & Condi 2014). By the time the basilica was constructed, the colony's foundation was nearly two generations in the past. The Augustan revolution had taken distinctive, and enduring, shape: his power had consolidated over the three decades since Actium, evolving from triumphant general to Pater Patriae, the title voted him in 2 BC by the Senate, equestrians, and the 'entire Roman people' (*RG* 35). This same year marked the dedication of the Forum of Augustus, which more than any other surviving physical monument embodies the essence of the *princeps*' power and authority, serving as perhaps the chief architectural and artistic theatre of Augustus's aspirations for Rome (Zanker 1990; Spannagel 1999; Ungaro 2007; Meneghini & Santangeli 2010; Shaya 2013). His forum complex as well as the many other changes he made to the old forum and throughout the city culminated centuries of experimentation and experience in manipulating public space for political ends, a contest in which shaping the past was a persistent motif (Russell 2015). The forum of Augustus employed Classical and Hellenistic artistic and architectural forms to celebrate the story of Rome as told by Augustus and his milieu, and its influence was far-reaching, as seen for example in Mérida, Italica, and Corduba (Mérida: Dardenay 2010; Italica: Peña Jurado 2007; Corduba: Jiménez & Carrillo 2011) and other provincial centres (Rose 2005; Geiger 2008, 192-197; Goldbeck 2015).[8] Those responsible for the Roman face of Corinth also drew on styles, themes and strategies developed in the capital city, adapting them to circumstances peculiar to the evolving culture of the early colony.

Until the construction of the basilica, Corinth's forum area was dominated by the remains of the South Stoa and the Temple of Apollo.[9] Probably dating to the first quarter of the 3rd century BC, the South Stoa measured

---

6   On the military power of the Greeks, specifically Athenians and Spartans, as viewed by Rome, Spawforth 2012, esp. ch. 3.

7   *Cf.* for Caesar's *clementia*: Caes. *BCiv* 3.98; Cic. *Att.* 9.16 and 8.13; Plut. *Caes.* 8.

8   Goldbeck 2015 comprehensively examines the influence of Augustus's Forum on the western empire, carefully distinguishing from site to site the extent of its 'Rezeption'.

9   Romano 2010; Scotton 2011; Scahill 2012. On the edge of what was to be the Forum was the Greek theatre, which also survived Mummius's sack at least in part: Williams & Zervos 1988, 108-120; Williams & Zervos 1989, 28-36.

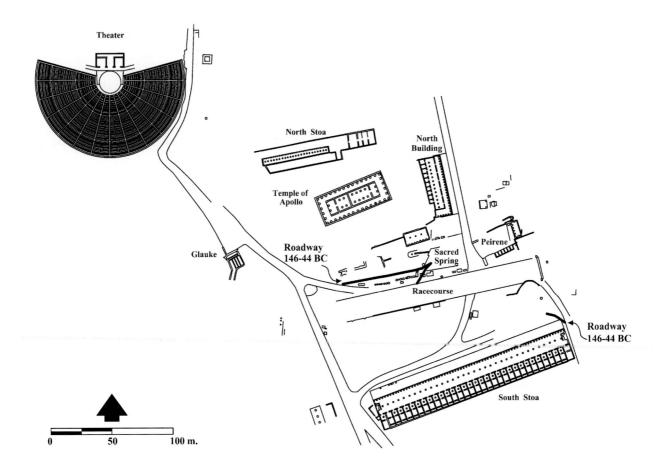

Figure 2. Central Corinth, 146-44 BC (Plan: David Gilman Romano, Corinth Computer Project).

an imposing 164 m. in length, running almost the entire length of what came to be the forum. Its condition and its use during the early imperial era is not certain, but it appears to have remained standing at least in part after 146 BC (Williams 1993, 37-38; Walbank 1997, 118-120; Scotton 2011; Scahill 2012). The Temple sits on a ridge that runs roughly parallel to the forum. At least part of its superstructure survived Mummius' destruction, but there was significant robbing of its blocks in the post-Roman period, which makes it difficult to ascertain how much was standing at the time of the Roman colonization (Frey 2015, 160-164; *cf.* Bookidis & Stroud 2004). Even in a ruined state, its visual dominance likely would have been magnified in the minds of the beholders by its antiquity. The temple, with its massive Doric monolithic columns, more than perhaps any other surviving building in Corinth would have embodied the Greek past.

Other buildings in forum area also survived in some form the destruction of 146 BC. These included the North Building, on the west side of the Lechaion Road near Peirene, the so-called Circular Monument, the Sacred Spring, and traces of the Hellenistic racecourse (Millis 2006; Romano 2010; Scotton 2011). The earliest documentation of a Roman presence in the forum area comes from a well in the South Stoa, perhaps indicating the beginning of some cleaning or building activity in the middle of Augustus's reign; but the earliest-documented actual architectural intervention in the vicinity takes place just north of the forum, around the Fountain of Peirene (Williams 1989; Slane 1986; Slane 2004; Scotton 2011; Robinson 2011). As Robinson has described, the renovations to the Fountain of Peirene, carried out between 10/9 BC and 5/4 BC, display an amalgamation of cultural and aesthetic themes (Robinson 2011, ch. 7, esp. 189-204). The Romans devised a new screen wall that helped to transform the fountain into a Roman civic monument, honouring its venerable past while concurrently securing its identifi-

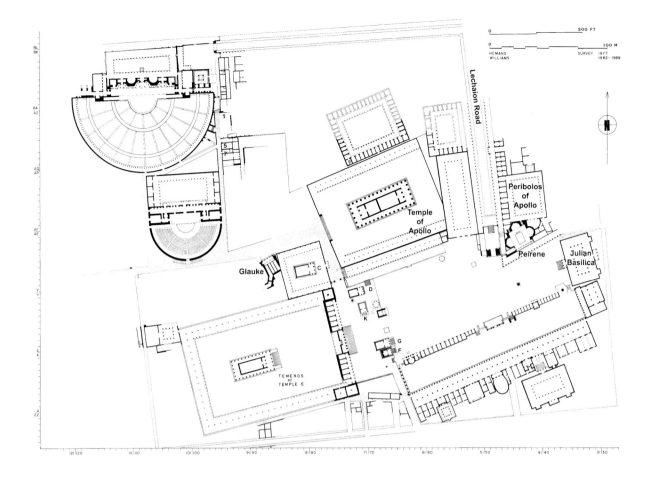

Figure 3. Central Corinth, orientation of existing and early Roman construction, mid-1st c. AD (Plan: David Gilman Romano. Corinth Computer Project).

cation as a Roman building. The sober Doric order of the lower level was surmounted by an Ionic order that in turn supported an arcade, a recurring feature in public Roman architecture beginning in the late Republic.

In laying out the new forum Roman engineers followed the general east-west orientation shared by the Temple of Apollo and the South Stoa, but shifted the orientation by 4.5 degrees when they laid out the principle new buildings of the Augustan era, which included the basilica on the east, several small temples to the west, and 'Temple E'.[10] None of these buildings line up with the central axis of either the Apollo Temple or the South Stoa. Although axial planning is the organizing principle for much new-built Roman public architecture in Rome and in the provinces, in Corinth's case the natural topography and pre-existing man-made features led to a multi-faceted plan.

3. The placement and architecture of the basilica

The basilica, which measures ca. 40 m. by 25 m., was tucked at the eastern end of the valley next to a north-south road and against a hillock, its long, western side flanking the Forum. In proportions and plan it resembles Vitruvius's description of the basilica he constructed for Fanum Fortunae (Vitr. *De arch.* 5.1.6-10), suggesting that the Corinthian *decuriones* probably turned to engineers and architects from Rome (Scotton 2012). It is possible that they were connected professionally to Vitruvius, whose books were probably used as a manual for at least some colonial city-building, as was the case

---

10 Romano 2010, 8-14, fig. 2.5. The Southeast Building, adjoining the Julian Basilica, dates either to the same time or shortly thereafter (Scotton 2012 for a preliminary assessment).

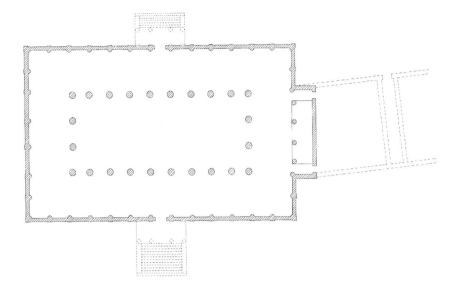

Figure 4. Julian Basilica, Floor plan. (Plan: P. Scotton).

at Fanum.[11] Although Vitruvius died around 15 BC, well before the Corinthian basilica was built, certain aspects reflect his thinking, but others do not. In his description of a 'normal' basilica, Vitruvius states that it should integrate with the forum space through a portico (Vitr. *De arch.* 5.1). This is not the case in Corinth: instead, the building's main entrance is raised 4.14 m. above the forum, with the hall sitting on a podium formed by the cryptoporticus. From forum floor to the top of the roof the building's height can be reconstructed at ca. 17 meters. The exterior of the basilica was covered in white stucco. Above the podium stood two superimposed, engaged Corinthian colonnades, ca. 5.91 and 2.96 m. tall respectively, with those on the upper level framing arcuated windows. The entrance from the forum into the basilica was up a broad staircase to a porch ca. 7.2 m. wide and 7.6 m. deep.[12] The impression of overall height would have been enhanced by the use of curvature in the design: by raising the north end above the south and displacing the apex of the curve northward the building would seem to rise even more from the surrounding landscape and structures.

Because of the Julian Basilica's tall podium on the side facing the forum, it occupies a singular role in the history of other early imperial basilicas, none of which show a similar feature. The design can be explained in part by the topography of the building site: the basilica sits at the eastern extremity of the Forum, where the ground begins a sharp rise to the east, so it was built to straddle the difference in ground level. On the west, the basement is above ground, necessitating a staircase from the level of the Forum to the main floor. On the east, the basement is below ground, and the main floor opens through the eastern door to street level. Either as a residual effect of this structural necessity, or intentionally, the façade towards the Forum was given a substantial lift in height thanks to the above-ground basement level, allowing the basilica a dominant role in defining the Forum. Its position anchored the long, narrow open space between it and the Roman temples at the opposite end, while its exceptional height enabled a visual challenge to the surviving Greek structures, especially the massive Temple of Apollo and South Stoa. The basilica's reconstructed height would have brought the rooftop almost to the same level as that of the Temple, even if this relationship was more apparent in plan and theory than in the viewer's experience, especially given the later building history of

---

11 Summary and bibliography for Vitruvius's education and career in Jones 2003, 33-46. Influence on the development of early imperial architecture ('a highly debatable subject'): Jones 2003, 6 and 11-13.

12 On the east side of the basilica there was a porch of similar dimension but only ca. 1.9 m. higher than as the north-south road passing next to the building.

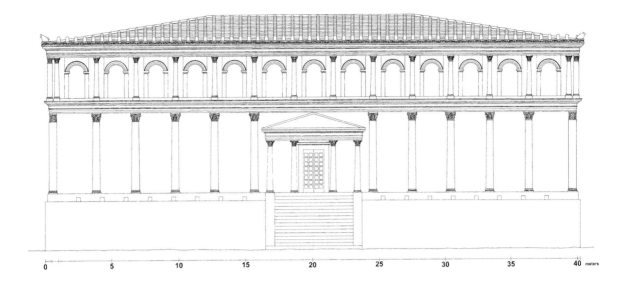

Figure 5. Julian Basilica, West façade. (Elevation: P. Scotton).

the area as it filled with structures. The Roman building's visual impact would have been enhanced by the richly articulated design of the façade, with its two-storey colonnade.

A comparison to this aesthetic comes from the Roman Forum in the position and appearance of the 'Tabularium', whose massive substructure and superimposed gallery provided a stage-like backdrop for the west end of the Roman Forum until at least partially blocked from sight by the later Temple of Concord and Temple of Divus Vespasianus.[13] Whether serving as Rome's record office or Sullan sanctuary,[14] the structure's role in organizing the Forum's space was the same: it imposed definition until its dominance was erased by later construction. In similar fashion, the Julian Basilica controlled the space of the Corinthian forum. Its position, framed by a rise in the ground level, provided a stage-like backdrop, visually dominant, and meaningful. As the first monumental administrative structure to be built in Corinth's centre, the basilica helped set the stage for all that followed, and would have played an outsized role, literally, in the new urban landscape. Not only did the basilica serve as visual notice on the Archaic Temple and the South Stoa that there was a new regime; it also made a powerful statement about the emerging Augustan formulations of government in early imperial Rome, where the increasingly elaborate structuring of the Forum mirrors political developments (Russell 2015). The architecture and the setting of the Corinthian basilica proclaimed it the seat of Roman authority, and its unusual scale announced its dominance of the formerly Greek landscape.

4. The sculptural assemblage: Romans as Greek heroes

The sculptural assemblage housed in the basilica appears to give a somewhat more nuanced approach to the relationship between Corinth and Rome. At least 11 marble statues and fragments thereof, dating to the Julio-Claudian period and representing Augustus and members of his family, were excavated in the basilica, some near where they probably stood at least at the time of the building's collapse (Scotton *et al.* 2014). Style and technique date several sculptures to the time of the building's construction or soon thereafter, the rest added during the reigns of Caligula, Claudius, and Nero in a process of agglomeration familiar from other Julio-Claudian statue groups (Rose 1997).

---

13   http://dlib.etc.ucla.edu/projects/Forum/reconstructions/Tabularium_1 (accessed 4/8/2017).
14   Coarelli 2010 joins others arguing against the traditional interpretation as Tabularium; he proposes instead a triple-temple sanctuary dedicated by Sulla, hence use of quotes in our article.

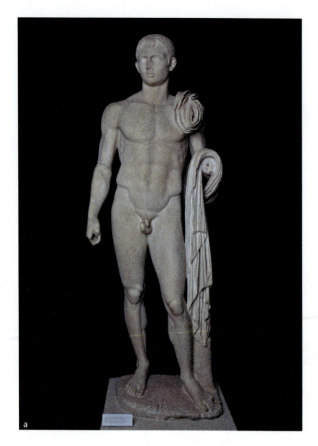 

Figures 6 a, b. Gaius and Lucius Caesar, Corinth Inv. S-1065 and 1080 (Photos: Petros Dellatolas. Courtesy of the American School of Classical Studies at Athens, Corinth Excavations).

As Rose and Boschung have demonstrated, these groups were an empire-wide phenomenon beginning in the reign of Augustus, and externally they offer many similarities (Rose 1997, Boschung 2002). However, the Corinthian group presents some anomalies that belie the emphatically Roman nature of the building in which they were housed, suggesting that the men responsible for commissioning these works of art wished to present a more nuanced view of the relationship between the Roman colony and Greek Corinth.

The basilica excavations produced a pair of statues identified securely as Augustus's adopted sons and heirs, Gaius and Lucius Caesar (Corinth Inv. S-1065 and S-1080: Pollini 1987, nos. 14 and 38; Vanderpool 2000). Gaius died in 4 AD at age 24, Lucius predeceased him in 2 AD at age 18; the Corinthian images were set up posthumously, perhaps not long after the completion of the basilica (Scotton *et al.* 2014). The statue types employ unambiguously the classical idiom, as seen by their notable similarity in pose and detailed measurements to the late fifth-century bronze known as 'Riace B', found in the sea off southern Italy (bronzes: Borelli and Pelagatti 1984; detailed comparison: Vanderpool 2000). The Corinthian portraits also resemble closely the Augus-tan-era Dioskouroi from the Theatre in Leptis Magna, which are depicted in almost the same schema and with identical measurements (Caputo 1976, 27-29, no. 7). An evocation of the Dioskouroi would resonate in the Greek and Roman worlds alike (Poulsen 1991; Geppert 1996; Vanderpool 2000). The Dioskouroi cult was observed in the Roman Forum, and they were patrons of the equestrian order as well as the *principes iuventutis*, informal titles awarded to both Gaius and Lucius. In Greece, the Dioskouroi were central to Spartan myth and ritual in Greek as well as in Roman times (Balzat 2010), and images of the Dioskouroi stood at the heart of Lysander's pan-Peloponnesian monument at Delphi celebrating his victory at Aegospotamoi (Paus. 10.9.7-10; Bommelaer 1971; Bommelaer 1981). The Twins also appear on Roman-era Spartan reliefs and elsewhere in the Peloponnese, often in stances similar to those seen for the Corinthian pair (Sanders 1993; Steinhauer 1993). Finally: the notion of 'twinning' symbolized by the Dioskouroi occurs in Augustan (and later) thinking about imperial succession (Champlin 2011).

The Corinthian statues are unique in depicting Gaius and Lucius in heroic nudity; where such information is preserved, other representations show Gaius togate, as in images from Gortyna, Ocriculum, or Carthage.[15] The explanation for the choice of statue type may lie in its relevance to local myth and cult, referring to the Peloponnesian (or Spartan) Dioskouroi rather than the Roman Castores. A very fragmentary 2nd-century AD inscription found in the basilica mentions the generosity of a member of the Spartan Euryclids, who either built or refurbished an *aediculam* and *statuam* (Kent 1966, no. 314). His ancestor C. Julius Eurycles was prominent among the supporters of Octavian at Actium and for his service was awarded Roman citizenship and control over Sparta (Bowersock 1961; Lindsay 1992; Spawforth 1996; Balzat 2008; Spawforth 2010; Millis 2013). He was disgraced late in the reign of Augustus, the dates debatable, but his reputation apparently was soon restored, probably no later than 15 AD. His son C. Iulius Laco and grandson C. Iulius Spartiaticus figured prominently in Corinth apparently from the reign of Claudius and later, serving as duovir and as president of the Isthmian games.[16] Given the prominence of the Euryclids from earliest years of Augustus' reign, and the documented presence from the reign of Claudius, possibly the family was involved in funding some aspect of the basilica, whether construction or dedications. It is known that the family traced its descent from the Dioskouroi (Spawforth 1996, esp. 173-174; 179, no. 15; Spawforth 2010), so if we were to draw up the ideal profile of a patron for the statues of Gaius and Lucius Caesar, a Euryclid would fit. The dedication would achieve dual aims: honouring Rome's leading family through a memorial to the deceased heirs, and evoking a heroic Spartan and Peloponnesian past as well as the family of the benefactor.

5. Romans as Greek generals

The basilica assemblage also included a relatively well-preserved cuirassed statue and a leg fragment from another in the same style (statue: Corinth Inv. S-1085 a, b: Johnson 1931, cat. 144; leg fragment: Corinth Inv. S-1081c: Johnson 1931, cat. 150). Given similarities in certain technical details to the statue of Gaius, the cuirassed figure was probably carved around the same time, and almost certainly represents a member of the imperial

family.[17] The inclusion of cuirassed figures was relatively rare in surviving Julio-Claudian imperial statue groups (Rose 1997, 74, with n. 25). Furthermore, its style and iconography find the best parallels in the world of Hellenistic arms and armoured figures. The cuirass type is Hellenistic, often used in late Republican and Julio-Claudian representations of Roman generals and *principes*, but appearing very rarely from the Flavian period onwards (Cadario 2004; Laube 2006). The version in Corinth is cylindrical, with a straight bottom edge in contrast to the bell-shaped curve on the lower edge of the armour worn by Augustus in his statue from Prima Porta.[18] The format with the straight edge appears much more frequently in Hellenistic representations than the one with the bell curve: compare the representation of Alexander on the mosaic from Pompeii depicting the battle at Issus (Picón & Hemingway 2016, 2, fig. 1), or the bronze statuette of Alexander on Bucephalos from Herculaneum (Picón & Hemingway 2016, 114-115, no. 15), or a pair of statues perhaps depicting several of Mithradates' officers or allies, found in the Samothrakeion in Delos and dated around 100 BC.[19] This version with the straight bottom edge lived on in the Julio-Claudian Aegean world not only in Corinth; it is also seen in groups from Tinos and Gortyna (Tinos: Queyrel 1986, nos. 30-33, 289-292, pls. 142-148; Gortyna: Cadario 2004, 285-291, pl. 34, 1-5). These as well as the Corinthian cuirass are retrospective in style, evoking a type that finds parallels beginning with Alexander.

As on the Prima Porta Augustus and the Tinos statues, the front of the Corinthian figure's cuirass is filled with figures. The execution is different, however, in that the Corinth figures are in exceptionally high relief and their limbs are almost entirely in the round, while the bodies twist from frontal to profile view, the feet projecting over the lower border of the cuirass. Albeit of lesser quality, the style of the relief resembles that of the neo-Attic 'Borghese Krater' in the Louvre, where the well-rounded figures fill the frieze panel, posing and dancing along its lower edge,

---

15   Gortyna and Ocriculum: Rose 1997, cat. 25.3, pl. 90; cat. 85.4, pl. 197; Carthage: Pollini 1987, cat. 10, pl. 12.1-4. *Cf.* togate head of Gaius in Schloss Fasanerie, Pollini cat. 26, pl. 28, 1-3. The Vicus Sandalarius altar, discussed below in connection with the statue of Augustus from the basilica, also depicts a togate Gaius.

16   Spawforth 1996, 174: C. Iulius Laco, duovir quinquennalis and Isthmian agonothete under Claudius, the duovirate probably falling in 41/2 AD; C. Iulius Spartiaticus, Laco's son, likewise duovir quinquennalis and Isthmian agonothete, holding the former post in 46/7 AD.

---

17   Scotton *et al.* 2014. There are arguments to be made that it represents Germanicus; the fragment of a pendant cuirassed figure in the basilica suggests the possibility of 'twinning', which in the case of Germanicus could be his adoptive brother, Drusus II. Suggested in Scotton *et al.* 2014, this will be fully explored in the publication of the Julian Basilica (see above, n. 1).

18   Prima Porta cuirass: Squire 2015, figs. 13-15 (with discussion and extensive earlier bibliography). Cuirassed figures in Ioannina and Thessaloniki also show the bell-bottom version: Ioannina: Faklari 2009, 131, fig. on 129; Thessaloniki: Karanastasi 1995, 216-220, fig. 58a.

19   Delos Museum A 4173, A 4242: Marcadé 1969, 331-333, pl. 75. Also of this type is the statue of Billienus in Delos, c. 100 BC, Marcadé 1969, 329-333, pl. 75. See also Cadario 2004 on Delos statues, 69-78, pl. 9, 1-2 (A 4173 and A 4242); 74-75, pl. 11, 3 (Billienus).

Figures 7 a, b. Cuirassed statue, Corinth Inv. S-1081; detail of breastplate (Photos: Petros Dellatolas. Courtesy of the American School of Classical Studies at Athens, Corinth Excavations).

drapery swirling in a motif of concealing and revealing, with feet occasionally projecting beyond the confines of the lower edge of the frieze.[20] In the centre of the Corinthian cuirass, a pair of winged Victories stride towards a trophy, their bodies twisting from front to profile, their drapery swirling open around their legs. They are depicted in the act of decorating a trophy with a round hoplite shield, a cuirass in the same Hellenistic style as that of the statue, and Hellenistic helmets resembling types seen on the balustrade reliefs of Pergamon's Sanctuary of Athena (Picón and Hemingway 2016, 188-189, figs. 109 a-b), the Telephos Frieze (Picón and Hemingway 2016, fig. 54), and the Great Altar of Pergamon, as worn by the giant identified as Otus (Charbonneaux 1973, fig. 291). Like the monuments set up by the Attalids, the Corinth statue's breastplate celebrates victories, the theme repeated by the trophy-carrying Nike who appears on the right shoulder strap. Although the Corinthian statue's motifs appear to be generic, an argument can be made that the Corinthian statue alludes to a specific historical event or series of events: Roman victories in Germania and Pannonia. Both Tiberius and Germanicus, both of whom are candidates as the subject of the Corinthian statue, eventually were awarded triumphs for their achievements against these enemies, the former in 12 A.D., the latter in 17 A.D. Even while Augustus was proclaiming peace, his armies were almost constantly on campaign, and the imagery of successful war and triumph is a key element of early imperial iconography (Hölscher 2006; Koortbojian 2006). In his conceptualization, the sculptor of the Corinthian statue drew on imagery that finds its best parallels in monuments celebrating Pergamon's victories over a barbarian enemy as well as Hellenistic kings.

While the armour and the motifs speak of military victory, the hand and arm positions send a different message. The right arm has been identified (Corinth Inv. S-1085a-b: Johnson 1931, cat. 144), and awaits restoration, but in preliminary studies it is evident that the hand and arm were held forward just above waist height, the hand held open, with the palm angled diagonally and up. This gesture invites various interpretations: it could

---

20   Photographs as well as bibliography: http://www.louvre.fr/en/oeuvre-notices/kylix-known-borghese-vase, accessed 4/4/2017. *Cf.* Picón and Hemingway 2016, no. 230, 285-286 (D. Roger). The Victory on the Belevedere alter, mid-Augustan in date, is also very similar in style to those on the Corinth statue: Kleiner 1992, 102-103, fig. 85.

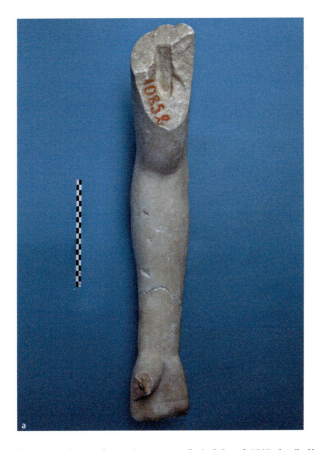 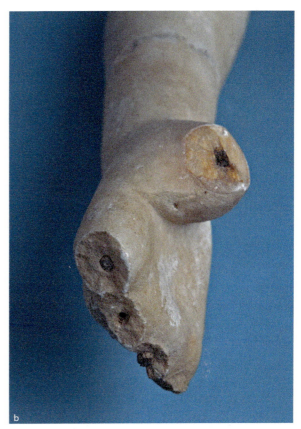

Figures 8 a, b. Arm from cuirass statue, Corinth Inv. S-1085; detail of hand (Photos: Petros Dellatolas. Courtesy American School of Classical Studies at Athens, Corinth Excavations).

indicate reconciliation, or friendship and alliance, as discussed by Rose and Buxton in their differing reinterpretations of the central, armoured figure on the breastplate of Augustus's statue from Prima Porta (Rose 2005; Buxton 2012); or a gesture of *clementia*, as may be the case for the depiction of Augustus extending his hand to barbarian chieftains and children on the cup from Boscoreale (Kuttner 1995). A fragment of a left hand holding an inverted sword, possibly sheathed, can also be associated with the Corinthian statue (Corinth Inv. S-1084: Johnson 1931, cat. 142): it would have been held in the position seen, for example, on the statue of Drusus the Elder in Caere (Boschung 2002, no. 25.5, pl. 69.1). The *parazonium*, symbol of rank and authority, is sheathed, inverted, and cradled, indicating the end of battle, reinforcing the message conveyed by the Corinthian figure's extended, open hand.

This statue (and its pendant) embodies the tension between war and peace in the new Augustan order, as conveyed by the art and architecture in the Forum of Augustus and by the *princeps* when he speaks of 'peace secured by Victory' (*RG* 13). In his studies of honorific portrait statues and civic identity in the Hellenistic world John Ma speaks of a military style and culture in the areas

Figure 9. Position of arm and hand, cuirassed statue (Photo: C. de Grazia Vanderpool).

Figure 10. Divus Iulius? Corinth Inv. S-1098 (Photo: Petros Dellatolas. Courtesy American School of Classical Studies at Athens, Corinth Excavations).

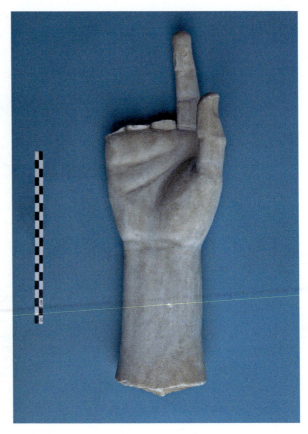

Figure 11. Right arm and hand. Corinth Inv. S-1095 (Photo: Petros Dellatolas. Courtesy American School of Classical Studies at Athens, Corinth Excavations).

of northern, central, and southern Greece as exemplified in the many fragments of bronze cuirassed figures found in Dodona (Ma 2013; Dodona: Katsikoudis 2006). It is noteworthy that – as we have seen – there is also a significant number of Julio-Claudian armoured statues from the same region as well as near islands such as Tinos and Naxos. That Rome could be construed as an heir to Hellenic military achievements is conveyed by Augustus himself: he included Apelles' painting of the triumphant Alexander in imagery attached to the Forum of Augustus (Plin. *HN* 35.10.27; 35.36.93-94; Rose 2005, 46) and celebrated the forum's inauguration with an immense *naumachia* that re-enacted the Greek victory at Salamis against the Persians (*RG* 23; Cass. Dio 55.10.7). The memory of Greeks as great warriors – above all Alexander as well as Athenians and Spartans – was evoked by placing their victories alongside Rome's own campaigns against Parthians and 'others' (*cf.* Spawforth 2012, esp. ch. 3). Through the Hellenistic style and embellishment of his armour, the Corinthian warrior was inserted into the same tradition, invested with the memory of Greek military valour. His gestures, however, convey the benefits accruing to those who make peace with Rome.

6. Divus Caesar and Augustus: Greek schemata, Roman virtues

The basilica assemblage also included a semi-draped statue in a type that is familiar from representations of Greek senior male deities and heroes, adapted for use in numerous Roman statues of private individuals as well as members of the imperial family (Hallett 2005). The figure, which can be restored as 2.50 m in height, the small end of colossal, was found close to the exedra in the south end of the basilica, and may have stood on the dais at least at the time the basilica was destroyed (Scotton 2011; Scotton *et al.* 2014; Vanderpool forthcoming 2017). The pose is stolid, his body frontal and almost without movement, the right arm probably held to one side and possibly projecting forward, the left arm bent and holding his drapery. By comparing technical details in the execution of the statue of Gaius we can establish that this figure belongs in the same general chronological framework, late in the reign of Augustus or early in that of Tiberius.

A closer look shows that the mantle is draped differently from the usual hip-mantle statues: its best parallel is a figure on the south panel of the Ara Pacis identified as Aeneas (Kleiner 1992, 93, 96, fig. 78), who wears the archaic 'toga sine tunica', used – according to Pliny – on statues representing the kings of Rome, and adopted – according to Plutarch – by Cato the Younger to evoke the early days of the Republic in his campaign to revive the *mos maiorum* (Plin. *HN* 34.23; Plut. *Cat. Min.* 6). As argued elsewhere (Vanderpool forthcoming 2017), the figure may represent Divus Iulius. If so, he is likened to a myth-historical figure such as Aeneas or Romulus, a founding father, a reference that would resonate in Corinth. The probable association with this statue of a fragmentary right hand and forearm (Corinth Inv. S-1095: Johnson 1931, cat. 151) may refine our understanding of the statue's meaning. The hand is held open, like that of the cuirassed statue; there is no trace of an object and the surfaces are equally finished on all sides. As already mentioned, the statue's right arm was not raised; its position was probably like that of the statue of Claudius from Olympia (Kleiner 1992, fig. 107): extended towards the viewer but open-handed in the case of the Corinthian figure. As we have already seen, the open-handed gesture is paralleled in Corinth on the cuirassed figure and is interpreted here as signalling the end of conflict, and *clementia*. If this reading of the cuirassed figure and the proposed statue of Divus Iulius is correct, then each embodies the remembrance of war and destruction, followed on by the benefits of peace.

Perhaps the best-known statue found in the basilica depicts the togate Augustus. Judging from the angle of the joint surface and drapery on the right arm, the missing lower arm projected obliquely from his right side, not towards the viewer. The position can be reconstructed by comparison with the 'Vicus Sandaliarius' altar, found in a precinct behind the Forum of Augustus and securely dated to 2 BC, the same year as the Forum's dedication (altar now in the Uffizi: Lott 2004, 144-146, 192-193, fig. 14 a-d; Koortbojian 2013, esp. 73-76, pl. 3.21; Marcatilli 2015). In the central panel, Augustus stands frontally, flanked by Gaius Caesar and a female figure of disputed identity. The *princeps*' toga is pulled over the back of his head, his right arm extends at an oblique angle from his body, and the hand holds a *lituus*. The schema is almost exactly that of the Corinthian statue, and both representations show Augustus as augur in the act of taking auspices: the altar may record a specific ceremony connected with Gaius Caesar's departure for the campaign against the Parthians later that year. Possibly both works of art derive from a common original: one candidate is a c. 11-meter-tall colossal statue, fragments of which were found in the Forum of Augustus.[21] In the proposed restoration, the statue is veiled and holds a *lituus*, representing Augustus

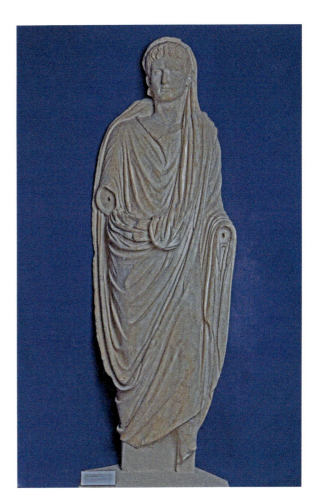

Figure 12. Augustus. Corinth Inv. S-1116 (Photo: Petros Dellatolas. Courtesy American School of Classical Studies at Athens, Corinth Excavations).

in his augural role.[22] Whether or not the Corinthian figure is directly connected with a schema devised for the Forum of Augustus, it remains a purely Roman conception, the physical expression of Augustus', and Rome's, authority, and the embodiment of Augustan *pietas*.

On the other hand, the portrait head of the Corinthian statue adds nuance to this statement of *romanitas*. In its conception, the head follows the widely-disseminated Prima Porta type, in which the gaunt traits of the young general and imperator as seen in his earliest portraits are glossed by those of a classical youth or deity (Boschung 1993; Pollini 1996). The togate body engaged in an ancient Roman ritual is linked by the classicized portrait type to another world, designating Augustus as an heir to the qualities and virtues embodied in classical forms. Among the crowd of portraits representing Augustus in this guise, the Corinthian representation stands out in its

---

21 http://en.mercatiditraiano.it/collezioni/percorsi_per_sale/sezione_del_foro_di_augusto/l_aula_del_colosso (accessed 4/9/2017).

22 Koortbojian 2013, 50-77, discussing augural roles of Julius Caesar as well as Augustus; Augustus and augural role: Dalla Rosa 2011.

Figure 13. Augustus, detail. Corinth Inv. S-1116 (Photo: I. Ioannidou and L. Bartzioti. Courtesy American School of Classical Studies at Athens, Corinth Excavations).

classicism, which could be termed 'self-conscious'. The crisp carving of the hair, which seems etched, finds its best parallel in works like the bronze Doryphoros in Naples or the Doryphoros from the theater in Corinth.[23] The hyper-classicism of the Corinthian portrait head could be a peculiarity of the artist's style; another possibility is that he deliberately exaggerated the style, reflecting – as we have seen – a local culture that was keenly aware of Corinth's Greek past.

7. Patrons in Corinth

The statues from the Corinthian basilica deployed iconography and style from the Roman and the Greek traditions to convey a narrative that blended elements of the Greek past with the Roman present, while the building made a strong statement of Roman authority. This program of architecture and art would have reached diverse audiences, from the simplest passer-by to the most sophisticated, whether of Greek background or other. Architecture, through its presence in, and control of, broadly accessible public space, would have had the greatest impact. Sculpture, enclosed in a privileged space and employing more sophisticated means, would have had a narrower impact. Who were those responsible for the overall conceptualization, and what were the sources of their inspiration? The decision to embark on a major building and artistic project in the centre of the city must have involved multiple layers of decision-making and funding. In Athens, Augustus and Agrippa initiated significant building activity (Spawforth 2012, esp. ch. 2), and the direct patronage of Augustus and his family was felt throughout the empire (Nicols 2013, 83-123). Through his example and through other means, including the enormous transfer of wealth from centre to periphery celebrated in his *Res Gestae* 15-18, Augustus would have encouraged the local elites to follow suit (Nicols 2013, 104-115). In Corinth this elite consisted predominantly of freedmen, many of whom were of Greek descent, with a smaller representation from two other groups: Roman citizens perhaps resident for many years in the Greek east as *negotiatores*, and members of the local Greek gentry (Spawforth 1996; Rizakis 2001; Millis 2010; Balzat & Millis 2014; Millis 2013; Pawlak 2014; Walbank 2014).

There is some epigraphical information from the building itself about patrons. Fragments dating to the mid-1st century AD of what may be an honour roll of donors includes the name of Gnaeus Babbius Philinus, a well-known freedman of Greek descent connected with other benefactions in Corinth (Kent 1966, no. 327; Millis 2014, 39-41). That there were multiple donors for different aspects of the building and its contents is suggested by the three names probably of freedmen that appear on an altar to Divus Augustus, set up soon after the building's construction (Kent 1966, no. 69; Scotton *et al.* 2014), and, as already noted, it is possible that the aristocratic Spartan Euryclids were also involved.

Contemporary Corinth also boasted the presence of important freedmen families initially associated with Marc Antony. In the years leading up to the construction of the basilica one of Corinth's leading citizens was M. Antonius Hipparchus, son of M. Antonius Theophilos, a freedman who served as Marc Antony's steward in Corinth.[24] As a young man, Hipparchus was the first of Antony's freedmen to go over to Octavian (Plut. *Ant.* 67.7), and he later served several terms as duovir. His long personal history with Augustus as well as (presumably) his sister Octavia and her children by Marc Antony may help explain several remarkable coin emissions. In 10/9 BC, Hipparchus and his fellow duovir M. Novius Bassus minted aes coinage that depicted Augustus on the obverse and on the reverse Julius Caesar, the first and only

---

23   Naples: Mattusch 2005, 276-277, figs. 5.187-5.190. Corinth: Sturgeon 2004, 117-120, pl. 33-a-d. The hair of the Corinthian Doryphoros is unevenly worked, with that over the front and especially the left side showing the greatest similarity to the Corinthian Augustus (Sturgeon 2004, pl. 33, a, b, d).

24   Spawforth 1996, 170, no. 4 a-c; Millis 2013, 46; Antonian network in Achaia: Rizakis 2001, 181-182.

known example of this combination in Roman Corinthian coins (Amandry 1988, 49-50, 142-144, pl. ix-x; RPC I, no. 1136). Shortly thereafter, in the momentous years 2/1 BC, Hipparchus and his colleague C. Servilius C.f. Primus coined a unique series depicting Augustus on the obverse, and on the reverse his heirs Gaius and Lucius Caesar (Amandry 1988, 50-51, pl. x-xi). The discovery of one of these coins in the foundation level of the basilica gives a terminus post quem for its construction (Scotton *et al.* 2014). The assiduousness of these honours is remarkable, suggesting the possibility that they are in thanks to the imperial family for favours done, such as financial assistance for the new basilica or other building projects. In any case, we may safely conclude that among the Corinthian magisterial elite responsible for conceptualizing the basilica and its sculptural programme were men closely connected to the *princeps*' family and inner circle in Rome.

8. Conclusion

The Julian Basilica was the local response to Augustus's empire-wide effort to give physical structure to the new political order, his own key monument being the roughly contemporary Forum of Augustus. Corinth's building becomes the visible face of Roman authority. Not only was Corinth an important colonial foundation; it was probably the capital of the province of Achaea. Especially in its early years, the basilica would have housed the main functions of both local and imperial administration.[25] There is also considerable evidence that the basilica was a locus of imperial cult activities beginning in the reign of Augustus (Scotton *et al.* 2014), and it may have provided – initially – a home for the administration of the historic Isthmian Games, a significant holdover from Corinth's Hellenic past.[26] Of the inscriptions from the basilica on statue bases dedicated to municipal officials, twelve include references to the Isthmian or Caesarian games, or both, through mention of the positions of *agonothetes* or *isogogeus*.[27]

Corinth's magisterial elite consisted of people with close ties to metropolitan Rome: in their manipulation of space, architecture, and art they drew on strategies devised in metropolitan Rome as exemplified in the contemporary Forum of Augustus, which employed a new artistic and architectural canon that drew on Classical and Hellenistic forms to refashion history and mythology. They would also have been aware of the Greek past, whether because of their own familial histories or because of Corinth's acknowledged and revered antiquity. They sought to blend the Roman with the Greek in creating their new city. By taking possession of, and co-opting the past they could fashion themselves as its heirs. The Julian Basilica was one tool in their efforts. It was given a commanding position and pride of place, challenging the Temple of Apollo as well as the South Stoa, thus weaving earlier Greek buildings with the Roman into a distinctively Roman urban fabric. The basilica's planners were also guided by local imperatives, as evidenced in the sculptural assemblage through the selection of types, iconography, and styles evoking the Greek past. The Julian Basilica appears to have been the first large-scale construction in the centre of Corinth but it was quickly followed by others, so that by the middle of the 1st century AD the remaining Greek structures had been enveloped, their visual pre-eminence at an end but their existence preserved. In characteristic Roman fashion the past had been edited, reformatted, and appropriated to consolidate the new social and political order, the blending accomplished by people who themselves belonged to culturally fluid populations.[28] The basilica and its sculptural assemblage document the complex identity of early Roman Corinth: Roman and at the same time Greek.

---

25 Until the construction of the basilica, there is no clear evidence in the archaeological record as to the location of the early colony's administrative centre including a curia for the decuriones. Perhaps political gatherings could be mobile, taking place in a variety of settings, as had been the case in Rome during much of the Republic (*cf.* Kondratieff 2010 on mobility of the praetor's tribunal in Rome).

26 Return of the Games to Corinth as early as 42 BC: Gebhard 1993; Gebhard 2005, esp. 182-189. See Kajava 2002; Del Basso *this volume*.

27 This number represents 20% of the 61 epigraphical references to the *agonothetes* with known find-spots in Corinth: the assessment comes from the analysis of findspots and inscriptions by Roncaglia and Scotton, to be published in the volume on the Julian Basilica in the Corinth excavation series (above, n. 1).

---

28 The theme of 'hybridity' and cultural 'collaboration' courses through recent work on Corinth and in general on early Roman colonies: see for example Thomas 2010; Wallace-Hadrill 2011; Millis 2010; Laird 2010; Sweetman 2011; Millis 2013. On interwoven identities: Walbank 2014, responding to Slane 2012.

References

Alroth, B. & C. Scheffer (eds) 2014. *Attitudes Towards the Past in Antiquity: Creating Identities. Proceedings of an International Conference Held at Stockholm University, 15-17 May 2009. Stockholm Studies in Classical Archaeology* 14, Stockholm.

Amandry, M. 1988. *Le monnayage des duovirs corinthiens, BCH Supplément* XV, Paris.

Balzat, J-S. 2008. Les Euryclides en Laconie. In: C. Grandjean (ed.), *Le Péloponnèse d'Épaminondas à Adrien, Actes du Colloque de Tours, 6-7 Octobre 2005*, Bordeaux, 335-350.

Balzat, J-S. . 2010. Prosopographie des prêtres et prêtresses des Dioscures de la Sparte d'époque imperial. In: A.D. Rizakis & C. E. Lepenioti (eds), *Roman Peloponnese III. Society, Economy and Culture under the Roman Empire: Continuity and Innovation, Meletemata* 63, Athens, 341-356.

Balzat, J.-S. & B.W. Millis 2014. M. Antonius Aristocrates: Provincial involvement with Roman power in the late 1st century B.C., *Hesperia* 82, 651-672.

Bastien, J.-L. 2008. Les temples votifs de la Rome Républicaine: Monumentalisation et célébration des cérémonies du triomphe. In: P. Fleury & O. Desbordes (eds), *Roma illustrata. Représentation de la ville*, Caen, 29-48.

Bommelaer, J.-F. 1971. Note sur les navarques et les successeurs de Polyclète à Delphes, *BCH* 95, 43-64.

Bommelaer, J.-F. 1981. *Lysandre de Sparte: Histoire et traditions, BEFAR* 240, Paris.

Bookidis, N. 2005. Religion in Corinth: 146 B.C.E. to 100 C.E. In: D.N. Schowalter & S. J. Friesen (eds), *Urban Religion in Roman Corinth: Interdisciplinary Approaches* (*Harvard Theological Studies* 53), Cambridge (MA), 141-164.

Bookidis, N. & R.S. Stroud 2004. Apollo and the Archaic Temple at Corinth, *Hesperia* 73, 401-426.

Borelli, L.V. & P. Pelagatti (eds) 1984. *Due bronzi da Riace: rinvenimento, restauro, analisi, et ipotesi di interpretazione*, Roma.

Boschung, D. 1993. *Die Bildnisse des Augustus* (*Das römische Herrscherbild* 1.2), Berlin.

Boschung, D. 2002. *Gens Augusta: Untersuchungen zu Aufstellung, Wirkung und Bedeutung der Statuengruppen des julisch-claudischen Kaiserhauses*, Mainz.

Bowersock, G.W. 1961. Eurycles of Sparta, *JRS* 51, 112-118.

Buxton, B. 2012. A new reading of the Prima Porta Augustus: the return of the Eagle of Legio V Alaudae, *Latomus* 338, 277-306.

Cadario, M. 2004. *La corazza di Alessandro. Loricati di tipo ellenistico dal IV secolo a.c. al II d.c.*, Milano.

Cadario, M. 2014. Preparing for triumph. Graecae Artes as Roman booty in L. Mummius' campaign (146 BC).

In: C.H. Lange & F.J. Vervaet (eds), *The Roman Republican Triumph: Beyond the Spectacle*, Rome, 83-101.

Caputo, G. 1976. *Le sculture del teatro di Leptis Magna*, Roma.

Champlin, E. 2011. Tiberius and the Heavenly Twins, *JRS* 101, 73-99.

Charbonneaux, J. 1973. *Hellenistic Art*, New York.

Coarelli, F. 2010. Substructio et tabularium, *PBSR* 78, 107-132.

Dalla Rosa, A. 2011. Dominating the auspices: Augustus, augury, and the proconsuls. In: J. H. Richardson & F. Santangelo (eds), *Priests and State in the Roman World*, Stuttgart, 243-269.

Dardenay, A. 2010. *Les mythes foundateur de Rome: Images et politique dans l'Occident romain*, Paris.

Davies, S. 2010. Carthage, Corinth, and 146 BCE: Shifting paradigms of Roman imperium, eScholarship. http://escholarship.org/uc/item/0fw661w0, accessed 1 September 2016.

Edlund-Berry, I. 2014. Attitudes towards the past in Antiquity: Creating identities. A summary of themes and ideas. In: B. Alroth & C. Scheffer (eds), *Attitudes Towards the Past in Antiquity: Creating Identities. Proceedings of an International Conference Held at Stockholm University, 15-17 May 2009. Stockholm Studies in Classical Archaeology* 14, Stockholm, 321-325.

Edmonson, J. 2011. A tale of two colonies: Augusta Emerita (Merida) and Metellinum (Medellin) in Roman Lusitania. In: R.J. Sweetman (ed), *Roman Colonies in the First Century of Their Foundation*, Oxford, 32-54.

Etienne, R. & J.-P. Braun 1986. *Ténos I: le sanctuaire de Poséidon et d'Amphitrite*, BEFAR 263, Paris.

Favro, D. 1996. *The Urban Image of Augustan Rome*, New York.

Friesen, S.J., D.N. Schowalter & J.C. Walters 2013. The local magistrates and elite of Roman Corinth. In: S.J. Friesen, S. James & D. Schowalter, *Corinth in Contrast: Studies in Inequality*, Leiden, 38-53.

Galinsky, K. (ed.) 2014. *Memoria Romana*, Ann Arbor.

Galinsky, K. (ed.) 2016. *Memory in Ancient Rome and Early Christianity*, Oxford.

Galinsky, K. & K. Lapatin (eds.) 2016. *Cultural Memories in the Roman Empire*, Los Angeles.

Gebhard, E. 1993. Isthmia in the Roman Period: The Isthmian Games and the Sanctuary of Poseidon in the early empire. In: T. Gregory (ed.), *The Corinthia in the Roman Period: A Symposium Held at The Ohio State University on 7-9 March 1991* (*JRA Supplement* 8), Ann Arbor, 78-94.

Gebhard, E. 2005. Rites for Melikertes-Palaimon in the early Roman Corinthia. In: D.N. Schowalter & S.J.

Friesen (eds), *Urban Religion in Roman Corinth: Interdisciplinary Approaches* (*Harvard Theological Studies* 53), Cambridge, MA, 165-203.

Gebhard, E. R. & M.W. Dickie 2003. The view from the Isthmus, ca. 20 to 44 B.C. In: N. Bookidis & C.K. Williams II, *Corinth XX, Corinth, The Centenary 1896-1996*, Princeton, 261-278.

Geiger, J. 2008. *The First Hall of Fame: A Study of the Statues in the Forum Augustum*, Leiden.

Geppert, S. 1996. *Castor und Pollux: Untersuchung zu den Darstellungen der Dioskuren in der römischen Kaiserzeit, Charybdis* 8, Münster.

Goldbeck, V. 2015. *Fora augusta. Das Augustusforum und seine Rezeption im Westen des Imperium Romanum, Eikoniká, Kunstwissenschaftliche Beiträge* 5, Regensburg.

Graverini, L. 2001. L. Mummio Acaico, *Maecenas: Studi sul mondo classico* 1, 105-148.

Hallett, C. 2005. *The Roman Nude: Heroic Portrait Statuary 200 BC – AD 300*, Oxford.

Haselberger, L. 2007. *Urbem adornare – Die Stadt Rom und ihre Gestaltumwandlung unter Augustus. Rome's Urban Metamorphosis under Augustus, JRA Supplement* 66, Portsmouth.

Hernandez, D.R. & D. Condi 2014. The formation of Butrint: New insights from excavations in the Roman forum. In: L. Përzhita, I. Gjipali, G. Hoxh & B. Muka (eds), *Proceedings of the International Congress of Albanian Archaeological Studies, Tirana*, 285-302.

Hölscher, T. 2006. The transformation of victory into power: From event to structure. In: S. Dillon & K. Welch (eds), *Representations of War in Ancient Rome*, Cambridge, 27-48.

James, S.A. 2013. The last of the Corinthians? Society and settlement from 146-44 BCE. In: S.J. Friesen, S.A. James & D.N. Schowalter (eds), *Corinth in Contrast: Studies in Inequality*, Leiden, 17-37.

Jiménez, A. & J.R. Carrillo 2011. Corduba/Colonia Patricia: The colony that was founded twice. In: R.J. Sweetman (ed.), *Roman Colonies in the First Century of Their Foundation*, Oxford, 55-74.

Johnson, F.P. 1931. *Corinth IX: Sculpture, 1896-1923*. Cambridge, MA.

Jones, M. 2003. *Principles of Roman Architecture*, New Haven.

Kajava, M. 2002. When did the Isthmian Games return to Corinth? (Rereading Corinth VIII.3.153), *CP* 97, 168-178.

Kantiréa, M., 2007. Les dieux et les dieux augustes. Le culte impérial en Gréce sous les Julio-claudiens et les Flaviens: études épigraphiques et archéologiques (*Meletemata* 50), Athènes.

Karanastasi, P. 1995. Ζητήματα της εικονογραφίας και της παρουσίας των Ρωμαίων αυτοκρατόρων στην Ελλάδα, *AE*, 209-226.

Katsikoudis, N. 2006. Δωδώνη. Οι τιμητικοί ανδριάντες, Ιωάννινα.

Kent, J.H. 1966. *Corinth VIII, Pt. 3: The Inscriptions, 1926-1950*, Princeton.

Kleiner, D.E.E. 1992. *Roman Sculpture*, New Haven.

Kondratieff, E., 2010. The urban praetor's tribunal in the Roman Republic. In: F. De Angelis (ed), *Spaces of Justice in the Roman World*, Boston, 89-126.

Koortbojian, M. 2006. The bringer of victory: Imagery and institutions at the advent of Empire. In: S. Dillon & K. Welch (eds), *Representations of War in Ancient Rome*, Cambridge, 184-217.

Koortbojian, M. 2013. *The Divinization of Caesar and Augustus*, Cambridge.

Kuttner, A.L. 1995. *Dynasty and Empire in the Age of Augustus: The Case of the Boscoreale Cups*, Berkeley.

Laube, I. 2006. *Thorakophoroi: Gestalt und Semantik des Brustpanzers in der Darstellung des 4. bis 1 Jhs. v. Chr.*, Rahden.

Lindsay, H. 1992. Augustus and Eurycles, *RhM* 135, 290-297.

Lott, J.B. 2004. *The Neighborhoods of Augustan Rome*, Cambridge.

Ma, J. 2013. *Statues and Cities: Honorific Portraits and Civic Identity in the Hellenistic World*, Oxford.

Marcadè, J. 1969. *Au Musée de Délos. Étude sur la sculpture hellénistique en ronde bosse découverte dans l'île* (*BEFAR Sér. Athènes* 215), Paris.

Marcatilli, F. 2015. L'altare del Vicus Sandaliarius agli Uffizi, *BaBesch* 90, 125-137.

Meneghini, R. & R. S. Valenzani 2010. *Scavi dei fori imperiali: il Foro di Augusto: l'area centrale*, Rome.

Millis, B.W. 2006. 'Miserable huts' in post-146 B.C. Corinth, *Hesperia* 75, 397-404.

Millis, B.W. 2010. The Social and Ethnic Origins of the Colonists in Early Roman Corinth. In: S.J. Friesen, D.N. Schowalter & J.C. Walters (eds), *Corinth in Context: Comparative Studies on Religion and Society*, Leiden, 13-35.

Morgan, C. 2014. Archaeology of memory or tradition in practice? In: B. Alroth & C. Scheffer (eds), *Attitudes Towards the Past in Antiquity: Creating Identities. Proceedings of an International Conference Held at Stockholm University, 15-17 May 2009. Stockholm Studies in Classical Archaeology* 14, Stockholm, 173-182.

Nicols, J. 2013. *Civic Patronage in the Roman Empire*, Leiden.

Pawlak, M. 2014. Corinth after 44 BC: Ethnical and cultural changes, *Electrum* 20, 143-62.

Peña Jurado, A. 2007. Reflejos del Forum Augustum en Italica. In: T. Nogales Basarrat & I. Rodà (eds), *Roma y las provincias: modelo y difusión. XI Coloquio Internacional de Arte Romano Provincial*, Roma, 323-345.

Pietilä-Castrén, L. 1987. *Magnificentia Publica: The Victory Monuments of the Roman Generals in the Era of the Punic Wars*, Helsinki.

Pollini, J. 1987. *The Portraiture of Gaius and Lucius Caesar*, New York.

Picón, C.A. & S. Hemingway (eds) 2016. *Pergamon and the Hellenistic Kingdoms of the Ancient World*, New York.

Popkin, M.L. 2016. *The Architecture of the Roman Triumph: Monuments, Memory, and Identity*, Cambridge.

Poulsen, B. 1991. The Dioscuri and ruler ideology, *SymbOslo* 66, 119-146.

Purcell, N. 1995. On the sacking of Corinth and Carthage. In: D.C. Innes, H. Hine, & C. Pelling (eds), *Ethics and Rhetoric: Classical Essays for Donald Russell on His Seventy-Fifth Birthday*, New York, 133-148.

Queyrel, F. 1986. Les sculptures. In: R. Etienne and J.-P. Braun, *Ténos I: le sanctuaire de Poséidon et d'Amphitrite* (*BEFAR* 293), Paris, 268-321.

Rizakis, A.D. 1997. Roman colonies in the province of Achaia: Territories, land and population. In: S.E. Alcock (ed.), *The Early Roman Empire in the East*, Oxford, 15-36.

Rizakis, A.D. 2001. La constitution des élites municipales dans les colonies romaines de la province d'Achaïe. In: O. Salomies (ed), *The Greek East in the Roman Context: Proceedings of a Colloquium Organised by The Finnish Institute at Athens; May 21 and 22, 1999. Papers and Monographs of the Finnish Institute at Athens* 7, Helsinki, 37-49.

Rizakis, A.D. 2010. Peloponnesian cities under Roman rule: The new political geography and its economic and social repercussions. In: A.D. Rizakis & C.E. Lepenioti (eds), *Roman Peloponnese III. Society, Economy and Culture under the Roman Empire: Continuity and Innovation (Meletemata* 63), Athens, 1-18.

Robinson, B. A. 2011. *Histories of Peirene: A Corinthian Fountain in Three Millennia*, Princeton.

Romano, D. G. 2010. Romanization in the Corinthia: Urban and rural developments. In: A.D. Rizakis & C. E. Lepenioti (eds), *Roman Peloponnese III. Society, Economy and Culture under the Roman Empire: Continuity and Innovation (Meletemata* 63), Athens, 155-172.

Rose, C.B. 1997. *Dynastic Commemoration and Imperial Portraiture in the Julio-Claudian Period*, Cambridge.

Rose, C.B. 2005. The Parthians in Augustan Rome, *AJA* 109, 21-75.

Russell, A. 2015. *The Politics of Public Space in Republican Rome*, Cambridge.

Sanders, J. 1993. The Dioscuri in post-Classical Sparta. In: O. Palagia and W.D.E. Coulson (eds), *Sculpture from Arcadia and Laconia*, Oxford, 217-224.

Scahill, D.R. 2012. The South Stoa at Corinth: Design, Construction and Function of the Greek Phase, Diss. University of Bath.

Shaya, J. 2013. The public life of monuments: The Summi Viri of the Forum of Augustus, *AJA* 117, 83-110.

Scotton, P. 2011. Imperial cult and imperial reconciliation. In: R.J. Sweetman (ed), *Roman Colonies in the First Century of Their Foundation*, Oxford, 75-84.

Scotton, P. 2012. The Basilica at Fano and the Vitruvian norm. In: L. Cavalier, R. Descat & J. des Courtils (eds), *Basiliques et Agoras de Grèce et d'Asie Mineure (Mémoires* 27), Bordeaux, 25-90.

Scotton, P., C. de Grazia Vanderpool & C. Roncaglia 2014. The imperial cult in the 'Julian Basilica' in Ancient Corinth. In: J.M. Álvarez, T. Nogales & I. Rodà (eds), *Centro y periferia en el mundo clásico. Actas del XVIII Congreso Internacional de Arqueología Clásica*, Mérida, 49-52.

Spannagel, M. 1999, *Exemplaria Principis. Untersuchungen zu Entstehung und Ausstatung des Augustusforums*, Heidelberg, 1627-1630.

Slane, K. 1986. Two deposits from the early Roman Cellar Building, Corinth, *Hesperia* 55, 271-318.

Slane, K. 2004. Corinth: Italian sigillata and other Italian imports to the early colony, *Early Italian Sigillata, Proceedings of the First International ROCT-Congress*, Leuven, 31-42.

Slane, K. 2012. Remaining Roman in death at an eastern colony, *JRA* 25 (2012), 442-455.

Spawforth, A. 1996. Roman Corinth: The formation of a colonial elite. In: A.D. Rizakis (ed), *Roman Onomastics in the Greek East: Social and Political Aspects: Proceedings of the International Colloquium on Roman Onomastics Athens, 7-9 September 1993 (Metemata* 21), Athens, 167-182.

Slane, K. 2010. C. Iulius Eurycles and the Spartan dynasty of the Euryclids. In: A.D. Rizakis & C. E. Lepenioti (eds), *Roman Peloponnese III. Society, Economy and Culture under the Roman Empire: Continuity and Innovation (Meletemata* 63), Athens, 129-154.

Slane, K. 2012. Greece and the Augustan Cultural Revolution, Cambridge.

Squire, M. 2015. Corpus imperii: verbal and visual figurations of the Roman 'body politic'. *Word & Image* 31, http://dx.doi.org/10.1080/02666286.2015.1047 669 (accessed 4/13/2017).

Stamper, J. W. 2005. *The Architecture of Roman Temples: The Republic to the Middle Empire*, Cambridge.

Steinhauer, G. 1993. Η εικονογραφία των Διοσκούρων στη ρωμαϊκή Σπάρτη. In: O. Palagia and W.D.E.

Coulson (eds), *Sculpture from Arcadia and Laconia*, Oxford, 225-235.

Sturgeon, M. C. 2004. *Corinth IX, Pt. 3: Sculpture: The Assemblage from the Theater*, Princeton, NJ.

Thomas, C. 2010. Greek heritage in Roman Corinth and Ephesos. In: S.J. Friesen, D.N. Schowalter & J.C. Walters (eds), *Corinth in Context: Comparative Studies on Religion and Society*, Leiden, 117-147.

Ungaro, L. 2007. The Forum of Augustus. In: L. Ungaro & M.P. Del Moro, *The Museum of the Imperial Forums in Trajan's Market*, Rome, Milano, 118-130.

Vanderpool, C. de Grazia 2000. Serial twins: Riace B and some Roman relatives. In: C. Mattusch, A. Brauer, and S.E. Knudsen (eds), *From the Parts to the Whole. I. Acta of the 13th International Bronze Congress Held at Cambridge, MA, May 28-June 1, 1996*, Rhode Island, 106-116.

Vanderpool, C. de Grazia 2003: Roman portraiture: The many faces of Corinth. In: N. Bookidis & C.K. Williams II, *Corinth XX, Corinth, The Centenary 1896-1996*, Princeton, 369-384.

Vanderpool, C. de Grazia Forthcoming 2017. Julius Caesar and Divus Iulius in Corinth: Man, memory, and cult. In: V. Di Napoli, F. Camia, V. Evangelidis, D. Grigoropoulos, D. Rogers, & S. Vlizos (eds), *What's New in Roman Greece? Recent Work on the Greek Mainland and the Islands in the Roman Period. Proceedings of a Conference held at Athens, 8-10 October 2015*, Athens.

Walbank, M.H. 1997. The foundation and planning of Roman Corinth, *JRA* 10, 95-130.

Walbank, M.H. 2010. The cults of Roman Corinth: Public ritual and personal belief. In: A.D. Rizakis & C. E. Lepenioti (eds), *Roman Peloponnese III. Society, Economy and Culture under the Roman Empire: Continuity and Innovation (Meletemata 63)*, Athens, 357-374.

Walbank, M.H. 2014. Remaining Roman in death at Corinth? A debate with K.W. Slane, *JRA* 27, 403-416.

Wallace-Hadrill, A. 2011. Pompeian identities: Between Oscan, Samnite, Greek, Roman, and Punic. In: E.S. Gruen (ed), *Cultural Identity in the Ancient Mediterranean (The Getty Research Institute. Issues and Debates)*, Los Angeles, 415-427.

Williams, C.K. II 1989. A re-evaluation of Temple E and the west end of the forum of Corinth. In: S. Walker and A. Cameron (eds), *The Greek and Roman Renaissance in the Roman Empire, Papers from the Tenth British Museum Classical Colloquium*, 156-162.

Williams, C.K. II 1993. Roman Corinth as a commercial center. In: T.E. Gregory (ed), *The Corinthia in the Roman Period: A Symposium Held at The Ohio State University 7-9 March 1991 (JRA Supplement 8)*, Ann Arbor, 31-46.

Williams, C.K. II & O.H. Zervos 1988. Corinth, 1987: South of Temple E and East of the Theater, *Hesperia* 57, 95-146.

Williams, C.K. II & O.H. Zervos 1989. Corinth, 1988: East of the Theater, *Hesperia* 58, 1-50.

Yarrow, L. 2006. Lucius Mummius and the spoils of Corinth, *Scripta Classica Israelica* 25, 57-70.

Zanker, P. 1990. *The Power of Images in the Age of Augustus*, Ann Arbor.

Ziolkowski, A. 1988. Mummius' Temple of Hercules Victor and the Round Temple on the Tiber, *Phoenix* 42, 309-333.

PART II

Competing with the Past

Heritage Societies? Private Associations in Roman Greece

Benedikt Eckhardt

Abstract

The history of private associations in the Roman imperial era is characterized by abundant variety and local developments, but also by common features that can be understood as provincial responses to imperial ideologies. While these common features can be detected in Roman Greece, particularly in the Roman colonies, they seem to be far less relevant in this region than in others. The article highlights this difference and attempts to explain it as the result of strategies of remembering. Both Romans and locals were aware of the mythological and religious traditions of Greece, which led to two particular local variants in the general history of associations under Rome: a tendency to build new associations on the basis of mythological models ('organizing the mythical past'), and a tendency to revive patterns of social organization that symbolically represented the Classical and Hellenistic past ('mythologizing the organizational past'). While Greece had a special status because of its literary tradition, the phenomena as such are not out of order with what happened in other regions; they are recreations of local history that could be (but did not have to be) embedded into an imperial ideology.

Keywords: associations, Romanization, history of institutions, imperial ideology, Roman Greece

1. Introduction

The history of the Greek city, if there ever was anything deserving that general label, is intricately connected to the history of private associations. In the Hellenistic period at the latest, *koina, thiasoi, synodoi* etc. were to be found in almost every major city and many smaller ones, providing both citizens and metics with an additional social context apart from the civic subdivisions. Rome also had an early history of associations, but before the late Republican period, their functions seem to have been more limited and their private nature can be doubted. When people in Italy, supposedly stirred up by an anonymous Greek, for the first time tried to build something approximating Greek cult associations, Roman authorities reacted hysterically, which led to the prosecution of thousands in the Bacchanalian affair of 186 BC (Livy 39.8-19; *CIL* I² 581). *Collegia* eventually became a relevant factor in Rome and Italy, but were regulated by a multitude of increasingly complex legal regulations. At the same time, Greeks kept assembling in their *thiasoi* and *synodoi* even after the Roman takeover, with little evidence for direct state supervision by imperial magistrates. The question naturally arises how Greek associations fitted (or did not fit) the social order guarded by Roman provincial administrators.

in: Dijkstra, T.M., I.N.I. Kuin, M. Moser & D. Weidgenannt (eds) 2017. *Strategies of Remembering in Greece under Rome (100 BC - 100 AD)*, Leiden (Sidestone Press).

The question as such is not entirely new. For Athens, the only place where a comparison between Hellenistic and later phenomena can be based on sufficient evidence, Marie-Françoise Baslez (2004) has provided a thorough discussion of associations in the imperial era. She notes several tendencies that set the associations of the Roman period apart from their Hellenistic predecessors: the members were relatively wealthy and normally Athenian citizens; founders and other leading figures played a much more important role; there was a more pronounced distinction between male and female members; finally, associations displayed a stronger focus on religious purposes, whereas ethnic or professional characteristics disappeared. Some of these observations are debatable. Men and women were sometimes listed separately in Hellenistic membership lists (*IG* II² 1297, 1298), and while some associations can plausibly be explained as professional or ethnic networks, their main identifying feature, i.e. the aspect of their group identity chosen for public representation, in the Hellenistic period was clearly religion (Gabrielsen 2007). But these are perhaps matters of degree, not substance, and Baslez's other observations still stand.

I nevertheless think that there remain many questions, for two reasons. First, it would be helpful to understand the Athenian data in the wider context of what was going on in the provinces of Achaea and Macedonia on the one hand, and in the rest of the Roman Empire on the other. Second and more specifically, looking for 'Strategies of Remembering' can help to reveal an aspect of the history of associations in Roman Greece that has hitherto been overlooked: the use of associations by both Roman administrators and local inhabitants for symbolically recreating a pre-Roman past. To approach these two issues, I first offer a brief sketch of a general model of Romanization and associations that seems to work for most regions of the empire (part two). I then turn to the evidence from Greece and note that it does not fit this model very well (part three). I then point to two strategies of remembrance at work in Greek associations of the Roman period: remembrance of religious and mythical tradition (part four) and remembrance of the early history of corporate organization in Greece (part five). I claim that this allows for the integration of Roman Greece into a general history of Romanization and associations that denies neither the local varieties nor the imperial ideologies surrounding private corporate organization (part six).

2. A model for associations and Romanization

If we try to identify the impact of Rome and imperial ideologies on the sphere of private corporate organization, we encounter a sceptical approach that prevails at least for the Eastern provinces. As associations had existed in the Greek world – and possibly beyond – long before the advent of Rome, one possible argument is that if there had been an influence, it would have been the other way round, from East to West (Cracco Ruggini 1976). Another, more recent approach has focused on the apparent irrelevance of Roman legal regulations on *collegia vel corpora* for the development of associations in the East (Arnaoutoglou 2002). When Caesar and Augustus ordered the dissolution of all but a couple of associations at Rome (Suet. *Iul.* 42.3; *Aug.* 32.1), they simultaneously flourished in Greece, Asia Minor and Egypt. And even if, as seems unlikely, the extension of the general ban on associations to the provinces only came with Septimius Severus (*Dig.* 47.22.1pr), new associations clearly did not cease to emerge even then. From this one might indeed conclude that Rome's influence on the history of associations in the Eastern provinces was marginal at best. However, this assessment, while pointing out important aspects, needs to be somewhat modified.

First, law was not irrelevant. While not as abundant as in Italy and the Western provinces, evidence for recognition procedures relating to the *ius coeundi* exists at least for Asia Minor – the *neoi* of Kyzikos (*CIL* III 7060), the *gerousia* of Sidmya (*TAM* II 175) and the *naukleroi* of Miletus (Ehrhardt & Günther 2013) all received such recognition from the emperor or the provincial governor, while the *fabri* of Nikomedeia failed to do so (Plin. *Ep.* 10.33-34). As for litigation, the events in Egypt under Flaccus and the case of the bakers of Ephesos both show that the prohibitive potential of Roman legal regulations could easily result in prohibitive action (Arnaoutoglou 2005, 207-212; IvE 215 with Perry 2015). Second, the focus on prohibitive aspects should not distract us from other ramifications the Roman imperial social order – supported by, but not limited to, Roman law – had on the development of associational culture in the provinces. I have argued elsewhere that the incentives provided through legal concepts like *collegium licitum*, *utilitas publica* and organization *ad exemplum rei publicae*, as well as the insecurity caused by the prohibitive aspects of the legal regulations, created a situation of isomorphic pressure (Eckhardt 2016a). The spread of associations that were all formed according to a somewhat similar pattern and oriented towards Rome does not contradict the policy evident from the legal regulations, but should be understood as an indirect effect. Agency in this process should mainly be attributed to the provincials themselves, who saw in these categories a way to receive status and recognition in an imperial world order. This comes close to what Clifford Ando (2010) has described in abstract terms as the creation of a homology between imperial and local structures, which ultimately leads to the creation of 'imperial identities'.

Associations in the Western provinces fit this model well. It is safe to assume that their very creation was tied to the establishment of Roman rule, and their role in connecting people to a Romanized public sphere has been noted in several studies (Verboven 2012; Tran 2012). A more complex question is how Roman concepts affected the associational culture of those regions where there was a long pre-Roman tradition of private corporate organization. Clearly, any answer has to be based on the development of corporate representation, as almost all relevant data come from inscriptions. At least some changes are clearly recognizable, most obviously the spread of professional associations. There were hardly any groups in the Hellenistic period outside Egypt whose members defined themselves primarily as practitioners of a craft or trade. In Greece, they first became a recognizable factor on 2nd century BC Delos under Roman influence (Rauh 1993). In the imperial era, professional associations are omnipresent not only in Egypt (where they had already existed in Ptolemaic times), but also in Asia Minor, Thracia and the cities of the Levant. They aspired and achieved a semi-public status, with seats in the theatres just like the *phylai*, treated in testaments on a par with civic institutions or the imperial *fiscus*, while at the same time declaring their loyalty to the emperors and their delegates through honorific decrees (on all this, see Van Nijf 1997). It is easy to imagine that these groups could be seen as fulfilling a 'useful' function for city and empire, regardless of their precise legal status.

Whereas groups advertising their professional links were flourishing under Rome, the default option for private organization in the Hellenistic period – groups defining themselves solely as worshippers of a deity – seems to have become less attractive. In Asia Minor, the typical designation of groups with theophoric names (*Apolloniastai, Athenaistai* etc.) largely disappears in the imperial period; in the Levant, a comparable form of self-designation only occurs once as a further qualification of a professional association (*SEG* 35.1572). In Thracia, recent finds alter the picture slightly (*Attiastai* and *Neomeniastai* in 3rd century AD Dionysopolis: Sharankov 2013), but the general conclusion remains valid. At the same time, other forms of organization with a religious denominator emerged, most importantly the many groups of *mystai* in Asia Minor – but in many cases, these were tied to the civic cult and/or the cult of the emperors, as is the case with *hymnodoi* (Eckhardt/Lepke forthcoming). The Roman order did not preclude organization for religious purposes, but privileges were accorded only to rather specific types. Among the groups with legal recognition, the only ones with a religious designator are *Augustales* (*CIL* V 4428; *AÉpigr* 2001, 853-854 with Camodeca 2001) and a cult group for Antinoos founded as an expression of loyalty to Hadrian (*CIL* XIV 2112 with

Bendlin 2011). While Roman law was not in itself a very restrictive factor – it even included a loophole for creating cult communities below the level of formal *collegia* (Dig. 47.22.1.1) – groups defining themselves merely as worshippers could not aspire to the quasi-civic status accorded to professional associations. Hence the general lack of attestations in the imperial period.

But Roman rule not only changed the primary designator of private corporate organization from religion to professions. It also facilitated the 'privatization' – at least to some degree – of organizational fields that had been decidedly civic in earlier periods. This becomes visible in the development of formal organizations tied to the gymnasium. While the phenomenon as such goes back to the 2nd century BC, it took on pace and significance in the Roman period, as *neoi* were increasingly integrated into the cities' strategies of showing their loyalty to Rome, and *gerousiai* became wide-spread as an additional, semi-public institution assembling Rome-friendly elites (Eckhardt forthcoming). Both groups could be officially acknowledged through Roman legal procedures (*CIL* III 7060; *TAM* II 175), and at least *gerousiai* could be founded by individuals (Engelmann 2012, 191-192 no. 11). Cities could thus underline their desire to participate in the Roman imperial order via newly defined corporate bodies, while local elites could find in these groups an additional source of distinction, particularly in light of the middle classes' tendency to claim civic space through professional associations.

What I have sketched here in very broad terms shows that some general insights into how associations could be integrated into the Roman imperial order are possible. At the same time, it is clear that no model should attempt to eradicate local variants, or to peg every piece of evidence according to preconceived categories. While historical models are necessary to avoid a mere antiquarian approach to the data, we have to be open for surprises and challenges in order to come to meaningful conclusions. For this particular model, the strongest challenge comes from Roman Greece.

3. The evidence from Roman Greece

It is easy to name a number of groups in Roman Greece that are unthinkable without the impact of Roman organizational concepts. We can point to a *collegium Larum domus divinae* at Corinth (*Corinth* VIII.3 62), a κολλήγιον Ἀυγουστάλων in Cassandreia (*SEG* 29.614; 46.746; Sverkos 2002, 174-179, esp. 176 n. 43), a κολλήγιον οὐρβανῶν in the same city (*SEG* 39.597; *cf. sodalicium urbanorum CIL* II 2428), the δοῦμος of the *compitalium* Ταύρου in Thessaloniki (*IG* X/2.1 860 with Łajtar 1992; *cf.* Republican *collegia compitalicia*), the ἀργεντάριοι (= *argentarii*) in Philippi (Pilhofer 2009, no. 410), the *Agrippiastai* of Sparta (*IG* V.1 374) or the resident Romans at Lokrian Opus (*IG* IX.1 283). For the prominence of corporations tied to the gymnasium and age groups, we can point to οἱ ἐκ τοῦ γυμνασίου and οἱ ἀλειφόμενοι ἐν ἀμφοτέροις τοῖς γυμνασίοις in Aegina (*IG* IV².2 974-975), or the ἱερὰ γερουσία of Hyettos (*IG* VII 2808). And since seat inscriptions for professional groups have been mentioned above as an important sign of a Romanized associational culture, the inscription of the λιθοκόποι in the theatre of Dionysos in Athens is a welcome addition (*IG* II² 5087). Clearly, most aspects discussed in the previous section can also be found in Roman Greece.

However, when compared to the evidence from Asia Minor, there are also important differences primarily related to the way religion figures in the inscriptions. The imperial cult does not seem to have been a point of interest for most groups. Instead, many associations chose the worship of other deities as their primary identifying marker, much like associations had done in the Hellenistic period. In Attica and Boeotia, some of them used traditional theophoric names (*Meikoniastai* in Athens *IG* II² 2776; *Herakliastai* in Liopesi *SEG* 31.122; *Herakleistai* in Pagai *IG* VII 192; *Heroiastai* in Akraiphia *IG* VII 2725); in Northern Greece, new terms like συνήθεια or θρησκεία (and plural designations derived from them) dominate the record. The term θίασος is also used with some frequency (below). The number of these groups, and the quantitative relation between them and professional associations, needs some explanation in light of the model developed above. The problem can be illustrated by a striking example: In Thessaloniki, a thriving port city where more associations are attested than in all other cities of the province of Macedonia combined, only four out of forty known associations (Nigdelis 2010 supplemented by Nigdelis 2016a) define themselves as professional groups (*IG* X/2.1 291; Nigdelis 2006, 184, 189, 248).

To be sure, several factors should be taken into account here. The professional groups attested at Thessaloniki (purple dyers, muleteers, crown-makers and gladiators) are such an arbitrary snapshot of the local economy that we must assume that there were other professional associations as well; the fact that the majority of the inscriptions comes from a funerary context may distort the proportions, as local professional groups may not have offered funerary services on the same scale as others. It is in any case likely that some associations functioned as professional networks, as has been argued for the *doumos* of Aphrodite Epiteuxidias (*SEG* 42.625; Voutiras 1992), but this is irrelevant in a model that focuses on representation. No matter how we put it, the lack of outspoken professional associations is notable. A more promising way to bring some order into a rather diverse set of data is the application of a basic legal distinction: we should expect

different results from Roman colonies than from free cities. Pliny's correspondence with Trajan on the *eranoi* of Amisus shows that a distinction was made between a *civitas libera*, where groups could be founded according to local law, and cities directly subject to Roman law, where severe restrictions applied (Plin. *Ep.* 10.92-93; *FIRA* I 21 § 106; *AÉpigr* 1986, 332 § 74). This same distinction explains the almost total absence of associations at Corinth, a Roman colony since 44 BC, and the flourishing of associations in Thessaloniki, a free city since roughly the same time. On the other hand, the types of associations that do appear in Roman colonies are often the same (Eckhardt 2016b, 649-653): *Augustales* and other groups related to emperor worship (like the *collegium Larum* mentioned above), a choice number of 'legitimate' *collegia* of professionals or temple administrators, and elite corporations like the *iuvenes*. Evidence from Corinth or Cassandreia fits this pattern well, and we will show that it also goes some way towards explaining evidence from Philippi and Dion. Still, the choice of religious identity markers throughout Greece is noteworthy, and the question arises how Roman Greece differed from Roman Asia Minor.

A solution might be sought in the old debate on Greek cultural resistance against Rome and Romanization. The main contributions to this discussion focus not on epigraphical data, but on a close reading of Greek authors like Plutarch or Pausanias (good overview in Veyne 2005, 163-257). Two insights can perhaps be singled out. First, it is appealing, but all in all too simplistic to claim that while the power became Roman, the culture remained Greek. There were of course hybrid forms and re-inventions, some of which will be discussed below. Second, Greeks did have a special sense of cultural superiority, religious tradition and (not national but) local history that set them apart from others. Educated Romans had learned enough about Greek history and literature to come to similar conclusions. As many of these traditions were tied to mainland Greece, it is perhaps not surprising to see less direct influence of Roman models of social organization here than in Thrace or Asia Minor.

With this in mind, I would like to offer a solution for a problem that I have admittedly created myself when I introduced my model. Those parts of the available evidence from Roman Greece that do not fit should at least in part be explained by the fact that corporate organization in this region was heavily influenced by strategies of remembering. Different approaches to associations had already sparked a cultural conflict in the Bacchanalian affair of 186 BC, and in the imperial era associations could still have an emblematic function in discourses on what was Greek and what was Roman. The strategies of remembering could, in my view, take two distinct forms. First, memory could be directed at local historical, mythical or religious tradition. A corporate organization could be in charge, or see itself as being in charge, of preserving such traditions by either embedding them into Roman imperial culture or by consciously emphasizing their pre-Roman origins (and hence non/pre-Roman character). Second, memory could be directed at the forms of corporate organization itself. Literary or documentary traces of local, pre-Roman traditions of social aggregation could be used to preserve or re-invent specific types of associations, which could then be either embedded into imperial culture or deliberately kept at a distance from it. We see this happening in other regions, *e.g.* in rural Phrygia or in Palmyra (Eckhardt 2016a, 163-167). It should not be surprising to find that in Greece use of this strategy was particularly attractive and widespread. If this has not been noted before, it is precisely because we had no overarching model that could have made Roman Greece appear peculiar, and hence call for an explanation of the evidence.

Preservation of local history and memory did not, of course, preclude the formation of corporate bodies that fitted the Roman order. The best-documented counter-example is the Athenian *ephebeia*, which can also serve as an example for both forms of memory combined into one institution: memory of organizational patterns and myth-historical memory (for the following: Wiemer 2011). In a process that began in the late Hellenistic period, the *ephebeia*, a civic institution for education and training of Athenian citizens, assumed many traits of a private club. Offices like the *kosmeteia* circulated in a closed circle of elite families, whose representatives synchronized their term of office with their sons' time as ephebes (which, in turn, was less bound to age criteria than it used to be). Catalogues of ephebes were erected not by the city, but by wealthy members or functionaries. The institution could even serve as a nodal point in a network of translocal, Rome-friendly elites, because being an Athenian was no longer a prerequisite for undergoing ephebic training at Athens. At the same time, the ephebes engaged in annual celebrations of Theseus' return from Crete and the battles of Marathon and (every four years) Plataea (on remembering the Persian Wars and Salamis and the *ephebeia*, see also Newby *this volume*). The memory of Athens' glory was upheld precisely in an institution that contributed to the continuous reproduction of Rome-friendly elites, perhaps comparable to the *collegia iuvenum* in the West, or the *neoi* of Asia Minor. This is an important example of what the 'embedding of the local in the imperial' (Ando 2010, 45) through a transformation of corporate bodies might look like in Greece: it took a form that intimately connected memory and innovation.

4. Organizing the mythical past

The *ephebeia* shows that historical and mythical traditions were consciously upheld in Roman Greece by corporate bodies that could play a pivotal role as 'heritage societies'. As mentioned above, the fact itself does not tell us much about the attitude towards Roman rule. Greek history and mythology could be upheld as an act of cultural resistance or demonstration of superiority, but they could also be integrated into a social order that gravitated towards Rome. This ambivalent function of mythology and religious tradition seems to explain some peculiarities in particular with regard to Dionysiac groups in Roman Greece.

We start with a well-known example from Physkos in West-Lokris. Around the middle of the 2nd century AD, the '*thiasos* of Amandos' had its *nomos* passed in two assemblies and inscribed on stone (*IG* IX.1² 670, ll. 4-21):

They shall give to the common fund 14 obols, not less. The common fund shall provide three lamps. A maenad shall not abuse or attack another maenad. Similarly, no cowherd shall abuse or attack another cowherd. But if someone does so, he shall give to the common fund a penalty of 4 drachmae per utterance. Similarly the one who does not come to the assembly although he is at home. And the one who does not come to the mountain (εἰς ὄρος) shall give 5 drachmae to the common fund. If the maenad does not bring --- on the holy night, --- she shall give to the common fund 5 drachmae. Similarly if a cowherd does not bring ---.[1]

We do not know who Amandos was, but he was clearly the founder or current leader of the association. The group called itself a *thiasos*. That it consisted of maenads and cowherds and embarked on processions 'to the mountain' suggests that *thiasos* should be taken here not just as a common term for associations, but as a term with a specific Dionysiac connotation. The *oreibasia* could be taken as evidence for an astonishing degree of cultic continuity, but caution is advisable. If someone in the Roman period wanted to create a Dionysiac group on the basis of Euripides and other literary traditions (but avoid the dangerous implications of uncontrolled women going to the mountains without male supervision) it would presumably have looked like this. Εἰς ὄρος, 'to the mountain', is of course known from Euripides' *Bacchae*. We also find it in Miletus, in a Hellenistic epigram that interacts with the literary tradition as well (*Milet* VI.2 733). *Boukoloi* can be found in several places either as a

---

1   τοὺς <θιασώτας> τῷ κοιν|[ῷ] δαπανᾶν δέκα τέσσαρας | [ὀβολ]-
 οὺς κὲ μὴ ἔλασον · τὸ κοινὸ[ν] | [παρ]έχεσθαι λύχνους τρῖς·
με|νάδα μαινάδι μὴ ἐπεγερθῆνε | μηδὲ λοιδορῆσε· ὁσαύτως
| μήτε βουκόλον ἐπεγερθῆνα[ι] | μήτε λοιδορῆσε· ἐὰν δέ τις, |
δώσι τῷ κοινῷ καθ᾽ ἓν ῥῆμα | προστίμου δ(ρ.) δ´· τὸν δὲ κατὰ
| σύνοδον μὴ συνελθόντα | ἐπειδημοῦντα ὁμοίως· | [ὁ δὲ] κεἰς
ὄρος μὴ συνελθὼν | [ἀποτ]ίσι τῷ κοινῷ δ(ρ.) ε´· μενὰς | [ἐὰν
μὴ] ἐνένκη τῇ εἱερᾷ νυκτ| ..6... ΤΡΙΑΣΙΕ, ἀποτίσι | [τῷ κοινῷ]
δ(ρ.) ε´· {ὁμοίως} δὲ κὲ | [βουκόλος] ἐὰν μὴ ἐν[ένκη] …

part of Dionysiac groups or as a designation for the group itself, as in Pergamon, where their meeting place has been identified (Schwarzer 2007). Maenads are more specific, as they are clearly tied to Greece in the literary and general mythological tradition. They could appear elsewhere, but only under the premise that they were actually Greek. Thus, the maenads who supposedly founded the three *thiasoi* of Magnesia on the Maeander (which seem to be institutions of the public cult) came from Thebes, as can be learned from a Hellenistic text re-inscribed in the 1st century AD (*I. Magnesia* 215; Henrichs 1978, 123-134).

Anne-Françoise Jaccottet notes that the *thiasos* of Amandos appears as a 'recreation on a more literary rather than an actually cultic basis' (2003, 256). It is an example of how memory and tradition could shape organizational choices in Roman Greece. This connection seems to be worth exploring, and the maenads are the most promising starting point. In Thessaloniki we know about an *archimainas* making a dedication to Dionysos Horophoros (Nigdelis 2006, 129). We do not know the organizational context in which she could call herself 'chief maenad', whether it was a civic cult or a private association. More evidence comes from the Roman colony of Philippi. A *thiasus maenadum regianarum* was involved in supplying a building with water (Pilhofer 2009, no. 340). The inscription was found below a bath erected in the 3rd century AD, but presumably refers to a previous building, most likely a sanctuary of Dionysos. The nature of the group is not entirely clear, not least because recent commentaries on the inscription (Jaccottet 2003, 61; Pilhofer ad loc.; Tsochos 2012, 96 n. 275) could make nothing out of *regianarum*. Jaccottet tentatively suggests a reference to the daughters of Kadmos (royal maenads), which would bring us back to Euripides. But no solution should ignore a coin mentioned by Amandry (1998, 24) that carries the legend LIBERI PATRO RECIANO. It seems that *re<c>ianarum* is an attribute that the maenads share with the god, perhaps a toponym that we do not know. In any case, it seems likely that this was a public cult group, not a potentially subversive assembly of Philippian women devouring raw flesh. Another inscription mentions the 'days of the maenads', a local festival to which the *thiasus maenadum* may have had some connection as well (Pilhofer 2009, no. 568). Their one activity we know of is a rather civilized one, connecting the sanctuary with the water-supply.

Their name (both elements, *thiasus* and maenads) suggests that these maenads were also, like the group from Physkos, a 'recreation based on literary models' (Jaccottet 2003, 61). But recreated by whom? The possibility should be envisaged that it was the Roman and Roman-oriented elite of the Roman colony of Philippi who chose this desig-

nation, as a reference to what they perceived to be local religious tradition. This suggestion could explain several aspects of Dionysiac cult groups in Northern Greece. To begin with, they are almost always called θίασος or, as in all cases from Philippi, *thiasus*, whereas no non-Dionysiac association in the province of Macedonia seems to have been called by that title. While the intimate connection between this particular designation for an association and the Dionysiac tradition seems obvious when we look at the myth, it did not exist before the Roman period. *Thiasos* as a term for corporate organization originally had nothing to do with Dionysos. In Classical Attica, it referred to a subdivision inside a phratry (*IG* II² 1237 with Hedrick 1990, 78-80), and in the Hellenistic period it became a standard designator for all kinds of religious associations. The restriction of the term to Dionysiac groups and its Latinization (as a *terminus technicus*) suggest a conscious attempt to shape an aspect of the organizational culture of Northern Greece according to literary models.

There is evidence to suggest that the groups in question were not mere private associations, but institutions related to the civic cult. In Philippi and Thessaloniki, several Dionysiac *thiasoi* could be named at the same time as recipients of donations or endowments, which means that there was an ordering principle in place that allowed donors to think of them as essentially one phenomenon (Pilhofer 2009, no. 524-525, possibly also 529 and 627 with Bartels 2006, 210; *IG* X/2.1 260, 506). In Dion, the *thiasus* of Liber Pater regularly appointed a temporary *aedilis*/ἀγορανόμος for the organization of a public festival (Jaccottet 2003, 45-49 no. 13-17); in the words of Pantelis Nigdelis, the group seems to have had a 'quasi-official' status (Nigdelis 2016b, 675-677; *cf.* Demaille 2008, 189-190). If there were any formal characteristics beyond the temporary festival, there is no trace of them. As a similar institution is attested as early as 7 BC in Beroia (*SEG* 48.751), the phenomenon was not restricted to Roman colonies; some imitation of cultic institutions and the trend to rediscover the mythological past may perhaps be assumed.

'*Thiasoi* of Asians' are known from Thessaloniki and from Lete in Mygdonia (*IG* X/2.1 309; *SEG* 35.751). A Dionysiac context is certain, but the groups also seem to have served as a sort of reservoir for immigrants from the province of Asia (most likely merchants), a common phenomenon in the Balkan region. Were they aware of Dionysos' mythical return to Greece *ex Asia*? In other regions of Greece, the terminology may have been somewhat less fixed and the function of the groups more varied. The three *thiasoi* mentioned in an inscription from Aegina together with *boule* and *demos* and the gymnasium-groups might have been civic subdivisions with no

76 STRATEGIES OF REMEMBERING IN GREECE UNDER ROME (100 BC - 100 AD)

connection to Dionysos (*IG* IV².2 971; but *cf. I. Magnesia* 215).[2]

Finally, there are occasional hints that Dionysiac associations were careful to present themselves as very traditional even when they did not use the term *thiasos*. In 2nd century AD Megara, the *palaion Bakcheion* set up an honorific stele for two female members of the local Romanized elite (*IG* VII 107). The decree is erected *eunoias charin*, which suggests a relationship between the women and the association, but it is rendered as a *psephisma boules* – again, the precise status of the group is debatable. The attribute *palaion* does not necessarily mean that there were other, more recently founded *bakcheia* in the city (none are attested), but can also be read as an assertion of local tradition. The same could be said for the *Bakcheion presbyteron* in 1st century AD Stobi (*IG* XII Suppl. 387); again, evidence for other groups is missing. Tradition also plays a key role in what is probably the best-known association inscription from antiquity, the *nomos* of the Athenian Iobakchoi (*IG* II² 1368; the 'best *bakcheion*', according to its self-praise). The members performed a sort of mythic drama, with the roles of Dionysos, Kore, Palaimon, Aphrodite and Proteurythmos assigned by lot (lines 121-127). The constellation was heavily influenced by mythological and other literary traditions, and the whole scene is somewhat reminiscent of the end of Xenophon's *symposium*. This association could legitimately be labelled a heritage society. At the same time, it clearly consisted of members of an upper class that would necessarily have to be oriented towards Rome. Its priest at the time when the inscription was set up was Herodes Atticus, one of the best-known members of the imperial elite.

Dionysos and his associations clearly had a visible place in the cities especially of Northern Greece, and the terminology used is suggestive of Greek tradition; we could say these associations were built 'by the book'. At the same time, the standardization and other indicators suggest that these were not always private initiatives, but that, paradoxically, the spread of organizations of maenads and other revellers could be an aspect of orientation towards Rome. The reorganization of (perceived) local traditions and its combination with purely Roman institutions like *Augustales* and *collegia Larum* would be a topic worthy of further study. Particularly interesting is the evidence from Philippi, where the Latin designation *cultores* (*cf. CIL* XIV 2112 mentioned above) designated cult groups for

Silvanus (consisting of slaves and freedmen, who could hardly have gathered in the middle of a Roman colony without the *placet* of their masters; Pilhofer 2009, no. 163-166), Jupiter Optimus Maximus (Nigdelis 2016c), Sarapis and Isis (with official functions in the context of the Asklepieia; Pilhofer 2009, no. 252, 307, 311 = *I. Philippi* II.1 54-55, 134), Cupido (a Roman re-imagination of Eros?; Pilhofer 2009, no. 350 = *I. Philippi* II.1 223) and one of the city's main gods, the Heros Aulonitis (Pilhofer 2009, no. 703e). But we have to move on to another, somewhat different strategy of remembering involving associations in Roman Greece.

5. Mythologizing the organizational past

We now turn to the commemoration of older forms of corporate organization, which were re-invented and filled with new meaning as remnants of the past. The obvious condition for showing this is a continuous record of associations over a long time span. In Greece, only Athens provides sufficient evidence, so this discussion will necessarily be Athenocentric, in the hope that some generalization from this arguably special case may be permitted.

One remarkable finding is that we know of six associations in Attica who called themselves *eranos* or *eranistai* (*IG* II² 1345; 1366; 1369; *SEG* 31.122; *SEG* 54.234; *AM* 67 [1942], 31 no. 30). This terminology does not appear elsewhere in Roman Greece; in fact it had never been widespread apart from clusters of evidence in Attica, Delos, Rhodes and Kos. Pliny's correspondence with Trajan (above) is an isolated example; we do not know if associations in Amisos called themselves *erani*. Literary references to Greek associations might have influenced the choice of words, most importantly Aristotle's note that 'there are associations which seem to have come into being for the sake of pleasure, like *thiasotai* and *eranistai*. For those have come into being because of sacrifice and community'.[3] With this quotation, we are drawn into the early history of Athenian associations.

As Christian Thomsen (2015) has emphasized, *eranistai* are among the oldest forms of private formal organization, epigraphically well attested already in the 4th century BC. *Eranos* as a corporate designation emerged later (mid-Hellenistic period) and for a while replaced the plural designation *eranistai* (Arnaoutoglou 2003, 70-87; Ismard 2010, 347-348). The apparent popularity of both terms in Roman Athens, not matched by epigraphic evidence elsewhere, suggests a conscious continuation of local tradition, and hence a strategy of remembering.

---

2   I exclude here a rather dubious reference to a *thiasos* of Aphrodite from Lechaion, one of Corinth's harbours (*SEG* 23.170), but should mention two other texts from the Corinthia where *thiasos* may have a Dionysiac connection and seems to be related to festivals in a similar way as in Dion (*Corinth* VIII.3 308, a fragment mentioning a θίασος and an ἀγορανόμος, and *SEG* 60.329, where the θίασος ἀρτοκρεωνικός can hardly be understood without assuming its connection to a festival).

---

3   Arist. *Eth. Nic.* 1160a: ἔνιαι δὲ τῶν κοινωνιῶν δι᾽ ἡδονὴν δοκοῦσι γίνεσθαι, θιασωτῶν καὶ ἐρανιστῶν: αὗται γὰρ θυσίας ἕνεκα καὶ συνουσίας.

This suggestion can be strengthened if we take a closer look at some of these groups. An inscription presumably set up in a sanctuary of Herakles in Acharnai or Cholargos records an unusually long list of association members, 83 men and 41 women (*SEG* 54.235). It was apparently begun in the 50s or 40s BC, contemporaneously with the bans on associations in the late Roman republic, and expanded in at least two stages until the late 1st century AD. It is introduced by the following text (lines 1-9):

To good fortune. When Lucius the younger of the deme Rhamnous was archon, the hieropoios and kosmetes Apollonios son of Antiochos inscribed the following eranistai, when Kallistratos was treasurer for the second time, and Demetrios was secretary for the second time. Thaleia was the archeranistria. Theodoros son of Metrodoros of the deme Paiania was the priest of Herakles.[4]

Apollonios served as both *kosmetes* and *hieropoios*. A 'keeper of the order' is known from the *ephebeia*, but also from private associations; we can compare the *eukosmos* of the Iobakchoi. It has been suggested that an increased emphasis on orderly behaviour can be read not least as a sign of awareness of Roman control (Arnaoutoglou 2016b), and we may indeed assume that associations were eager to show that they were far from creating illegitimate *coetus*. More interesting for our purposes is Apollonios' other office. *Hieropoioi* are well-known from Attic inscriptions; taken over from the civic cult, they are among the regularly attested offices in Athenian private associations (Arnaoutoglou 2003, 107-108). However, to the best of my knowledge, all epigraphic evidence for them comes from the late Archaic to mid-Hellenistic period. The institution was thus already out-dated when the stele was originally set up, and the archaizing effect could only have become more visible over the course of time. Just like the term *eranistai*, the use of *hieropoios* can be understood as a conscious mnemonic choice. Such designations connected associations to the early history of local corporate organization. The fact that this particular inscription was visible and in use more than a century after its original installation shows that the epigraphic monuments themselves gave access to the past and offered ways to revive it.

Another example can be found in a much more informative inscription, possibly from the deme Paiania and dated to the late 1st or early 2nd century AD (*SEG*

31.122). It contains the statutes of the *synodos* of *Herakliastai en limnais* and refers to that association repeatedly as an *eranos* (lines 38 and 44, in a part of the inscription written by a different hand). The remarkable details start already with the ἔδοξε-formula at the very beginning, which shows that the rules were not democratically voted for, as would be expected from a Hellenistic association, but that they were single-handedly imposed by the *archeranistes* Marcus Aemilius Eucharistos. He had apparently deposited a sum of money, not to be touched by anyone, that allowed for the founding of the association, which explains his personal influence. The document contains a number of regulations, some of which are procedurally and legally more advanced than those found in Hellenistic documents (e.g. there were annual contractors for wine and pork who had to give sureties and were fined the *duplum* if they did not provide the goods in time). But I would like to single out a somewhat less obvious passage (lines 27-29):

Ten praktores shall be appointed on compulsion from the association. If some members do not wish to serve (ὑπομένειν) as praktores, ten shall be chosen by lot from the body of members.[5]

The compulsory aspect of the first sentence is somewhat modified by the second (or rather, the compulsion is somehow passed on to others). Perhaps ὑπομένειν should be understood as 'stay in office' rather than 'serve', which would mean that there was an initial appointment of ten *praktores* who could then later be replaced by members chosen by lot. The relevant aspect for our purposes is that *praktores* are not otherwise attested in associations, and that apart from this inscription, the latest epigraphical attestation of *praktores* in Attica can be dated no later than 348 BC (*Agora* 16, no. 56). We may assume that the *praktores* of the association had to do with collecting money, presumably fines (as membership fees had to be paid to the treasurer). The obligatory tax collectors of Roman Egypt, also called *praktores*, come to mind, so the term itself (and even an element of compulsion) was not alien to the Roman period. But as the epigraphic evidence just discussed reminds us, there was also a board of *praktores* in Classical Athens who were chosen by lot, most likely ten in number (one from each *phyle*), as in this association. Evidence for this institution comes from 5th and 4th century BC inscriptions as well as from Andocides and Demosthenes (Hansen 1980, 160). It would thus not only have been known to the educated, but also acknowledged as a reference to the time

---

4 [Ἀγα]θῆι Τύχηι. Ἐπὶ Λευκίου Ῥαμνουσίου νεωτ[έρου] ἄρχοντος | Ὁ{ι} ἱεροποιήσας καὶ κοσμητεύσας Ἀπολλώνιος Ἀντιόχου τούσ|δε ἀνέγραψεν ἐρανιστὰς ταμιεύοντος τὸ δεύτερον Καλ|λιστράτου, γραμματεύοντος δὲ Δημητρίου τὸ δεύτερον. | ἀρχερανίστρια | Θάλεια. | ἱερεὺς Ἡρακλέους | Θεόδωρος Μητρο|δώρου Παιανεύς.

5 κατασταέσθ{ωσαν}αι δὲ ἐπάνανκες ἐκ τῆς συνόδου πράκ|τορες δέκα. ἐὰν δέ τινες μὴ θέλωσιν πράκτορες ὑπομένειν κληρούσθω|σαν ἐκ τοῦ πλήθους δέκα. Transl. E. Lupu, *NGSL* 5.

of Athens' greatness. This throws new light on the well-known tendency of associations to replicate state patterns and build 'cités en miniature' (Baslez 2006, 157). This association at least seems to have taken its cue not from current state patterns, but from a political context that had ceased to exist a long time ago. The same seems to be true of the *eranistai* with their *hieropoios*.

There is further evidence for exact terminological continuities between very early and very late association inscriptions from Athens that are difficult to explain if not by conscious imitation. A case in point are the regulations on absence, which distinguish between *apodemountes* and *epidemountes* and contain exculpation clauses in case of illness or grief; while they do become more sophisticated over time, they are phrased in a very similar way by the *orgeones* of Bendis (ca. 330 BC), a group of *Heroistai* (57/56 BC) and the Iobakchoi (164/165 AD) (*IG* II² 1361, 1339, 1368). Similarly, a *dokimasia* of future members is almost unattested in associations outside Attica, but does appear, always under this designation, in inscriptions issued by, again, the *orgeones* of Bendis, the Iobakchoi, and a *synodos* of *eranistai* (2nd century AD; *IG* II² 1369). Other archaisms may escape us. To give just one example, the *synodos* of *eranistai* had among its magistrates a *homoleitor* appointed for life (and in charge of a *heroon*); this certainly looks like an ancient term, but one that is not attested otherwise.

Two additional inscriptions from Athens, both of a somewhat later date, deserve to be highlighted. The first one, from 162/163 AD (*IG* II² 1351), is a decision by 'the [*orge*]*ones* around' someone beginning with S, possibly the Syrian goddess. It seems to have concerned a list of names. The second inscription, from the Piraeus, is dated to the beginning of the 3rd century AD and contains much more information (*IG* II² 2361). It is a list of *orgeonai* and priestesses, set up by the *hymnetes* of Euporia Thea Belela and 'the gods around her'; all in all, we have 42 names, mostly Athenian citizens. In four or five cases it can be shown that two (or in one case four) members come from the same family. Mentioned first after a male and a female priest is a *pater orgeonikes synodou*.

Orgeones are even older than *eranistai*. They seem to be mentioned in the Solonian law on associations quoted in a rather corrupt form in the Digest (*Dig.* 47.22.4), which states that contracts entered in the context of several forms of social aggregation, including ἱερῶν ὀργίων (or, ὀργεῶνες, according to several emendations proposed) are valid as long as they do not contradict state law. Like other elements of Solonian legislation, this law has occasionally been regarded as unauthentic, as a possible invention of the late Hellenistic or early Roman period (Arnaoutoglou 2003, 44-57; 2016a; against this Ismard 2010, 44-57).

This may well be true for the law in this form, but that a regulation on *orgeones* was regarded as actually written down on the Solonian *axones* at least in the 1st century AD seems to emerge clearly from a note by Seleukos, who in his discussion Περὶ τῶν Σόλωνος ἀξόνων explained that *orgeones* are associations (*syllogoi*) for heroes or gods (*FGrHist* 341 F 1). In a fragment presumably relating to the Periclean law on citizenship, Philochoros famously notes that *orgeones* should be admitted into phratries (*FGrHist* 328 F 35a; Periclean context: Andrewes 1961). From this note it can be inferred that at least in the 450s, *orgeones* were not private associations (otherwise, we would reach the unacceptable conclusion that joining or founding a private association was equivalent to becoming a citizen of Athens). They were rather an older form of organization presumably based on descent, now to be integrated into the framework set out by Pericles. However, from the last third of the 4th century BC onwards, there can be no doubt that *orgeones* were private associations, formed by both citizens and metics. The *orgeones* are therefore a prime example of the emergence of private networks out of constituent parts of Greek civic organization in the late Classical and early Hellenistic period. If we accept the Solonian law, we can even follow Gabrielsen (2016) in understanding their history from the late 4th century BC onwards as 'the return of the private network'. However, they did remain a local phenomenon. Apart from the numerous attestations from Attica, we only find the term in two inscriptions from Lemnos (*IG* XII.8 19, 21; 4th century BC), where Athenian cleruches had been settled earlier, and in two further texts from Megara (now attributed to Eleusis; IG II³ 646) and Teos (Pottier & Hauvette-Besnault 1880, 164 no. 21; 2nd century BC).

It is all the more remarkable to find *orgeones* and an *orgeonike synodos* at such a late date, at a time when the term had long fallen out of use even in Athens. We should explain this as a conscious choice, one that took into account the history of associational life in late Classical and early Hellenistic Athens, which was presumably still visible in inscriptions standing on the streets or even in sanctuaries. In addition, the Solonian law on associations was known, as shown by its quotation in the Digest, and Arnaoutoglou has rightly pointed to the restoration of Solon's laws in the time of Hadrian (Arnaoutoglou 2003, 55-57). An official sanction of local traditions of corporate organization is conceivable. We cannot know the intentions of the people involved. But an assertion of local tradition in light of an increasingly unified system of associational life in the empire is one possible explanation. Much like the mythological past, the organizational past became a local feature worthy of preservation.

6. Conclusion

Greece will never fit the model sketched in the first section perfectly, but at least some of the deviations can now be seen in a different light. The abundant evidence for religion as a primary designator of group identities can be explained, at least in a significant number of cases, in the context of strategies of remembering. Precisely how these interacted with Roman expectations is a difficult question. Memory and tradition could work both ways; they could 'embed the local in the imperial', as most of the evidence in part four suggests, or refuse to do so. Romans and Greeks may also have had different opinions on that. Our approach to this question will ultimately depend on other factors, namely how we generally view the Greeks in the Roman period, as reluctant Romanizers, outspoken opponents even, or rather as people who did participate in the culture of isomorphism, but in their own way (as did, *mutatis mutandis*, people in other regions of the empire). At the very least, I think we can show that Greeks were not immune to the challenges posed by an imperial framework surrounding private corporate organization, however much they chose to cultivate the differences.

Acknowledgment

I thank Kimberley Czajkowski for correcting my English.

References

Amandry, M. 1998. Le monnayage de la Res Publica Coloniae Philippensium. In: U. Peter (ed.), *Stephanos nomismatikos. Edith Schönert-Geiss zum 65. Geburtstag*, Berlin, 23-31.

Ando, C. 2010. Imperial Identities. In: T. Whitmarsh (ed.), *Local Knowledge and Microidentities in the Imperial Greek World*, Cambridge, 17-45.

Andrewes, A. 1961. Philochoros on Phratries, *JHS* 81, 1-15.

Arnaoutoglou, I.N. 2002. Roman Law and *collegia* in Asia Minor, *RIDA* 49, 27-44.

Arnaoutoglou, I.N. 2003. *Thusias heneka kai sunousias. Private Religious Associations in Hellenistic Athens*, Athens.

Arnaoutoglou, I.N. 2005. *Collegia* in the Province of Egypt in the First Century AD, *AncSoc* 35, 197-216.

Arnaoutoglou, I.N. 2016a. The Greek Text of D. 47.22.4 (Gai 4 *ad legem duodecim tabularum*) Reconsidered, *Legal Roots* 5, 87-119.

Arnaoutoglou, I.N. 2016b. Θόρυβος, εὐστάθεια και το κανονιστικό πλαίσιο των αθηναϊκών λατρευτικών σωματείων, *EHHD* 46, 23-78.

Bartels, J. 2006. Lateinische Grabinschriften aus Philippi: Corrigenda, *ZPE* 157, 199-212.

Baslez, M.-F. 2004. Les notables entre eux. Recherches sur les associations d'Athènes à l'époque romain. In: S. Follet (ed.), *L'Hellénisme d'époque romaine. Nouveaux documents, nouvelles approches (Ier s. a.C. – IIIe s. p.C.)*, Paris, 105-120.

Baslez, M.-F. 2006. Entraide et mutualisme dans les associations des cités grecques à l'époque hellénistique. In: M. Molin (ed.), *Les regulations sociales dans l'antiquités*, Rennes, 157-168.

Bendlin, A. 2011. Associations, Funerals, Sociality, and Roman Law: The *collegium* of Diana and Antinous in Lanuvium (CIL 14.2112) Reconsidered. In: M. Öhler (ed.), *Aposteldekret und antikes Vereinswesen. Gemeinschaft und ihre Ordnung*, Tübingen, 207-296.

Camodeca, G. 2001. Albi degli Augustales di Liternum della seconda metà del II secolo, *AION(archeol)* N.S. 8, 163-182.

Cracco Ruggini, L. 1976. La vita associativa nelle città dell'Oriente greco: tradizioni locali e influenze romane. In: D. Pippidi (ed.), *Assimilation et résistance à la culture gréco-romaine dans le monde ancien*, Bucharest, 463-491.

Demaille, J. 2008. Les P. Anthestii: une famille d'affranchis dans l'élite municipale de la colonie romaine de Dion. In: A. Gonzales (ed.), *La fin du statut servile? Affranchissement, libération, abolition. Vol. I*, Besançon, 185-202.

Eckhardt, B. 2016a. Romanization and Isormorphic Change in Phrygia: The Case of Private Associations, *JRS* 106, 147-171.

Eckhardt, B. 2016b. The Eighteen Associations of Corinth, *GRBS* 56, 646-662.

Eckhardt, B. forthcoming. The Young, the Old and the Blessed. Corporate Bodies of Elite Reproduction in Roman Asia Minor, forthcoming in a conference volume edited by S. Skaltsa & C.A. Thomsen.

Eckhardt, B. & A. Lepke forthcoming. Mystai und Mysteria im kaiserzeitlichen Kleinasien. In: M. Blömer & B. Eckhardt (eds), *Transformationen paganer Religion in der römischen Kaiserzeit. Rahmenbedingungen und Konzepte*, Berlin.

Ehrhardt, N. & W. Günther 2013. Hadrian, Milet und die Korporation der milesischen Schiffseigner. Zu einem neu gefundenen kaiserlichen Schreiben, *Chiron* 43, 199-220.

Engelmann, H. 2012. Inschriften von Patara, *ZPE* 182, 179-201.

Gabrielsen, V. 2007. Brotherhoods of Faith and Provident planning: The Non-Public Associations of the Greek World, *MHR* 22, 183-210.

Gabrielsen, V. 2016. Associations, Modernization and the Return of the Private Network in Athens. In: C. Thiersch (ed.), *Die athenische Demokratie im 4. Jahrhundert. Zwischen Modernisierung und Tradition*, Stuttgart, 121-162.

Hansen, M.H. 1980. Seven Hundred *Archai* in Classical Athens, *GRBS* 21, 151-173.

Hedrick, C. 1990. *The Decrees of the Demotionidai*, Atlanta.

Henrichs, A. 1978. Greek Maenadism from Olympias to Messalina, *HSPh* 82, 121-160.

Ismard, P. 2010. *La cité des réseaux. Athènes et ses associations, VIe – Ier siècle av. J.-C.*, Paris.

Jaccottet, A.-F. 2003. *Choisir Dionysos. Les associations dionysiaques ou la face cachée du dionysisme, Vol. II: Documents*, Zürich.

Łajtar, A. 1992. Ein zweiter Beleg für δοῦμος in Thessalonike, *ZPE* 92, 211-212.

Lupu, E. 2009 (= NGSL). *Greek Sacred Law. A Collection of New Documents*, 2nd ed., Leiden.

Nigdelis, P.M. 2006. *Επιγραφικά Θεσσαλονίκεια I*, Thessalonike.

Nigdelis, P.M. 2010. Voluntary Associations in Roman Thessalonikē: In Search of Identity and Support in a Cosmopolitan Society. In: L. Nasrallah, C. Bakirtzis & S.J. Friesen (eds), *From Roman to Early Christian Thessalonikē. Studies in Religion and Archaeology*, Cambridge MA, 13-47.

Nigdelis, P.M. 2016a. Τετραδισταί in a Funerary Inscription from Roman Thessaloniki, *GRBS* 56, 475-484.

Nigdelis, P.M. 2016b. The *Nonae Capratinae* in Dion and Religious Associations and Public Festivals in Roman Macedonia, *GRBS* 56, 663-678.

Nigdelis, P.M. 2016c. HARPALIANI: A New Village of the Roman Colony of Philippi. In: B. Takmer, E.N.A. Arca & N.G. Özdil (eds), *Vir Doctus Anatolicus. Studies in Memory of Sencer Şahin*, Istanbul, 640-650.

Perry, J. 2015. 'L'État intervint peu à peu': State Intervention in the Ephesian 'Bakers' Strike'. In: V. Gabrielsen & C.A. Thomsen (eds), *Private Associations and the Public Sphere*, Copenhagen, 183-205.

Pilhofer, P. 2009. *Philippi. Band II: Katalog der Inschriften von Philippi*, 2nd ed., Tübingen.

Pottier, E. & A. Hauvette-Besnault 1880. Inscriptions d'Érythrées et de Téos, *BCH* 4, 153-182.

Rauh, N. 1993. *The Sacred Bonds of Commerce. Religion, Economy and Trade Society at Hellenistic Roman Delos*, 166-87 B.C., Amsterdam.

Schwarzer, H. 2007. Die Bukoloi in Pergamon. Ein dionysischer Kultverein im Spiegel der archäologischen und epigraphischen Zeugnisse. In: I. Nielsen (ed.), *Zwischen Kult und Gesellschaft: Kosmopolitische Zentren des antiken Mittelmeerraumes als Aktionsraum von Kultvereinen und Religionsgemeinschaften*, Augsburg, 153-167.

Sharankov, N. 2013. Inscriptions. In: I. Lazarenko, E. Mircheva, R. Encheva, D. Stoianova & N. Sharankov, *The Temple of the Pontic Mother of Gods in Dionysopolis*, Varna, 47-64.

Sverkos, I.K. 2002. Παρατηρήσεις σε μια νέα επιγραφή από το territorium της ρωιμαϊκής αποικίας της Κασσάνδρειας (Πρινοχώρι), *Tekmeria* 7, 167-180.

Thomsen, C.A. 2015. The *Eranistai* of Classical Athens, *GRBS* 55, 154-175.

Tran, N. 2012. Associations privées et espace public. Les emplois de *publicus* dans l'épigraphie des collèges de l'Occident romain. In: M. Dondin-Payre & N. Tran (eds), *Collegia. Le phénomène associatif dans l'Occident romain*, Paris, 63-80.

Tsochos, C. 2012. *Die Religion in der römischen Provinz Makedonien*, Stuttgart.

Van Nijf, O.M. 1997. *The Civic World of Professional Associations in the Roman East*, Amsterdam.

Verboven, K. 2012. Les collèges et la romanisation dans les provinces occidentales. In: M. Dondin-Payre & N. Tran (eds), *Collegia. Le phénomène associatif dans l'Occident romain*, Paris, 13-46.

Veyne, P. 2005. *L'empire Gréco-romain*, Paris.

Voutiras, E. 1992. Berufs- und Kultverein: Ein δοῦμος in Thessalonike, *ZPE* 90, 87-96.

Wiemer, H.-U. 2011. Von der Bürgerschule zum aristokratischen Klub? Die athenische Ephebie in der römischen Kaiserzeit, *Chiron* 41, 487-537.

Performing the Past: Salamis, Naval Contests and the Athenian *Ephebeia*

Zahra Newby

Abstract

A number of ephebic reliefs displayed in Athens during the late 1st to 3rd centuries AD feature references to a *naumachia* in either words or images. This article explores the history to these reliefs by looking at the roles played by Athenian ephebes in naval displays during the late Hellenistic period, and at the changes which occurred in both terminology and display under the Roman Empire. In both the late Hellenistic and the Roman period there is a clear association made between naval activities and the memory of the battle of Salamis in 480 BC. The rituals performed by the Athenian ephebes during festivals and at sites associated with this famous sea-battle ensured its continued remembrance throughout this period. Yet we also find an increased emphasis on the martial nature of the ephebes' activities, through use of the term *naumachia*, during the Roman period, which made the link to Salamis increasingly specific, perhaps in relation to the sponsorship and interests of Roman emperors.

Keywords: ephebeia, festivals, naumachia, Salamis, Athens, Persian Wars

1. Introduction

One of the concerns of this volume is the way in which cities and individuals adopted various strategies to keep alive the memory of the past in the Roman period. Almost as soon as they had ended, the Persian Wars cast a long and glorious shadow. As a symbol of Greece's great fight against the barbarian, the Persian wars acted as an example of Panhellenic unity and co-operation, though this memory could also be manipulated to create divisions and hierarchies between individual Greek city-states. In this article I examine the inscriptions and reliefs set up to commemorate the activities of Athenian ephebes, to explore one aspect of the ways in which the enduring legacy of the Persian Wars was experienced and re-performed from the Hellenistic to Roman periods.

The Persian Wars are a *leitmotif* in Greek history, cropping up repeatedly in cultural discourse from the 5th century BC well into the late Roman period. The memory of the famous victories in which the Greeks came together to defeat the barbarian Persians was kept alive through both verbal and visual means, recorded in speeches and histories, and

in: Dijkstra, T.M., I.N.I. Kuin, M. Moser & D. Weidgenannt (eds) 2017. *Strategies of Remembering in Greece under Rome (100 BC - 100 AD)*, Leiden (Sidestone Press).

recalled through physical monuments.[1] They could also be used for a variety of purposes, both to draw together the Greek city states by appealing to the common Pan-hellenic cause, but also to enhance the reputation of individual poleis through reference to victories in which they had played the major role, such as Thermopylae for the Spartans, or Salamis and Marathon for the Athenians. In this article I investigate the resonance of Athens' naval victory at Salamis in 480 BC as it was experienced and re-performed through the activities of the Athenian ephebes. While there may have been continuity of practice between these periods, the commemoration of ephebic actions clusters around two specific periods, the late 2nd century BC, and the late 1st to early 3rd centuries AD.

In a paper on the mechanisms of memory in Ancient Greece, Simon Price distinguished two key ways in which memories were constructed, which he termed 'Inscribed Memory (objects and texts), and also per-formative Embodied Memory (ritual and other formal-ized behaviour)' (Price 2012, 17). In this article I wish to explore how different forms of remembering worked together, by examining the symbiotic relationship between monuments, words and ritual actions in the context of memories of Athens' victories against the Persians. I am interested in thinking about how recalling the past can help to shape social identities in the present.[2] Rather than adopting one particular theoretical approach to this, I seek to explore the material with the following questions in mind: how did the actions of the Athenian ephebes keep the memory of the past alive, and whose interests did this serve? The self-image of the ephebes and the wealthy families they came from, a wider sense of communal civic identity, and the interests and enthusiasms of external powers are all factors at play here. Through examination of the activities of the Athenian ephebes we can see how rituals, monuments and evocative places helped to keep alive the memory of Athens' military past, and re-embody her victories in the performances of the gilded youth of the city.

Permanent physical memorials for the battles at Marathon and Salamis seem to have been set up in the course of the 5th century BC and are recorded in ora-torical texts from the 4th century BC where they serve as evidence of Athens' past prowess (West 1969; Rabe 2008, 101-110). Xenophon (Xen. *An.* 3.2.13) cites the

trophies as proofs (*tekmeria*) of the victories which the Athenians had won over Xerxes by both land and sea, but also cites the freedom which the city enjoys as the chief sign of these victories. In Plato's *Menexenus* (Plat. *Menex.* 245a) the trophies at Marathon, Salamis and Plataea seem to hold a didactic function, since we are told that the Athenians refrained from giving direct aid to the Persians against the Spartans (in the 390s BC), lest they bring shame upon these trophies. The value of the victory at Salamis as a model to live up to is also expressed in an inscription commemorating a soldier killed fighting at Salamis c. 250 BC, who is said to recall the excellence of the ancestors who slayed the Persians (Moretti 1967, 50-51, no. 24). In his account of the Syracusan campaign at the end of the 5th century BC, the 1st-century BC historian Diodorus Siculus also suggests that the Athenian commander, Nicias, spurred on his troops by reminding them of the trophies erected at Salamis and urging them not to betray the reputation of their fatherland (13.15.2). These victories were clearly used as a paradigm of coura-geous behaviour, and served to encourage emulation of this in the current generation.[3]

The enduring importance of Athens' Persian war history, and especially her naval victories, in the Roman period can be seen in the works of Philostratus, who presents the sage Apollonius of Tyana rebuking the Athenians for dancing away their reputation as the victors of Salamis (Philostr. *VA* 4.21). In the *Lives of the sophists* (Philostr. *VS* 2.9, 584) Philostratus also records a speech by Aelius Aristides in the mid-2nd century AD on the theme 'Isocrates tries to wean Athens from the sea'. These texts suggest that Athens' naval victories, as well as the land victory at Marathon, were still keenly remembered in the 1st to 3rd centuries AD.[4] As we shall we, this naval heritage is evoked in the texts and monuments commem-orating the activities of the Athenian ephebes from the late 3rd century BC until the 3rd century AD, but also undergoes important changes of emphasis. Both continu-ity and change can be seen in the strategies by which the Athenian ephebes remembered their past.

2. Celebrating the Persian Wars in the Hellenistic ephebeia

The Athenian ephebeia is often seen as experiencing its peak in the 4th century BC, during which it lasted for two

---

1 Jung 2006; see Loraux 1986, esp. 155-171, on funerary orations; West 1969, Hölscher 1998, 163-169 and Rabe 2008, 101-110 on victory monuments. On memorials to the Athenian war dead more generally see Stupperich 1977; Low 2010 and Arrington 2015. For discussion of the use made of the Persian wars in the Roman period see Spawforth 1994 and 2012, 103-141; Alcock 2002, 74-86.

2 For a discussion of the theoretical approaches to this question, and the issues at stake, see Alcock 2002, 1-35, especially 1, n. 1 on the theories of Jan Assmann and others.

3 Compare Roller 2004 on the use of monuments and narratives to encourage emulation of famous *exempla* in a Roman context.

4 On the role Marathon played in discourses of the past during this period see Jung 2006, 205-224; Gomez 2013; Bowie 2013 and Athanassaki 2016. I propose to return to the potential tensions between Athenian commemorations of Marathon and Salamis in a future paper.

years and involved the majority of the city's youths, paid for at public expense. In contrast, the Hellenistic ephebeia has been viewed in terms of decline (Pélékidis 1962, 155-182). Reforms at the start of the 3rd century made participation voluntary, reduced the term to one year, and gave ephebes the responsibility for paying for their own armour. These changes seem to have led to a drastic reduction in the size of the ephebeia from around 600 youths per year in the 4th century to a low of c. 20-60 per year from 229-167 BC, and can also be associated with an oligarchization of the institution (Perrin-Saminadayar 2007, 31-58). While the numbers may have been small, however, the institution itself gained increased visibility at this time. A number of lengthy epigraphic texts were set up in the Athenian agora during the course of the 3rd and 2nd centuries at the instigation of the demos, publicly praising the ephebes and their instructors. These show that while the ephebes continued to train in military exercises they also played a visible role in the religious and civic life of the city, marching in religious processions and attending meetings of the assembly (Perrin-Saminadayar 2007, 50-52).[5] Prosopographic analysis also suggests that a high proportion of the ephebes came from notable families, and that many went on to hold a political career after their service in the ephebeia (Perrin-Saminadayar 2007, 63-89). In the course of the 2nd century the ephebeia was also opened up to youths from non-Athenian families, attested as *xenoi*, and later *epengraphoi*, on ephebic decrees from 123/2 onwards, and leading to a corresponding increase in the overall number of ephebes (Perrin-Saminadayar 2007, 248-253).

Amongst their many religious duties were a number of sacrifices and processions in honour of Athens' ancient war dead. The ephebic decree in honour of the ephebes of 123/2 BC (*IG* II² 1006, lines 22-23) praises them for running a race in armour from the *polyandrion* (the communal tomb in the Cerameicus) at some point during the Epitaphia festival; they also paraded in armour both at this festival and at the Theseia. Literary references to an *agon* commemorating the war dead go back to the 4th century BC (Lys. 2.80; Pl. *Menex.* 249b), while vases labelled as 'prizes at the games for those killed in the war' dating to the 5th century suggest that these games had a long history (Vanderpool 1969).[6] A few lines later the same ephebic degree also praises the ephebes for visiting the tomb at Marathon to offer a crown and a sacrifice in honour of those who had died in the war for freedom (*IG* II² 1006, lines 26-27). It is within this wider context of honouring the warriors of the past, as well as showcas-

ing their own military readiness, that we should see the actions discussed below.

During the late Hellenistic period Athenian ephebes were extensively involved in activities on the island of Salamis in honour of the hero Ajax, and in memory of the famous naval battle here. Ajax's cult seems to have had a long history on the island; according to Herodotus the Athenians had called on him for help in the battle of Salamis (Hdt. 8.64.2) and it is likely that a festival in his honour was celebrated after the victory here, if not before (Mikalson 1998, 184). This festival was probably revived after the return of Salamis, along with other possessions, to Athenian ownership in 229 BC though the actions of Diogenes, who hitherto had acted as Macedonian governor of Attica. For his role in securing Athens' freedom Diogenes was honoured as a benefactor, and the ephebes seem to have played an important role in perpetuating his memory. A new 'Diogeneion' gymnasium in which the ephebes trained was named after him, while decrees from the end of the 2nd century BC show that the ephebes celebrated a festival named after him and offered sacrifices to him (*IG* II² 1011, lines 14-15; 1028, lines 23-24; 1029, line 14; Habicht 1997, 179-180).

A decree of 214/3 BC, honouring the ephebes of the previous year, gives us a brief glimpse of ritual activities taking place on Salamis, referring to the ephebes' presence on Salamis, a procession in honour of Democratia, a long race in honour of the eponymous hero, and a fragmentary reference restored as an allusion to a *hamilla*, or contest (*SEG* 29.116, lines 17-21). Much fuller references come around a century later, in a series of decrees dating to the years from 127/6 to 96/5 BC.[7]

These decrees list a variety of activities, though not all in the same order or with the same details. *SEG* 15.104, lines 21-23, of 127/6 BC (T25) refers to the ephebes making a voyage to Salamis for the contest of the Aianteia, sacrificing to Zeus of the Trophy, sacrificing to Ajax and Asclepius and running a torch race. A fragmentary word starting alpha mu at l. 132 in the decree honouring the ephebes for their activities on Salamis is restored as a reference to a contest of the boats, ἄμ[ιλλαν τοῖς πλοίοις, but more concrete references to naval contests appear a few years later. A number of decrees describe the ephebes participating in the festivals Mounichia, Diisoteria and Aianteia, which all took place in the vicinity of Mounichia and Salamis.

IG II² 1006 + 1031 is dated to 122/1 BC (T26) and describes the ephebes of the previous year. At lines 28-32 their activities at Salamis and Mounichia are described:

---

5 On the ephebes' military role, see Kennell 2009b.
6 Compare Diod. Sic. 11.33.3, associating the *epitaphios agon* with the aftermath of the Persian Wars.

7 Perrin-Saminadayar 2007, 199-248 collects the epigraphic evidence, providing texts and translations for many, though not all. I follow his dates here and indicate his catalogue numbers by T, but follow the texts as given in *IG* II².

PERFORMING THE PAST   85

ἀνέπλευσαν δ[ὲ καὶ] ἐπὶ τρόπαιον καὶ ἔθυσαν τῶι Διὶ τῶι Τρο- | [πα]ίωι καὶ τῆι πομπεῖ τῶν μεγάλων θεῶν ἐποιήσαντο τ[ῶν πλοίων τὴν ἅμιλλαν· π] εριέπλευσαν δὲ καὶ [τοῖς Μου]νιχίοις εἰς τὸν λιμένα τὸν ἐμ Μου- | [νιχίαι ἁμ]ιλλώ[μεν]οι. ὁμ[ο]ίως δὲ καὶ τοῖς Διϊσωτηρίοι[ς]· ἀπ[έπλευσαν δὲ καὶ ἐπὶ τὰ Αἰ]άντεια κἀκεῖ [π]οιησάμ[ενοι ἅμ]ιλλαν τῶν πλοίων καὶ πομπεύ- | [σαντε]ς καὶ θύσαν[τες τ]ῶι Αἴαντι ἐπηνέθησαν ὑπ[ὸ τοῦ δήμου τοῦ Σαλαμινίω] ν καὶ ἐστεφ[αν]ώθησ[αν] χ[ρ]υσῶι σ[τεφά]νω ἐπὶ τῶι εὐτάκτως καὶ | [εὐσ]χημόνως πεποιῆσθ[αι] τὴν ἐπιδ[η]μίαν·

They sailed up to the trophy and sacrificed to Zeus Tro[pa]ios, and in the procession of the great gods they made [the contest of the boats].[8] They sailed around into the harbour of Mounichia for the Mounichia festival and competed; likewise for the Diisoteria. They [sailed] away [for the Ai]anteia and there, having made a contest of the boats and having processed and sacrificed to Ajax they were praised by [the people of Salamis] and crowned with a golden crown for having completed their stay in good order and in a becoming fashion.

IG II² 1008, lines 17-24 of 118/7 BC (T28) has a similar order of events: the ephebes sailed to the trophy and sacrificed to Zeus Tropaios, competed in the harbour during the procession of the Great gods, then sailed to Salamis to take part in the Aianteia where they took part in a naval contest, sacrifices and processions. The boats are said to have double rows of oars (line 76), while another decree calls the boats 'the sacred ships', ταῖς ἱεραῖς ναυσίν (*IG* II² 1011, line 16, T31), and later praises the ephebes for bringing the boats into dry dock (line 19, *cf. IG* II² 1028, line 37 of 101/0 BC, T32). In this inscription (*IG* II² 1011, lines 15-18) the ephebes are praised for sailing around to Mounichia, sailing to Salamis and performing a contest of boats, ἅμιλλαν τῶν πλοίων, winning a long race in Salamis against the inhabitants and sacrificing to Ajax and Asclepius.

Most of the inscriptions have the same order for the events, depicting a series of rituals in which the ephebes first sailed to the trophy, then came back to Mounichia, sometimes for naval contests, before returning to Salamis for the Aianteia, which again sometimes includes naval contests. The prefixes applied to the verbs in *IG* II² 1006 strongly suggest that there was a set itinerary for these activities, which here include naval contests both in the harbour at Mounichia and at Salamis (lines 28-32). Here we are told that the ephebes sailed out to the trophy (ἀνέπλευσαν), then sailed around (περιέπλευσαν)

into the harbour of Mounichia before they sailed off (ἀπέπλευσαν) to the Aianteia, where they performed a naval contest. Other contests, presumably also naval, took place at the Mounichia and the Diisoteria festivals.[9] The attention to the geographical itinerary here strongly suggests that the description follows the actual order of events closely. Others, which mix up the order of the rituals, may do so in order to group them together geographically, putting all the actions on Salamis together, and all those on the mainland together (e.g. *IG* II² 1009 + 2456 + 2457, lines 21-24).

The festivals and rituals referred to here all have close connections with the celebration of the victory over the Persians at Salamis in 480 BC. The festival of Artemis Mounichia took place on 16 Mounichia, the anniversary of the battle of Salamis. Plutarch (Plut. *de glor. Ath.* 349f) tells us that this day was dedicated to the goddess Artemis because it was then that she shone on the Greeks as they were conquering at Salamis.[10] The festival of Ajax at Salamis seems to follow immediately after that at Mounichia, and would also appear to be associated with the victory at Salamis. Indeed, it took place in the very area where the victory was won, and honoured a hero who was believed to have given his support to the Athenians on the day of the battle, as Herodotus attests (Hdt. 8.64.2). The dating of the trophy ceremony is less clear, but perhaps occurred on the day before the Mounichia festival, if we follow the order set out in *IG* II² 1006.[11]

The trophy itself was located on the island of Salamis on the tip of the Cynosoura promontory, where there is a cutting of around 1.8 m² in the rock (Wallace 1969, 301-302; Culley 1977, 296-297; Rabe 2008, 104-106). This seems to be the remains of a monument which was still visible from Athens in the eighteenth century (Stuart & Revett 1762, ix). Wallace (1969, 302) noted other cuttings on the island of Leipsokoutali, which lies across the strait from Cynosoura, and suggested that they may have been the foundation for another trophy mentioned by Plutarch (Plut. *Arist.* 9.2), identifying this island as Psyttaleia. The fact that the so-called Attic restoration decree, discussed further below, locates the trophy on Salamis, along with the sanctuary of Ajax and the *polyandrion*, shows that the trophy visited by the ephebes was the structure located on the Cynosoura promontory (*IG* II² 1035, lines 28-30; Culley 1975; 1977, 285-286; Rabe 2008, 105). Herodotus (Hdt. 8.121) records that

---

8   The restoration is justified by the reference to the contest again later in the inscription at lines 71-72.

9   Note that Perrin-Saminadayar 2007, 208 punctuates the text at line 30 differently. In either case, however, contests are said to take place at both festivals.

10   The same date appears in Plut. *Lys.* 15, but in *Cam.* 19 he gives the date as 20 Boedromion. See Bowie 2013, 245.

11   For discussion of the dating of these festivals see Mommsen 1898, 452-3; Deubner 1932, 204-5, 228; Pélékidis 1962, 247-249.

a captured trireme was dedicated to Ajax at Salamis, alongside two others dedicated at the Isthmus and Sounion respectively. West (1969, 16-17) suggests that the stone monument on Salamis was a permanent replacement for this initial trophy. It seems to have taken the form of a marble column on a square limestone base, sharing a similar form to the Marathon trophy (Vanderpool 1966, Rabe 2008, 101-104). That it carried a replica of a trireme as a visual reference to the ship which had preceded it, and the naval victory it commemorated, as Culley (1977, 297) suggests, is an attractive idea, but cannot be confirmed. While the date at which the stone monument was set up is uncertain, references to a trophy here in 4th-century BC texts (Pl. *Menex.* 245a, Xen. *An.* 3.2.13, Lycurg. *Leoc.* 73) suggest that it was probably erected in the course of the 5th century BC, along with the trophy at Marathon. It was still surviving in the 2nd century AD, when it was seen by Pausanias (Paus. 1.36.1).

At the end of the 2nd century BC, then, possibly in a continuation of practices revived after the return of the island in 229 BC, the ephebes were a very visible presence in the religious rituals in the area of Salamis, participating in sacrifices, processions and contests. These activities included naval voyages along the coast and between the mainland and Salamis, and some form of naval contest. The inscriptions use a variety of terms to refer to the boats. In *IG* II² 1011, line 16 the boats used for the voyage around the coast are referred to as sacred ships, ταῖς ἱεραῖς ναυσίν, while the contest is referred to as ἅμιλλαν τῶν πλοίων, the contest of the boats. A little later (line 19) the ephebes appear bringing into dry dock boats described as ἀφρακτῶν, boats without hatches. This may suggest that special boats were reserved for the activities during these festivals. In *IG* II² 1008, line 76 the boats are described as having two banks of oars, πλοίοις δικρότοις, and it is possible that they were reduced size replicas of warships.

The nature of the naval contests is similarly vague. They are usually referred to as *hamillai ploion*, contests of the boats, which most scholars gloss as races or regattas. A similar term is used in a list of prizes for the Panathenaia festival which is dated to the 380s BC (*SEG* 53.192, 139-42; Shear 2003). Here the term νικητήρια νεῶν ἁμίλλης, 'prizes for the contest of the ships' heads a list of prizes awarded to victorious teams. This shows that the contest at the Panathenaia was performed in teams made up of various Athenian tribes. This is the only secure reference to naval contests at the Panathenaia and we do not know how long they formed part of the Panathenaic contests. A reference in Plato the Comic Poet, which is cited in Plutarch's *Life of Themistokles* (Plut. *Them.* 32.4-5) via Diodorus the Periegetes' work *On Tombs*, gives the tomb of Themistokles on the coast of Piraeus as being a good place to watch the 'contest of the ships' (ἅμιλλα τῶν νεῶν). Since Plato the Comic Poet dates to the end

of the 5th century BC, a few decades before the Panathenaic prize list, this might refer to contests during the Panathenaia. It is interesting, however, that Plutarch cites it as part of his discussion of the location of the tomb of Themistokles, famous for his role in the naval victory at Salamis. For Plutarch's later audience, the reference to naval contests in this area might instead have evoked the contests performed as part of festivals honouring the memory of Salamis, and not those of the Panathenaia.

3. Salamis and naval activities under Augustus

References to ephebic activities on Salamis appear on the ephebic decrees until the mid-90s BC but then disappear until the later 1st century AD. On the basis of this, and Dio Chrysostom's report that 'those who disparage their city and the inscription on the statue of Nicanor are accustomed to say that it actually bought Salamis for them' (Dio Chrys. *Or* 31.116), earlier scholarship accepted the idea that Athens had lost Salamis in the wake of the First Mithradatic War (see Habicht 1996 for details). It was assumed that it was subsequently returned to the city by the agency of one C. Julius Nicanor, who is acclaimed on four Athenian statue bases as a new Homer and new Themistokles (*IG* II² 3786-3789). More recent scholarship has cast doubt on this, suggesting that there is no positive evidence that the island was ever lost, and suggesting that Nicanor's role may instead have been to buy back certain private lands for public use (Habicht 1996, 86; Bowersock 2002, 11-16; Jones 2005, 169-72).

These activities are usually placed in the Augustan period, along with the restoration decree, *IG* II² 1035, which describes the restoration of Attic sanctuaries and sacred lands to public use (Culley 1975, 1977; Schmalz 2007-8). As already mentioned, the restoration decree references places on the island of Salamis, including the sanctuary of Ajax and the promontory where the trophy and mass tomb (*polyandrion*) were located. It also mentions a number of sites at Piraeus, including one associated with 'the voyage of the sacred [ships]', as well as dry docks in the Grand Harbour (*IG* II² 1035, lines 31-37, 45-46; Culley 1977, 285-6, 291-298). The dry docks are mentioned after reference to a shrine 'founded by Themistokles before the sea-battle of Salamis', which situates them in relationship to that famous battle. This concern for the restoration of spaces closely associated with the events of the Persian Wars suggests that the enduring or revived memory of those events played an important role in the communal self-image of Athens at this period. Yet, the promotion of the past at this time can also be closely associated with the interests of the emperor Augustus. As Hölscher (1984) and Spawforth (2012, 103-105) have shown, Augustus used the battle of Salamis as a parallel to his own naval victory over Antony at Actium. Athens' keenness to restore sites associated with the memory of the Persian wars might then have been provoked in part by the emperor's own interest in reviving the memory of this past, as a glorious precedent for his own victories (Spawforth 2012, 107-111). The use of the past to gain attention and favour from Rome can be seen elsewhere a little later, in the claims of various Asia Minor cities recorded in Tacitus' reports of debates in the senate under Tiberius (Tac. *Ann.* 3.60-63; 4.55-56).

Ephebic decrees and honorific inscriptions give no details of ephebic naval activities between 96 BC and the late 1st century AD. However, the reference in the restoration decree to the voyage of the sacred ships (*IG* II² 1035, lines 36-37: τὸν παράπλουν τῶν ἱερῶν | [νεῶν) shows that some ritual naval activities were still taking place in this period. In earlier years the ephebes had performed voyages in sacred boats around the area, and so it seems reasonable to assume that they were involved in this voyage too. Whether they also performed in naval contests is less clear. There is no specific reference to *hamillai* at this time, though it is possible that contests were still occurring but were not recorded in the ephebic decrees, which underwent a change in form now.

One tantalising question is what possible relationship there might be between ephebic naval activities at Athens and the mock naval battle between Greeks and Persians which Augustus held in Rome in 2 BC (*Mon. Anc.* 23; Ov. *Ars am.* 1.171-172; Dio Cass. 55.10). Graindor (1927, 128-129) long ago suggested that the emperor might have been influenced by seeing the ephebic naval contests at Athens, and that it was in this period that they changed from a regatta to a naval battle, though in fact the word *naumachia* does not appear in ephebic inscriptions until the end of the first century AD. Raubitschek (1954, 319) even suggests that Nicanor played a role in the contests, earning him the name 'the new Themistokles'. The evidence is patchy and we can only draw inferences from what survives. It is clear that the restoration decree strengthened the memory of and spaces associated with Athens' Persian War past, perhaps under the impetus of Augustus' interest in linking his own victories with this venerable history. Given that the ephebes were earlier involved in sacred voyages and naval contests as part of festivals commemorating the Persian Wars, it seems quite plausible that some form of naval contests took place in Athens at this time too. It is less clear whether they now took the form of mock naval battles, inducing Augustus to copy this at Rome, or whether instead it was the emperor's innovation to convert naval manoeuvres alluding to the past into a full-blown recreation of a famous battle. I suspect the latter, and that it was this crystallisation of the link between naval supremacy and a re-enactment of the past which encouraged later ephebic contests to include more direct references to battle skills and the memory of the famous sea-battle at Salamis.

4. The ephebic *naumachia* of the 1st to 3rd centuries AD

Finally, we turn to the performance and celebration of Athens' naval victories in the activities and monuments of the Athenian ephebes of the later Roman period.[12] As Perrin-Saminadayar (2004) and others have noted, during the Roman imperial period the epigraphic habit of the Athenian ephebes underwent a significant change in form.[13] In place of public decrees honouring the ephebes and their leaders and giving detailed accounts of their activities, which we have hitherto been drawing on, we find ephebes or ephebic officials setting up lists of the ephebes for a particular year. The place in which these lists were displayed also differed. While the Hellenistic decrees were set up in the public space of the agora, many of the later lists of the 1st to 3rd centuries AD have been found clustered around the area of the church of St. Demetrios Katephoris, built into the post-Herulian wall, and are thought to have been displayed within the Diogeneion gymnasium, which was the seat of the ephebeia in the Hellenistic and Roman periods (Wiemer 2011, 501).[14] A series of portrait herms was also found here, many set up by the ephebes in honour of their leaders (Lattanzi 1968; Krumeich 2004). Perrin-Saminadayar (2004, 103) characterizes this shift in representation as marking a form of privatization of the ephebeia in which it became dominated by wealthy families and their concerns; yet, as Wiemer notes (2011, 512-514), while the institution was certainly dominated by elite families in this period, it still acted as a miniature mirror of the state and should not be characterized purely as an elite club. Instead, the military and civic functions of the ephebeia remained strong, with the ephebes playing a continued role in religious processions, and presenting themselves both as military protectors of the city and as its future magistrates and leaders (Wiemer 2011; 506, 510-514; *cf.* Kennell 2009a, 331-336).

---

12 This section draws on my earlier discussion of the Athenian ephebeia in Newby 2005, 168-201, esp. 179-92 on the *naumachia*. For other discussions of the Athenian ephebeia in the Roman period see Perrin-Saminadayar 2004 and Wiemer 2011, whose discussion of the ephebeia's military associations at 490-499 reaches similar conclusions to Newby 2005, apparently separately. See also Kennell 2009a for a broader discussion of ephebic institutions in the Roman period. The inscriptions relating to the period are collected in the unpublished PhD-thesis of Wilson 1992.

13 Reinmuth 1955: 226-228 gives an earlier overview of the changing pattern of ephebic inscriptions. See also Wiemer 2011, 501-506.

14 *IG* II² 1079, lines 41-43 specifies that the decree should be set up in three copies, one at the Eleusinion, one in the Diogeneion and one at Eleusis. Further see Frantz 1979, 200-201.

As we will see, one very public role which the ephebes continued to fulfil in the religious life of the city was their involvement in civic festivals. A detailed list of festivals appears in *IG* II² 2119, dated to AD 180-191.[15] Interwoven into this list are some events which seem to have been performed on a civic level, and not purely within the ephebeia. Indeed, the very first victory mentioned is that of all the ephebes in the race to Agras (lines 127-129: τὸν | πρὸς Ἄγρας δρόμον ἅπαν-|τες οἱ ἔφηβοι). Graindor (1922, 214-215) identifies this as the race in armour held as part of the festival of Artemis Agroteria, and suggests that the ephebes may have competed against those of the previous year. A reference to the torch race contest 'to the heroes' (ἐπὶ τοῖς ἥρωσι) in line 227 also suggests involvement in the Epitaphia festival (Graindor 1922, 214). Here, however, we shall investigate the evidence for their involvement in naval contests held as part of the Aianteia and Mounichia festivals.

References to naval contests appear in both textual and visual form on ephebic stelai from the late 1st century AD and are marked by a change in vocabulary from references to *hamillai* (contests) to use of the verb *naumacheo* (fight at sea). They were discussed by Follet (1976, 339-343) who saw a reference to a *naumachia* in either word or image as a reference to the Great Panathenaia festival and thus as evidence of dating to a Panathenaic year. This means of dating has been accepted by others, but deserves challenge. As both Shear and I have argued (Newby 2005, 179-180; Shear 2012, 165-166), there is no persuasive link between the *naumachiai* referred to in these stelai and the *neon hamilla* which appeared on the list of prizes for the Panathenaia in the early 4th century BC (*SEG* 53.192, lines 139-142). Follet based her argument on one of the latest stelai which shows the head of Athena and two Panathenaic amphorae at the top of the stele, and a sketch of a boat with the labelled figure 'naumachos Herennius Dexippos' at the bottom (*IG* II² 2245, line 477, fig. 1). Yet while this particular stele can thus be dated to a year in which the Great Panathenaia was held, there is no reason to link the *naumachia* image itself with that festival, or to assume that other references to *naumachiai* must come from Panathenaic years. Instead, there is persuasive evidence to link them with the festivals at Salamis and Mounichia which helped to keep alive the memory of the victories won during the Persian Wars (Newby 2005, 179-192).

Figure 1. Ephebic stele of AD 255/6 showing the naumachos Herennius Dexippos in a boat at the bottom. IG II² 2245, Athens Epigraphic Museum 10038. After: Graindor 1924, pl. 82.

---

15 Below I give the dates in *IG* II² and Follet 1976, 341-342. Note that many of the latter rely on Follet's association of scenes or references to a *naumachia* with a Panathenaic year, an association which I reject (she is followed by Byrne 2003, 530; 523-524). See further below and Shear 2012 on the implications of this for the wider dating of Athenian inscriptions.

References to a naval contest appear on 14 reliefs or inscriptions, in either visual or verbal form.[16] One of these is an uninscribed relief dated to the Hadrianic period, showing a scene of the crowning of the kosmetes at the top with a boat holding eight men at the bottom (Athens National Museum 1468; Rhomiopoulou 1997, 46; Newby 2005, fig. 6.2). Here all the youths are calmly seated and the overall impression is that they are commemorated for involvement in a rowing race or perhaps even simply a sacred voyage. Elsewhere, however, texts and images tell a different story. The earliest references to a naval contest appear in two inscriptions from the reign of Domitian, *IG* II² 1996 and 1997. Both inscriptions carry visual images of boats, roughly scratched at the bottom of *IG* II² 1996, and only partially preserved on *IG* II² 1997. The textual references to the *naumachia* are likewise fragmentary. On *IG* II² 1996 τὴν ἐν Σ[αλαμῖνι ναυμαχίαν ἐνί]κων has been restored at l. 9. The line seems to refer to a victory of the two sons of the kosmetes, Straton son of Straton and Menandros son of Straton, both of the deme Epikephisia. This relief comes from the year of the archonship of Domitian. The other inscription, *IG* II² 1997, was indentified by Wilson as referring to the *naumachia* (1992, E125). He suggests that ναυμάχ in line 5 should be restored as ναυμάχ[ον or ναυμάχ[ίαν, i.e. as a reference to the *naumachia*, rather than as ναυμάχ[ου, son of Naumachos, a suggestion followed by Byrne (2003, 523-4) who follows Wilson in dating the inscription to AD 91/2.

Further evidence comes from the Hadrianic period. In addition to the uninscribed relief NM 1468, which is dated stylistically, two other inscriptions from this period refer to the *naumachia*. The first is *IG* II² 2024, an inscribed herm portrait which is dated to the archonship of Hadrian, and was set up by M. Annius Thrasyllus to his fellow-ephebes. He singles out for particular mention his fellow-ephebe Titus Flavius Philathenaios. Both hold Athenian as well as Roman citizenship. Thrasyllus is from the Cholleidai deme while Philathenaios is from the Eupyridai deme. They thus come from the same tribe, Leontis (Whitehead 1986, 370). While the front of the herm is taken up with lists of the ephebes enrolled for the year, on the right hand side of the shaft a brief inscription identifies a number of victors. We are told that in the Germanikeia T. Claudius Thraseas of Melite won the encomium, while Annius Thrasyllus won the torch race. After a space, the inscription goes on to mention the *naumachia* and the names of M. Annius Thrasyllus of

Cholleidai and T. Flavius Philathenaios of Eupyridai (lines 133-137). We are not told of the festival in which this victory occurred, but given that the Germanikeia does not include a *naumachia* in other inscriptions it seems to have been during a separate event.

It may be significant that two of these pieces of evidence come from periods when the emperors Domitian and Hadrian were acting as archon for the city. As we have already seen, Augustus took a particular interest in the Athenian past, setting his own foreign policy in the long tradition of struggles against the East (Spawforth 2012, 103-106). Roman visitors were often keen to experience the relics and monuments attesting to the past. Festivals which recalled that past might, then, have received a particular boost from the presence of the emperor in the city, especially in the case of Hadrian who had a profound impact on Athens' religious life (Shear 2012).[17]

While these early references to the *naumachia* are somewhat fragmentary and elusive, more detailed evidence comes from mid-2nd to mid-3rd centuries AD. A vivid visual rendering of the contest is found on a relief set up by two ephebic team captains in 163/4 (*IG* II² 2087, Oliver 1971, 69-70, no. 4; fig. 2). In turn the names of the ephebes making up each team (*systremma*) are listed, followed by the victories of its members in various ephebic competitions. The *naumachia* is not explicitly mentioned in the text, but the bottom of the relief is dominated by a vividly carved image of a boat, containing five youths who are naked except for a chlamys around their shoulders. The central three are shown seated and rowing, while the other two stand on the prow and the stern, carrying their oars on their shoulders. There is a great sense of action in the scene; the figure to the left of the relief, who stands on the prow, looks to the left as if keeping watch, the seated rower next to him looks up to the other standing ephebe for a command, while he in turn strides towards the back of the boat and brandishes his oar as if he might use it to repel boarders. We are clearly in the midst of the contest here, in contrast to the other images which tend to show the team at rest, holding the prizes of victory. This scene is also the most detailed depiction of the boat used in the *naumachia*. On the prow of the boat, to the left of the relief, appears a three-pronged ram, similar to those which equipped Athenian warships (Morrison *et al.* 2000, 167; 221-223; a surviving example is in the Piraeus archaeological museum). A similar ram also appears on the boat guided by Herennius Dexippos shown at the bottom of *IG* II² 2245 (fig. 1).

This suggests that the boats used in these contests may have been smaller replicas of a warship, equipped with a bronze ram for attacking other ships. The teams

---

16 Text only: *IG* II² 2024, line 136; 2119, line 223; 2198, line 18. Text and Image: *IG* II² 1996, line 9; 1997, line 5; 2130, lines 48-49; 2167, lines 17-18; 2208, line 146; 2245, line 477. Image only: *IG* II² 2087; 2106; 2124; 2248; National Museum 1468 (uninscribed relief).

17 It is unclear whether Domitian actually visited Athens, but he certainly promoted its interests: Oliver 1981, 417-418.

Figure 2. Relief set up by two ephebic team captains. IG II² 2087, National Archaeological Museum, Athens 1466. © Hellenic Ministry of Culture and Sports / Archaeological Receipts Fund and National Archaeological Museum.

Figure 3. Ephebic list showing the naumachia at the bottom. IG II² 2130, National Archaeological Museum Athens 1470. © Hellenic Ministry of Culture and Sports / Archaeological Receipts Fund and National Archaeological Museum.

themselves consisted of 12 ephebes and it is likely that all would have participated in the *naumachia*. The relief condenses this to fit the space, but still gives a vivid sense of the team-work necessary for the contest. Whether these teams competed in other ephebic events as well is unclear – the fact that the *naumachia* dominates this relief may suggest that it was the most important event in which they participated (Oliver 1971, 73).

Elsewhere other images of boats appear on some of the ephebic lists, and where the victors are named they can sometimes be identified with the team captains of the various *systremmata*, as in *IG* II² 2208, discussed below. *IG* II² 2130, dated to AD 192/3 or 195/6, is one of the most impressive and detailed ephebic lists (fig. 3). At the top of the relief, beneath a pediment holding the remains of a flying figure, is a well-carved relief panel showing from left to right a runner in the torch race, a pair of athletes wrestling and the remains of a standing figure who can be identified as Herakles, standing in the pose of the Farnese type (Newby 2005, 183-186). Beneath this is a neat inscription, listing the officials in charge of the ephebes, and the ephebes who undertook specific roles, before listing all the ephebes by tribe. The inscription is laid out over four columns, but at the bottom of the two left-hand columns a space was left which was subsequently carved with an image of a ship, facing right.

The boat carries three ephebes. The one at the stern is shown rowing, while the central one brandishes a crown and holds a palm over his shoulder. The figure at the front holds up his oar. This relief is now divided into two parts, with the right-hand section conserved at the Ashmolean in Oxford. This section preserves the prow of the ship, here too equipped with a protruding ram (Graindor 1924, pl. 66). Immediately above the boat is a labelling inscription, which runs as follows (lines 48-49):

Φιλιστείδ[ης Ͻ Πειρ]αιεὺς καὶ Πο Αἴλ
Κορνήλιος Παλ ναυμαχ[ήσαντε]ς Μουνίχια
συνεστεφανώθησαν

Philisteides, [son of Philisteides of Pir]aeus and Publius Aelius Cornelius of Pallene, having competed in the naval battle at the Mounichia, were jointly crowned.

Figure 4. Ephebic list with a scene of the naumachia at the bottom. IG II² 2208, National Archaeological Museum Athens 1465. © Hellenic Ministry of Culture and Sports / Archaeological Receipts Fund and National Archaeological Museum.

As Kapetanopoulos (1992-1998, 217) and Shear (2012, 166) show, there is no compelling reason to read Mounichia here as a locative (as Follet 1976, 341), and instead it should be understood as a reference to the Mounichia festival. This, then, is evidence that naval competitions continued to be held as part of the Mounichia festival in the imperial period. The change in terminology, however, from references to a *hamilla* to use of the verb *naumacheo* suggests a change in emphasis in these competitions, focussing more strongly on their martial character. As we have seen above, the visual depictions also reinforce this sense of an allusion to battle, through the active poses of the figures, and the prominence in some of the images of rams, similar to those which adorned warships.

Another ephebic list, *IG* II² 2208, further testifies to the importance which this competition was given within the many activities in which the ephebes participated (fig. 4). This list is dated to AD 215/6 by Byrne (2003, 533) and like *IG* II² 2130 is notable for its monumentality. The main text is flanked by two columns while above a scene of the crowning of the kosmetes is flanked by crowns, indicating the mutual honouring of the kosmetes and the ephebes (Newby 2005, 174, 186-187). At the bottom of the relief, below the lists of names, is a heading, carved in the same size of letters as were used in the initial heading identifying the ephebic officials (line 146). Though fragmentary, this can be confidently restored as reading οἱ [ναυ[μαχ]ήσαντε[ς], 'those who competed in the naval battle'. Beneath this heading are images of two boats; a further two probably occupied the space to the right of the panel. Above each is a name label (col I. line 77, col II, line 147, col III, line 168). From left to right we find Aurelius Dositheos, son of Thales; Aurelius Herakleides, son of Thales and Aurelius Anthos, son of Teimon. The first two are the sons of the kosmetes for the year, named in lines 6-7 as Aurelius Dositheos, son of Dositheos, also called Thales, of Pambotadai. All three ephebes played an active part in the running of the ephebeia. All are listed as gymnasiarchs while Aurelius Herakleides and Aurelius Anthos both acted as *systremmatarchai*, and the sons of the kosmetes also acted as agonothetes of various festivals (lines 80-2, 95-6, 103-5).

It seems likely that it was their role as captains of the teams which competed in the naval battle which led to them being hailed here as *naumachesantes*. The images which lie beneath these names further this impression of the importance of these individuals. In each boat we see only two figures; one rows, while the other stands holding up his oar. Here it is the active figure of the *systremmatarches* who is praised, with the contribution made by the rest of the team reduced to a single rower. The type of boat, however, is very similar to that shown on *IG* II² 2130, having a similar plume at the stern and a pointed ram on the prow.

The visual evidence suggests that this *naumachia* was indeed some kind of naval battle. The tactics used in sea battles were primarily ramming and boarding of the enemy ships. The presence of sharp rams on these boats, and the active pose of the ephebes who stand brandishing their oars, suggests that these contests might have showcased those skills. Perhaps the aim was to board a rival boat, and to prevent yourself being boarded. The extent to which this was an actual contest, with winners and losers, is harder to ascertain. The majority of the inscriptions referred simply to competing in the event (using the verb *naumacheo*), but one inscription may refer to a victory here (*IG* II² 2198, lines 18-20):

[ναυμ]αχής ἐνί
-ς Ἀχαρνεύς
[συστρεμματά]ρχαι

Kirchner expands the text to read ναυμαχήσ(ας) ἐνί(κα), 'having competed in the sea-battle, he won', which would credit the unnamed ephebe from Acharnai as winning a victory in the *naumachia*, rather than just competing in it.[18] A list of the *systremmatarchai* then follows. This suggests that the ephebic teams were closely associated with the *naumachia*, and that winners may have been identified in the contest. The overall impression from the other inscriptions, however, is that it was taking part in the sea-battle which was of primary importance. While the imperial reliefs are elusive about the context in which this type of contest took place, with only one referring to the Mounichia and another plausibly restored to read 'at Salamis', it seems reasonable to assume that these *naumachiai* are the later successors to the Hellenistic *hamillai* which took place within the context of festivals commemorating the battle of Salamis: the Aianteia, Mounichia and the voyage to the trophy on Salamis. The change in terminology seems to suggest a change in focus, from a race to a display of fighting skills, perhaps involving boarding or warding off other ships. Whether the *naumachia* was a precise re-enactment of the battle of Salamis is less clear. I suggest that it was probably a display of naval military skills within the context of festivals recalling the Persian wars, and in the space where the Battle of Salamis had occurred. This would have evoked the memory of that famous battle and shown that the Athenian ephebes were the rightful heirs of their famous forefathers.

It is worth dwelling briefly here on composition of the Athenian ephebeia in this period. From the late Hellenistic period the ephebeia was opened up to non-Athenians, named on the inscriptions first as *xenoi*, then *epengraphoi*, and in many periods these youths actually seem to dominate (Perrin-Saminadayar 2007, 248-53; Baslez 1989). In the *systremmata* relief discussed above, one team is made up entirely of Athenians, while the other includes non-Athenians too. If the *naumachia* was a team event, it seems inevitable that non-Athenian citizens would also have competed in it, which might have diluted the message suggested here, namely that the *naumachia* was used as a way of keeping alive the memory of Athenian naval prowess and its most famous achievement. However, it is notable that when particular individuals are mentioned as *naumachos* they can overwhelmingly be identified as Athenian citizens. Both the ephebes named as *naumachesantes* on *IG* II² 2130 are Athenian citizens, and they include the son of the ephebic antikosmetes; on *IG* II² 2208 two sons of the kosmetes, from the deme Pambotadai, appear as naval victors, while on *IG* II² 2245 the *naumachos* Herennius

Dexippos is the son of the famous Athenian historian P. Herennius Dexippos, whose role as agonothetes of the Panathenaia is alluded to in the imagery at the top. While non-Athenians certainly participated in the ephebeia in large numbers (Baslez 1989), and must have played a role in the naval contests, it was predominantly the sons of leading Athenian families who advertised their role in the *naumachia* on stelai and used it to present themselves as true Athenians, reliving the values and glories of the past in the Roman present.

5. Conclusions

From the 5th century onwards Salamis always seems to have played an important role in Athenian self-identity, alongside the memory of the Battle of Marathon, and trophies celebrating both battles could be used to urge the Athenians to emulate their heroic forefathers. From the 3rd century BC onwards, the role of commemorating Salamis seems to have been handed especially to the Athenian ephebes, who participated in a number of naval events during festivals associated with the victory, including voyages and contests. These displays reasserted the memory of the Athenian tradition of naval supremacy and situated it within the specific context of the memory of the Battle of Salamis. What happened to these activities in the 1st century BC is unclear, but it seems as though they were given a new lease of life in the restoration decree, which mentions the sacred ships as well as the sanctuary of Ajax and the trophy on Salamis. This seems to show some form of naval activity occurring in the period of Augustus. Whether this influenced Augustus' decision to recreate the sea-battle at Rome, or was in its turn influenced by Augustus' actions cannot be reconstructed. It is possible that the influence went both ways, and that Augustus had seen the displays at Athens and crystallized the implicit link of naval prowess with the battle at Salamis when he decided to recreate this battle in Rome. The more overtly military character which the contests take on later might then have been encouraged and prompted by the use to which Salamis and other Persian war battles were put in the services of imperial ideology.

In the changing history of ephebic naval contests at Athens we can see both continuity and change between the Hellenistic and Roman periods. In both periods the memory of Salamis continued to be important, and the ephebes were given the chief role in embodying and keeping alive the symbolism of Salamis through their ritual activities. Yet the increased focus on military skills which is implied by the use of the word *naumachia*, the very word used to describe the battle of Salamis in the restoration decree (*IG* II² 1035, line 46), and the visual portrayal of boats with rams on Roman-period reliefs also suggests that the link between ephebic displays and

---

18   *IG* II² 2198, p. 589. Follet 1976, 418, line 122 restores the line differently as [καὶ ἐναυ]μαχησε Νι-, seeing Νι as the start of the ephebe's name. *IG* II² 1996, line 9 may also refer to a victory in the naumachia, if the restoration as τὴν ἐν Σ[αλαμῖνι ναυμαχίαν ἐνί] κων is correct. See above.

the past was made more concrete and explicit in this period. This change is parallel to the increased violence shown in the ephebeia at Sparta in this period, with its famous whipping contest (Kennell 1995, esp. 78-84; Newby 2005, 150-167), while the more explicit link to the sea-battle at Salamis fits into Roman desires to see old Greece as a place of the past, to be enjoyed as touristic 'theme-park' celebrating 'the glory that was Greece'.

At the same time the memory of Salamis was not just a means to attract Roman attention. The fact that wealthy ephebes and officials put their resources into advertising their involvement, or that of their offspring, in such contests shows that it brought them prestige and pride amongst their peers. Thus the memory of the past, and the re-performance of the past in ritual activities were also means to ensure elite self-representation, helping to assert an individual's claims to be a true Athenian citizen and a rightful inheritor of Athens' naval supremacy. We cannot disentangle these two strands: memories of the past helped

to shape contemporary civic identities for the cities of the eastern Roman provinces, but commemoration and recollection was always done in the awareness of a number of different audiences, comprising both one's fellow citizens and incomers from the wider Roman world. Together, rituals, monuments and inscribed records helped to keep alive the memory of the past, and assert its continued relevance both to the citizens of Athens and to its foreign visitors.

Acknowledgements

I am grateful to the editors of this volume for inviting me to contribute to the conference on which it is based and for their helpful comments on my paper, as well as to the conference participants for their questions and discussion. In particular, I thank Sam Heijnen for discussion of the restoration decree, and Sean Byrne for long ago pointing me towards Wilson's dissertation.

References

Alcock, S.E. 2002. *Archaeologies of the Greek Past. Landscape, Monuments, and Memories.* Cambridge.

Arrington, N.T. 2015. *Ashes, Images and Memories. The Presence of the War Dead in Fifth-Century Athens,* Oxford.

Athanassaki, L. 2016. Who was Eucles? Plutarch and his sources on the legendary Marathon-runner (*de Gloria Atheniensium*347CD). In: J. Opsomer, C. Roskam & F.B. Titchener (eds), *A Versatile Gentleman. Consistency in Plutarch's Writing,* Leuven, 213-228.

Baslez, M.-F. 1989. Citoyens et non citoyens dans l' Athènes Impériale au Ier et au IIe siècles de notre ère. In: S. Walker and A. Cameron (eds), *The Greek Renaissance in the Roman Empire*, London, 17-34.

Bowersock, G. 2002. The new Hellenism of Augustan Athens. *AnnPisa* 7.1, 1-16.

Bowie, E. 2013. Marathon in the Greek Culture of the Second Century AD. In: C. Carey & M. Edwards (eds), *Marathon 2,500 years. Proceedings of the Marathon Conference 2010, BICS* Supplement, London, 241-253.

Byrne, S.G. 2003. *Roman Citizens of Athens*, Leuven.

Culley, G.R. 1975. The Restoration of Sanctuaries in Attica: *IG* II² 1035, *Hesperia* 44, 207-223.

Culley, G.R. 1977. The Restoration of Sanctuaries in Attica, II, *Hesperia* 46, 282-298.

Deubner, L. 1932. *Attische Feste*, Berlin.

Follet, S. 1976. *Athènes au IIe et au IIIe siècle: Études chronologiques et prosopographiques*, Paris.

Frantz, A. 1979. A public building of late Antiquity in Athens (*IG* II² 5205), *Hesperia* 48, 194-203.

Goméz, P. 2013. Marathon et l'identité grecque au IIe s. apr. J-C: du mythe au lieu commun. In: A. Gangloff (ed.), *Lieux de mémoire en Orient grec à l'époque impériale*, Bern, 79-94.

Graindor, P. 1922. Études sur l'ephébie attique sous l'Empire, *MusB* 26, 165-228.

Graindor, P. 1924. *Album d'inscriptions attiques d'époque impériale*, Gand.

Graindor, P. 1927. *Athènes sous Auguste.* Le Caire.

Habicht, C. 1996. Salamis in der Zeit nach Sulla, *ZPE* 111, 79-87.

Habicht, C. 1997. *Athens from Alexander to Antony*, transl. D.L. Schneider, Cambridge, MA.

Hölscher , T. 1984. Actium und Salamis, *JdI* 99, 187-214.

Hölscher, T. 1998. Images and political identity: the case of Athens. In: D. Boedecker & K.A. Raaflaub (eds) *Democracy, Empire and the Arts in Fifth-century Athens*, Cambridge, MA, 153-183.

Jones, C.P. 2005. An Athenian document mentioning Julius Nicanor, *ZPE* 154, 161-172.

Jung, M. 2006. *Marathon und Plataiai. Zwei Perserschlachten als «lieux de mémoire» im antiken Griechenland*. Göttingen.

Kapetanopoulos, E. 1992-1998. The Reform of the Athenian Constitution under Hadrian, *Horos* 10-12, 215-237.

Kennell, N.M. 2009a. The Greek ephebate in the Roman period, *International Journal of the History of Sport* 26, 323-342.

Kennell, N.M. 2009b. Review of Perrin-Saminadayar 2007, *BMCR*, http://bmcr.brynmawr.edu/2009/2009-09-43.html, accessed 3 April 2017.

Krumeich, R. 2004. 'Klassiker' im Gymnasion. Bildnisse attischer Kosmeten der mittleren und späten Kaiserzeit zwischen Rom und griechischer Vergangenheit. In: B.E. Borg (ed.), *Paideia: The World of the Second Sophistic*, Berlin, 131-155.

Lattanzi, E. 1968. *I ritratti dei cosmeti nel museo nazionale di Atene*. Roma.

Loraux, N. 1986. *The Invention of Athens. The Funeral Oration in the Classical City*, trans. A. Sheridan, Cambridge, MA.

Low, P. 2010. Commemoration of the war dead in classical Athens: remembering defeat and victory. In: D.M. Pritchard (ed.), *War, Democracy and Culture in Classical Athens*, Cambridge, 341-358.

Mikalson, J.D. 1998. *Religion in Hellenistic Athens.* Berkeley.

Mommsen, A. 1898. *Feste der Stadt Athen in Altertum.* Leipzig.

Moretti, L. 1967. *Iscrizioni storiche ellenistiche* I, Firenze.

Morrison, J.S., J.F. Coates & N.B. Rankov 2000. *The Athenian Trireme. The history and reconstruction of an Ancient Greek Warship*, 2nd ed., Cambridge.

Newby, Z. 2005. *Greek Athletics in the Roman World. Victory and Virtue.* Oxford.

Oliver, J.H. 1971. Athenian Lists of Ephebic Teams, *ArchEph* 1971, 66-74.

Oliver, J.H. 1981. Roman emperors and Athens. *Historia* 30, 412-423.

Pélékidis, C. 1962. *Histoire de l'éphébie attiques des origines à 31 avant Jésus-Christ*, Paris.

Perrin-Saminadayar, É. 2004. L'éphébie attique de la crise mithridatique à Hadrien: miroir de la société athénienne? In: S. Follet (ede), *L'Hellénisme d'époque romaine. Nouveaus documents, nouvelles approches (Ier s. aC – IIIe. s. pC)*, Paris, 87-103.

Perrin-Saminadayar, É. 2007. Éducation, culture et société à Athènes. Les acteurs de la vie culturelle athénienne (229-88). Un tout petit monde. De L'archéologie à l'histoire, Paris.

Price, S. 2012. Memory and ancient Greece. In: B. Dignas and R.R.R. Smith (eds), *Historical and Religious Memory in the Ancient World*, Oxford, 15-32.

Rabe, B. 2008. *Tropaia.* τροπή *und* σκῦλα *– Entstehung, Funktion und Bedeutung des griechischen Tropaions.* Tübingen.

Raubitschek, R.E. 1954. The New Homer, *Hesperia* 23, 317-319.

Rhomiopoulou, K. 1997. Ελληνορωμαϊκά γλυπτά του εθνικού αρχαιολογικού μουσείου, Αθήνα

Roller, M.B. 2004. Exemplarity in Roman culture: the cases of Horatius Cocles and Cloelia, *CP* 99, 1-56.

Schmalz, G.C.R. 2007-8. Inscribing a ritualized past. The Attic restoration decree *IG* II^2 1035 and cultural memory in Augustan Athens, *Eulimene* 8-9, 9-46.

Shear, J. 2003. Prizes from Athens: The List of Panathenaic Prizes and the Sacred Oil, *ZPE* 142, 87-108.

Shear, J. 2012. Hadrian, the Panathenaia and the Athenian Calendar, *ZPE* 180, 159-172.

Spawforth, A.J.S. 1994. Symbol of unity? The Persian-Wars tradition in the Roman empire. In: S. Hornblower (ed.), *Greek Historiography*, Oxford, 233-47.

Spawforth, A.J.S. 2012. *Greece and the Augustan Cultural Revolution*, Cambridge.

Stuart, J. & Revett, N., 1762. *The Antiquities of Athens* I, London.

Stupperich, R. 1977. *Staatsbegräbnis und Privatgrabmal im klassischen Athen*. PhD Dissertation Westfälischen Wilhelms-Universität, Münster.

Vanderpool, E. 1966. A Monument to the Battle of Marathon, *Hesperia* 35, 93-106

Vanderpool, E. 1969. Three prize vases, *ArchDelt* 24, 1-5.

West III, W.C. 1969. The trophies of the Persian Wars, *CP* 64, 7-19.

Wallace, P.W. 1969. Psyttaleia and the Trophies of the Battle of Salamis. *AJA* 73, 293-303.

Whitehead, D. 1986. *The demes of Attica, 508-7-ca.250 BC: a political and social study*, Princeton.

Wiemer, H.-U. 2011. Von der Bürgerschule zum aristokratischen Klub? Die athenische Ephebie in der römischen Kaiserzeit. *Chiron* 41, 487-537.

Wilson, P. 1992. *A corpus of ephebic inscriptions from Roman Athens 31BC-267AD.* PhD Dissertation, Monash University, Melbourne.

Greek Panhellenic *Agones* in a Roman Colony: Corinth and the Return of the Isthmian Games

Lavinia del Basso

Abstract

In 146 BC L. Mummius removed the administration of the Isthmian Games from Corinth and awarded it to nearby Sikyon. However, shortly after its re-foundation as a Roman colony, Corinth recovered its Panhellenic festival and hosted it in its urban centre for almost a century. This article discusses how the return of the Isthmian Games provides additional evidence against the fully 'Roman nature' of the colony. The recovery of the festival prompted the reintroduction of the original pine crown in order to show the continuity with Corinth's prestigious legacy, and to reinforce its claim on the *agonothesia* of the Panhellenic contests. Moreover, the existence of a cult for Melicertes during the 'urban Isthmian phase' is addressed in light of a previously neglected inscription. The article also explores the impact of the Isthmian Games on the topography of early Roman Corinth, linking the refurbishment of the *archaion gymnasion* and of the surrounding area to the return of the Panhellenic festival.

Keywords: Roman Corinth, Isthmian Games, Panhellenic prizes, gymnasia, cult of Melicertes

1. Introduction

The Isthmian Games were held every two years under the administration of Corinth in the sanctuary of Poseidon on the Isthmus. The famous and well attended Panhellenic festival played an important role during the late Republican period when it served as a location for the first diplomatic approaches between Rome – the rising political and military power – and the Greek world (Borimir 2001, 32-34). After the successful war against the Illyrians (229/8 BC), an episode that marked a shift of interest towards the Eastern part of the Mediterranean, the Roman authorities sent embassies to Athens and Corinth, in order to establish diplomatic relationships with the two prestigious poleis. Corinth invited some Roman representatives to attend the Isthmian Games (Polyb. 2.12). The participation, crowned by the victory in the stadion of an otherwise unknown Plautus (Cass. Dio 8.19), was highly significant; it implied that the Greek world recognized Rome as a political peer on a stage of Panhellenic relevance (Simpsons 2016, 87-89). The role of the Isthmian festival as a place of communication and negotiation between Rome and the Greek poleis reached its peak some years later, with the famous 'declaration of freedom' that T. Quinctius Flamininus announced to the overcrowded stadium (Plut.

in: Dijkstra, T.M., I.N.I. Kuin, M. Moser & D. Weidgenannt (eds) 2017. *Strategies of Remembering in Greece under Rome (100 BC - 100 AD)*, Leiden (Sidestone Press).

Vit. Flam. 10.3-10).[1] Given these premises, it is hardly surprising that the Roman authorities showed a particular interest in the Isthmian Games after Corinth's defeat in 146 BC.

2. The 'Sikyonian phase' of the Isthmian Games (146 BC – 46 BC)

Several ancient authors provide gloomy descriptions of Corinth after its capture: it is said that the city was deprived of its autonomy, plundered and destroyed, the surviving inhabitants sold as slaves and its hinterland transformed in *ager publicus* or gifted to nearby Sikyon (Wiseman 1979, 491-496; Gebhard & Dickie 2003, 261-265).[2] However, the excavations show that the material damages were not as extensive as the literary sources imply (Gebhard & Dickie 2003, 266-277; James 2014b, 17-37): for example, the discovery of locally produced and imported pottery dated to the 1st century BC provides clear evidence that Corinth was still inhabited during this period (James 2014a, 47-63). Still, even though the city was not as 'prostrata ac diruta' (Cic. *Fam.* 4.5.4) as the ancient authors suggest, it is undeniable that it suffered a major institutional break between 146 BC and the establishment of the Roman colony in 46 BC (Alcock 1993, 24-33). This is because in 146 BC L. Mummius also deprived Corinth of the presidency of the Isthmian Games and awarded it to Sikyon, which was a faithful Roman ally during the war against the Achaean league (Paus. 2.2.2). The choice was quite significant since the festival was part of the prestigious *periodos* and its possession was highly regarded (Paus. 2.2.2). Unfortunately, no extant literary or epigraphical sources deal directly with the 'Sikyonian phase' of the Isthmian Games. Therefore, many aspects of the Panhellenic contest during this period remain unknown, such as their organization and funding, the identity of the athletes who took part in the competitions, or the ways Sikyon dealt with the public in attendance and the related logistical issues. Pausanias' description of the agora of Sikyon provides a possible hint, in that he describes an altar of Poseidon Isthmios near the bouleuterion (Paus. 2.9.6).[3] It is possible that this cult was introduced when the city obtained the *agonothesia* of the Panhellenic festival (Mylonopoulos 2003, 205-206).[4] A senatorial decree from Delphi shows that in 135 BC the Isthmian-Nemean guild of the Artists of Dionysos, involved in a bitter quarrel with the Attic guild, held a meeting in Sikyon rather than in the locations chosen by the Roman Senate, Argos and Thebes (FdD 3.2.70; *SIG*[3] 705); the choice of Sikyon was perhaps due to its role as the administrative headquarter of the Isthmian Games. Moreover, the existence of the Isthmian Games in this period is confirmed indirectly by the athletes listed as *Isthmionikai* or *periodonikai* on the honorary statues set up in their hometowns or in other Panhellenic sanctuaries (Farrington 2012, 22-23).

That said, the location of the Isthmian festival under the Sikyonian administration is still uncertain. The sanctuary of Poseidon on the Isthmus suffered severe damages in 200 BC and during Mummius' siege (Gebhard & Dickie 2003, 265). According to Polybius L. Mummius undertook the restoration of the stadium (Polyb. 39.6.1). In 45 BC Cicero mentions that a statue of A. Postumius Albinus, one of the ten commissioners charged with the reorganization of Greece after 146 BC, stood in the sanctuary (Cic. *Att.* 13.32.3). Both authors hint at the fact that the sanctuary was not completely abandoned; thus far, however, the excavation was unable to find proof for restorations or building activities before the middle of the 1st century AD (Gebhard 1993, 75-94; Gebhard & Dickie 2003, 265).[5] Therefore, most scholars conclude that the Isthmian festival was hosted in Sikyon itself (Gebhard 1993, 75-77; Lolos 2011, 279-282). The polis was equipped with a stadium and a theater for the athletic and musical contests (Lolos 2011, 279-282): its gymnasium could be used for training as well as competitions (Wacker 1996, 223).

In 46 BC, Corinth was re-established as *Colonia Laus Iulia Corinthiensis* on its previous location, and shortly after it recovered the presidency of the Isthmian Games. In the following paragraph I address the meaning of the Panhellenic festival in the new institutional context of the Roman colony.

---

1   Other ancient sources: Polyb. 18.44-46; Livy, *Epit.* 32.10-33.15; Val. Max. 4.8.5; App. *Mac.* 9.4.

2   Strab. 8.6.23; *Anth. Pal.* 9.151 (Antipater of Sidon); *Anth. Pal.* 7.297 (Polystratus); Cic. *Fam.* 4.5.4; Livy. *Per.* 52; *Anth. Pal.* 9.284 (Crinagoras of Mitylene); Vell. Pat. 1.13.1; Just. *Epit.* 34.2.1- 6; Paus. 2.1.2; Oros. 5.3; Aur. Vict. *De vir. ill.* 3.60.

3   The excavations of the agora of Sikyon have so far found no traces of this altar.

4   The author argues that the presence of Poseidon in the agora is an exception rather than the norm, and that the closeness of the altar to the bouleuterion is similar to the situation at Olympia (altar of Zeus Horkios – bouleuterion). See the sanctuary of Nemean Zeus in the agora of Argos (Paus. 2.20.3), which could have been introduced when the city gained the administration of the Nemean Games.

5   It must be noted, though, that several areas of the Isthmian sanctuary are still unexcavated.

3. The Roman colony of Corinth and the 'urban Isthmian Games'

The rebirth of Corinth as a Roman colony, set in motion under Caesar and set in place by Marc Antony and Augustus, led to several changes. The new city adopted Roman laws, institutions, cults, Rome's religious calendar and Roman-style entertainment (Walbank 1997, 95-96);[6] Latin was used for public documents (Millis 2010, 23-30). The colonists became the new civic elite thanks to their Roman citizenship (Millis 2010, 13-35), while the local inhabitants were downgraded to the status of *incolae* (Walbank 1997, 95-96).[7] According to several Greek authors Roman Corinth was perceived as a foreign entity in the surrounding Greek milieu, and its new inhabitants were accused of downgrading the city's ancient and glorious legacy with their libertine status (Strab. 8.6.23).[8] These literary accounts have been taken at face value by some scholars, without paying proper attention to the scope of the narrative or the authors' personal biases.[9] As a result, early Roman Corinth has been seen as the ultimate 'imago Romae', gradually undergoing a 'hellenization process' (i.e. the introduction of Greek elements such as cults, myths and language) that reached its peak during the Antonine period (Kent 1966, 18-19; Walbank 1997, 95-96).[10] This view has been challenged by recent studies: they show that the re-foundation of Corinth as a Roman colony did not result in the adoption of a 'ready-made cultural package' from Rome (Pawlak 2013, 143-162).[11] Rather, it seems that the new colonists, for the most part Roman freedmen of Greek origins who were able 'to manoeuvre effectively in both the Greek and Roman worlds' (Millis 2010, 36), were fully aware of the prestigious history and the rich cultural tradition of the ancient Greek polis, and that they were willing to incorporate all elements that could help them to shape their civic identity (Pawlak 2013, 143-162).

Figure 1. Duoviral coin of Cn. Publilius and M. Antonius Orestes (40 BC; RPC 1, 1123). After the Classical Numismatic Group, Inc. (www.cngcoins.com/Coin.aspx?CoinID=118300).

In this context, the return of the Isthmian Games under Corinthian control provides a useful example of how the new inhabitants and magistrates of Roman Corinth recovered ancient or even long-lost features of the Panhellenic festival in order to show continuity between the Greek polis of classical period and the new Roman colony. This strategy of remembering, that can be found also in other fields, such as civic coinage (Papageorgiadou-Bani 2004) and urban topography (Robinson 2013, 341-384), was used 'to promote their (i.e. the colonists') status not as interlopers but as legitimate successors and inheritors of the Greek city' (Millis 2010, 13) and to increase the colony's prestige among the Greek world.

The recovery of the Panhellenic festival did not coincide with its return on the Isthmus as in Classical times; some, if not all of the activities of the *panegyris* now probably took place in Corinth itself until well into the second quarter of the 1st century AD, hence the definition of 'urban Isthmian Games'. The exact year when the *agones* returned to Corinth is not known, but it is clear that it must predate the first known Isthmian victory list of 3 AD (Merritt 1931, 14-18, n. 14). Gebhard convincingly suggested that Corinth regained the administration of the festival shortly after its foundation as a Roman colony (Gebhard 1993, 81-82). She noticed that the coinage of the duovirs of 40 BC shows a pine wreath encircling the abbreviated name of the city on the obverse and a *praefericulum* on the reverse (*RPC* 1, 1123).[12] Since the pine crown was the traditional prize for the Isthmian victors, Gebhard suggests that the recovery of the Isthmian Games happened shortly after the establishment of the Roman colony.

---

6   Several authors (Dio Chrys. *Or.* 31.121; Philostr. *VA* 26; Luc. *Demon.* 33) held the Roman colony of Corinth responsible for spreading Roman spectacles in Greece; see Spawforth 1994, 151-168.

7   For changes affecting the territory see Rizakis 1997, 15-36.

8   Other ancient sources: Polyb. 39.2; *Anth. Pal.* 9.284; Paus. 7.15.1-16.8.

9   Alcock 1993, 24-33 on the impact of the loss of *eleutheria* upon the negative judgement of Greece under the Roman rule in ancient Greek authors and the consequences of these depictions in modern historiography.

10 The idea of a 'hellenization process' comes from Favorinus (Dio Chrys. *Or.* 37.25): the author praises the citizens of Corinth because, though Romans, they managed to 'hellenize' themselves, adopting Greek culture, language and values. For the influence of Favorinus' *Korinthiakos* in Corinth's historiography see Millis 2010, 14-17.

11 The expression 'ready-made cultural package' is used by Woolf 1998, 11.

12 The *duoviri quinquennales* of this year were Cn. Publilius and M. Antonius Orestes. The pine crown also appears on the issues struck by P. Aebutius and C. Pinnius between 39 and 36 BC. Gebhard 1993, 81, n. 15 identifies the vase as a hydria and interprets it as a symbol for athletic competitions; however, since the vase has only one handle, it seems better to identify it with a *praefericulum*, as in *RPC* 1, 1123.

It is impossible to know whether the return of the festival under Corinth's control was already included in Caesar's colonial plans or if it was prompted by the local elite.[13] In any case, it is clear that the new inhabitants were proud of their Panhellenic *agones:* not only did they use Isthmian-related themes on their coins, but the *agonothesia* of the Games also became the highest civic office, and the *ornamenta agonothetica* the most prestigious honour of the colony (Camia & Rizakis 2008, 238). Like the other three contests of the *archaia periodos* (Olympia, Delphi and Nemea), the Isthmian Games attracted a large public from the entire Mediterranean; they were also an important source of income for the city (Spawforth 1989, 196; Camia 2011, 41-76), and a stage of great relevance for both the athletes and the organizers. It is hardly surprising that the task of agonothete, though burdensome, attracted not only the members of the Corinthian elite, but also wealthy benefactors from other poleis.

As mentioned before, the new inhabitants of the colony resumed some of the ancient customs to shape their new identity and to show themselves as the legitimate successors of the old, illustrious polis, rather than a group of foreign ethnic origins, of dubious social status, and diverse cultural backgrounds (Pawlak 2013, 150-153).[14] The choice of the pine wreath as the Isthmian prize is one of the ancient customs that was deliberately reintroduced by the colonial elite to suggest continuity with Corinth's prestigious past.[15]

The Isthmian prizes are the subjects of one of Plutarch's *Table-talks* (Plut. *Quaest. conv.* 5.3, trans. Clement & Hoffleit 1969):

> *Why the pine was held sacred to Poseidon and Dionysus; originally the victor's crown at the Isthmia was of pine, later of celery, now again of pine.*

The learned accounts gathered by Plutarch and some scattered mentions in other literary sources allow us to trace modifications in the shape and quality of the Isthmian wreaths. According to all extant sources, the pine crown was the original prize for the Isthmian winners (Broneer 1962, 259-260). As for the other Panhellenic festivals, the choice of a specific plant was linked

Figure 2. The Attic victory list IG II² 3145. After The Metropolitan Museum of Art, New York (Rogers Fund 1959, inv. n. 59.11.19).

to the founding myth of the *agones* (Paus. 8.48.2-3): the Corinthian king Sysiphus organized the first athletic competition to honor his nephew Melicertes, upon finding his dead body under a pine tree on the Isthmus (Plut. *Quaest. conv.* 5.3.675-676; Paus. 2.1.3).[16] In the second quarter of the 5th century BC, the time of Pindar, the Isthmian winners had been given a wreath of *selinon,* i.e. celery (Broneer 1962, 259).[17] Plutarch's guests mention several reasons for this change: Plutarch himself accepts the idea that the Corinthians copied the celery crown of the Nemean Games out of rivalry (Broneer 1962, 259).

Finally, 'in recent times' the celery wreath was replaced again with the original pine crown. Neither Plutarch nor other sources give a more precise chronology or an explanation for this change. Broneer (1962, 259-263), comparing the literary accounts with the epigraphical data, suggested that the original pine wreath was reintroduced in the first half of the 2nd century BC, mentioning the Attic victory monument *IG* II² 3145 as evidence.

The document, now in the Metropolitan Museum of Art, is a large, fragmentary marble stele set up by a victorious athlete from Rhamnous, whose accomplishments are shown through the depictions of the prizes. Among them, there is a pine wreath inscribed with the name *Isthmia*.[18] According to the first editor, the inscription was produced in the first half of the 2nd century BC; the date was accepted by Broneer, who consequently placed the reintroduction of the pine crown in this period (Broneer 1962, 261). L. Robert was the first to voice his doubts regarding the date of the Attic inscription, attributing it to the 2nd century AD on palaeographical grounds (Robert & Robert 1960, 157; Robert & Robert 1961, 162; Robert & Robert 1963, 132). L. Robert's theory was confirmed

---

13 Pawlak 2013, 51 suggests that the return of the Games probably required the intervention of Roman authorities. See Braaden (1966, 326-329) for the involvement of L. Mummius in the choice of the administrators for the Nemean Games.

14 Pausanias (2.1.2) refers to the old inhabitants of Corinth as *Corinthii* and distinguishes them from the citizens of *Colonia Laus Iulia Corinthiensis,* implying the higher ethnic and social status of the former over the latter.

15 The revival of the Isthmian pine crown as 'instrument de l'hellénisation' is mentioned by Pièrart (1998, 106-107), accepting the traditional chronology established by Broneer (1962).

16 After his death, Melicertes became a god with the name of Palaemon and received a cult on the Isthmus; for the various versions of this myth See Pachey 2004, 135-180.

17 Pind. *Ol.* 13.33; Pind. *Nem.* 4.88; Pind. *Isthm.* 2.16; Pind. *Isthm.* 8.64

18 *IG* II² 3145: *in vaso oleario:* Παναθήναια; *in corona pinea:* Ἴσθμια; *in scuto:* ἐξ Ἄργους ἀσπίς; *in corona apii:* Νέμ[εα] / [– – – Ἀλε]ξάνδρου Ῥαμνούσιος ἀνέ[θηκε].

some years later by Follet, who identified the victorious athlete with Athenaios, son of Alexandros, of the deme of Rhamnous, cosmete of the ephebes in 145/6 AD (Follet 1976, 212).[19]

What this means is that there is no extant evidence that the Isthmian pine crown was reintroduced in the late Hellenistic period; its first known depiction is on the aforementioned coinage of the duovirs of 40 BC. Admittedly, the switch from celery to pine could have happened during the rather obscure 'Sikyonian phase'. In my opinion, however, the reintroduction of the original pine crown is a strategy of remembering that fits better within the cultural context of early Roman Corinth.[20] The plant linked the Panhellenic Games with their foundation myth. Its purpose was to present the Corinthians as the legitimate owners of the Isthmian festival. The choice of the original 'Corinthian' pine instead of the 'Nemean' celery allowed the Roman colonists to show themselves as the rightful 'heirs of Sisyphus' and increased the legitimacy of their claim over the presidency of the Isthmian Games. Unfortunately, it is not possible to identify the specific agents of this change; as mentioned earlier, the new citizens of Corinth were for the most part Roman freedmen of Greek origins (Millis 2010, 21-36), so that it is possible that they played a role in this and other recoveries of ancient Corinthian traditions. In sum, at the time of the establishment of the Roman colony of Corinth the city's prestigious past was carefully adapted to present needs.

4. The recovery of the Isthmian Games and Corinthian cults

The relocation of the Isthmian Games seems to be connected with a revival of two other important cult traditions. It seems that the new inhabitants of Corinth also revived the myth of Melicertes. According to Gebhard, the baby child had been the recipient of a cult since the Archaic period. The rituals were discontinued during the 'Sikyonian' and the 'urban' phases of the Games; they were reintroduced when the Isthmian festival returned on the Isthmus, around the middle of the 1st century AD (Gebhard 1993, 78-94). On the other hand, Pièrart suggests that the cult was introduced for the first time around the middle of the 1st century, because the exca-vations have found no certain proof of its existence in the previous periods (Piérart 1998, 103-109). It is hence difficult to ascertain whether the child hero was honoured with a cult during the 'urban Isthmian phase' and whether his myth played a role in shaping the landscape of early colonial Corinth.[21]

We know from the victory lists that the *Kaisareia* – a festival for Augustus, held together with the Isthmian Games – included a torch race at the latest during the Neronian period, and possibly already in 3 AD (Wiseman 2015, 230-231). A duoviral issue of the Augustan period depicts a torch on the obverse and an athlete with a palm branch on the reverse, which could refer to the same competition (*RPC* 1, 1135). Moreover, during the excavations of the gymnasium of Corinth three fragments of marble torches were found; this is important because the restoration of this building in the early Roman period is closely connected to the recovery of the Isthmian Games. There is no evidence that the *lampas* was performed to honour Melicertes, yet several coins of the 2nd century AD combine a torch or a torch bearer on the obverse with the baby hero on his dolphin on the reverse (Wiseman 2015, 231, n. 175). Therefore, it is possible that the torch race during the Caesarean Games was established for Melicertes, even though other gods cannot be excluded.

Another possible piece of evidence for a cult of Melicertes in the 'urban Isthmian phase' is a dedication from Kos, set up by the flute-player Ariston for Bacchus and Apollo; the man won a pine crown at the Isthmian Games 'upon playing fast for Palaemon' (Segre 1993, n. 234: 'καὶ πίτυν ἐξ Ἰσθμοῖο Παλαίμονι πυκνὰ λαλεῦσαν'). The inscription has been generically assigned to the 1st century BC on palaeographical grounds; the pine wreath dates it after the establishment of the Roman colony. The document seems to refer to musical contests that were held for the baby hero during the festival. It would be interesting to know whether the revival of these ancient Corinthian traditions had an influence on Roman culture at a broader level; Melicertes is widely featured in Augustan poetry (Pachey 2004, 135-180),[22] even though he was already known during the Republican period (Plaut. *Rud.* 160-162).

Another Corinthian hero closely related to the Isthmian Games is Bellerophon, who famously tamed Pegasus near the Peirene spring. In the Hellenistic period

---

19 Athenaios is mentioned in *IG* II² 1765, 2052, 2055 and *IG* III 74: he was *prytanis* of the Aiantis tribe, *xystarch* for life in Bythinia and *ieronikes* in an unknown discipline. See also Amandry 1980, 231-233 for the renaming of the Argive *Heraia* as ἡ ἐξ Ἄργους ἀσπίς at the end of the 1st century BC and during the Imperial period.

20 See also Blech 1982, 134 who suggests that the pine crown was reintroduced when the Games returned to Corinth even though he does not explain its meaning within the context of the Roman colony.

21 Roman Corinth certainly preserved the memory of king Sisyphus, uncle of Melicertes and founder of the Isthmian Games, whose ancient palace still stood on top of Acrocorinth during the Augustan period (Strab. 8.6.21); however, there is no proof that the acropolis was integrated in the celebration of the Isthmian Games. For the grave of Sisyphus in the sanctuary of Poseidon on the Isthmus, see Paus. 2.2.

22 On the founding of Roman colonies and their influence on Augustan literature, see Gros 1990, 548-549.

it was customary for the Isthmian victors to drink from the renowned source (Robinson 2011, 35). This 'Isthmian toast' is depicted on a Julio-Claudian silver cup, found in Berthouville (France): a naked athlete, wearing a pine crown and holding a palm branch, approaches the personified Peirene spring (Robinson 2011, 32-34; Robinson 2013, 356-357).[23] The pine crown places the episode in contemporary Corinth and suggests that the drinking ritual was still known and possibly performed during the Roman period.

In sum, the return of the Isthmian Games from Sikyon and the recovery of these ancient Corinthian memories played an important part in the 'hellenization' of early Roman Corinth, and they were instrumental in showing the continuity between the ancient polis and the new colony.[24] However, after Actium it became the only Panhellenic festival to be associated with the Caesarean Games, thus creating a link between the Greek prestigious tradition and the Roman *princeps* (Kantirea 2007, 184-187; Pawlak 2013, 151; Farrington 2012, 29). The first known mention of this festival is an honorary statue set up by a Corinthian tribe for M. Antonius Aristokrates, agonothete of the Isthmian and Caesarean Games.[25] Aristokrates was an Argive rhetor, *duovir* in the Roman colony of Dyme in 39-36 BC (*RPC* I, 1285) and a well-known supporter of Marc Antony, who probably gave him Roman citizenship. For Aristokrates the *agonothesia* of the Isthmian and Caesarean Games was not only a way to increase his prestige locally, but also a stage to display his allegiance to the new Augustan regime (Balzat & Millis 2013, 663-664). The inscription was set up before the end of the 1st century BC, indicating that the Caesarean Games were soon added to the Panhellenic festival (Balzat & Millis 2013, 663-664). The establishment of this new competition was probably a local initiative (Kantirea 2007, 185), ratified by the Roman authorities, in order to please the *princeps,* and it is tempting to link its introduction to M. Antonius Aristokrates himself.[26]

5. The 'urban Isthmian Games' and the topography of early Roman Corinth

Even though the idea of an 'urban Isthmian phase' is generally accepted, the possible venues for the various competitions have been discussed only in recent times. In 29 BC, Strabo describes the sanctuary of Poseidon on the Isthmus as the place 'where the Corinthians used to celebrate the Isthmian Games' (trans. Jones 1924), suggesting that during this period the Panhellenic festival was held elsewhere (Strab. 8.6.22). A fragmentary statue base of Cn. Cornelius Pulcher mentions that he was the first agonothete '*qui Isthmia ad Isthmum egit*' around the middle of the 1st century AD.[27] The excavations at Isthmia confirm that the sanctuary was restored in that period, when ritual activities were resumed (Gebhard 1993, 82-89; Marty 1993, 117-121). This has led many scholars to conclude that when Corinth recovered the presidency of the Isthmian festival, the competitions were held in the city centre and not on the Isthmus (Gebhard 1993, 82).[28] It is not known why the inhabitants of Corinth did not refurbish the sanctuary of Poseidon at an earlier date; it is possible that the large expenses for the settlement of the colony and for the restorations of the public buildings discouraged them from undertaking further projects for the sanctuary of Poseidon.

The victory catalogue of 3 AD included athletic, equestrian and musical competitions, implying the presence of buildings or provisional structures to host them; another required feature was an altar for Poseidon.[29] Moreover, the city had to provide accommodation for the athletes and for the *theoroi*, as well as for the public in attendance. Panhellenic festivals were a valuable source of income, since they attracted large crowds who required lodgings, food and water, hygienic facilities and entertainments (Borimir 2001, 32-67). Unfortunately, only a few of these activities can be associated with known spaces or buildings in Corinth.

---

23 Robinson also suggests (Robinson 2011, 207-209) that the later marble revetment of the Peirene, sponsored by Antonius Sospes and his family (*Corinth* VIII 3, n. 170), was related to the *agonothesia* of the Isthmian Games that Sospes exceptionally held three times.

24 Significantly, the victory lists of the Isthmian Games are written in Greek whereas the vast majority of the public inscriptions are in Latin; see Kent 1966, 18; Millis 2010, 23-24; for a different opinion, see Kantirea 2007, 186 who suggests that the use of Greek is related to the large number of athletes and visitors from Asia Minor, who would have been less familiar with Latin.

25 *Corinth* I-1973-4: M̲[---] Antonio / <A>ristocratę / agonothę(te) Isthmion / et Cae[sa]reon tribus / Iulia.

26 See C. Sosius, another partisan of Marc Antony who was pardoned by Augustus and showed his allegiance to the *princeps* by restoring the temple of Apollo Medicus, closely related to the *gens* Iulia.

---

27 Kent 1966, n. 153. The inscription is broken in the section mentioning the agonothete's name; it has been restored as L. Castricius Regulus (25 AD) in the *editio princeps* by Kent and as Cn. Publicius Regulus (*duovir* in 50/51 AD) by Gebhard 1993, 87. Kajava 2002, 168-176 proposes Gn. Cornelius Pulcher (around 43 AD); the restitution is further improved by Camia & Kantirea 2008, 386.

28 Gebhard 1993, 83 also suggests that the Caesarean Games were held in Corinth even after the return of the Isthmian Games to the sanctuary of Poseidon.

29 The only inscription related to Poseidon/Neptunus are *Corinth* VIII 2 nn. 2-3 (Babbius' Fountain) and *Corinth* VIII 3, n. 156 (honorary statue for *Aulus Arrius Proculus,* priest of Neptunus Augustus and agonothete of the Isthmian and Caesarean Games, 39 AD); in the latter case, there is no evidence that the cult of Neptunus Augustus was related to the god of the Isthmus. For the cult of this god in Corinth see also Dubbini 2011, 152-156.

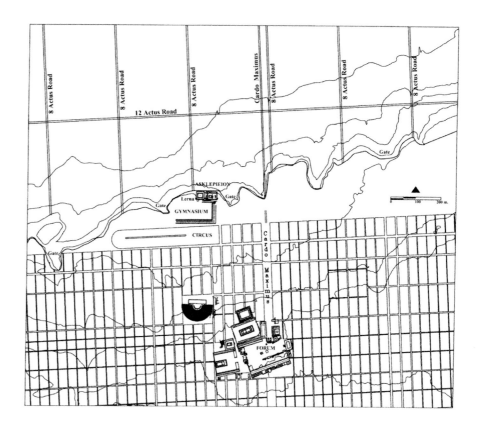

Figure 3. Plan of Corinth with the gymnasium area on N. After Romano 2003, 289.

The theatre, hastily repaired in the early years of the Roman colony, was probably used for the musical (and later poetic) contests (Gebhard 1993, 82-89). During its excavations, a fragmentary head of a male adult wearing a pine crown dated to the Augustan period was found; the statue could represent either an Isthmian official or an Isthmian victor (Sturgeon 2004, 133-137). D.G. Romano has suggested that the recently discovered Augustan circus, in the northern area of the city, hosted the equestrian events of the Panhellenic Games (Romano 2005, 608-609). The use of a circus, a quintessentially 'Roman' building (Dodge 2008, 133-146), to house a Greek Panhellenic contest would be quite interesting; however, the existence of a stadium in another area of the city cannot be ruled out. As for the athletic competitions, B. A. Robinson proposes that the athletic competitions took place in the Roman Forum (Robinson 2013, 356-357).[30] The northern part of this area was occupied by a dromos from the 5th century BC until the sack of Corinth; the racetrack was probably used for the ritual agones that accompanied the various stages of male civic integration (Dubbini 2011, 212). Excavations in this area brought to light some fragmentary Hellenistic inscriptions related to the Isthmian games, probably honorary statues for local athletes that stood along the dromos (*Corinth* VIII.I 790; *Corinth* I-1969-3).[31] However, the entire Forum area was paved during the Augustan period (Laird 2010, 84), making the surface unsuitable for athletic purposes.

On the northern edge of the city centre stood the *archaion gymnasion* mentioned by Pausanias (Paus. 2.4.5; Wiseman 2015, 194-195).[32] It was a large open court surrounded by stoai on three sides and provided with draining systems; the excavations were limited to a small and badly preserved area. The few architectural remains that were

---

30   For the use of *fora* for games during the late Republican period, see Vitr. *De arch.* 5.1-2.
31   Williams 1970, 38-39 suggests that the dromos was also used as a training area for local athletes (a similar space for equestrian activities was in the agora of Elis, according to Paus. 6.24.2). For the structures see also Romano 1993, 86-90.
32   For an alternative location see Williams 2013, 22-24, who suggests that the ancient gymnasium stood in the area immediately north of the theatre.

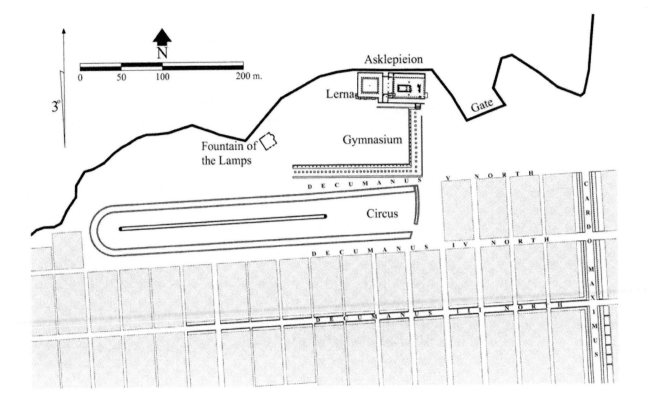

Figure 4. Plan of the 'ancient gymnasium'. After Romano 2005, 603 (courtesy of the Trustees of the American School of Classical Studies at Athens).

discovered were dated between the end of the 1st century AD and the beginning of the 2nd century AD (Wiseman 1967, 27-28; Wiseman 1967b, 408-409; Wiseman 2015, 194-195).

Even though the investigations failed to bring to light previous phases, there are indications that the area was used as an athletic facility already at the end of the 1st century BC. Thus the gymnasium is surrounded by other buildings that underwent restorations or were rebuilt from the ground after the foundation of the Roman colony: on its northern side the Asklepieion (Melfi 2014, 747-776), the Fountain of Lerna and the Fountain of the Lamps (Wiseman 1972, 5), the circus on its south (Romano 2005, 585-611) and a Hellenistic *balaneion* on the west side (Wiseman 1972, 9-16). It would be quite unusual that such a large space in the middle of a crowded area was left unused until the end of the 1st century AD. Moreover, as Wiseman suggests, the springs and the bath were restored to provide the athletes with water to drink and for hygienic purposes in this period (Wiseman 2015, 196-197). Last but not least, several herms inscribed with Isthmian victory lists were found in this area, including the already mentioned inscription of 3 AD.[33] Even though herms could also be displayed in other public contexts, such as baths, theatres or circuses (Wrede 1985, 32-49), it is quite probable that these were originally set up in the gymnasium (Wiseman 2015, 199-200). Pausanias reports that the lists of the *Olympionikai* in the gymnasium of Elis spurred the local youth to train even harder, in order to achieve the same results as the famous victors of the past (Paus. 6.6.3); the Isthmian herms in the gymnasium of Corinth probably played a similar role.

It can be suggested that the area of the *archaion gymnasion* was not abandoned during the early years of the Roman colony: it probably featured structures used by the local

---

33   *Corinth* VIII.1, n. 14 (3 AD); *Corinth* VIII.1, n. 15 (from the gymnasium area; end of the II century AD); *Corinth* VIII.3, n. 228 (from the Lerna fountain); Corinth I-1970-39 (from the *balaneion;* late Julio-Claudian period; on this inscription, see *cf.* now Wiseman 2015).

youth for their daily trainings[34] as well as by the athletes during the festivals (Wiseman 2015, 196-197). An early restoration of the archaic gymnasium in the newly established Roman colony could have been prompted by the return of the Isthmian Games and the need of adequate buildings to host the events.[35]

5. Conclusions

Shortly after its establishment as a Roman colony, Corinth recovered its prestigious Isthmian Games. The new Roman citizens revived some of the festival's ancient or even long-lost traditions to create a sense of continuity between the present and the city's illustrious past. For example, they replaced the 'Nemean' crown of celery with the original 'Corinthian' pine wreath, that provided a link with the founding myth of the Isthmian Games; they reintroduced torch-races and musical competitions for Melicertes and the 'toast' from the Peirene Spring for the Isthmian victors. The revival of these memories allowed the new Roman colonists to show the continuity between the ancient and the present Panhellenic festival and reinforced their claims over its prestigious *agonothesia*. Even though it is difficult to ascertain the impact of the Isthmian Games on early Corinth's landscape, it can be suggested that they prompted the restoration of the *archaion gymnasion* and of the surrounding area. These strategies of remembering show that early Roman Corinth was not an exact copy of Rome on provincial soil, as previously assumed; from the very beginning its new inhabitants revived ancient myths and cultural traditions and used them to shape their new identity as Roman citizens (mostly of Greek libertine origins) of Corinth.

Acknowledgements

I would like to thank the organizers of the workshop for inviting me, all those in attendance for the useful suggestions, and the editors for their invaluable remarks. I would also like to thank Prof. E. Lippolis and Prof. D. Palombi, who supervised my thesis on early Roman Corinth, for their advice; Dr. D. Russo for sending me an otherwise inaccessible article, and Dr. L. Zamboni for his patience and support. None of the aforementioned is responsible for the author's opinions or mistakes.

References

Alcock, S.E. 1993. *Graecia Capta. The landscapes of Roman Greece*. Cambridge.

Amandry, M. 1988. *Le monnayage des duovirs corinthiens, BCH Supplément XV*, Paris.

Amandry, P. 1980. Sur les concours argiens. In: *Études argiennes, BCH Supplément VI*, Athènes, 211-253.

Balzat, J.S. & B. Millis 2013. M. Antonius Aristocrates: Provincial Involvement with Roman Power in the Late 1st Century BC, *Hesperia* 81, 651-672.

Blech, M. 1982. *Studien zum Kranz bei den Griechen*. Berlin.

Borimir, J. 2001. Isthmian amusements, *CIIre* 8, 32-67.

Bradeen, D. 1966. Inscriptions from Nemea, *Hesperia* 35, 320-330.

Broneer, O. 1962. The Isthmian victory crown, *AJA* 66, 259-263.

Camia, F. 2011. Spending on the *agones:* the financing of festivals in the cities of Roman Greece, *Tyche* 26, 41-76.

Camia, F. & M. Kantirea 2008. The imperial cult in the Peloponnese. In: A.D. Rizakis & C. Lepenioti (eds), *Roman Peloponnese. Vol. 3. Society, Economy and Culture Under the*

---

34 It is uncertain whether the Roman colony of Corinth also established the *ephebeia;* the only hint of its existence is a fleeting remark of Epictetus about an ephebarch (Arr. *Epict. diss.* 3.1.34).

35 A similar pattern can be found in Nikopolis, where the gymnasium was built in the Augustan period in relationship with the establishment of the *Aktia* (Strab. 7.7.6).

Roman Empire: Continuity and Innovation, Meletemata 63, Athens, 375-406.

Camia, F. & Rizakis, A. 2008. Magistrati municipali e svolgimento delle carriere nelle colonie romane della provincia d'Acaia. In: C. Berrendoner, M. Cébeillac-Gervasoni & L. Lamoine (eds), *Le quotidien municipal dans l'Occident romain,* Paris, 233-245.

Clement, P.A. & Hoffleit, H.B. 1969. *Plutarch. Moralia, Volume VIII: Table-Talk, Books 1-6. Loeb Classical Library 424.* Cambridge, MA.

Di Napoli, V. 2014. *Teatri della Grecia romana: forma, decorazione, funzioni,* Atene.

Dodge, H. 2008. Circuses in the Roman east: a reappraisal. In: J. Nelis-Clément & J.M. Roddaz (eds), *Le cirque romain et son image,* Bordeaux, 133-146.

Dubbini, R. 2011. *Dei nello spazio degli uomini: i culti dell'agora e la costruzione di Corinto arcaica,* Roma.

Farrington, A. 2012. *Isthmionikai. A catalogue of Isthmian victors,* Hildesheim.

Ferrary, J.L. 1988. *Philhellénisme et impérialisme: aspects idéologiques de la conquête romaine du monde hellénistique, de la seconde guerre de Macédoine à la guerre contre Mithridate.* Rome.

Gebhard, E.R. 1993. The Isthmian Games and the sanctuary of Poseidon in the Early Empire. In: T.E. Gregory (ed), *The Corinthia in the Roman Period: including the papers given at a symposium held at the Ohio State University on 7-9 March, 1991, JRA Supplement VIII,* Ann Arbor, 78-94.

Gebhard, E. & Dickie, M.W. 2003. The view from the Isthmus ca 200 to 44 BC. In: C.K. Williams II & N. Bookidis (eds), *Corinth XX: the Centenary 1896-1996,* Princeton, 261-278.

Gros, P. 1990. Le premier urbanisme de *Colonia Iulia Carthago.* Mythes et réalités d'une fondation césaro-augustéenne. In: *L'Afrique dans l'Occident romain (Ier siècle av. J.C.-IVe siècle ap. J.C.): actes du colloque organisé par l'École française de Rome sous le patronage de l'Institut national d'Archéologie et d'art de Tunis (Rome, 3-5 décembre 1987). Publications de l'École française de Rome 134,* Rome, 547-570.

James, S.A. 2014a. Bridging the gap: local pottery production in Corinth, 146-44 BC. In: P. Guldager Bilde & M.L. Lawall (eds), *Pottery, people and places: study and interpretation of Late Hellenistic pottery,* Aarhus, 47-63.

James, S. A. 2014b. The last of the Corinthians? Society and settlements from 146 to 44 BC. In: S. J. Friesen, S.A. James & D. Schowalther (eds), *Corinth in contrast: studies in inequality,* Leiden, 17-37.

Kajava, M. 2002. When did the Isthmian games return to the Isthmus? (Rereading Corinth 8. 3. 153), *CP* 97.2, 168-178.

Kantirea, M. 2007. *Les dieux et les dieux augustes. Le culte impérial en Grèce sous les Julio-claudiens et les Flaviens. Études épigraphiques et archéologiques,* Athènes.

Kent, J.H. 1966. *Corinth VIII, Pt. 3: The Inscriptions, 1926-1950,* Princeton.

Laird, M. L. 2010. The emperor in a Roman town: the base of the Augustales in the Forum at Corinth. In: S.J. Friesen, D. Schowalter & J. Walters (eds), *Corinth in context: comparative studies on religion and society,* Leiden, 67-116.

Lolos, Y. 2011. *Land of Sikyon: archaeology and history of a Greek city-state,* Princeton.

Melfi, M. 2014. Religion and Society in Early Roman Corinth: a Forgotten Coin Hoard and the Sanctuary of Asklepios, *Hesperia* 83, 747-776.

Meritt, B.D. 1931. *Corinth VIII, Pt. 1: Greek Inscriptions, 1896-1927,* Cambridge, MA.

Millis, B. W. 2010. The social and ethnic origins of the colonists in early Roman Corinth. In: S.J. Friesen, D. Schowalter & J. Walters (eds), *Corinth in context: comparative studies on religion and society,* Leiden, 13-35.

Mylonopoulos, J. 2003. *Heiligtümer und Kulte des Poseidon auf der Peloponnes,* Liège.

Pachey, C.O. 2004. *Baby and child heroes in ancient Greece,* Urbana.

Papageorgiadou-Bani, H. 2004. *The numismatic iconography of the Roman colonies in Greece. Local spirit and the expression of imperial policy,* Athens.

Pawlak, P. 2013. Corinth after 44 a.C.: ethnical and cultural changes, *Electrum* 20, 143-162.

Pièrart, M. 1998. Panthéon et hellénisation dans la colonie romaine de Corinthe: la redécouverte du culte de Palaimon à l'Isthme, *Kernos* 11, 85-109.

Rizakis, A. 1997. Roman colonies in the province of *Achaia.* Territories, land and population. In: S.E. Alcock (ed), *The early Roman empire in the East.* Oxford, 15-36.

Rizakis, A. 2001. La constitution des élites municipales dans les colonies romaines de la province d'Achaïe. In: O. Salomies (ed.), *The Greek East in the Roman context : proceedings of a colloquium organised by The Finnish Institute at Athens, May 21 and 22, 1999. PMFIA VII,* Helsinki, 37-49.

Robinson, B.A. 2013. Playing in the sun: hydraulic architecture and imperial display in imperial Corinth, *Hesperia* 82, 341-384.

Robert, J. & Robert L. 1960. Bulletin épigraphique. *REG* 73, 134-133.

Robert, J. & Robert L. 1961. Bulletin épigraphique. *REG* 74, 119-268.

Robert, J. & Robert L. 1963. Bulletin épigraphique. *REG* 76, 121-192.

Romano, D.G. 2005. A Roman circus at Corinth, *Hesperia* 74, 585-611.

Sassu, R. 2014. *Hiera chremata. Il ruolo del santuario nell'economia della polis,* Roma.

Segre, M. 1993. *Iscrizioni di Kos, vol. 1. Monografie della Scuola Archeologica di Atene e delle Missioni Italiane in Oriente VI.* Roma.

Simpson, G. 2016. *Rome spread its wings: territorial expansion between the Punic wars,* Barnsley.

Spawforth, A.J.S. 1989. Agonistic festivals in Roman Greece. In: S. Walker & A. Cameron (eds), *The Greek renaissance in the Roman Empire: papers from the tenth British Museum Classical Colloquium. BICS Supplement LV,* London, 193-197.

Spawforth, A. J. S. 1994. Corinth, Argos, and the Imperial Cult: Pseudo-Julian, Letters 198, *Hesperia* 63, 211-232.

Spawforth, A.J.S. 1996. Roman Corinth: The Formation of a Colonial Elite. In: A.D. Rizakis (ed.), *Roman Onomastics in the Greek East: Social and Political Aspects. Proceedings of the International Colloquium on Roman Onomastics Athens, 7-9 September 1993,* Athens, 167-182.

Sturgeon, M.C. 2004. *Corinth IX, Pt. 3: Sculpture: the assemblage from the theater,* Ann Arbor.

Wacker, C. 1996. *Das Gymnasion in Olympia: Geschichte und Funktion,* Würzburg.

Walbank, M.E.H. 1997. The Foundation and Planning of Early Roman Corinth, *JRA* 10, 95-130.

Williams, C.K. 2013. In Corinth with Pausanias as a guide. In: W.D. Niemeier (ed.), *The Corinthia and the northeast Peloponnese: topography and history from prehistoric times until the end of antiquity,* München, 11-25.

Wiseman, J.R 1967. Excavations at Corinth. The gymnasium area. 1965, *Hesperia* 36, 13-41.

Wiseman, J.R. 1969. Excavations at Corinth. The gymnasium area.1967-1968, *Hesperia* 38, 64-106.

Wiseman, J.R. 1972. Excavations at Corinth. The gymnasium area, *Hesperia* 41, 1-42.

Wiseman, J.R. 1979. Corinth and Rome I: 228 BC-267 AD. In: *ANRW II 7.1,* Berlin, 438-548.

Wiseman, J.R. 2015. Agonistic festivals, victors and officials in the time of Nero: an inscribed herm from the gymnasium area of Corinth. In: E.R. Gebhard & T.E. Gregory (eds), *Bridge of the untiring sea: the Corinthian Isthmus from Prehistory to Late Antiquity, Hesperia Supplement* XLVIII, Athens, 193-226.

Woolf, G. 1998. *Becoming Roman: the origin of provincial civilization in Gaul,* Cambridge.

Wrede, H. 1985. *Die antike Herme,* Mainz am Rhein.

PART III

Honouring Tradition

Heroes of Their Times. Intra-Mural Burials in the Urban Memorial Landscapes of the Roman Peloponnese

Johannes Fouquet

Abstract

The practice of honouring civic benefactors in the public space of the city was a phenomenon that developed into a decisive characteristic of Greek cities from the late Classical period onwards. The *euergetai* usually were awarded with the erection of an honorary statue, whereas in rare cases they were granted the extraordinary right to be buried inside the city boundaries. When engaging with these honorary monuments recent scholarship has commonly adopted the analytical category of 'space', with a particular focus on visual and performative aspects. By the (re)contextualization of these monuments in the architecturally framed space of the city criteria like materiality, visibility or proximity to public thoroughfares are considered as indicators of social relevance. In contrast, this article aims to shift the focus from the perception of space only as a physical entity to a conceptualization that includes its function as a medium of collective memory condensed into urban memorial landscapes. This is argued in the case of three intra-mural burials from Roman Messene, Mantineia and Argos.

Keywords: burials, honorary practices, memorial topographies, Roman Peloponnese

1. Introduction

On the Ides of March of the year 44 BC Caesar was slain, the dictator was dead. The Romans, however, did not celebrate his murderers as restorers of *libertas* as much as the conspirators had hoped. When public opinion eventually turned against M. Iunius Brutus and C. Cassius Longinus, the leaders of the conspiracy, they found themselves forced to flee to the eastern Mediterranean. How different was the reception that they experienced, according to Cassius Dio, in Athens! It culminated in the vow by the Athenian demos to set up two bronze statues for the murderers on the agora, close to the famous statue group of the Tyrannicides. Through their deed the two Roman senators had become emulators of Harmodios and Aristogeiton, as Cassius Dio explains.[1] And

---

1   Cass. Dio 47.20.4; Plut. *Brut.* 24.1. The Tyrannicides supposedly stood on the north side of the Athenian Agora, while the exact position is uncertain, see Wycherley 1957, 93-98.

in: Dijkstra, T.M., I.N.I. Kuin, M. Moser & D. Weidgenannt (eds) 2017. *Strategies of Remembering in Greece under Rome (100 BC - 100 AD)*, Leiden (Sidestone Press).

indeed, the fragment of a statue base for Brutus found in the agora seems to confirm Dio's narrative.[2]

How exceptional this event must have been is clarified by two Athenian honorary inscriptions from the early Hellenistic period. Both texts mention the provision that the accompanying statues could be placed anywhere on the agora, except near the Tyrannicides.[3] Apparently, the immediate area around this *lieu de mémoire* of the Athenian democracy was intentionally kept free from other monuments.[4] From a pragmatic perspective, this public conduct was aimed at ensuring the visibility of the monument that would otherwise have been cluttered up by other statues. More importantly, however, it controlled or rather prevented an appropriation of the in terms of social capital highly desirable prominence inherent to this focal point of civic identity.[5] The Tyrannicides remained an exclusive *topos epiphanestatos* of the Athenian memorial topography.

Archaeological research on the public practice of honouring civic benefactors, a decisive feature of Greek city life since the 4th century BC, has traditionally been guided by a physical conception of space. By this methodological approach, i.e. the (re)contextualisation of honorific monuments in the built space of the cities, criteria like materiality and visibility have been – and this needs to be stressed – quite rightly acknowledged as indicators of prestige and social status.[6] However, as the case of the Tyrannicides has highlighted, a complementary understanding of space as an ideational entity that was conceptualised by oral and literal interpretation into mental maps of remembrance and collective civic identity seems to provide further insights into the public honorary practices of the Greek cities.[7] In this conceptual

framework, spatial proximity must not only be considered as an indicator of semantic connotation, but also, according to Pierre Bourdieu, as symbolic profit of distinction in the contested physical and social space.[8]

In what follows, the previous considerations will be applied to a selected group of intra-mural burials on the Roman Peloponnese. Even though this phenomenon of Greek memorial culture experienced a distinct increase since the Hellenistic period, the actual number of these burials in the Greek motherland and in particular on the Peloponnese during the Roman period is considerably smaller than for example in contemporary Asia Minor.[9] It is safe to assume that alongside the actual monument, the benefactors were usually honoured with a public cult as well that perpetuated their remembrance in a way similar to the civic heroes of the mythical past.[10] Despite this per se close relation with memorial topography, it is remarkable that intra-mural burials have so far been analysed primarily on the basis of a physical conception of space. The conclusion reached by Catharina Flämig in her study of funerary architecture in Roman Greece, that all of the intra-mural burials distinguished themselves by a conspicuous setting in the urban fabric, is, in the end, hardly surprising.[11] In some cases this setting might have been related to the already mentioned cultic and ritual performances at the grave, *e.g. pompai* or funeral games as attested by a Late Hellenistic inscription for a civic benefactor in the stadium of Messene.[12] Beyond this point of view, however, there is more to be said about intra-mural burials and the way they were entangled in urban memorial topographies.

2. A heroon in the gymnasium of Messene
A paradigmatic example for the entanglement of physical and memorial spaces is one of the several heroa in the gymnasium of Messene.[13] This often discussed building was constructed on the south end of the stadium on a

---

2   *SEG* 17.75; *cf.* Krumeich & Witschel 2009, 208-209; Ma 2013, 104.

3   *IG* II² 450, frg. b l. 11-12: πλὴν παρ᾽ Ἁρμόδιον καὶ Ἀριστογείτον[α]; *IG* II² 646.

4   It is thus not surprising that only Antigonus Monophthalmus and Demetrius Poliorcetes, the apostrophied *soteres* of Athens, were accorded this honour before the end of the 4th century BC, see Diod. Sic. 20.46. Krumeich & Witschel 2009, 208 with n. 141 speculate about the possibility that a statue of Sulla was placed as well near the Tyrannicides in the early 1st century BC. On the role of the Tyrannicides in Sullan ideology in Athens see also Kuin *this volume*.

5   The concepts of 'isolation' and 'prominence' regarding the spatial conception of honorary statues are discussed by Ma 2013, 113-118. On civic identity in analogy to approaches of urban sociology to understand cities as autonomous cultural phenomena see Löw 2008, esp. 73-87, 90-91; Zimmermann 2015.

6   See, however, Lafond 2006, 195-202; Krumeich & Witschel 2009 for a more comprehensive approach. *Cf.* Bourdieu 1991, 26-28 for the concept of 'angeeigneter physischer Raum' as indicator of social status.

7   Still fundamental: Nora 1984. For the semantic relation of social and physical space: Bourdieu 1991, esp. 28-29.

8   Bourdieu 1991, 31. Ma 2013, 118-121 concerning 'proximity' as 'metaphor for abstract relationship' (119).

9   Schörner 2007; Flämig 2007, 19-24; for the Hellenistic period most recently Fröhlich 2013, esp. 299 with additions to the incomplete catalogues of Schörner and Flämig.

10 Schörner 2007, 130-138; but methodological caveat by Fröhlich 2013, 236. See Lafond 2006 on urban memorial topographies in the cities of the Roman Peloponnese.

11 Flämig 2007, 20. *Cf.* the topographical analysis by Schörner 2007, 20-37 and the conclusion reached by Cormack 2004, 45: 'burial in privileged, prestigious space within the fabric of the city'.

12 *IG* V,1 1427; *cf.* Themelis 2000, 168-170; Müth 2007, 122-123. On cultic and ritual performances related to heroa in general: Schörner 2007, 130-138.

13 Besides the building in question all other heroa are of Hellenistic date: Themelis 2000, 114-136; Müth 2007, 110-119; Fröhlich 2013, 227-228, 297-298.

more than 7 m tall podium that was bonded into the outer face of the older city wall (fig. 1-2). The tomb with a length of 11.6 m and a width of 7.44 m was built of local limestone and has been reconstructed as a tetrastyle prostylos in plan with a Doric order (fig. 3). Individual elements of the architecture and the architectural decoration betray Hellenistic influences.[14] Apart from workshop traditions, especially the choice of the Doric order might be interpreted as an intentional retrospective emphasis, not at least because the actual construction date is much later: several grave stelai of the 1st century BC to the 1st century AD that were reused in the podium and, in particular, a stratigraphically relevant Neronian coin of 68 AD provide evidence for a secure *terminus post quem*.[15] Furthermore, a sarcophagus of the middle 2nd century AD found among the ruined structure suggests that it was used as a burial place by this period at the latest.[16]

The question of who was buried in this building has already been extensively discussed in research. There are sound arguments for an identification with the influential Messenian family of the Saithidai (yet epigraphically not attested before the Late Hellenistic period), not least because Pausanias mentions a hero cult for one of their members in the gymnasium.[17] The honorand is commonly identified with Tiberius Claudius Saethidas Caelianus who in his career under Trajan and Antoninus Pius served as *helladarches* of the Achaean *koinon* and *archiereus* of the Imperial cult, in addition to being an eminent civic benefactor.[18] As a consequence, the heroon must probably be dated to the middle of the 2nd century AD, as has been convincingly suggested before by Nino Luraghi.[19]

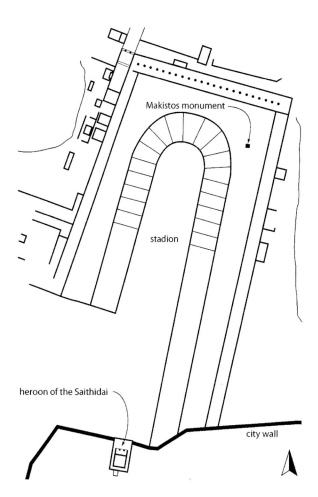

Figure 1. The gymnasium of Messene, redrawn after: P. Themelis, Ἀνασκαφή Μεσσήνης, Prakt 2007, fig. 1.

---

14 Cooper 1999; *cf.* Themelis 2000, 102-113; Flämig 2007, 175-176 no. 76; Müth 2007, 119-124; Schörner 2007, 243-245 cat. A 20. On the burial type of the 'temple grave' in Roman Greece: Flämig 2007, 45-51 concluding that it was common only in the 2nd century AD.

15 On the grave stelai: Themelis 2000, 108. The stratigraphical investigations on the east side of the podium carried out by Frederick A. Cooper and Pieter Broucke are unpublished so far. The coin was found in a layer of limestone chips that was directly related to the building process at the heroon.

16 Themelis 2000, 107; Flämig 2007, 176; Schörner 2007, 244.

17 Paus. 4.32.2: Αἰθίδαν δὲ ἐμαυτοῦ πρεσβύτερον ὄντα εὕρισκον, γενομένῳ δὲ οἱ χρήμασιν οὐκ ἀδυνάτῳ τιμαὶ παρὰ Μεσσηνίων ὑπάρχουσιν ἅτε ἥρωι. On the emendation of (S)aethidas: Themelis 2000, 108-109; Baldassarra 2007, 36 with n. 58; Luraghi 2008, 194. More reluctant Flämig 2007, 176; Müth 2007, 121-122. The alternative identification as heroon of Aristomenes (see below) proposed by Cooper 1999, 195-196 has been persuasively refuted by Themelis 2000, 110-112; Müth 2007, 123-124. On the family of the Saithidai: Baldassarra 2007, 36-42 (with relevant literature); Luraghi 2008, 191-194.

18 On Caelianus see Rizakis *et al.* 2004, 521-522 no. 156.

19 Luraghi 2008, 197. In favor of a Neronian dating now Themelis 2013, 143.

So much for the heroon itself. Of far more interest to this article is the description by Pausanias following his comments on the hero cult of (S)aithidas. In the vicinity (ἐνθαῦτα) he noticed another heroon, where Aristomenes, the legendary paragon of Messenian liberty in the wars against Sparta, was buried.[20] The monument, which according to Pausanias consisted of a column above the actual grave, has not been securely identified so far.[21] In spite of the lack of confirming evidence, Frederick Cooper's assumption is still appealing, that the heroon of Aristomenes might have acted as an off-centre turning post in the stadium.[22] A striking spatial and visual relation with

---

20 Paus. 4.32.3: καὶ Ἀριστομένους δὲ μνῆμά ἐστιν ἐνταῦθα. On Aristomenes: Ogden 2004, esp. 33-36; *cf.* Lafond 2006, 188-190.

21 See Müth 2007, 126. Themelis 2000, 28-40 identified the heroon of Aristomenes with the so-called heroon K4 that is located outside the gymnasium complex and close to its propylon.

22 Cooper 1999, 197 who, however, considered this as an indication that the heroon of the Saithidai has to be identified with the heroon of Aristomenes. On turning posts in Greek stadia: Miller 1980, esp. 159-160.

Figure 2. The restored podium of the heroon and the Messenian city wall (photo author).

Figure 3. The restored heroon, view from north (photo author).

this monument could, after all, be the explanation for the unconventional setting of the heroon of the Saithidai that is located significantly off the axis of the stadium (fig. 1).

Be that as it may, it is certainly no accident that Pausanias' description suggests a certain proximity between the two monuments. While the Saithidai could apparently enjoy the prominence of Aristomenes' tomb, this claim to Messene's civic identity and its myth-historical past certainly must have been in some way or other a matter of contention. Indeed, there was another family of the Messenian elite who definitely traced back their origins to this heroic figure and may well have set up a statue for its putative ancestor in the 2nd-3rd century AD.[23] In the case of the Saithidai the juxtaposition evidently reinforced a self-representation of the family that was based on military virtue in the interest of the city. This claim finds its expression in the sculptural decoration of the heroon itself. Attached to its pediment was an *imago clipeata* with the bust of a male figure wearing a cuirass (fig. 4) whose identification, not at least due to the missing head, remains open to speculation.[24] It might represent Caelianus himself or even one of his two grandsons, Tiberius Claudius Saithidas Caelianus (II) and Tiberius Claudius Frontinus Niceratus who served as military tribunes in the Roman legions during the Antonine period.[25] In any case, in view of general trends in the funerary sculpture of Roman Greece where aspects of civil life seem to have prevailed, this is a rather unusual iconography, while the emphasis on and the remembrance of military virtue are common topoi in the Hellenistic gymnasium.[26] And in Messene, the monument for the fallen in the battle of Makistos of the 3rd century BC, which stood in front of the east portico of the gymnasium, is perfectly in line with this.[27] While certain military aspects of the *ephebeia* seem to have lasted into the Roman period, the contemporary elite discourses that valued the renowned military deeds of

Figure 4. Imago clipeata with male figure in cuirass, after: Themelis 2000, 106 fig. 91.

the classical Greek past might have been another driving force behind the demonstration of military prowess by the Saithidai.[28]

In this respect, it is very remarkable how the claim of a normative behaviour was reinforced by family remembrance. According to Pausanias, oral tradition identified the image on a stele that must have stood close to the heroon either with the honoured benefactor himself or with one of his ancestors, (S)aithidas the Elder, who had successfully defended Messene against a Macedonian attack in 214 BC.[29] Without any clear evidence it is impossible to reconstruct whether or not this conflation of two family members was a popular attribution or rather intentionally emphasized, *e.g.* by an inscription on the stele. The setting of the heroon on the city walls that (S)aithidas the Elder had defended might, however, point to the latter, as Luraghi has argued.[30] For the public image of the family it probably made no difference at all in the end.[31]

---

23   On this Messenian family: Baldassarra 2007, 28-36. The statue base inscribed with 'Ἀριστομένης' was reused as building material in a proto-byzantine church southeast of the theatre of Messene. See Themelis 2000, 28-31 with fig. 25 for the dating.

24   Themelis 2000, 107. If the missing head can be restored with a male portrait head of the Antonine period that was found close by, as has been tentatively suggested by Themelis, remains uncertain. In contrast, Themelis 2013, 143 now argues for a Neronian date of the *imago clipeata*.

25   Peter Broucke has kindly informed me that certain technical aspects leave no doubt about the assignment to the heroon. It cannot be excluded, however, that the *imago clipeata* was part of a later alteration. On Tiberius Claudius Saithidas Caelianus (II) see Rizakis *et al.* 2004, 522-524 no. 157; on Tiberius Claudius Frontinus Niceratus see Rizakis *et al.* 2004, 518-519 no. 150.

26   On the few examples of military iconography in Attic and Laconian grave reliefs: von Moock 1998, 59-60; Papaefthimiou 1992, 44-47, 65-68. On military training in the Hellenistic gymnasium: Kah 2004, esp. 69-74.

27   Müth 2007, 124-125.

---

28   On military aspects of the *ephebeia* in the Roman period: Kennell 2010, 205-206, 215-216. On the significance of past Greek military virtues: Spawforth 2012, 103-141.

29   Paus. 4.32.2: εἰσὶ δὲ τῶν Μεσσηνίων οἳ τῷ Αἰθίδᾳ χρήματα μὲν γενέσθαι πολλὰ ἔλεγον, οὐ μέντοι τοῦτόν γε εἶναι τὸν ἐπειργασμένον τῇ στήλῃ, πρόγονον δὲ καὶ ὁμώνυμον ἄνδρα τῷ Αἰθίδᾳ· Αἰθίδαν δὲ τὸν πρότερον ἡγήσασθαι τοῖς Μεσσηνίοις φασίν, ἡνίκα ἐν τῇ νυκτὶ Δημήτριός σφισιν ὁ Φιλίππου μηδαμῶς ἐλπίσασιν αὐτός τε καὶ ἡ στρατιὰ λανθάνουσιν ἐσελθόντες ἐς τὴν πόλιν.

30   *Cf.* Luraghi 2008, 197-199 on the inscription and the setting.

31   On the social significance of ancestry in Roman Greece: Lafond 2006, 164-169.

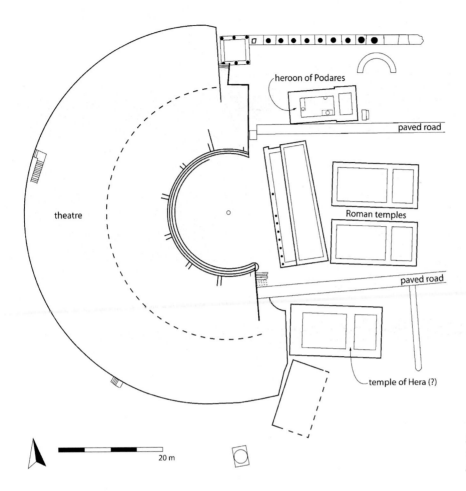

Figure 5. Plan of the west end of the Mantineian agora, redrawn after: Fougères 1898, 167 fig. 37.

3. Heroa on the agorae of Mantineia and Argos

Related to the heroon of the Saithidai is the case of an intra-mural burial of the late 1st century AD on the agora of Mantineia, for which, according to Pausanias, the pre-existing heroon of Podares had been reused.[32] Pausanias writes that Podares lost his life as *polemarchos* in the battle at Mantineia against Thebes in 362 BC, and subsequently was awarded with a public burial as he had distinguished himself as one of the bravest in battle.[33] That this burial included a public cult seems plausible but remains open to speculation due to the vague remarks by Pausanias.[34]

Unfortunately, the state of archaeological research on the agora of Mantineia is highly problematic, as the publication of the excavations carried out by Gustave Fougères in the late 19th century leaves many questions unanswered. However, there is good reason to identify the heroon with a building on the west side of the agora and in front of the northern *analemma* of the theatre (fig. 5-6). The remains of this temple-like prostyle structure with dimensions of about 12 m x 5 m constitute a foundation of rubble stones and a few blocks of the wall socle.[35] In its 'cella' Fougères found two cremation burials along the long sides and a sarcophagus made of spolia in front of the rear wall. It contained a corpse of unknown sex and a considerable number of grave goods, which

---

32 Paus. 8.9.9-10.
33 *Cf.* Fröhlich 2013, 242 who highlights the exceptionality of this honour in this period.
34 Paus. 8.9.10: Ποδάρην δὲ ἐπ' ἐμοῦ τὸν ἀρχαῖον ἐτίμων οἱ Μαντινεῖς [...]; *cf.* Fröhlich 2013, 243.
35 Fougères 1898, 190-192. The hypothesis by Schörner 2007, 44-45 with n. 353; Schörner 2014, 158 that the prostyle facade was a Roman addition to the heroon is not substantiated by any evidence.

Figure 6. The heroon of Podares after a clean-up in 2012 (courtesy of exploring-greece.gr).

have been tentatively dated to the Imperial period without, however, being published in detail so far.[36] Several stamped tiles found in the vicinity of the building confirm the identification with the heroon of Podares.[37]

A serious disadvantage for our understanding of this monument is certainly the lacking evidence for its commonly accepted construction date in the 4th century BC, which is exclusively based on Pausanias' remarks.[38] While the documentation by Fougères offers no information on stratigraphy, the architecture and building techniques do not exclude a dating to the late Classical period.[39] The dating of the stamped tiles indicates that in this case, the monument was renovated in the Roman period.[40]

The renovation of the monument might have been part of the events that Pausanias dates to the period three generations before his own lifetime, i.e. around the late 1st century AD. A descendant of Podares with the same name, who according to Pausanias lived recently enough to obtain Roman citizenship, was honoured with a burial inside the older heroon. It can be cautiously identified with the already mentioned sarcophagus. Its prominent setting in front of the rear wall, but also an inscription that according

---

36 Fougères 1898, 192-193. According to Fougères the plinth of an equestrian statue 'de travail hellénique' had been reused for the lid of the sarcophagus. On the basis of Fougères' descriptions Schörner 2007, 216-217 Kat. A4; Schörner 2014, 158 highlighted the chronological significance of several glass *unguentaria* for a possible Roman dating of the burial. A revision of the whole complex of small finds is urgently required.

37 *IG* V² 321.2: 'Ποδάρεος δαμόσιος'; *cf.* Fougères 1898, 191.

38 Fougères 1898, 191; followed by *e.g.* Jost 1985, 131; Schörner 2008, 217. In contrast, Luraghi 2008, 199-200 with n. 36 speculated on a Roman construction date.

39 According to Fougères 1898, 191 the walls of the monument were built 'sans doute' with mud brick. However, there seems to be no cogent evidence for this assumption if, as Fougères suggests himself, another course of stone blocks followed above the blocks of the wall socle preserved *in situ*. While two temples behind the skene of the theatre were according to Fougères (1898, 190) built on a foundation of rubble stones and mortar, the mortarless construction technique of the Podareion might be an indication for a pre-Roman date.

40 Fr. Hiller von Gaertringen commented in *IG* V² 321.2: 'Lateres ei Podari conveniunt qui duobus aevis ante Pausaniam vixit (…)'.

HEROES OF THEIR TIMES | 117

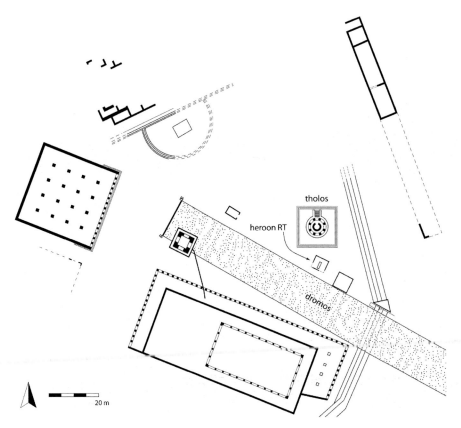

Figure 7. Plan of the agora of Argos, redrawn after: Pariente et al. 1998, 230 fig. 4.

to Pausanias was changed on this occasion, seem to point to a general rearrangement of the monument.[41] Although we can only suspect, it seems plausible that the new inscription still related to the remembrance of the older Podares, which, after all, was the decisive factor for the present honour. And, in fact, this might have been the case before as the second cremation burial in the heroon seems to indicate. Even though there is no evidence concerning its date, Pausanias knew of a grandson of the older Podares who fought as one of the commanding officers in the war against the Spartan king Agis in the 3rd century BC.[42] It is thus tempting to interpret the heroon as a monument in honour of this family, which was in use for centuries.[43] However, how well-founded the claim to ancestry of the Roman citizen Podares really was, escapes our understanding. As has been pointed out before, putative associations with famous ancestors of Greek history were a common feature of elite self-representation at the time.[44]

Here, we might expect that the rearranged heroon puts forward a decisive claim to military virtue as did the Saithidai at Messene, but evidence is lacking. The rudimentary described grave goods, among other things writing utensils and instruments associated with sport and personal hygiene, seem to point to an elite background characterized by education and training in the gymnasium.[45] Could this possibly indicate that Podares died at young age, perhaps as an ephebe? Again, the evidence is slight, but two cist burials of the Augustan period from the periphery of the agora at Eretria that contained the corpses of two male youths offer a close parallel in the selection of grave goods.[46] Finally, the premature death of a promising youth who was tragically denied the chance

---

41   Paus. 8.9.9. Schörner 2007, 87 mistakenly commented that this inscription was found by Fougères.
42   Paus. 8.10.5.
43   *Cf.* Fröhlich 2013, 242-243 In contrast, Schörner (2007, 86) thought both cremation burials to date to the 4th century BC.
44   Luraghi 2008, 200-201; Spawforth 2012, 40-41.
45   *Cf.* Schörner 2007, 87; Schörner 2014, 158.
46   See Psalti 1997, 402-403; Psalti 2010, 289-290.

Figure 8. The so-called heroon RT on the agora of Argos (courtesy of the Εφορεία Αρχαιοτήτων Αργολίδας, ΥΠΠΟΑ).

to live up to the remembrance of his ancestors might have prompted the public burial on the agora of Mantineia.[47]

Even more difficult to comprehend is an intra-mural burial on the agora of Argos. The monument with dimensions of about 5.4 m x 5 m has only been preserved slightly above its foundation level. The actual burial chamber is bordered on three sides with a core of *opus caementicium*, while the outer facade was constructed with a course of partially reused limestone blocks (fig. 7-8).[48] For the reconstruction of the missing superstructure, the altar tomb of Lucius Castricius Regulus in Kenchreai, which was built under Tiberius, seems to provide a good parallel.[49] Accordingly, the self-representation of the honoured benefactor and, ultimately, of the wider family is decisively different from the preceding examples insofar as this architectural burial type was inspired by Italian influences.[50] Besides the interred corpse, the sex and identity of which remain unknown, only a few of the once apparently wealthy grave goods have been preserved.[51] The dating of the burial to the second half of the 1st or the early 2nd century AD is based on a small group of *unguentaria*.[52] That the burial chamber was set against the interior south face of

---

47   See Fröhlich 2013, 229-230 on other examples of the Late Hellenistic period.
48   P. Marchetti 1977, 677-678; Marchetti & Kolokotsas 1995, 31-32 with pl. 7 and plan 2; Pariente *et al.* 1998, 219. The tomb went unnoticed by Flämig 2007 und Schörner 2007. Besides this burial on the agora Piérart 2010, 33 with n. 130 has recently argued that the so-called 'thermes A' in their first building phase were a 'monument privé à la gloire d'une des grandes familles'; followed by Fröhlich 2013, 292. This hypothesis is based on three sarcophagi that were found in a crypt-like chamber in the building complex. Regarding the desperate state of publication the question whether these sarcophagi really were part of the original plan remains unsolved. The same applies to the function of the large peristyle courtyard and the annex rooms for which Piérart's identification offers no substantial explanation.
49   On the tomb at Kenchreai see Willson Cummer 1971, esp. 225 fig. 7 and 227 fig. 8 for the reconstruction of its superstructure; Flämig 2007, 159-161 no. 44.
50   On the burial type of the so-called 'altar tomb' and its Italian provenance: Flämig 2007, 42-45 (with literature).
51   See Piérart & Touchais 1996, 80-81.
52   Abadie-Reynal 2007, 288 no. 18.

Figure 9. The crypt and corridor of the tholos (photo author).

the limestone blocks, and thus might have been accessible in some way or other, could possibly indicate that ritual performances took place at the grave.

Particularly interesting is again the setting of the monument in between the dromos to the south and a monumental tholos to the north (fig. 7). The close proximity has already prompted Patrick Marchetti to suppose that the honoured benefactor was, in fact, identical with the donor of the round building. It replaced an undated predecessor in the late 1st century AD.[53] This is without doubt an appealing hypothesis, but the controversial function of the tholos allows space for further speculation, since the interpretation as a nymphaion, which had been suggested by the excavators, was convincingly refuted by Marcel Piérart. In the late 1st century AD Argos simply had no sufficient water supply by which the fountain could have been fed.[54] Considering the unusual architecture of the building that combined a crypt of about 1 m in diameter in its substructure with a corridor opening onto the north facade (fig. 9), the alternative interpretation as a heroon put forward by Piérart seems all the more worth considering. At any rate, the architecture of the Antonine heroon of Palaimon at Isthmia offers striking parallels for this feature.[55]

On his way across the agora Pausanias mentions a remarkable number of heroa for various figures of the local Argive mythology. Only a few of them have actually been found in the excavations by the Εφορεία Αρχαιοτήτων Αργολίδας and the École

---

53 Marchetti & Kolokotsas 1995, 32.
54 Piérart 1999, esp. 255-256; *contra* Marchetti & Kolokotsas 1995, 205; Marchetti 2010, 53. The archaeological evidence for a water reservoir to the north of the tholos that Marchetti & Kolokotsas 1995, 27, 53 and Marchetti 1998, 358 with fig. 3 postulated, is vague at best. According to the authors, it collected the water of the intermittent river Charadros by which the fountain was fed. Rightly sceptical: Piérart 1999, 265. How from a hydrostatic perspective the water was transferred from the hypothetical reservoir to the outlets of the fountain reconstructed 3.5 m above the contemporary ground level remains obscure.
55 Piérart 1999, esp. 255-259 referring to the Palaimonion at Isthmia. The implications of such an interpretation for the architectural reconstruction of the tholos at Argos cannot be discussed in this article.

française d'Athènes so far.[56] Especially the myth of Danaos, the legendary king of Argos, and his family was ubiquitous in the memorial topography of Roman Argos, which, according to Patrick Marchetti, 'avait été systématiquement structuré en référence à la légende des Danaïdes'.[57] Accordingly, the Palinthos, as the tomb of Danaos on the agora was called, certainly must have been a prominent monument. While Pausanias is rather vague about its setting, Strabo located it right in the middle of the agora.[58] The identification with the tholos is tempting, and the more so since it was, from what we know so far, the first building on the agora almost completely rebuilt with marble in the Roman period.[59] The semantic association of the Danaids with water might, finally, have facilitated the transformation of this monument into a fountain in a second building phase in the later 2nd century AD.[60]

All in all, we might suspect that the heroon on the agora of Argos followed the pattern already observed in the case of Messene. The extraordinary social status of the honoured benefactor was not only expressed by his public burial on a central spot in the open square – and that with remarkable Roman overtones -, but also was reaffirmed by the close proximity to a *lieu de mémoire* of the Argive memorial topography. If the contemporary rebuilt tholos, maybe paid for by the honouree, really was the tomb of Danaos remains, however, open to speculation.

4. Conclusion

Even though the evidence of the intra-mural burials presented here is in many ways not straightforward, the picture emerging from the assembled mosaic of stones and fragments broadly agrees with the observations initially made on the case of the Tyrannicides. It also has become clear that besides visibility and materiality the allusion to the collective *memoria* of the city could be turned – in the sense of Bourdieu – into a symbolic profit of distinction in the physical and social space. The meaningful analogy that was established on the basis of spatial proximity to a specific *lieu de mémoire*, and probably through ephemeral performative acts (such as funerary cults) as well, reinforced above all the normative behaviour of the honouree in accordance with civic ethics such as concern for public prosperity, defence of civic *eleutheria* and military virtue, the latter certainly tinged with retrospective overtones of the great deeds of the classical past. In this regard, the intra-mural burials were, of course, no exception to contemporary elite mentalities. The assimilation with prominent figures of civic history or figures of local mythology is, after all, a well-known aspect of the public honorary practice of Roman Greece.[61] In an

---

56 A synopsis of the monuments mentioned by Paus. 2.19.3-22.7 is provided by Piérart 1998, 342-348. On the heroon of the Seven against Thebes: Paus. 2.20.5; *SEG* 37.283; see Pariente 1992. On the tomb of Phoroneus: Paus. 2.20.3; *SEG* 56.418; see most recently Piérart 2013.

57 Marchetti 2001, 458 n. 15 (with quote); *cf.* Aupert 2001, 453-454; Lafond 2006, 215; Spawforth 2012, 169-170, 174-175, esp. 177-179.

58 Strab. 8.6.9.

59 Plausibly Piérart 1999, 256-259. An alternative identification of the Palinthos with the so-called 'salle hypostyle' on the west side of the agora was proposed by Marchetti 2010, 51 Anm. 107. However, the argument is hardly convincing as it is based a) on the highly problematic hypothesis that the agora extended all the way to the west to the foothills of the Larisa and b) on a base for a statue of Danaos (*SEG* 28.397) reused in a Late Roman wall of the 'salle hypostyle'. In contrast, the architecture of this building is clearly in line with other public assembly halls, as *e.g.* the Thersilion in Megalopolis or the bouleuterion in Sikyon. On the urban development of Roman Argos and the Roman Peloponnese in general see the forthcoming publication of my Heidelberg PhD thesis: J. Fouquet, 'Das Eigene im Fremden. Stadtentwicklung und urbane Lebensformen auf der kaiserzeitlichen Peloponnes'.

60 On the second building phase of the tholos: Marchetti & Kolokotsas 1995, 143-144. Furthermore, Piérart 1999, 259-261 tried to substantiate the identification with the tomb of Danaos in the light of a highly fragmentary inscription (*SEG* 32.282) preserved on one of the architrave blocks of the tholos. If, however, the waterworks mentioned in the text are indeed part of Hadrian's building programme, who, in turn, was according to Piérart associated as *ktistes* with Danaos, is pure speculation.

61 Lafond 2006, 208-217.

Argive inscription from the Trajanic period, for instance, Claudia Philomathia who raised three sons to adulthood was honoured for her outstanding mother's role with the title of νέα Ὑπερμνήστρα, the role model *par excellence* for marital virtues in Argive mythology.[62]

At the same time, the discussed cases enhance our understanding of other, far more fragmentarily preserved intra-mural burials, *e.g.* the heroon of the prominent senator and civic benefactor Caius Iulius Eurykles Herculanus at Sparta. From this monument dated to the years after Herculanus' death in 136/7 AD a few architectural pieces have been reused in the late Roman fortification wall of the acropolis about 190 m to the east of the theatre.[63] While it cannot be excluded that the heroon stood on the agora on the Palaiokastro hill, as has been suggested before, a place near the theatre, where the graves of Leonidas and Pausanias and a stele with the names of the fallen in the battle of the Thermopylae recalled the city's glorious past in the Persian wars, seems worth considering in light of the presented results.[64]

Ultimately, the example from Sparta clearly illustrates the limits of memorial culture as well. With the construction of the fortification wall in the early 5th century AD the symbolism of Eurykles' heroon finally had become meaningless for Spartan civic identity. Contrary to the previously discussed 'heroes' of the Roman period, whose remembrance was woven into the urban memorial topographies, it was the longevity of the classical *lieux de mémoire* that prevailed: around the time when Eurykles' monument was razed, the city of Megara in the person of the local bishop reinstated the memory of the citizens fallen in the Persian wars by a renovation of their heroon in the city.[65] The benefactors of the Roman period thus remained but 'heroes' in their times.

Acknowledgements

A first draft of this article was read by Paul Scotton who has also kindly improved the English. All shortcomings remain, of course, my own. I would like to express my sincere gratitude to Pieter Broucke who kindly provided me insight into his unpublished manuscript on the heroon at Messene. Furthermore, I would like to thank Petros Themelis, the Εφορεία Αρχαιοτήτων Αργολίδας and exploring-greece.gr for granting me permission to reproduce the images as indicated.

---

62   *SEG* 16.259, l. 8; *cf.* Lafond 2006, 215; Spawforth 2012, 176-177.
63   On the heroon of Eurykles Herculanus (*IG* V¹ 489, 575): Spawforth 1978, 249-255; Flämig 2007, 213-214 no. I 3 (possibly on the agora). The tomb went unnoticed by Schörner 2007. On Eurykles Herculanus: Rizakis *et al.* 2004, 286-294 no. 462.
64   Paus. 3.14.1.
65   *IG* VII 53; *cf.* Schörner 2014, 154-155, 158.

References

Abadie-Reynal, C. 2007. La céramique romaine d'Argos (fin du IIe siècle avant J.-C. – fin du IVe siècle apres J.-C.), Athènes.

Aupert, P. 2001. Architecture et urbanism à Argos au Ier siècle ap. J.C. In: J.-Y. Marc & J.-C. Moretti (eds), Constructions publiques et programmes édilitaires en Grèce entre le IIᵉ siècle J.-C. et le Iᵉʳ siècle ap. J.-C., Actes du colloque organisé par l'École Française d'Athènes et le CNRS, Athènes 14-17 mai 1995, Athènes, 439-454.

Baldassarra, D. 2007. Famiglie aristocratiche di Messene imperiale: il contributo dell'epigrafia. In: G. Cresci Marrone & A. Pistellato (eds), *Studi in ricordo di Fulviomario Broilo, Atti de convegno, Venezia, 14-15 ottobre 2005,* Padua, 25-62.

Bourdieu, P. 1991. Physischer, sozialer und angeeigneter physischer Raum. In: M. Wentz (ed.), *Stadt – Räume, Die Zukunft des Städtischen, Frankfurter Beiträge* 2, Frankfurt, 25-34.

Cooper, F.A. 1999. Curvature and other architectural refinements in a Hellenistic heroon at Messene. In: L. Haselberger (ed.), *Appearance and essence. Refinements of classical architecture: curvature, Proceedings of the Second Williams Symposium on Classical Architecture held at the University of Pennsylvania, Philadelphia, April 2-4, 1993,* Philadelphia, 185-197.

Cormack, S. 2004. *The space of death in Roman Asia Minor,* Wien.

Flämig, C. 2007. *Grabarchitektur der römischen Kaiserzeit in Griechenland,* Rahden/Westf.

Fröhlich, P. 2013. Funérailles publiques et tombeaux monumentaux *intra-muros* dans les cités grecques à l'époque hellénistique. In: M.-Cl. Ferriès, M.P. Castiglioni & F. Létoublon (eds), *Forgerons, élites et voyageurs d'Homère à nos jours, Hommages en mémoires d'Isabelle Ratinaud-Lachkar,* Grenoble, 227-309.

Fougères, G. 1898. *Mantinée et l'Arcadie orientale,* Paris.

Jost, M. 1985. *Sanctuaires et cultes d'Arcadie,* Paris.

Kah, D. 2004. Militärische Ausbildung im hellenistischen Gymnasion. In: D. Kah & P. Scholz (eds), *Das hellenistische Gymnasion, Wissenskultur und gesellschaftlicher Wandel* 8, Berlin, 47-90.

Kennell, N. 2010. Citizen Training Systems in the Roman Peloponnese. In: A.D. Rizakis & C.E. Lepenioti (eds), *Roman Peloponnese III. Society, Economy and Culture under the Roman Empire, KERA Meletemata* 63, Athens, 205-216.

Krumeich, R. & Ch. Witschel 2009. Hellenistische Statuen in ihrem räumlichen Kontext: Das Beispiel der Akropolis und der Agora von Athen. In: A. Matthaei & M. Zimmermann (eds), *Stadtbilder im Hellenismus, Die hellenistische Polis als Lebensform* 1, Berlin, 173-226.

Lafond, Y. 2006. *La mémoire des cités dans le Péloponnèse d'époque romaine (IIe siècle avant J.-C.-IIIe siècle après J.-C.)*, Rennes.

Löw, M. 2008. *Soziologie der Städte*, Frankfurt am Main.

Luraghi, N. 2008. Meeting Messenians in Pausanias' Greece. In: C. Grandjean (ed), *Le Péloponnèse d'Epaminondas à Hadrien, Colloque de Tours, 6-7 octobre 2005*, Bordeaux, 191-202.

Ma, J. 2013. *Statues and cities. Honorific portraits and civic identity in the Hellenistic world*, Oxford.

Marchetti, P. 1977. Le monument rond, *BCH* 101, 675-677.

Marchetti, P. 1998. Le Nymphée d'Argos, le Palémonion de l'Isthme et l'agora de Corinthe. In: A. Pariente & G. Touchais (eds), *Άργος και Αργολίδα. Τοπογραφία και πολεοδομία, Πρακτικά διεθνούς Συνεδρίου, Αθήνα – Άργος 28.04.-01.05. 1990*, Ελληνογαλλικές έρευνες 3, Paris, 357-366.

Marchetti, P. 2001. Le substrat dorien de l'Apollon Palatin. In: J.-Y. Marc & J.-C. Moretti (eds), Constructions publiques et programmes édilitaires en Grèce entre le IIe siècle J.-C. et le Ier siècle ap. J.-C., Actes du colloque organisé par l'École Française d'Athènes et le CNRS, Athènes 14-17 mai 1995, Athènes, 455-471.

Marchetti, P. 2010. L'épigraphie argienne et l'oligarchie locale du Haute-Empire. In: A.D. Rizakis & C.E. Lepenioti (eds), *Roman Peloponnese III. Society, Economy and Culture under the Roman Empire, KERA Meletemata* 63, Athens, 43-57.

Marchetti, P. & K. Kolokotsas, 1995. *Le Nymphée de l'agora d'Argos. Fouille, études architecturale et historique*, Paris.

Miller, S.G. 1980. Turns and lanes in the ancient stadium, *AJA* 84, 159-166.

von Moock, D.W. 1998. Die figürlichen Grabstelen Attikas in der Kaiserzeit. Studien zur Verbreitung, Chronologie, Typologie und Ikonographie, Mainz.

Müth, S. 2007. Eigene Wege. Topographie und Stadtplan von Messene in spätklassisch-hellenistischer Zeit, Rahden/Westf.

Nora, P. 1984. Entre mémoire et histoire, la problématique des lieux. In: P. Nora (ed.), *Les lieux de mémoire, I. La République*, Paris, XVI-XLII.

Ogden, D. 2004. Aristomenes of Messene. Legend of Sparta's nemesis, Swansea.

Papaefthimiou, W. 1992. Grabreliefs späthellenistischer und römischer Zeit aus Sparta und Lakonien, München.

Pariente, A. 1992. Le monument argien des „Sept contre Thèbes'. In: M. Piérart (ed.), *Polydipsion Argos. Argos de la fin des palais mycéniens à la constitution de l'État classique*, Fribourg (Suisse) *7-9 mai 1987, BCH Suppl.* 22, Athènes, 195-229.

Pariente, A., M. Piérart & J.-P. Thalmann. 1998. Les recherches sur l'agora d'Argos: résultats et perspectives. In: A. Pariente & G. Touchais (eds), *Άργος και Αργολίδα. Τοπογραφία και πολεοδομία, Πρακτικά διεθνούς Συνεδρίου, Αθήνα – Άργος 28.04-01.05 1990*, Ελληνογαλλικές έρευνες 3, Paris, 211-231.

Piérart, M. 1998. L'itinéraire de Pausanias à Argos. In: A. Pariente & G. Touchais (eds), *Άργος και Αργολίδα. Τοπογραφία και πολεοδομία, Πρακτικά διεθνούς Συνεδρίου, Αθήνα – Άργος 28.04-01.05 1990*, Ελληνογαλλικές έρευνες 3, Paris, 337-356.

Piérart, M. 1999. Les puits de Danaos et les fontaines d'Hadrian. In: J. Renard (ed.), *Le Péloponnèse. Archéologie et Histoire, Actes de la rencontre internationale de Lorient, 12-15 mai 1998*, Rennes, 243-268.

Piérart, M. 2010. Argos romaine: La cité des Perséides. In: A.D. Rizakis & C.E. Lepenioti (eds), *Roman Peloponnese III. Society, Economy and Culture under the Roman Empire, KERA Meletemata* 63, Athens, 19-41.

Piérart, M. 2013. Le tombeau de Phorôneus et le culte des Épitélides à Argos. In: M.-C. Ferriès, M.P. Castiglioni & F. Létoublon (eds), *Forgerons, élites et voyageurs d'Homère à nos jours, Hommages en mémoires d'Isabelle Ratinaud-Lachkar*, Grenoble, 311-329.

Psalti, A. 1997. Οικόπεδο Α. Αλεξανδρή, *ArchDelt* B 52, 402-403.

Psalti, A. 2010. Zwei Gräber aus der römischen Kaiserzeit. In: Ch.M. Pruvot, K. Reber & T. Theurillat (eds), Ausgegraben! Schweizer Archäologen erforschen die griechische Stadt Eretria. Eine Ausstellung der Schweizerischen Archäologischen Schule in Griechenland in Zusammenarbeit mit dem Antikenmuseum Basel und Sammlung Ludwig, Basel, 289-290.

Rizakis, A.D., S. Zoumbaki & C.E. Lepenioti 2004. *Roman Peloponnese II. Roman personal names in their social context. Laconia and Messenia, KERA Meletemata* 36, Athens.

Schörner, H. 2009. *Sepulturae graecae intra urbem. Untersuchungen zum Phänomen der intraurbanen Bestattungen bei den Griechen*, Möhnesee.

Schörner, H. 2014. Revival of the intra-urban burial in Greek poleis during the Roman imperium as a creation of identity. In: B. Alroth & Ch. Scheffer (eds), *Attitudes towards the Past in Antiquity: Creating Identities. Proceedings of the International Conference Held at Stockholm University, 15-17 May 2009, Stockholm Studies in Classical Archaeology* 14, Stockholm, 151-162.

Spawforth, A.J.S. 1978. Balbilla, the Euryclids and memorials for a Greek magnate, *BSA* 73, 249-260.

Themelis, P. 2000. Ήρωες και ηρώα στη Μεσσήνη, Βιβλιοθήκη της εν Αθήναις Αρχαιολογική Εταιρεία 210, Αθήνα.

Themelis, P. 2013. The 'Doryphoros' of Messene. In: V. Franciosi & P. Themelis (eds), *Pompei/Messene. Il 'Doriforo' e il suo contesto, Mediterraneo: miti, storie, armonie* 2, Napoli, 125-209.

Willson Cummer, W. 1971. A Roman tomb at Corinthian Kenchreai, *Hesperia* 40, 205-231.

Wycherley, R.E. 1957, *The Athenian Agora 3: Literary and epigraphical testimonia*, Princeton.

Zimmermann, M. 2015. Neue Perspektiven der Stadtforschung: Städtische Physiognomien im Horizont der Mikroregion. In: A. Matthei & M. Zimmermann (eds), *Urbane Strukturen und bürgerliche Identität im Hellenismus, Die hellenistische Polis als Lebensform* 5, Heidelberg, 400-405.

Public Statues as a Strategy of Remembering in Early Imperial Messene

Christopher Dickenson

Abstract

Under the Roman Empire the poleis of Greece were setting up honorific statuary monuments with increasing frequency. Statues of emperors and members of the imperial family, of local politicians and benefactors are attested in all areas of public space from agoras to bathhouses, from gymnasia to theatres. While these monuments were intended to perpetuate the memories of contemporary individuals, they stood in settings that were also home to older statues, which served as focal points for remembering, or reinventing, local history and identity. Our best source for these monuments is, of course, Pausanias. The tendency in modern scholarship has been to see the impact of all these statues on public space in negative terms – monuments of emperors advertised foreign oppression; monuments for members of the local elite signalled the end of democracy; both took up space where day-to-day activity had once taken place; and the survival of old historic monuments transformed civic centres into museum-like spaces for backward looking introspection. This article challenges this vision and argues that public monuments played a dynamic role in defining relations of power both vis-à-vis Rome and within the polis at the local level. It makes the case that examining the spatial setting of monuments and looking at the interplay of meaning – both intended and fortuitous – between different types of statue in the same spatial setting adds new layers of understanding regarding their political significance. The case study, Messene, is studied using archaeological, epigraphic and literary evidence. Messene is ideally suited for thinking about the range of ways in which monumental space could be used to shape political realities in Greece under the Empire.

Keywords: Messene, portrait statues, honorific statues, public space

1. Introduction

Portrait statues were everywhere in the cities of Roman Greece. Sculpted in marble and bronze, set up to honour benefactors, to commemorate emperors and as votive offerings to the gods, statues of men, and to a lesser extent women, could be seen in all of the polis' public spaces – in the agora, in sanctuaries, in theatres, gymnasia and alongside major thoroughfares. Some statues were survivals from the distant past. Pausanias' description of Greece contains many references to statues from Classical or even Archaic times that could still be seen in the poleis of his day. Many more represented people who were

in: Dijkstra, T.M., I.N.I. Kuin, M. Moser & D. Weidgenannt (eds) 2017. *Strategies of Remembering in Greece under Rome (100 BC - 100 AD)*, Leiden (Sidestone Press).

still alive or had been alive within living memory. Portrait statues shared the polis' public spaces with countless other statues representing gods, heroes and figures of myth. It is doubtful whether any urban societies in history – with the exception of Imperial Rome itself – were home to as many statues as the Greek cities of the Roman Empire.

This phenomenon has certainly not gone unnoticed in modern scholarship and portrait statues have been much discussed from a range of different approaches. However, it is only recently – surprisingly so – that scholars have begun to pay much attention to the relationship between portrait statues and their spatial context.[1] How portrait statues derived meaning from, and were viewed and experienced in, their setting are still issues that are not well understood. This article aims to deepen understanding of the connection between the setting and meaning of public portrait statues by focusing on a city that lends itself particularly well as a case study: Messene in the southern Peloponnese. Messene is a good place for asking questions about public portrait statues because of a fortuitous combination of several factors: (i) a particularly rich and useful description by Pausanias, (ii) the absence of a modern settlement above the ancient site, (iii) a high degree of preservation of ancient buildings and monuments, (iv) widespread excavation in recent years, and (v) the exemplary level of publication of the excavations albeit for some material still, as yet, in preliminary form.

Messene is also an inherently fascinating city to study for a number of reasons. The city was founded in the late Classical period, when the Thebans freed the region from Spartan subjugation. For our theme of 'remembering', Roman Messene is of particular interest because the city had a rather different relationship to its past than cities such as Athens where there had been continuity of habitation since time immemorial or Corinth, which had been resettled very recently by the Romans. Unlike the Roman period Corinthians the Messenians could lay claims to a continuous historic and mythic tradition that stretched back into the Archaic period and beyond, when their ancestors had fought against the Spartans; unlike the Athenians, however, because of the relatively late dates at which the city was founded and at which their traditions first became fossilized in the form of written sources, the Messenians in Hellenistic and Roman times had more freedom to reinvent their traditions to serve the needs of the present. Messene is also interesting for our purposes because, to judge from its monumental architecture, the city clearly thrived under the Roman Empire.[2] Messene, however, is largely absent from the extant literary sources of the period so that we are largely dependent on the ar-

chaeology and epigraphy from the site to reconstruct its post-Hellenistic history.[3]

Moving through three of the city's major public spaces – its agora, sanctuary of Asklepios, and gymnasium – the discussion here will explore how thinking about the spatial context of different types of portrait statue can deepen our understanding of the meanings they might have carried for the ancient Messenians. A fourth public space, the theatre, is not discussed because all secure evidence for statues there dates to the 2nd century AD or later. By looking at potential connections between statues that stood in the same location – and between statues and other monuments – and by thinking about the potential audience statues would have had in different settings the aim is to deepen our understanding of how portrait statues were used to define relations of power at the local level and to accommodate the realities of rule by the outside imperial power.

The discussion is also a challenge to the tendency in modern scholarship to think of statues and other monuments as belonging to discrete categories. Investigating honorific statues, private dedications, votive statues, statues of emperors, ideal sculpture, cult statues and so on, in isolation is certainly useful but the trade-off is that up to now very little attention has been paid to ways in which the boundaries of these categories were fluid and could overlap. The fact that all these types of statue could be found throughout the public spaces of the Roman period polis created much potential for interplay of meaning between them – and between statues and other types of monument such as tombs and *heroa* – which could be exploited through placement in significant locations or through choices made concerning their appearance. Examples of statues from Messene will be used here to suggest ways in which ambiguities between honorific and votive portraits, between local and imperial portraits, between mortal and divine statues, between statues and grave monuments and – crucially for the theme of this book – between new and old statues, may have been drawn on to give them meaning.

In keeping with the scope of the volume the focus here will be on the late Hellenistic and early Imperial period. To appreciate the ways in which portrait statues set up at that time fed off the associations of their setting for meaning it will be necessary at certain points to say something of earlier monuments that were still standing. Occasionally we will also cast our glance ahead to the centuries that followed to consider how the meaning of the monuments set up in our period might have changed over time or have influenced the placement of later statues. Archaeological, epigraphic and literary evidence will be drawn upon both

---

1   For example Ma 2013, esp. chs 3 and 4, Dillon & Baltes 2013, van Nijf 2011, Höghammar 1993.
2   On the city's economy see Themelis 2010b.

3   See Roebuck 1941 for Messenian history down to 146 BC and Luraghi 2008 chapters 8 and 9 for the Roman period.

126   STRATEGIES OF REMEMBERING IN GREECE UNDER ROME (100 BC - 100 AD)

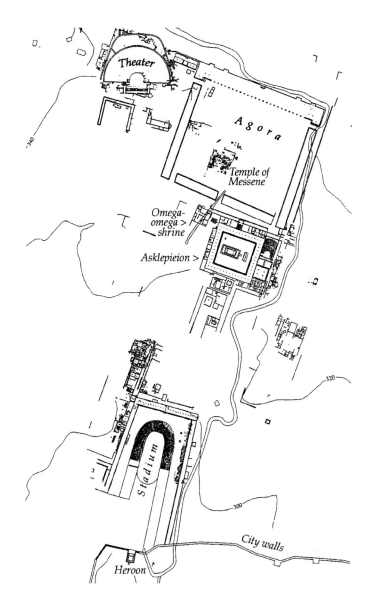

Figure 1. Map of the central area of Messene (reproduced by permission of Petros Themelis).

to trace the presence of statues in particular spaces and to draw inferences about the use of those spaces. The evidence for statues is drawn from a database of public monuments in Roman Greece that I am currently developing (https://romangreece.classics.ox.ac.uk). The discussion is divided into two sections, the first dealing with statues of locals, the second with statues of emperors. My own words of caution about pigeonholing statues by subject matter highlight the artificiality of the distinction, but the evidence from Messene is such, as we shall see, that breaking it down in this way usefully allows different questions to be explored. I shall, however, consider ways in which the boundaries of meaning between the two categories overlapped.

2. Statues of locals

The agora was usually a prime location for setting up portrait statues in a Greek city (Ma 2013, 75-9 and 142-8 and Dickenson 2017b). At Messene the agora has only recently been systematically excavated and is still incompletely known (see Figure 1). It was an enormous square covering some 2.9 hectares, divided into a series of terraces running east-west, and surrounded on all four sides by stoas (see Themelis 2010a, Themelis 2012). Enough sculpture and inscriptions have been found to suggest that the square

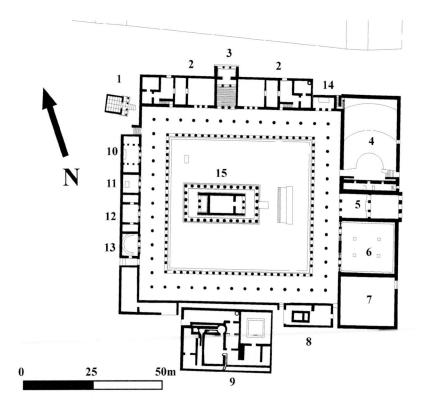

Figure 2. Map of the Messenian Asklepieion (1. Temple of Artemis Orthia, 2. Sebasteion, 3. North Propylon, 4. Ekklesiasterion, 5. East Propylon, 6. Bouleuterion, 7. Archive, 8. Tomb of Damophon?, 9. Bathhouse, 10. Oikos K (of Artemis), 11. Oikos M (of Tyche), 12. Oikos N (of Epaminondas, Thebes and Herakles), 13. Oikos Ξ (of Apollo and the Muses), 14. Fountain, 15. Temple of Asklepios).

was indeed an important setting for statues but the evidence is very fragmentary. My database currently includes evidence for twenty-three portrait statues of locals mentioned in publications of the excavations. The agora's commercial function is attested to by an inscription naming various stoas by products sold in them (*SEG* 23.205; *SEG* 23.207; *SEG* 35.343; see also Migeotte 1985) and by measuring tables found *in situ* in the north stoa (Themelis 2012, 37-44). This means that any statue set up there would have stood amid the hustle and bustle of daily life. The inscriptions, however, are typically too badly preserved to know why people were granted statues or what their background was. Some of the statues found in the agora area may have been votive offerings set up in the various sanctuaries that stood within the square.[4] There is much better *in situ* evidence from the agora for statues of emperors as we shall see in the next section.

To the south of the agora lies the well-preserved, mid-Hellenistic Asklepieion complex, a peristyle court with a Doric temple in its centre and series of rooms behind the colonnade on three of its sides (see Figure 2) (for an overview see Themelis 2015, 77-93 and Dickenson 2017a, 130-142). Asklepios was an important deity at Messene as reflected in a tradition presented with scepticism by Pausanias that the god was considered to be a 'citizen' of the city (Paus. 2.26.7). On the west a row of 'oikoi' housed statues of gods and heroes, almost all by the celebrated local artist Damophon.[5] Pausanias mentions these statues and substantial pieces of were found during the excavations (Paus. 4.31.10. Themelis 2015, 136-142 and Themelis 1996). The nature of these deities suggests a coherent sculptural programme intended as an expression of Messenian identity (Luraghi 2008, 277-285): they included Apollo (Asklepios' father), Herakles the father of the Dorians, the Tyche of the City and a personification of Thebes, the city whose army had liberated Messenia. There was also a statue of the Theban general Epaminondas, seen at Messene as the city's founding hero (see Luraghi 2008, 216) (although Pausanias' curious comment that the statue was made of iron, unlike the rest which were

---

4   On the temples see Themelis 2010a, 110-118 and Themelis 2012, 44-7.
5   For the architecture of this wing see Chlepa 2001.

of stone, and was not by Damophon raises the possibility that it was added later).

Damophon is the Hellenistic artist about whom we possess the most information but all of that information is to be found in Pausanias.[6] It is likely that Pausanias learned most of what he knew about Damophon at Messene, which suggests a considerable degree of local pride in the artist in the 2nd century AD. A column monument bearing seven proxeny decrees in honour of Damophon was found to the south of the Asklepieion, which suggests it would still have been standing in Pausanias' day. It stood next to a group-grave housed within a small building, which may have been the tomb of Damophon and his family.[7] Damophon's continued fame under the Empire must have given the statues in the Asklepieion a new layer of meaning. In addition to their sacred and historical connotations, by the height of the Roman Empire they also helped preserve the memory of the celebrated local artist who had lived centuries before and had repaired Pheidias' Zeus at Olympia (Paus. 4.31.6) and who, as evidenced by the proxeny decrees, had conferred fame and political capital upon the city. Such associations surely made the Asklepieion an attractive place for setting up new portrait statues in our period.

Under the Principate the northern wing of the Asklepieion served as a Sebasteion (see the next section). The eastern rooms consisted of a small theatre labelled the 'ekklesiasterion' by the excavators, a so-called 'bouleuterion' and possibly a public archive (Themelis 2015, 82-87; Birtacha 2008). These rooms provide good grounds for seeing the Asklepieion as a centre of politics and administration rather than a healing shrine like Asklepieia elsewhere.[8] In addition to its sacred statues the sanctuary was also home to the largest concentration of portrait statues known for the city.

The foundations of some 140 bases and several exedra monuments were found in the central courtyard (see Figure 2) (Themelis 2015, 77). Many of them – possibly the majority – surely supported portrait statues but as only a handful of inscriptions were discovered that might have belonged to these monuments little can be said about who their subjects were, when they were set up or whether they were for the most part votive or honorific in nature; both private (*SEG* 23.218, 23.224,) and public (*SEG* 23.211; *SEG* 23.212; 23.213) dedications were found there. Modern scholarship has, however, arguably drawn too sharp a distinction between the two kinds of portraits. If these were honorific statues they would have carried religious connotations by virtue of their location in a sanctuary; if they were votive dedications they would, like honorific statues, have preserved the memory of their subjects for future generations. The bases were clearly distributed to allow movement around the precinct and toward the altar so we should imagine – as scholars have for similar concentrations of statues elsewhere (e.g. Dillon & Baltes 2013) – that at festival times this host of statues created a powerful sense that the subjects of the monuments the city's living population were standing among as participants in the religious rites.

Rather better contextual evidence for the ways in which portrait statues drew on their setting for meaning was discovered in the northernmost of the western *oikoi*, the room dedicated to the worship of Artemis (see Figures 3 and 6).[9] Pieces of the cult statue, mentioned by Pausanias, were found within the room, together with its base, the bases of thirteen other statues, several inscribed with votive dedications, and eight of the stone statues they supported, all but one of them headless but otherwise substantially preserved. These statues fall into two groups – five life-size young girls and three approximately two-thirds life-size priestesses. The statues of the girls have been dated somewhere between the 1st century BC (Themelis 1994, 115; Connelly 2007, 151; Loube 2013, 105 n.551; Bobou 2015, 59) and the 1st century AD (Brulotte 1994 1, 245; Zunino 1997, 41; Melfi 2007, 286), the priestesses to the 2nd or 3rd centuries AD.[10] The statues have been used as important evidence for reconstructing the cult of Artemis practiced here (see Themelis 1994).

Most of the inscriptions are very brief but one of them (*SEG* 23.220) is an epigram written in the first person as though the statue's subject, a girl called Mego, were speaking (see Figure 4). It presents her statue – also discovered, see Figure 5 – as a dedication by her parents following her service in Artemis' cult and expresses daughterly gratitude to her parents. The inscription mentions that Mego carried a torch and the sacred *bretas* of the goddess; the left arm of the statue, discovered separately from the body, shows the girl carrying the small cult statue (Themelis 1994, 115-116 and fig. 19). These duties were such that they could surely only be performed by one girl each year; the dedication of a statue in the small room must have been an even more jealously guarded privilege. The statue points to elite status which is confirmed by the fact that Mego's parents are mentioned in the inscription as serving as priests (ἱερατεύσαντες) in the cult. Her father, Damonikos, is also known to have served as gym-

---

6   On Damophon see Themelis 1993; Themelis 1996; Smith 1991, 240-241; Pollitt 1986, 165-167.

7   See Themelis 2003, 40-46 on the column and tomb; *cf.* Boehringer 2001, 278 and 2007 Fröhlich 2007, 208-210 who argue that the tomb was probably not Damophon's.

8   As do Papahatzis 1967/8; Orlandos 1976, 38; Felten 1983, 82-93; Torelli 1998, 471; Themelis 2015, 77 and Dickenson 2017a, 130-142. *Cf.*, however, Riethmüller 2005, 164-165.

9   For the archaeology of the room see Chlepa 2001, 10-69.

10   Themelis 1994, 111-115; Bobou 2015, 60 though *cf.* Connelly 2007, 157 who places one of them much earlier.

Figure 3. The Oikos of Artemis (photograph by the author).

Figure 4. The base of Mego's statue (photograph by the author).

nasiarch and to have set up statues of himself and his brother in the propylon of that building (*SEG* 46.416 and 417; see Themelis 2015, 211; Ma 2013, 229 and Baldassara 2010). Deploying portrait statues at multiple locations is a strategy of elite self-promotion known for other Greek cities.[11] The statue of Mego was thus both a religious and a political monument – it displayed piety toward the goddess while at the same time advertising the status of the family. The same is surely true of the statues of the other girls. Their low number (and even if some have been lost it is clear that the room could not have held many more) attests that statues can only have been dedicated in exceptional circumstances and not every year. The importance of a girl initiate's family would

---

11   E.g. at Termessos: van Nijf 2011.

Figure 5. Mego's statue (photograph by the author).

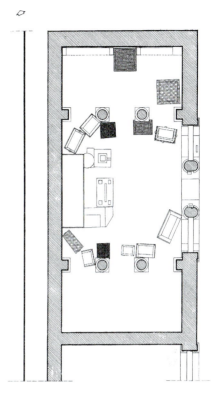

Figure 6. Plan of the Artemision (reproduced by permission of Petros Themelis).

almost certainly have played some role in the decision as to whether to grant her a statue.

The statues of the priestesses are of interest here because they provide clues as to how the memory of the statues of the girls was experienced in later centuries. Eleven of the bases – all three priestesses, three girls and five anonymous bases – were discovered in a broken circle with the statue of Artemis at its apex opposite the entrance (see Figures 3 and 6). We cannot know when the arrangement was created: was it planned from the beginning and then developed over time? Or does it represent some late rearrangement? We can be sure, however, that the placement made sense when the priestess statues were added in the 2nd or 3rd centuries. The new statues were clearly positioned in relation to the older ones to articulate a connection between them. Perhaps the prestige of the priestesses was enhanced by emphasizing the long continuity of the cult; perhaps there was a religious significance with the priestesses understood as joining the girls of centuries past and the goddess herself in a sacred dance.[12] Other readings are no doubt also possible. It seems clear, however, that the meaning of the new statues was created through the context in which they stood and through tapping into the historical, sacred and political associations of the monuments they stood among.

The final public space to which we turn is the impressive gymnasium/stadium complex on the southern edge of the city. The running track, lined by embanked seating for the length of its east and the first third of its west side, ended at the wall of the city. The space at the top of the embankment was surrounded by a Pi-shaped colonnade with a series of rooms, including a recently excavated palaestra, at the rear on the west (see Figure 7)(see Themelis 2001b, Themelis 2009 and now Themelis 2015, 106-119). The gymnasium was both the place where young men went through the formative experience of education that would make them into citizens and the setting for a number of important local festivals when presumably the whole population would come together to witness and take part in competitions and other festivities in honour of the gods (Themelis 2001b). This made the gymnasium a powerfully charged location for setting up portrait statues.

From the period of Augustus the complex was entered from the north through a Doric propylon where, as already mentioned, Damonikos set up statues of himself and his brother during his tenure as gymnasiarch. Evidence for a handful of other portrait statues dating to our period has been found in the gymnasium including: a group monument for a husband and wife (*SEG* 52.402; see

---

12 As suggested by Themelis 1994, 101 and 122 and Connelly 2007, 153-154. *Cf.*, however, Loube 2013, 112-113.

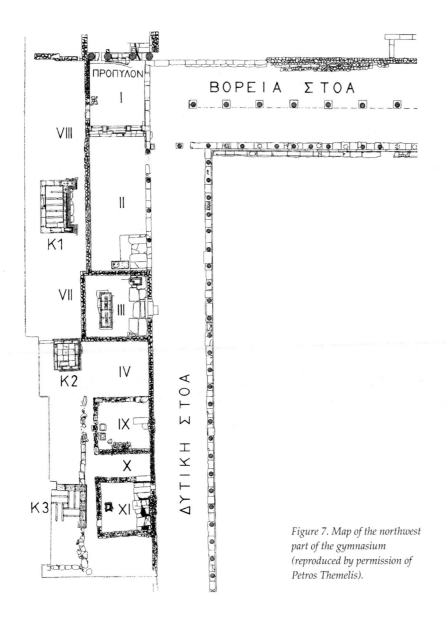

Figure 7. Map of the northwest part of the gymnasium (reproduced by permission of Petros Themelis).

Themelis 2010b, 104; Themelis 2002, 52), two bases for gymnasiarchs from the 2nd or 1st century BC,[13] a 2nd or 1st century BC statue of an athlete who won the *dolichos* at Isthmia as a boy and at the Lykaia in Arcadia as a man,[14] and an early 1st century AD statue for one Dionysios, son of Aristomenes, the base found in situ in one of the western rooms (*SEG* 52.404).

The base for one of the gymnasiarchs was reused for a statue of a man called Theon (*SEG* 47.400). This is not the only example of recycling of bases at Messene. This has little to do with the practice of re-inscribing bases of figures from the distant past, known at places such as Oropos and Athens, which Dio Chrysostom railed against in his 31st Rhodian Oration and which has been the attention of some important recent scholarship.[15] While that phenomenon seems to have had to do with capitalising on the honour of association with a prestigious figure or artist by repurposing old statues,

---

13   *SEG* 43.159 and an inscription mentioned by Themelis 2001a, 200 as being discovered in 1996 but unpublished.
14   *SEG* 46.410. On the festival see Mahoney 2016, 206-265 and on this inscription 223-224.
15   See Platt 2007, Fernoux 2017, Shear 2007 and Moser *this volume*.

at Messene more pragmatic considerations were clearly at work. The base of Theon's statue was turned so that the original text was no longer visible. All memory of the original monument was thereby obliterated; this was simply the recycling of a conveniently shaped block of stone. The interest of this evidence for our purposes is that it shows how soon after being set up monuments were sometimes taken down. The men whose statues had originally stood atop these bases had no doubt hoped they would stand for eternity but they were dismantled within a generation or two. Presumably this was more likely to happen if the families of honorands were no longer interested in, or able to, preserve their ancestor's monuments because they had died out or had fallen from prominence.

Theon's statue (see Figure 8), set up in the mid-late 1st century AD in Room IX, suggests several ways in which the boundaries between different types of statue – honorific, funerary and sacred – could be blurred. The man has been identified as a member of one of Messene's leading families, which can be traced in the epigraphic record from the Augustan period into the 2nd century AD (Fröhlich 2007, 214-216; Luraghi 2008, 307 n. 58). Not only the base but the marble statue itself, missing the head, were discovered. The body stands in the familiar arm sling pose, popular since Aeschines' 4th century statue for portraying men of politics (Smith 1998, 65-66; Richter 1965, 212-215, figs 1369-1390). The honorific associations of the pose and costume thus chime with the inscription, which presents the statue as a dedication by the polis. The inscription also, however, refers to Theon as a 'hero', which suggests funerary connotations and that the statue was erected posthumously. At Messene there were strikingly large numbers of funerary monuments within the civic centre, most of them Hellenistic group-graves of people who had died fighting for the city (Fröhlich 2007 and Themelis 2001a). The largest concentration of public tombs was in the gymnasium. One, labelled Tomb K3 by the excavators, stood behind the room in which Theon's statue was found and had been used for the secondary burial of a namesake and presumed ancestor of his (Themelis 2015, 113 and Luraghi 2008, 307 n. 58). Theon himself was possibly also buried in the gymnasium; at the very least his statue must have been intended to tap into the funereal associations of the place, to create connections with grave monuments of the past and, more specifically, with his own forebears.

Theon's statue was found in the same room as a very well-preserved statue interpreted as Hermes.[16] Statues of similar type often served as grave markers in the Hellenistic and Roman period Greek east and are usually also identified as Hermes (although Christopher Hallett has

Figure 8. Theon's statue (photograph by the author).

questioned the certainty of that identification and has suggested that these 'tomb portraits' were not intended as representations of the god at all, see Hallett 2005, 36-41). Dionysios, son of Aristomenes, whose statue was mentioned above, and which stood in a different room (Room XI) of the gymnasium, may also have been represented in a similar guise because the base was found together with fragments of a Hermes of the Andros type.[17] Dionysios, like Theon, is honoured as a 'hero' on his base (*SEG* 47.399). Theon's statue standing next to the 'Hermes' therefore almost certainly would have called to mind the world of the cemetery.

In another room of the complex, Room III, a statue of Hermes stood alongside a statue of Herakles. Enough of the Herakles was found to identify it as of the Farnese type; only small fragments of the Hermes survive but it was clearly of a different type to the two already mentioned, assuming that those were representations of the god. These must be the statues that Pausanias saw in the gymnasium, which he says were by Egyptian artists and the focus of

---

16 Themelis 2015, 132-133; *cf.* Palagia 2010, 434-435 who identifies it as Diomedes.

17 Themelis 1997, 97-99; Themelis 2000, 137-140. Note that Hallett (2005) has also questioned whether the famous Hermes of Andros really was a statue of the god.

(religious) honours (Paus. 4.32.1). Both pieces of information are confirmed by epigraphic discoveries within the building. An inscription gives the names of these Egyptian artists and an inscribed lintel over the door refers to the room as a 'naos'.[18] It is worth considering the way that these statues, and the Hermes in particular, may have informed the way in which the two other 'Hermes' statues of the gymnasium were viewed and experienced.

Modern scholars have tended to see statues of mortals represented in divine guise as at worst affectation, at best, as allegorical statements about their subject's perceived qualities (e.g. Hallet 2005, *passim*). I suggest that situations like that in the gymnasium at Messene present a challenge to such restrictedly secular line of interpretation. A visitor to the gymnasium was confronted with a representation of Hermes in statuary form that he/she was expected of recognise as a manifestation of the god. Is it not then likely that his/her viewing of representations of men in a guise that closely resembled that same god, in the same artistic medium, of the same material, in other rooms of the same complex would have called to mind some of the connotations of that 'cult' statue? Even if Hallett is right and statues of mortals such as these were not meant as representations of Hermes at all, surely the ease with which they have been accepted as such in modern literature is only possible because of ambiguity between mortal and divine representation that the sculpture was playing with. It is surely not far-fetched to attribute some degree of sacred significance to these statues of mortals. At the very least the decision to portray them in this way implies the message that they had achieved a closeness to the gods that other men had, which is, after all, no more than the use of the word 'hero' on one of the bases – and on Theon's – suggests.

To argue that civic portrait statues could be experienced as having a degree of religious power is not to imply that there were no other ways of experiencing them and, indeed, the combination of Theon's statue and the Hermes may itself have called to mind more quotidian associations. A bundle of papyrus rolls beside Theon's left foot advertised his learning, and the obvious interpretation is that he was a gymnasiarch, like the man whose base his statue usurped. In that light the nudity of the accompanying statue of Hermes may have evoked the costume of the ephebes who were in the gymnasiarch's charge. Strikingly an early 3rd century AD stele from Athens shows nude ephebes crowning a himation figure in exactly the same pose as Theon's, and also with papyrus scrolls by his left foot; the man here is a *kosmetes*, the magistrate responsible for training the ephebes at Athens.[19] Once again it is not necessary to posit a single overriding meaning for Theon's

statue. The statue could simultaneously conjure up the civic, funerary, religious and gymnasial sphere, taking its meaning from the spatial context in which it stood and from the other monuments with which it shared that space.

I have already mentioned the statue of a Dionysios son of Aristomenes that stood in one of the rooms of the gymnasium, which portrayed the deceased as a Hermes of the Andros type. The man belonged to another of Messene's leading families who are also well attested in the epigraphic record. This family took their name, and claimed descent, from Aristomenes, the legendary leader of the resistance to the Spartans in the Second Messenian War.[20] To think about the deeper meaning of that statue it is worth considering its relationship to two monuments to the hero that are known to have stood in the gymnasium or its vicinity. Pausanias saw the tomb of Aristomenes, where he was worshipped as a hero, which has tentatively been identified with a site of cultic activity discovered by excavations just to the north of the gymnasium (Paus. 4.32.3-6; Themelis 2001a, 203). He also saw a statue of Aristomenes within the gymnasium (Paus. 4.32.6). It is well documented that local elite families were keen to cultivate links to illustrious ancestors in Roman Greece (Spawforth 2012,40-41; Luraghi 2008, 200-201): Aristomenes' family was surely no exception. The lengthy accounts of Aristomenes' daring escapades in Pausanias' description of the city (Paus. 4.6.3 and 4.14-26; see also Langerwerf 2009) suggest that Pausanias was drawing on a local informer and it is tempting to suppose that these stories were being cultivated by the family that bore his name. At other cities in Roman period Achaia local elite families are known to have taken particular pride in the public tombs of legendary or mythical ancestors (Dickenson 2016 and Fouquet *this volume*) and Nino Luraghi has suggested the Aristomenes family at Messene did so (Luraghi 2008, 322). Any visitor to the gymnasium who saw the statue of Dionysios son of Aristomenes there would have had to pass the tomb on entering the complex so their viewing of the statue would likely have prompted recall of the family's distinguished lineage.

Themelis has suggested that the statue of Aristomenes in the gymnasium may have stood atop the large column on the east side of the terrace above the seating (Themelis 2015, 115 and fig. 123). The suggestion cannot be proved but so prominent a spot would certainly have been appropriate. Although the column might be possible to date, with Pausanias as our only hard evidence for Aristomenes' statue it is impossible to say when it was set up. It might have been an old monument but it is also possible that it was erected in the Roman period, perhaps even not long

---

18   See Themelis 2001b, 125-126 for transcriptions and translations.

19   *IG* II² 2208. The stele is discussed by Newby *this volume*.

20   For the evidence for the family see Luraghi 2008, 318-323.

134   STRATEGIES OF REMEMBERING IN GREECE UNDER ROME (100 BC - 100 AD)

Figure 9. The tomb of the Saithidai in the stadium (photograph by the author).

before Pausanias' visit, either by the Aristomenes family themselves or forces wishing to flatter them. Whether the statue in the gymnasium was older or younger than that of Dionysios there must have been some resonance of meaning between them. The one emphasised the family's distinguished place in the myth-history of the city, the other commemorated their contemporary significance. The fact that both men were presented in statuary form elided any sharp distinction between them. Even accounting for the likelihood that Aristomenes' statue looked very different from Dionysios' – it is hard to imagine Aristomenes was also portrayed as a Hermes – and almost certainly did occupy a more highly visible location, both were presented as sculpted likenesses. The implication is that Dionsysios shared something of the heroic stature of his ancestor, which is precisely what the use of the word 'heros' on his base proclaims.

Whatever the sacred connotations of these monuments they served a clear political purpose, working to legitimate and enhance the standing of the Aristomenes' family within the community. As the place where young male citizens passed through their ephebic training and people from all walks of life gathered for festivals in honour of the gods the gymnasium was well chosen as a location for perpetuating their memory. This close association between the Aristomenes family and the gymnasium probably goes some way towards explaining why the elite family who by the 2nd century AD seem to have surpassed them in prominence, the Saithidai, staked a claim to the space by placing their family mausoleum there. The small Doric temple-like building was set up in the 1st century AD – and thanks to modern reconstruction stands again – at the end of the running track, exerting an imposing presence and dominating the space (Themelis 2001b, 120-121 and Luraghi 2008, 311-314 and Flämig 2007, 20-21) (see Figure 9).

3. Statues of Roman rulers

Discussion of statues of Roman rulers at Messene must begin in the late Republic with a group monument set up to honour Sulla and two of his associates in the east of the agora near the Temple of Messene. The monument consisted of three bronze statues on a single large limestone base with three separate dedications by the demos to Sulla, an 'imperator' Lucius Licinius Murena (identified as a brother to the consul of 62 BC and also known from an inscription from Rhodes *IG* XII 1.48) and a Gnaeus Manlius Agrippa, otherwise unknown and not thought to be related to his famous namesake, Augustus' friend and general.[21] The monument must have been erected sometime in the late 80s BC after Sulla's victory over Mithridates.[22] Nothing is known of Messene's involvement in that war (see Luraghi 2008, 264) but the fact that Sulla and Murena are thanked as 'euergetai' on the base need not mean the city had taken the Roman side. Sulla was also honoured for his 'goodwill' (*eunoia*) at Athens, a city that he had notoriously and brutally sacked (*IG* II² 4103. For Sulla's sack of Athens see Plut. *Vit. Sull.* 14.3-6 and Hoff 1997); an associate of Sulla's, one Quintus Lutatius, was even given a statue at Athens in the agora atop a column monument in front of the Stoa of Attalos (Thompson 1950, 318; Merrit 1954, no. 36). Whatever Messene's relationship with Rome at this time, the prominent location of this monument made a powerful statement about the city's perception of its position with respect to Roman power. In granting Sulla a statue on the agora the city was effectively treating him like a Hellenistic king.[23]

The first evidence for honouring emperors at Messene comes with the conversion of the northern wing of the Asklepieion complex into a Sebasteion. An architectural study of the rooms carried out by a Japanese team has recently been published (Hayashida, Yoshitake *et al.* 2013, 65-69). An Augustan inscription to do with the repair of public buildings in the city was found in the Asklepieion and mentions the 'Sebasteion' by name as the location where the text was to be set up.[24] This makes it one of the few actual attestations of the word in antiquity.[25] Another inscription mentioning a 'Kaisareion' as part of the Asklepieion must refer to the same building (*IG* V¹ 1462). The presence of the *Sebasteion* is one of the reasons for thinking of the Asklepieion as a political complex because the imperial cult was often accommodated in or near buildings of government and administration.[26] We would expect the Sebasteion to have housed statues of the

imperial family as at imperial cult centres elsewhere such as the Julian Basilica at Corinth,[27] the Metroon at Olympia (Price 1984, 160) or the so-called Sebasteion at Boubon (Kokkinia 2008, 6-12). The only evidence for sculpture consists of fragments of a single over-life-sized statue, possibly of Augustus (Price 1984, 148 n. 48; Orlandos 1976, 29). It is of course possible that other statues were destroyed or removed at some point. The Asklepieion was, as we have seen, a focal point for Messenian identity as expressed through statues of gods, heroes and local men and women. Setting up statues of emperors within the complex created resonances with the sacred and civic connotations of the older monuments, while emphasising the power of the imperial house. Dedicating the northern wing of the Asklepieion to emperor worship, in effect, gave the emperors a tutelary role analogous to that of the deities assembled in the *oikoi* of the western wing.

Elsewhere in the city Messene provides very good evidence for a phenomenon as yet unattested elsewhere in Greece – the clustering of statues of emperors in dynastic or thematic groups. The first such cluster concerns three bronze statues of the same emperor, Nero, which were set up in front of the Arsinoe Fountain just outside the northwest entrance to the agora. The statues were dedicated by representatives of three different local elite families: a Ti. Claudius Aristomenes (*IG* V¹ 1450), a Ti. Claudius Saithidas (*SEG* 41.353) and a Kleophatos son of Aristeus (*IG* V¹ 1449). The first two are, of course, members of the two local elite families mentioned in the preceding section. One of the two men is almost certainly mentioned in another inscription as the principle benefactor of a major remodelling of the fountain to include statues of the *sebastoi*, presumably a group of statues of Julio-Claudian emperors (*SEG* 46.418). Frustratingly only the first part of the name ('Tiberio…') is preserved so both Ti. Cl. Saithidas (Baldassarra 1999, 148 and Felten & Reinholdt 2001, 319) and Ti. Cl. Aristomenes (Themelis 1995, 56-57) have been suggested as restorations. Excavations have confirmed that the fountain was indeed renovated in the mid-1st century – the colonnade along the front was dismantled, two round basins were added and an exedra set up at the rear, which must have carried the new statue group (Reinholdt 2009; the renovations are discussed on 130-134. See also Themelis 74-77 and Longfellow 2011, 112). We see here a precursor of the slightly later trend of honouring emperors with statues in monumental fountains or nymphaia (Longfellow 2011). Whether or not a statue of Nero was also included in the group monument inside the fountain the message of dynastic continuity was clear. At the same time Nero's multiple representations in a prominent location in front

---

21   *SEG* 48.494-6; the monument is discussed by Themelis 2001a, 205-206.

22   Dohnicht & Heil 2004 date it to 83-81 BC, Themelis 2001a, 205-6 to post-81 BC.

23   For statues of kings on agoras see Dickenson 2013, 64-67.

24   *SEG* 35.343; *SEG* 23. 205; *SEG* 23.207; Themelis 2015, 91; see also Hänlein-Schäfer 1985, 162-164 and Alcock 1993, 182-183, 185.

25   In Greece a *Sebasteion* is also attested at Gytheion – *SEG* 11.923. See also Camia & Kantiréa 2010, 379.

26   See Price 1984, 109 and 134-135; Evangelidis 2008; Dickenson 2017, 274, 281 and 283-286.

27   Johnson 1931, de Grazia Vanderpool 2003, 375-377 and de Grazia Vanderpool & Scotton *this volume*.

of the building emphasised the pre-eminence of the reigning emperor.

The Arsinoe for whom the fountain was named was not, Pausanias tells us (Paus. 2.26.7 and 4.31.6), a Ptolemaic queen but the daughter of Leukippos and, according to local mythology, the mother of Asklepios, an extremely important deity at Messene as we have seen. The association of statues of the Julio-Claudians, and especially Nero, with the monument weaved the power of the ruler into the myth-history of the community at a location that would have been a hub of activity as the principle source of water in the civic centre. The statues also, of course, emphasized the position of the three local benefactors within the community and their connection to the imperial house. Two of the three had Roman citizenship. The dedications by Ti. Cl. Aristomenes and Kleophatos further emphasise that connection by mentioning that both men were priests of the cult of the emperor and the goddess Roma; they also, incidentally, record that they served as agoranomoi which might give an additional, partial explanation for the location of the statues at the entrance to the square. The inscription by Ti. Cl. Saithidas refers to him as *philokaisar* as if compensating for a lack of official position connecting him to the emperor by stressing his personal devotion to the ruler. We may perhaps detect here something of the rivalry that would, in the case of the two better-attested families at least, persist into the time of the Antonines. The inscription naming the man responsible for renovating the fountain is also believed to have come from a statue base which, because it shows signs of being worn by water, is thought to have stood somewhere within the fountain (Reinholdt 2009, 131) thereby also advertising this man's local position and his links with the ruling dynasty. Monuments to honour emperors and their families were rarely exclusively about imperial power but were often closely entwined with the articulation and negotiation of local power relations as the renovations of the Arsinoe fountain well illustrate.

It is also worth noting that two of the three bases were found in situ, the third very nearby and that Nero's name was not removed from any of the texts. The right hand side of one (*SEG* 41.353) is missing but it is the surviving part of the stone that bears Nero's name. This all suggests that the statues continued to stand for a long time after Nero's fall from power. Harriet Flower has demonstrated that attitudes to Nero's memory in the generation after his death were complex, that destruction of his monuments and erasure of his name from inscriptions was not universal and that it is hard to discern patterns to explain where and in what circumstances they were allowed to survive.[28] The decision not to obliterate his memory at

Messene may have been taken because of local enthusiasm for the emperor, but equally it may also have had something to do with the continued influence of at least two of the families responsible for setting them up.

The next cluster of imperial statues found at Messene is a recently discovered, and not yet fully published, set of monuments for the Flavians, all set up by the polis inside the north stoa of the agora at the building's western end (see Figure 10). There were statues of Vespasian, Titus, Domitian and Domitia Longina (Themelis 2013). Monuments to this dynasty are unusual in Greece and no similar concentration has been found elsewhere. There is no evidence for a particular connection between these emperors and the city. Curiously, however, evidence from Megalopolis hints at a possible parallel that might explain why they were set up. A bilingual inscription found at Megalopolis commemorates Domitian's restoration of a stoa there following a fire (*CIL* 3.13691, which appears first on the stone, and *IG* V, 2 457). The inscription has sometimes been linked to the so-called Stoa of Philip, a building that occupies an analogous position to the stoa at Messene on the city's agora and which exhibits striking similarities to that building in terms of its size, protruding wings and exedras at the rear.[29] It is tempting to speculate that Domitian might also have made a benefaction at Messene to do with the building in which the statues were set up.

The location of the statues means that they would have been among the first monuments anybody would have seen on entering the agora from the direction of the Arsinoe fountain even if they would have been partially obscured by the columns of the stoa. While Nero's statues had not been removed, visitors to the agora were forcibly reminded that his power had been eclipsed by the new rulers. The commercial character of the agora and the north stoa in particular has been remarked on in the first section here. The statues of these emperors were thus placed at the heart of civic life where the Messenians would have seen them in their day-to-day comings and goings. The agora was, as we have seen, also a popular place for honouring locals although, unlike the emperors, their statues have rarely been found in anything like an in situ context.

The familial grouping of the statues of the Flavians, and particularly the presence of Domitian's wife, was presumably intended to emphasise the hoped for continuity of the new royal house. Two of the bases, however, bear a stark reminder that that hope was not realised. The name of Domitian has been removed from his own base and that of his wife (see Figure 11). Obliteration of Domitian's

---

28 Flower 2006, 197-233. See also Hoët-Van Cauwenberghe 2007 and Varner 2004, 79-81.

29 On the building see Dickenson 2017, 73-74; Schultz 1892, 59-66; Coulton 1976, 256; Lauter & Spyropoulos 1998, 122-125; and now Lauter-Bufe 2014.

Figure 10. The row of statue bases for the Flavians (photo by the author).

Figure 11. The base for Domitian's statue (photo by the author).

Figure 12. The base for the statue of Domitia Longina (photo by the author).

name from inscriptions and destruction of his monuments was carried out more systematically and on a far greater scale than for any previous victim of *damnatio memoriae* (Flower 2006, 235-255 Varner 2004, 111-135). Whether the Messenians were carrying out official instructions or acting spontaneously in response to similar actions elsewhere is impossible to say. The fact that the bases, unlike those of Nero, were dedicated by the polis perhaps meant that they lacked local defenders to stand in the way of their destruction. With the erasure of the names the statue of Domitian himself was also certainly torn down: both the crowning and supporting blocks of the base have been badly damaged, the latter in a way that could only have occurred after the crowning block had been removed (Figure 11). Domitia's base is better preserved and the letters of the offending name carefully chiselled away which suggests that her statue was allowed to remain (Figure 12). The care taken here suggests the intention was not so much to destroy all memory of Domitian as to remember the disgrace of his fall. The fact that his base was found in situ suggests that it was left to stand in its ruined state beside the intact monuments of his father, brother and wife. This act of *damnatio memoriae* was then as much a strategy of remembering as of forgetting.

The practice of setting up statues of emperors in dynastic groups at Messene would continue into the 2nd century AD. Substantial fragments of three marble statues were discovered in the theatre, which the excavators have identified as Trajan, Hadrian and Lucius Verus (Themelis 2015, 59 and figs. 34-36). A row of bases for statues of Antoninus Pius, Marcus Aurelius, and Faustina the Younger has been discovered along the south side of the Temple of Messene, the personified city goddess, on the agora (*SEG* 52.405; *IG* V. 1.1451 and *SEG* 52.405). It is worth noting that while these statues were dedications by 'the Greeks' they were paid for by various members of the Saithidas family – descendants of one of the men who had set up one of the statues of Nero – who in that period reached the apogee of their local power and prestige. Several reasons can be posited for setting these statues up near the temple. Firstly, and most pragmatically, the temple's location on the agora again assured the high visibility of these statues in the day-to-day life of the community. In Hellenistic times the temple had served as a location for setting up records of important political communications (see Themelis 2010a, 114-116; Themelis 2012, 45-47). Pausanias tells us that the interior of the temple was decorated by paintings showing early mythical kings of Messene (Pausanias 4.31.11-12). Nino Luraghi argues persuasively that the original meaning of these paintings was rather different and that Pausanias has misread them in light of contemporary political realities (Luraghi 2008, 269-275). Nonetheless the royal connotations of the temple in his day might partly explain why

this was deemed a particularly suitable spot for setting up statues of emperors. At the same time proximity to the temple also possibly gave these statues a more religious aura than those of the Flavians in the north stoa. For our purposes the main relevance of these statues of the Antonines is that they joined an older statue of Claudius that had been set up there during the reign of that emperor by an old man called Charidamos, son of Kraton, who is known to have had an illustrious local political career in the first half of the 1st century AD (*SEG* 55.515. For the man's career see Themelis 2010b, 103). This juxtaposing may have been intended to underscore the legitimacy of the imperial system through emphasising its longevity; at the same time it may be significant that Claudius represented the dynasty under which the Saithidai had gained the Roman citizenship. In either case we are presented here with another glimpse of how a statue set up in the early part of the Empire was remembered and continued to give meaning to its setting in later times.

To return finally to the last major public space in the city, the gymnasium/stadium complex, it is striking that no evidence for statues of emperors has been found there. Absence of evidence is rarely evidence for absence but the fact that so many other statues and other monuments have been found in the gymnasium suggests at the very least that it was not a major showcase for imperial statues. An Augustan period inscription that mentions contests in honour of the first emperor suggests that imperial cult festivals were held in the gymnasium (*SEG* 23.206, discussed by Spawforth 2012, 212-213). In terms of its monuments, however, the gymnasium seems to have been reserved as a privileged place for the expression of local identity. The absence of imperial monuments no doubt increased the impact of monuments of the Aristomenes family and the tomb of the Saithidai. Within the stadium, whether as ephebes engaged in training, as athletes competing on the track or as spectators, even during the games in honour of the emperor, Messene's citizens would have found themselves confronted with imposing reminders of the realities of local power.

4. Conclusions

The aim here has been to show how our understanding of the portrait statues that were so ubiquitous in the Roman period polis can be deepened through examining the spatial context in which they were set up. I have suggested ways in which statues were deliberately positioned to create purposeful connections with other monuments in order to influence the meanings that were ascribed to them when viewed in their spatial context. Old statues could lend meaning to new ones as in the case of the votives of the Artemision or the statues of the Antonines set up beside the statue of Claudius near the Temple of

Messene; portrait statues could take on funerary or even divine connotations through their proximity to tombs or statues of gods, as in the cases of the statues of Theon and Dionysios in the gymnasium. Statues of emperors were as much statements of local as of imperial power. Local families sought to enhance their visibility on the public stage through deploying different types of statues in different locations, a strategy adopted by Damonikos the gymnasiarch in the 1st century. Strategic placement of statues by elite families like the descendants of the hero Aristomenes undoubtedly played an important role of cementing their position within the community. An argument running through the discussion was that we should rethink the categories that modern scholarship imposes on the ancient material and recognise that as they were experienced in their ancient setting distinctions between different types of statue were often ambiguous. Exploiting ambiguity through the placement of statues was no small part of what gave them their meaning.

Setting up a statue of any kind is always an act of commemoration, an intention to perpetuate a particular memory for future generations. The array of statues that was strung out through the public spaces of an ancient city like Messene constituted a rich and ever evolving tapestry of civic memories through which local identity was expressed and defined, through which power relations within the local community were negotiated and contested and through which sense was made of relations to higher powers both in this world and the world of the gods. This tapestry was continually being edited as statues, or statue groups, were set up, moved or taken away, like stiches or complex motifs being added or unpicked. Each and every new stitch was at some small level a 'strategy of remembering'. We can no longer reconstruct the entire complex range of meanings that public portrait statues must have held for ancient viewers but by continually adjusting our perspective to view the individual stitches now as part of the tapestry as a whole, now within the part of the design where they were placed, we can at least come a step closer to understanding their importance within Roman period polis culture and society.

Acknowledgement

The research that led to this article was supported by a Marie Curie Intra-Urban Fellowship for Career Development.

References

Alcock, S.E. 1993. *Graecia Capta – The Landscapes of Roman Greece*, Cambridge.

Baldassarra, D. 1999. *Famiglie aristocratiche di messene in epoca imperiale,*. Tesi di Laurea, Venice.

Baldassara, D. 2010. La famiglia di Damonikos di Messene. In: R.W.V. Catling, F. Marchand & M. Sasanow (ed.), *Onomatologos: Studies in Greek Personal Names presented to Elaine Matthews,* Oxford, 172-180.

Birtacha, P. 2008. Μεσσήνη: το ωδείο και το ανατολικό πρόπυλο του Ασκληπιείου, Athens.

Bobou, O. 2015. *Children in the Hellenistic World: Statues and Representation*, Oxford.

Boehringer, D. 2001. *Heroenkulte in Griechenland von der geometrischen bis zur klassischen Zeit: Attika, Argolis, Messenien*, Berlin.

Brulotte, E.L. 1994. *The Placement of Votive Offerings and Dedications in the Peloponnesian Sanctuaries of Artemis, 2 Vols.* PhD Dissertation, University of Minnesota.

Camia, F. & M. Kantiréa 2010. The Imperial Cult in the Peloponnese. In: A. D. Rizakis & C.E. Lepenioti (eds), *Roman Peloponnese III. Society, Economy and Culture under the Roman Empire: Continuity and Innovation. Meletemata 63*, Paris, 375-406.

Chlepa, E.-A. 2001. Μεσσήνη: το Αρτεμίσιο και οι οίκοι της δυτικής πτέρυγας του Ασκληπιείου, Athens.

Connelly, J.B. 2007. *Portrait of a Priestess: Women and Ritual in Ancient Greece*, Princeton.

Coulton, J. J. 1976. *The Architectural Development of the Greek Stoa*, Oxford.

de Grazia Vanderpool, C. 2003. Roman Portraiture: The Many Faces of Corinth. In: C.K. Williams II & N. Bookidis (eds), *Corinth XX: The Centenary: 1896-1996*, Princeton, 369-384.

Dickenson, C. P. 2013. Kings, Cities and Marketplaces – Negotiating Power through Public Space in the Hellenistic World. In: C.P. Dickenson & O.M. van Nijf (eds), *Public Space in the Post Classical World. Caeculus, Papers on Mediterranean Archaeology and Greek and Roman Studies*, Leuven, 37-75.

Dickenson, C.P. 2016. Contested Bones: the Politics of Intraurban Burial in Roman Greece. *Ancient Society* 46, 95-163.

Dickenson, C.P. 2017a. *On the Agora – The Evolution of a Public Space in Hellenistic and Roman Greece (c. 323 BC – 267 AD)*, Leiden.

Dickenson, C.P. 2017b. The Agora as Setting for Honorific Statues in Hellenistic and Roman Greece. In: O.M. van Nijf & A. Heller (eds), *The Politics of Honour in the Greek Cities of the Roman Empire*, Leiden, 432-454.

Dillon, S. & E.P. Baltes 2013. Honorific Practices and the Politics of Space on Hellenistic Delos: Portrait Statue Monuments Along the Dromos. *AJA* 117, 207-246.

Dohnicht, M. & M. Heil 2004. Ein Legat Sullas in Messenien. *ZPE*, 235-242.

Evangelidis, V. 2008. The Architecture of the Imperial Cult in the Agoras of the Greek cities, *Egnatia* 12, 125-144.

Felten, F. 1983. Heilgtümer oder Märkte? *AK* 26, 84-104.

Felten, F. & C. Reinholdt 2001. Das Brunnenhaus der Arsinoe in Messene. In: V. Mitsopoulos-Leon (ed.), *Forschungen in der Peloponnes. Akten des Symposions anläßlich der Feier '100 Jahre Österreichisches Archäologisches Institut Athen' Athen 5.3-7.3.1998. Österreichisches Archäologisches Institut. Sonderschriften. Band 38*, Athens, 307-323.

Fernoux, H.-L. 2017. La gestion des statues honorifiques à Rhodes à la fin du Ier siècle ap. J.-C. d'après le Rhodiakos de Dion de Pruse (Or. XXXI) In: O.M. van Nijf & A. Heller (eds,), *The Politics of Honour in the Greek Cities of the Roman Empire*, Leiden, 81-108.

Flämig, C. 2007. *Grabarchitektur der römischen Kaiserzeit in Griechenland*, Rahden.

Flower, H.I. 2006. *The Art of Forgetting: Disgrace and Oblivion in Roman Political Culture*, Chapel Hill.

Fröhlich, P. 2007. Les Tombeaux de la ville de Messène et les grandes familles de la cité à l'epoque hellénistique. In: C. Grandjean (ed.), *Le Péloponnèse D'Épaminondas À Hadrien – Colloque de Tours 6-7 Octobre 2005*, Paris, 203-227.

Hallett, C.H. 2005. *The Roman Nude: Heroic Portrait Statuary 200 B.C.-A.D. 300*, Oxford.

Hänlein-Schäfer, H. 1985. *Veneratio Augusti: eine Studie zu den Tempeln des ersten römischen Kaisers*, Rome.

Hayashida, Y., R. Yoshitake & J. Ito 2013. *Architectural Study of the Stoas of the Asklepieion at Ancient Messene*, Fukuoka.

Hoët-Van Cauwenberghe, C. 2007. Condamnation de la mémoire de Néron en Grèce: Réalité ou mythe?' In: Y. Perrin (ed.), *Neronia VI: Rome, l'Italie et la Grèce, Hellénisme et philhellénisme au premier siècle après J.-C: actes du VIIe Colloque international de la SIEN (Athènes, 21-23 octobre 2004)*, Brussels, 225-249.

Hoff, M.C 1997. Laceratae Athenae: Sulla's Siege of Athens in 87/6 BC and its Aftermath. In: M.C. Hoff & S.I. Rotroff (eds), *The Romanization of Athens. Proceedings of an International Conference Held at Lincoln, Nebraska (April 1996)*, Oxford, 33-51.

Höghammar, K. 1993. *Sculpture and Society: A Study of the Connection Between the Free-Standing Sculpture and Society on Kos in the Hellenistic and Augustan Periods*, Stockholm.

Johnson, F.P. 1931. *Corinth IX: Sculpture 1896-1923*, Cambridge, MA.

Kokkinia, C. 2008. Introduction. In: C. Kokkinia (ed.), *Boubon: The Inscriptions and Archaeological Remains: A Survey 2004-2006. Meletemata 60*, Athens, 1-25.

Langerwerf, L. 2009. Drimakos and Aristomenes. Two Stories of Slave Rebels in the Second Sophistic. In: S. Hodkinson (ed.), *Sparta: Comparative Approaches*, Swansea, 331-359.

Lauter, H. & T. Spyropoulos 1998. Megalopolis. 3. Vorbericht 1996-1997. *AA*, 415-451.

Lauter-Bufe, H. 2014. *Die Stoa Philippeios in Megalopolis*, Mainz.

Longfellow, B. 2011. *Roman Imperialism and Civic Patronage: Form, Meaning, and Ideology in Monumental Fountain Complexes*, Cambridge.

Loube, H.M. 2013. *Sanctuaries and Cults of Artemis in Post-Liberation Messene: Spartan Mimeses?* PhD Dissertation, University of Ottawa.

Luraghi, N. 2008. *The Ancient Messenians – Constructions of Ethnicity and Memory*, Cambridge.

Ma, J. 2013. *Statues and Cities: Honorific Portraits and Civic Identity in the Hellenistic World*, Oxford.

Mahoney, K. 2016. *The Royal Lykaian Altar Shall Bear Witness: History and Religion in Southwestern Arcadia*. PhD Dissertation, University of Pennsylvania.

Melfi, M. 2007. *Il santuario di Asclepio a Lebena*, Athens.

Merrit, B.D. 1954. Greek Inscriptions. *Hesperia* 23, 233-283.

Migeotte, L. 1985. Réparation de monuments publics à Messène au temps d'Auguste. *BCH* 109, 597-607.

Orlandos, A. 1976. Νεώτεραι έρευναι εν Μεσσήνη. In: U. Jantzen (ed.), *Neue Forschungen in griechischen Heiligtümern*, Tübingen, 9-38.

Palagia, O. 2010. Sculptures from the Peloponnese in the Roman Imperial Period. In: A. D. Rizakis & C.E. Lepenioti (eds), *Roman Peloponnese III. Society, Economy and Culutre under the Roman Empire: Continuity and Innovation. Meletemata 63*, Paris, 431-445.

Papahatzis, N. D. 1967/8. Το Ασκλεπιείο της Μεσσήνης ώς κέντρο της δημοσιάς ζωής της. In: A. Orlandos (ed.), Χαριστήριον εις Αναστάσιον Κ. Ορλάνδον, Athens, 363-365.

Platt, V.J. 2007. Honour Takes Wing: Unstable Images and Anxious Orators in the Greek Tradition. In: Z. Newby & R. Leader-Newby (eds), *Art and Inscriptions in the Ancient World*, Cambridge, 247-271.

Pollitt, J.J. 1986. *Art in the Hellenistic Age*, Cambridge.

Price, S.R.F. 1984. *Rituals and Power: The Roman Imperial Cult in Asia Minor*, Cambridge.

Reinholdt, C. 2009. *Das Brunnenhaus der Arsinoë in Messene: Nutzarchitektur, Repräsentationsbaukunst und*

Hydrotechnologie im Rahmen hellenistisch-römischer Wasserversorgung, Vienna.

Richter, G.M.A. 1965. *The Portraits of the Greeks. Volume II*, London.

Riethmüller, J.W. 2005. *Asklepios: Heiligtümer und Kulte. 2 Vols*, Heidelberg.

Roebuck, C. 1941. *A History of Messenia from 369 to 146 BC*, Chicago.

Schultz, R.W. 1892. 'Chapter III. Architectural Description and Analysis.' In: E. Gardner & R.W. Schultz, *Excavations at Megalopolis 1890-91*, London, 15-68.

Shear, J. L. 2007. Reusing Statues, Rewriting Inscriptions and Bestowing Honours in Roman Athens. In: Z. Newby & R. E. Leader-Newby (eds), *Art and Inscriptions in the Ancient World*, Cambridge, 221-246.

Smith, R.R.R. 1991. *Hellenistic Sculpture: A Handbook*, New York.

Smith, R.R.R. 1998. Cultural Choice and Political Identity in Honorific Portrait Statues in the Greek East in the Second Century A.D, *JRS* 88, 56-93.

Spawforth, A. 2012. *Greece and the Augustan Cultural Revolution*, Cambridge.

Themelis, P. 1993. Damophon von Messene. Sein Werk im Lichte der neuen Ausgrabungen. *AK* 36, 24-40.

Themelis, P. 1994. Artemis Ortheia at Messene – the Epigraphical and Archaeological Evidence. In: R. Hägg (ed.), *Ancient Greek Cult Practice from the Epigraphical Evidence – Proceedings of the Second International Seminar on Ancient Greek Cult Organized by the Swedish Institute at Athens 22-24 November 1991*, Stockholm, 101-122.

Themelis, P. 1995. Ανασκαφή Μεσσήνης. *PAE*, 55-86.

Themelis, P. 1996. Damophon. In: O. Palagia & J.J. Pollit (eds), *Personal Styles in Greek Sculpture*, Cambridge, 154-185.

Themelis, P. 1997. Ανασκαφή Μεσσήνης. *PAE*, 79-113.

Themelis, P. 2000. Ήρωες και ηρώα στη Μεσσήνη, Athens.

Themelis, P. 2001a. Monuments guerriers de Messène. In: R. Frei-Stolba & K. Gex (eds), *Recherches récentes sur le mond hellénistique – actes du colloque en l'honneur de Pierre Ducrey (Lausanne, 20-21 novembre 1998)*, Bern, 199-215.

Themelis, P. 2001b. Roman Messene. The Gymnasium. In: O. Salomies (ed.), *The Greek East in the Roman Context. Proceedings of a Colloquium Organised by the Finnish Institute at Athens, May 21 and 22, 1999*, Helsinki, 119-126.

Themelis, P. 2002. Ανασκαφή Μεσσήνης, *PAE*, 21-55

Themelis, P. 2003. *Heroes at Ancient Messene*, Athens.

Themelis, P. 2004. Μεσσήνη. *Ergon*, 24-32.

Themelis, P. 2009. Das Stadion und das Gymnasion von Messene. *Nikephoros* 22, 59-78.

Themelis, P. 2010a. Die Agora von Messene. In: H. Frielinghaus & J. Stroszeck (eds), *Neue Forschungen zu griechischen Städten und Heiligtümern: Festschrift für Burkhardt Wesenberg zum 65. Geburtstag. Beiträge zur Archäologie Griechenlands 1*, Möhnessee, 105-126.

Themelis, P. 2010b. The Economy and Society of Messenia under Roman Rule. In: A.D. Rizakis & C.E. Lepenioti (eds), *Roman Peloponnese III. Society, Economy and Culture under the Roman Empire: Continuity and Innovation. Meletemata 63*, Paris, 89-110.

Themelis, P. 2012. The Agora of Messene. In: V. Chankowski & P. Karvonis (eds), *Tout vendre, tout acheter. Structures et équipments des marchés antiques. Actes du colloque d'Athènes, 16-19 juin 2009*, Paris, 37-47.

Themelis, P. 2013. Μεσσήνη. *Ergon*, 24-27.

Themelis, P. 2015. *Ancient Messene*, Athens.

Thompson, H.A. 1950. Excavations in the Athenian Agora: 1949. *Hesperia* 19, 313-337.

Torelli, M. 1998. L'Asklepieion di Messene, lo scultore Damofonte e Pausania. In: G. Capecchi (ed.), *In memoria di Enrico Paribeni*, Rome, 465-483.

van Nijf, O.M. 2011. Public Space and Political Culture in Roman Termessos. In: O. M. van Nijf & R. Alston (eds), *Political Culture in the Greek City After the Classical Age. Groningen-Royal Holloway Studies on the Greek City After the Classical Age. Vol. 2*, Louvain, 215-242.

Varner, E.R. 2004. *Mutilation and Transformation: Damnatio Memoriae and Roman Imperial Portraiture*, Leiden.

Zunino, M.L. 1997. *Hiera Messeniaka. La storia religiosa della Messenia dall'età micenea all'età ellenistica*, Udine.

Shortages, Remembering and the Construction of Time: Aspects of Greek Honorific Culture (2nd century BC – 1st century AD)

David Weidgenannt

Abstract

Several inscriptions from Roman Greece mention shortages of food or related phenomena. But it is not the crises themselves that these inscriptions aim to present. More importantly, they want to inform us about the successful solution to these problems in the context of local euergetism. Drawing on the sociological theories of Karl-Siegbert Rehberg, I aim to highlight the institutional character of euergetism and the mechanisms that kept this institution alive. Although in many cases we do not know about the continuing relationship between *euergetes* and recipient after the inscriptions had been engraved, the honorary inscriptions try to create the impression of a perpetual system that could be relied on in future times of need. Therefore, the explicit reference to potential critical situations in inscriptions not only presented the actual solution, but was also a method to reassure communities of their capacity to solve future problems, and a way to incentivize contributions by prospective benefactors. Seen from this angle, honorary decrees and honorary inscriptions were not only strategies of remembering, but also strategies for future action.

Keywords: shortages, euergetism, honorific decrees, epigraphy, institutionalism

1. Introduction

In his earliest civic speech (Dio Chrys. *Or.* 46), probably given during the reign of Vespasian,[1] Dio Chrysostom finds himself in a rather uncomfortable situation. A grain shortage in his native city of Prusa had caused severe disturbances that led to conflict between the wealthy orator and those who felt that their needs were not satisfied. From his oration we can infer that the shortage of grain did not lead to an overall scarcity, but rather that

---

1   Dessau 1899, 83-84 argued, *contra* von Arnim 1898, 205-207 (time of Domitian), for the reign of Vespasian, accepted by von Arnim 1899, 374-376. Since then, this date has been accepted, *cf.* Desideri 1978, 131-133; Jones 1978, 134; Swain 1996, 207 n. 69; Bekker-Nielsen 2008, 177. Bresson 2016, 394 n. 52 mistakenly dates the speech to the year of the proconsulship of Varenus Rufus in 105/6 AD.

in: Dijkstra, T.M., I.N.I. Kuin, M. Moser & D. Weidgenannt (eds) 2017. *Strategies of Remembering in Greece under Rome (100 BC - 100 AD)*, Leiden (Sidestone Press).

the price rose so much that it seemed unbearable for parts of the local populace (46.10).[2] In this situation Dio was made a scapegoat, having recently bought public land and built colonnades and workshops on it (46.9). In the eyes of his angry opponents this was a clear sign of a financial capacity that could – and should – be put to better use in this time of need. Two further accusations were levelled at him: firstly that he was hoarding wheat without selling it, and secondly that he refused to lend money for buying grain, despite being very rich himself:

Again, no man is more blameless than I am in connexion with the present shortage. Have I produced the most grain of all and then put it under lock and key, raising the price? Why, you yourselves know the productive capacity of my farms – that I rarely, if ever, have sold grain, even when the harvest is unusually productive, and that in all these years I have not had even enough for my own needs, but that the income from my land is derived exclusively from wine and cattle. Nay but, some one may claim, though I lend money, I am unwilling to supply it for the purchase of grain. There is no need for me to say anything on that score either, for you know both those who lend money in our city and those who borrow.[3]

The situation quickly escalated: together with another man Dio was threatened with stones and fire (46.6), and the mob even tried to invade his home, though it stopped short of attacking the house. Furthermore, during his oration he was confronted by an angry crowd trying to interrupt his speech by causing an uproar, and in the very

first paragraph he already addresses their anger against him (46.1).

When dealing with written copies of oral speeches, it is almost always impossible to determine which parts of the speech have been altered before publication in a written form. But even if not every detail of the written speech corresponds with the actual historical situation in Prusa, we know from other examples that Dio's case is not an imaginary scenario, but part of day-to-day life in ancient cities during the Hellenistic and Imperial periods.[4]

Several other instances of social tensions in relation with alleged food shortages are known.[5] Nevertheless, it is almost impossible to quantify the effect of food shortages on local populations.[6] If Dio is to be believed, the price of grain in Prusa seems to have been higher than usual, but not so high that people could not afford grain at all (46.10).[7]

Even if a shortage of grain did not necessarily lead to starvation, a fear of shortage could equally result in social tensions too. As Paul Erdkamp has shown, it was not only supply and demand that affected the polis economy, but also certain social values.[8] Thus, it was not only in the interest of the poorer citizens to have enough grain at a 'fair price';[9] providing cheap grain was also a way for the wealthy to maintain and strengthen their position in the social hierarchy.[10]

Remarkably, most of our sources do not deal with the actual crises connected to the food supply, namely shortages and ensuing riots. Peter Garnsey remarks that 'the evidence is predominantly epigraphic and weighted towards the successful resolution of food crises rather than

---

2   For this episode see Jones 1978, 19-25; Stahl 1978, 163-166; Garnsey 1988, 77, 258 with n. 25; Erdkamp 2005, 278; Quaß 1993, 253-254; Zuiderhoek 2009, 68; Colpaert 2014, 193-197. For the methodological problems of evaluating the effects of food crises see Garnsey 1988, 6-7, 19. The decades since the publication of Peter Garnseys seminal work on *'Famine and Food Supply in the Ancient World'* (Garnsey 1988), have provided new insights into the socio-economic implications of (shortages of) food and their manifold effects in the context of polis politics: see Quaß 1993, 229-269; Garnsey 1999; Erdkamp 2002; 2005, 258-316; Zuiderhoek 2008, esp. 172-177; 2009, 66-70; 2017, 144-146, 189. An older view can be found in Jones 1940, 217-218.

3   Dio Chrys. *Or.* 46.8: καὶ μὴν τῆς γε νῦν ἀπορίας οὐδεὶς μᾶλλον ἐμοῦ ἀναίτιος. πότερον γὰρ σῖτον ἁπάντων πλεῖστον γεωργῶν κατακέκλεικα τούτων, αὔξων τὴν τιμήν; ἀλλ᾽ ἐπίστασθε αὐτοὶ τὴν δύναμιν τῶν ἐμῶν χωρίων, ὅτι σπάνιον εἴ ποτε ἀπεδόμην σῖτον καὶ τοῦθ᾽ ὅταν ὑπερβάλῃ τῷ πλήθει, ἐν δὲ τοῖς τοσούτοις ἔτεσιν οὐδὲ τὸν ἀρκοῦντα ἔχω, ἀλλ᾽ ἔστι μοι ἡ πᾶσα ἐπικαρπία ἐξ οἴνου καὶ βοσκημάτων. ἀλλ᾽ ἀργύριον δανείζων οὐ βούλομαι παρέχειν εἰς τὴν τοῦ σίτου ὠνήν. οὔκουν οὐδὲ περὶ τούτου οὐδέν με δεῖ λέγειν· οἴδατε γὰρ ὑμεῖς καὶ τοὺς δανείζοντας ἐν τῇ πόλει καὶ τοὺς δανειζομένους. The translations of passages from Dio *Or.* 46 are from Lamar Crosby/Loeb. Unless otherwise noted, all other translations are my own.

4   This does not mean that every shortage led to brutal civic unrest: see Garnsey 1988, 30 with the comment of Erdkamp 2002, 97 and Zuiderhoek 2008, 173-174 with n. 49 for social tensions with further literature.

5   *Cf.* Philostratus' descriptions of food riots in Athens (*V S* 1.23.1) or in Aspendos (*V A* 1.15; on this event see Garnsey 1988, 76-77. Raeymaekers 2000 points out the fictitious character of the episode, i.e. neither time nor space are authentic). Further examples are collected in Garnsey 1988, 14-16 (esp. 15 n. 8), 29-31, 76; Erdkamp 2002; Bresson 2016, 335-336, 394-395.

6   See n. 2.

7   For the prices of staple foods see Garnsey 1988, 24-25 (on the price during shortages); Sosin 2002, 137-142 (on the price of grain in the Hellenistic Aegean); Erdkamp 2005, 283-306 (on price regulations); Bresson 2016, 254-259, 325-338, 422-427. For the close relationship between price setting and moral behaviour see Erdkamp 2002, 109-110 with n. 61 and 64.

8   See Erdkamp 2002 and 2005, 312-313, where he uses the concept of moral economy (for a recent perspective see Streeck 2007).

9   For the idea of a 'fair price' see *e.g.* Arist. [*Ath.Pol.*] 51.3. Bresson 2016, 331-332 has pointed out that 'fair' does not always mean 'cheap', although both aspects are often closely connected.

10   For this aspect see Garnsey 1988, 86; Erdkamp 2002, 115; 2005, 269, 315-316; Zuiderhoek 2008, 172-177. This must not necessarily mean that wealthy citizens were always eager to pay.

their less cheerful aspects' (Garnsey 1988, 30, see also 37-38). To this group of epigraphical testimonies belong several honorary decrees from mainland Greece, which under Augustus became the Roman province of Achaea.

In these inscriptions, benefactors are honoured for a number of reasons, including for contributing to the food supply of several cities, thereby avoiding a more serious disaster or at least reassuring the local populace.[11] Yet, they do not necessarily offer a detailed and accurate historical account of food shortages and their solution. Instead, they reveal how (potential) critical situations were remembered in the context of other benefactions, and how the language of honorary decrees shaped or should shape the perception of food crises and their solution, thus reflecting on the broader honorific genre.[12]

Based on examples from Boeotia, the Argolid, and Arcadia from the 2nd century BC to the 1st century AD, I examine the way shortages and countermeasures were presented in epigraphic contexts, and how these representations may be read as idealized narrations of the way the polis and its benefactors dealt with (potentially) critical situations. Drawing on Karl-Siegbert Rehberg's

concept of institutional mechanisms, I show how the language of honorary decrees created the impression of a perpetual system that could – at least according to the text – be relied on in future times of need. In this context, the construction of an 'eternal benefactor' and the inclusion of family members in euergetic relationships can be interpreted as a way not only to highlight the benefactor's deed, but also to show the city's perception of euergetism in general.[13]

2. Euergetism and the creation of *Eigenzeit*

Euergetism was not a one-off engagement. Being one form of gift exchange, it is characterised by a high degree of reciprocity,[14] which means that every action of the *euergetes* entailed a reaction on the side of the recipient and vice versa.[15] For the benefactors the public honours received meant an accumulation of prestige and an acknowledgement of their social status. These encouraged them to act as *euergetai* again, thus changing the governing principle of *do, ut des* into *das, ut dem*.[16] The same holds true for the cities, which were interested in keeping the exchange alive as well.

This reciprocity has in recent scholarship been embedded in concepts of social relationships. Nino Luraghi and Angelos Chaniotis referred to the term 'social capital', thereby borrowing heavily from Bourdieu.[17] This is very useful as it helps to describe the – in economic terms – often unequal relationship between *euergetes* and recipient. Whereas the *euergetes* mainly invests either

---

As Erdkamp 2005, 278 notes, 'the line between voluntary gifts and coerced contributions often becomes very thin.' The example of Dio shows that strong social ties – after all, the mob knows where he lives – within local contexts could facilitate the enforcement of moral expectations (*contra* Erdkamp 2002, 113; for a modern perspective see Streeck 2007, 19). Avoiding civic unrest also meant, in Roman times, avoiding the involvement of the Roman rulers (see Erdkamp 2005, 315 with n. 244).

11 These inscriptions use very different terminologies for food shortages (for the terminology in general see Garnsey 1988, 18-20; Kohns 1994, 839-840): 2nd century BC: *IG* VII 4132 (with *SEG* 41.435) lines 8-10 (Acraephia): σιτοδε|[ί]ας τε πλεονάκις γ[ε] γενημέν[η]ς [ἀπω]λ[είας] τε ὅσων|περ χρείαν εἶχεν ὁ δ[ῆ]μος; *IG* V 2, 437 line 6 (Megalopolis): σιτοδείαις σίτου; 1st century BC: *IG* IV², 1 65 lines 5-7 (Epidaurus): σιτοπωλοῦντος αὐτοῦ πλειονά|κις, ὅταν ἦν χρεία, βλάπτοντος τὸν ἴδιον βίον χάριν τοῦ πᾶσιν συμφέ|ροντος; *IG* IV 2² 750 lines 8-13 (Megara): [τοῦ μὲν] σιτωνικοῦ κατ[αναλισκο]|μένου εἰς [στρατι]ωτικὰς οἰκονομ[ίας περὶ] | [πό]λεμον, ἔτ[ι δὲ τῶ]ν πειρατᾶν ἐπε[χρομένων] | κα[ὶ κ] ατατρεχ[όντω]ν τὰν χώραν, ἅμ[α καὶ ἐν]|δείας οὔσας δ[ιὰ τὴν] ἀριστοπολ[ιτείαν] – – – -|[π]αρέχων ἱκανὸν σ[ῖ]τον, *cf.* Rigsby 2010 for date and place and for the text Thonemann 2008 (= *SEG* 57.310); FdD III.4 55 lines 3-4 (Delphi): καὶ ἐν τῶι ἐνεστακότι δὲ ἐνι[αυτῶι, δεινᾶς χρ]είας γενομένας [τᾶι πόλει] | [ἁμ]ῶν διὰ τὸν περιεστα{κοτα}κότα και[ρόν, παρακληθ]εὶς ὑπὸ τῶν πολιτᾶν ὅπως χοραγήση [σ]ῖτον Καφισίας; 1st century AD: *SEG* 15.330 lines 47-58 (Acraephia): ἐν τῆ τῆς χώρας ἀπωλείᾳ […] καὶ | τοῖς μὲν εἰθισμένοις ἀτάκτως ὑπουργεῖν | τῇ πόλι καπήλοις τε καὶ μαγείροις καὶ ἀρτοκό|ποις ἐκ τῶν ἰδίων ἐπήρκεσαν δόντες τοῖς | μὲν ἀρτοκόποις σῖτον; *IG* V 2, 516 lines 16-17 (Lycosura): ἀφορίας καρπῶν γε|νομένας; 2nd century AD: *SEG* 11.492 line 7 (Sparta): ἐν σπάνει ὅτε ὁ μέδιμνος ἐγένετο * μ´.

12 For this rather constructivist approach to honorary decrees see the important study from Wörrle 1995, esp. 241. See also Rehberg 1998, 397. For the use of rhetorical devices see also Zuiderhoek 2009, 145, 152; Ma 2013, 58-60.

13 The decrees mentioning shortages of food serve here only as a case study. The questions posed could and should be applied to honorific decrees in general, but this goes far beyond the limits of this article and its temporal and geographical scope. Since decrees mentioning shortages present only a small fraction of all extant honorary decrees and since the passages mentioning shortages are part of much longer texts, I cannot draw far-reaching conclusions. I nevertheless hope to offer one possibility of how these texts and passages can be read.

14 The reciprocal character of euergetism is treated by Van Nijf 1997, 116-120; Domingo Gygax 2003 (for Hellenistic times see esp. 197-199); 2006, esp. 271-274; 2009, esp. 184 for 'chains of gifts and counter-gifts'; Zuiderhoek 2007, 203-207; 2009, esp. 113-153; Colpaert 2014, esp. 186-193; Domingo Gygax 2016, *e.g.* 2-3, 12.

15 For proleptic honours see Domingo Gygax 2009 and Domingo Gygax 2016, 45-57.

16 For the stressful situation of nearly infinite obligations, not only to serve the public, but also to surpass other benefactors in Hellenistic times see Wörrle 1995, esp. 246-247 and Domingo Gygax 2009, 175-178.

17 See Luraghi 2010; Chaniotis 2013. Domingo Gygax 2009, 175 uses the term 'symbolic capital' (Zuiderhoek 2009, 114 with other examples). For a very concise introduction to Bourdieu's different forms of capital see Bourdieu 1983. Zuiderhoek 2009, 119-122 refers to David Beetham's model of political legitimacy without really clarifying the shortcomings of Bourdieu's scheme (119).

money or goods whose value can be translated into a sum of money (i.e. both are quantifiable), the recipient pays back in a social currency whose value is not easily quantifiable, at least not in terms of money. Euergetism is a relationship of exchange in which material and symbolic values are intertwined and which rests on the visible connection between the two. This connection is not ontological in the sense that it exists naturally from the beginning, and it is not natural in the sense that, once established, it necessarily lasts forever. More precisely, euergetism only exists in an institutionalized form,[18] and can be described as a relatively stable and recurring pattern of behaviour in social contexts (Rehberg 1998, 386).

As Rehberg (1998, 386-387) has shown, institutions are characterized by 'institutional mechanisms', which help to legitimize them and keep them alive.[19] In the case of euergetism, the implicit assumption about gift and counter-gift is not the only relevant institutional mechanism; another form is the creation of *Eigenzeit*, an institutionally generated temporality with different notions of duration, past, present, and future (Rehberg 1998, 400-401). These notions can also be found in honorary decrees, which, sometimes in the form of repetitive formulations, include their own version of *Eigenzeit*.[20] By this means the reciprocal character of euergetism could be reinforced and was made visible in public in the form of inscriptions and monuments, which served as permanent and legible testimonies for the (alleged) functioning of the institution. While the different strategies of how benefactors and their benefactions were remembered could be interpreted as nothing more than retrospective summaries of good deeds, they clearly carried with them certain implications for future action.[21]

3. Kapon, son of Brochaos

In the first half of the 2nd century BC a citizen of the Boeotian city of Chorsiae proposed:

In the archonship of Kallixenos, [...son of...]kleis proposed: since Kapon, son of Brochaos of [...], is continually well disposed toward the city of the Chorsians for all time, and there being a grain shortage throughout Boeotia, and all the poleis having voted against the export of grain, he made an advance to the polis of two hundred kophinoi, and he brought the grain to the polis. And later, when there was a lawsuit against our polis [...] wishing to prove in every way his goodwill and the favour he has for the Chorsians, and when there was no money in the treasury, he made an advance to the polis of a not inconsiderable sum of money, and the loan being great, some citizens acting as guarantors, he remitted to the polis five hundred drachmas of that loan. And he is continually useful with regard to the needs of private individuals all the time. So that the polis may appear grateful and honour fully according to worth those who do any good deed, it was resolved by the damos that he should be proxenos and benefactor of the polis of the Chorsians, both he and his descendants [...].[22]

There is no doubt that the population of Chorsiae had every reason to honour Kapon. He had helped the city in a time of need, provided grain and partly forgiven a debt.

---

18 Lately, Christel Müller (Müller 2011, esp. 359-360) chose the concept of New Institutional Economics (NIE) to explain the relationship of euergetism and financial aspects in Hellenistic times. She too highlighted the institutional character of euergetism.

19 Rehberg 1998, 386: '*Institutionelle Mechanismen* sind analytisch herauszuarbeitende Formen der Stabilisierung von Sozialbeziehungen [...].' This works not only on the level of euergetism in general, but also on the level of individual elite members and families, who yearned for social recognition and its perpetuation (see Zuiderhoek 2009, 138, 151).

20 These 'texts' are also representatives of the whole institution of euergetism and of very individual official conferments: for the significance of text and publication see Rehberg 1998, 388 and Zuiderhoek 2009, 126.

21 The aspect of continuity is also stressed in Zuiderhoek 2009, 137, 152: 'Honorific monuments, inscriptions and statues all served to provide a façade, or at least a sense, of continuity, precisely because such continuity was in reality often lacking.' (137). Further examples can be found in Quaß 1993, 52 n. 157.

22 [Καλ]λιξένω ἄρχοντος, | [-------------]κ[λ]εῖος ἔλεξε· ἐπιδεὶ Κάπων Βρόχαο | [----- εὔν]οος ἐὼν [διατ]ελῆ τῆ πόλι Χορσιείων, | [ἐν παντὶ κ]ηρῦ, κὴ [σ]πανοσιτίας γενομένας περὶ | [τὰν Βοιωτ]ίαν κὴ τᾶν πολίων πασ[ά]ων ἀπεψαφισμέ-|[νων τ]ὰν τῶ [σ]ίτω [ἀπο]στ[ο]λὰν, προέχρεισε τῆ πό-|[λι πο]υρῶν κοφίνως διακατίω[ς κ]ὴ κατέστασε | [τὸν] σῖτον τῆ πόλι· [κὴ] οὔ[σ]τερ[ον] δίκας ἐώσας τῆ πό-|[λι] ἁμέων [...], βειλόμε-|[ν]ος ἐκ παντὸς τρό[πω] ἀποδί[κ]νουσθη τὰν εὔνυ-|αν κὴ ἤρεσιν ἂν ἔχ[ι π]οτὶ Χορσιείας, οὐκ ἐόντων | χρειμάτων ἐν τ[ῦ] κ[υ]ν[ῦ], προέ[χρ]εισε [τ]ῆ πόλι χρεί|ματα οὐκ ὀλίγα, κὴ δανίω μεγάλω γενομένω, | κὴ τῶν πολιτά[ω]ν πιθόντων αὐτόν, ἀφεῖλε τὰν | πόλιν δραχμὰς πεντακατίας· ἔτι δὲ κὴ τῶν ἰ[δ]ι[ω]τάων τὺς κ[α] χρείαν ἐχόντως εὐχ[ρ]ειστεῦεν | διατελῆ ἐν παντὶ κηρῦ· ὅπως ὦν κὴ ἁ πόλις φή|νειτη εὐ[χ]άριστος ἐῶσα κὴ τιμεῶσα καθόλου | [κ]ὰτ ἀξίαν [τ]ὼς ἀγαθόν τι ποιέ[ο]ντας αὐτάν· δ[ε]|[δό]χθη τῦ δάμυ· πρόξενόν τε εἶμεν κὴ εὐεργέ|[τ]α τᾶς πόλιος Χο[ρσιεί]ω[ν αὐτὸν κὴ] ἐκγ[όν]ως, | [-----------------------------]. Text and translation (modified by author) follow Mackil 2013, 448-449. For the text and its different datings see *IG* VII 2383; Roesch 1965, 256-261 (= *SEG* 22.410; ed., tr., comm.; date: 200-180 BC); Moretti 1967, 168-170, no. 66 (= *SEG* 25.515; ed., tr., comm.; date: early 2nd century BC); Migeotte 1984, 41-44 no. 10 (= *SEG* 34.1690; ed., tr., comm.; date: ca. 200-180 BC); Gehrke 1993, 150-151, 151 n. 42 (= *SEG* 43.214; date: early or first third of the 2nd cent. BC); Müller 2005, 101-105 (= *SEG* 55.551; date: 170-160 BC); Knoepfler 2006, 653-654 no. 194 (before or after 172/1 BC); Mackil 2013, 448-453 (ed., tr., comm.; date: ca. 171-160 BC). A concise version of Mackils analysis is Mackil 2015, 499-500.

For a small city with only a limited amount of arable land a food shortage could lead to a severe crisis.[23] We know that some years earlier the city already had received a loan from Thisbe, and it is very likely that the honorary decree should be dated to a time shortly afterwards.[24]

When looking at the general structure of the text, we can see that the document has a typical opening with the dating formula ([Καλ]λιξένω ἄρχοντος) and the naming of the mover of the motion ([------------]κ[λ]εῖος ἔλεξε), followed by a short catalogue of the benefactor's deeds beginning with ἐπιδεί, before moving to the hortatory intention and the resolution formula.[25]

The catalogue of deeds is framed by the repetition of a participle with the verb διατελῇ (= διατελεῖ) and the prepositional construction ἐν παντὶ κηρῦ. This forms an interesting contrast with the following list of the services Kapon has already rendered. While his deeds are clearly narrated as past actions, διατελῇ evidently assumes that his behaviour will also be the same in the future or, more precisely, in every necessary circumstance (ἐν παντὶ κηρῦ).[26] Whereas the first διατελῇ describes his behaviour towards the city, the second one relates to private persons, thereby stressing that not only individuals, but also the city collective were beneficiaries of Kapon's good deeds.

Therefore, the inscription is more than a one-time testimony to Kapon's previous goodwill: the inscription makes distinct assumptions about his future behaviour. That this future mattered is also evident from the inclusion of his ἔκγονοι, who may have been awarded the title εὐεργέτης as well. The city of Chorsiae extended the reciprocal relationship with Kapon to his descendants, who thus became part of the reciprocal system of good deeds and public honours, before even performing the services expected of them.[27] This in turn meant that they had a debt to pay off. In the case of Kapon this was worth the effort. His family became one of the most prominent families of the region and stayed influential until the end of the 2nd or the beginning of the 3rd century AD. Although we have no further information about the relationship between this family and Chorsiae, we know that members of this family served in religious positions and later had close ties to the imperial house.[28]

It is therefore no surprise that Dio, while trying to win the goodwill of the Prusians, refers back to his predecessors:[29]

Now with reference to my father, there is no need for me to tell whether he was a good citizen, for you are always singing his praises, both collectively and individually, whenever you refer to him as being no ordinary citizen. You should know, however, that these words of praise of yours are of no use to him; on the other hand, when you give your approval to me, his son, then you have been mindful of him too. [...] Being descended, then, from such forebears, even if I were an utter knave myself, yet surely on their account I should merit some consideration instead of being stoned or burned to death by you.[30]

---

23 For the economic situation in Chorsiae see Migeotte 1984, 42 with n. 91. In the first third of the 2nd century, Boeotia faced a severe shortage of grain: see Roesch 1965, 258-259; Moretti 1967, 169; Gehrke 1993, 145-148; Quaß 1993, 243; Walsh 2000, 301-302 (= *SEG* 50.1694 with a comment by Angelos Chaniotis, who, *pace* Walsh, draws attention to warfare as a possible cause for the shortage); Mackil 2014, 61-62.

24 *SEG* 3.342; see Roesch 1965, 252-256; Moretti 1967, 163-168 no. 65; Migeotte 1984, 45-48 no. 11. For the temporal but not necessarily causal relation between these two inscriptions see Müller 2005, 103-104.

25 In general: Klaffenbach 1957, 67-83, esp. 75; McLean 2002, 229-232; Ma 2013, 58-60. For the hortatory clause see also Luraghi 2010, 250-251.

26 For the form διατελῇ see Blümel 1982, 176. Although the use of a participle with a form of διατελείν is to some extent part of the stereotypic language of honorary decrees, this does not mean that it has no hermeneutic value. The use of διατελείν in other tenses than present hints at an awareness for its different semantics: see *e.g.* imperfect in *SEG* 25.540 lines 2-3 (Aulis): ἕνεκα κὴ εὐνοίας ἇς ἔχων | διετέλι ἐν τὰν πόλιν; (for the form διετέλι see Blümel 1982, 185); aorist and present in *IG* IV², 1 66 with Peek 1969, 16-17 no. 21 lines 25-26: ὅμως Ε[ὐ]|άνθης διετέλεσε πωλῶν πᾶσιν and lines 55-56: ἀρετᾶς ἔνε|[κ]εν καὶ εὐνοίας ἇς ἔχων διατελεῖ. Dietrich 1973, 213 has shown that the periphrasis with διατελείν and present participle denotes a combination between a retrospective and prospective view, stressing the continuity before and after a certain moment ('die kontinuative Schau', 196). For the continuous aspect of διατελέω see also Kühner *et al.* 1904, 63-66 (bes 64: 'immerwährend, unausgesetzt, stets'); Schwyzer *et al.* 1950, 392 ('fortwährend'), 450; Adrados 1992, 453; Bentein 2016, 62, 74.

27 For these honours in advance see Domingo Gygax 2003, 191-192; Luraghi 2010, 249-252 with n. 6.

28 For the family of Kapon see Gehrke 1993, 150-152. Knoepfler 1999 (= *SEG* 49.513), 242 with n. 67 (and again Knoepfler 2006, 653-654) argued that Kapon was a native of Phokis. Although this cannot be ruled out, it is more likely that Kapon was from Boeotia (see Mackil 2013, 451 for the discussion).

29 For the importance of genealogy see Quaß 1993, 40-79; Lafond 2006, 164-169; Zuiderhoek 2009, 62-63, 140-146 (mostly focusing on the so-called 'ancestor clause', which presents the honorand's pedigree and highlights the accomplishments of his ancestors); Ma 2013, 155-239 (esp. 233-239 for public monuments; Ma emphasizes the role of the elite for the display of genealogy without adequately considering the benefits for the polis, who itself could have been interested in family continuity).

30 Dio Chrys. *Or.* 46.2-4: Περὶ μὲν γὰρ τοῦ πατρὸς οὐδὲν ἐμὲ δεῖ λέγειν εἰ ἀγαθὸς ἦν. ἀεὶ γὰρ εὐφημεῖτε αὐτὸν καὶ κοινῇ καὶ καθ ἕκαστον, ὅπου ἂν μνησθῆτε, ὡς οὐ φαῦλον πολίτην. δεῖ μέντοι εἰδέναι ὑμᾶς ὅτι οὐδὲν ὄφελος ἐκείνῳ ἐστὶ τούτων τῶν ἐπαίνων· ἀλλ' ὅταν ἡμᾶς τοὺς ἐξ αὐτοῦ ἀποδέχησθε, τότε κἀκείνου μέμνησθε. [...] ἐκ τοιούτων δὴ ὄντες ἡμεῖς, εἰ καὶ σφόδρα πονηροὶ ἦμεν, ἀλλά τοι δι' ἐκείνους ἐντροπῆς τινος ἄξιοι ἦμεν, οὐχὶ λευσθῆναι ὑφ' ὑμῶν οὐδὲ καταφλεχθῆναι.

Here we can see the double-edged consequences of family remembrance: While Dio wants to use his ancestors to save his own skin, the angry crowd recalls the family's lavish wealth that justifies their demands.

4. Euanthes, son of Eunomos

An inscription from the Asclepieion in Epidaurus dating to the 1st century BC further demonstrates that the prediction of future behaviour and the presentation of family ties (that is to say: benefactors in the making) mattered.[31] We know that the sanctuary fell upon especially hard times in the 1st century BC. Livy reports that Epidaurus 'is now rich in the traces of gifts of which it has been robbed, but then [sc. in the time of Aemilius Paullus] was rich in the gifts themselves which the sick had consecrated to the god as payment for health-giving remedies'.[32] This was the result of the sanctuary being plundered by Sulla and later by Cilician pirates.[33] Both aimed at improving their financial situation at the expense of the sanctuary's wealth.

The honorary decree for Euanthes, son of Eunomos and descended from one of the major families of Epidaurus (the so-called *gens magna*), belongs in this context:[34] Not only did he serve as agonothete and *agoranomos* on several occasions, but he also provided grain for the local people while a Roman garrison was installed in the city of Epidaurus, which led to a widespread shortage of grain (*IG* IV², 1 66, lines 28-29: γενηθείσας ὁλοσχερεστέρας ἐν τᾶι πόλει | σπάνιος σίτου). This in turn resulted in a steep rise of the wheat price. Euanthes managed at his own expense to sell a *medimnos* to the local people at five and later four drachmas instead of ten.[35] The inscription even informs us that this was not a one-time commit-

ment: he continued to sell *medimnoi* at this low price throughout the year (*IG* IV², 1 66, lines 32-33: διετέλε[ι π]ω[λῶν] […]|[…] δι' ἐνιαυτοῦ), as the Roman garrison stayed more than ten months (*IG* IV², 1 66, lines 33-34: μεινάντων τῶν στρατ[ιω]|τᾶν πλέον [ἢ μ]ῆνας δέκα).[36] He even managed to have the city released from its obligation to supply troops (*IG* IV², 1 66, lines 45-47). That the supply of food was a real concern for Epidaurus can be inferred from another 1st century BC inscription that honours a certain Aristobulus who frequently sold grain in times of need, thereby risking his own means for the benefit of the public.[37] It is impossible to tell if this inscription is related either to the presence of the Roman garrison or to Sulla's plundering of the place. But it is evident that in 1st century BC Epidaurus the local elites assumed their responsibilities in times of need.

As in the Boeotian inscription, the verb διατελεῖ is present in the decree for Euanthes as well.[38] We should not dismiss it as a meaningless formula written in stone. Euanthes was not only awarded a statue in the sanctuary of Apollo Maleatas and Asclepius (*IG* IV², 1 66, lines 51-52), it was also decreed that in the course of the contests for the gods, a crown was to be publicly awarded to him 'because of his excellence and his goodwill, which he shows continually towards the city.'[39]

Moreover, the decree states that this was not the only occasion on which Euanthes' past deeds were praised and his future actions anticipated. During the Dionysia, after the drink-offering and the crowning of the *euergetes*, a herald was to announce a slightly altered proclamation:

The city of the Epidaurians crowns Euanthes, son of Eunomos, the Epidaurian, with a golden crown because of his excellence and his nobility, which he continually shows towards the city.[40]

This meant that Euanthes' future behaviour was not only predicted, it was also officially promised to all those present at the festival.

As in the case of Kapon, Euanthes' descendants also became inscribed in the reciprocal relationship of euergetism. His ἔκγονοι shared the privilege of the *proedria*. This, too, was more than just a written testimony of the

---

31 The text follows *IG* IV², 1 66 with Peek 1969, 16-17 no. 21. For the inscription in the context of the 1st century BC see Rostovtzeff 1998, 751; Garnsey 1988, 248; de Souza 1999, 146-147; Melfi 2007, 69-70, 169 Nr. 360. For the date of the decree (74/73 BC) see now Rigsby 2010, 311-312.

32 Liv. 45.28: *nunc uestigiis reuolsorum donorum, tum donis diues erat, quae remediorum salutarium aegri mercedem sacrauerant deo* (Transl.: Schlesinger/Loeb).

33 For Sulla see Diod. Sic. 38.7; App. *Mith.* 54; Paus. 9.7.5. The (economic) situation of the sanctuary in the 1st century BC is very hard to assess. Melfi's account of Sulla's plundering (Melfi 2007, 68) is incomplete in that she leaves out the compensation that Sulla gave to the sanctuaries for his confiscations: see Rostovtzeff 1998, 742 with n. 7; Larsen 1959, 365, 426-427; Dignas 2002, 117-118; Eckert 2016, 105-110. For the pirates see Plut. *Pomp.* 24.5 and de Souza 1999, 146-147.

34 For this family and their genealogy see *IG* IV², 1 XXV with Box 1933 and Broadbent 1968, 18-23.

35 *IG* IV², 1 66, lines 31-33. For the price of grain see above n. 7. Sosin 2002, 136 (on *IG* IV², 1 66 see 136 n. 32) has shown that the inscriptions mentioning shortages of food offer a chronological account of the events: (1) price increase followed by (2) the intervention of the *euergetes* and (3) price decrease.

36 See Quaß 1993, 131-132, 251.

37 *IG* IV², 1 65, lines 5-7; for the inscription and its context see Rostovtzeff 1998, 751; Quaß 1993, 243 n. 968 and 969; Melfi 2007, 67. See also n. 11.

38 For the different connotations of different tempora see above n. 26.

39 *IG* IV², 1 66, lines 54-56: στεφ[α]νοῖ | [ἁ] πόλις ἁ τῶν Ἐπιδαυρίων <Εὐάνθη Εὐνόμου Ἐπιδαύριον> χρυσῶι στεφάνωι ἀρετᾶς ἕνε|[κ]εν καὶ εὐνοίας ἇς ἔχων διατελεῖ εἰς αὐτάν.

40 *IG* IV², 1 66, lines 69-72: ἁ πόλις ἁ τῶ[ν Ἐπι]δαυρίων στεφανοῖ Εὐάνθη Εὐνόμου Ἐπιδαύριον χρυσῶ | στεφ[ά]νωι ἀρετᾶς ἕνεκεν καὶ καλοκαγαθίας ἇς ἔχω[ν] | διατελεῖ εἰς αὐτάν.

city's gratitude: Euanthes' descendants became part of a well-staged act at the festival of Apollo and Asclepius, in which they, together with Euanthes, were called to the *proedria*.[41] They also shared with him the προπομπεία at the same festival (*IG* IV², 1 66, lines 64-67). Like Euanthes himself, they enjoyed exemption from taxes, tributes and liturgies for future times.[42] These public honours had a twofold intention: on the one hand, the Epidaurians extended their honours to Euanthes' family and thereby highlighted the importance of his deeds, on the other hand, his descendants were now obliged to act as Euanthes had done and provide help in times of need.

A later testimony attests to the success of this system: the city of the Epidaurians honoured two of his descendants, Polykrates and his father Euanthes, with bronze statues (*IG* IV², 1 647-649 with Peek 1969, 124 no. 282). The inscription for Polykrates explicitly calls him *euergetes* (*IG* IV², 1 647, line 4). Unfortunately, the exact nature of the services that Polykrates provided for his native city is unknown. Both statues shared a base with another statue (for the base see Griesbach 2014, 63-64, Table 12a). This last statue was set up in honour of the aforementioned Euanthes, the *euergetes* from *IG* IV², 1 66 and grandfather and great-grandfather respectively of Euanthes and Polykrates, who, at the time when the statue and the inscription were fashioned, was probably already deceased.[43] The monument therefore spans four generations of one family on a single base. Thus, as late as the 1st century AD, Euanthes was still a point of reference for the euergetism of his family. That this was not only a family matter is obvious: it was not his family who set up the statue. The polis of the Epidaurians set up all three statues, thereby making family continuity in connection with euergetic behaviour visible to everybody.[44]

5. Xenarchos, son of Onasikratos
Another example from the Roman imperial period illustrates the same deliberate intention to display family con-

tinuity. An honorary decree from Lycosura[45] announces that a certain Xenarchos 'gives crops, as often as the city is under pressure because of a lack of corn, and sells them sufficiently for a lower price'.[46] We do not know to what extent Lycosura was affected by a shortage, but the text (line 13: ὁσάκις) suggests that Xenarchos would supply the city with corn in future times as well.[47]

Xenarchos further 'promised in the name of himself, his wife, and his family to renovate the temple [sc. of Despoina] by himself'.[48] Here, too, the favour was returned, not only by the Lycosurians but also by the people from Megalopolis. He was awarded the *proedria* at the local contests (*IG* V 2, 515B, line 31). Further, it was decreed that statues of him, his wife Nikippa and their family be set up, and that pictures on gilded shields be installed in the sanctuary of Despoina and in the temple for the emperor.[49] As in Epidaurus, we have to envision a statuary group encompassing at least two generations.[50] The composition implied euergetist continuity too. The assumption that Xenarchos, his wife, and his family would behave as *euergetai* is also evident in the honorary inscription:

The polis of the Megalopolitans [set up] *Xenarchos and Nikippa and their family, who are benefactors throughout their whole life.*[51]

This mutual relationship corresponds with the interests of both Xenarchos and the local people. When Xenarchos promised to renovate the temple in the name of his family, this implied that the future generations could also gain prestige from his deed. As Dio's speech and the example

---

41 *IG* IV², 1 66, lines 59-64. For this case see Gauthier 1985, 23 n. 49.

42 *IG* IV², 1 66, lines 72-74.

43 *IG* IV², 1 649. The inscription gives no clear evidence whether Euanthes was still alive or not: *cf.* lines 3-4 (συμβουλε[ύο]ντα τὰ κρά|τιστα ἐν παντὶ καιρῶι) with *e.g.* lines 6-7 (εὐεργετηκότα πολλὰ καὶ μεγάλα τὰν πόλιν). Could συμβουλε[ύο]ντα also be συμβουλε[ύσα]ντα?

44 *IG* IV², 1 649, lines 1-3 even has a papponymikon [Εὐάνθη] | Εὐνόμου Ἐπιδαύρ[ιον, Ε]ὐά[νθεος] | υἱωνόν. See Quaß 1993, 62-65 for further examples.

45 *IG* V 2, 515B. For the inscription see: Jost 1985, 174 with n. 5 (*cf.* the different dating on 185 with n. 6); Quaß 1993, 243 with n. 969; Tsiolis 2011, 276 with n. 17. See now Billot 2008, 141, 154 with n. 160 and Kantiréa 2016, 38-39 favouring an earlier date (early Augustan, first half of the 1st century AD) for the inscription.

46 *IG* V 2, 515B, lines 13-14: παρέχεται δὲ καί, ὁσάκις ἂν ἁ πόλις θ[λίβητ]αι [καρ]|πῶν ἐνδίᾳ, τὰ γενήματα καὶ πρὸς ἐλάσσονος τιμᾶς δι[αρκῶ]ς πωλῶ[ν].

47 Although Greek inscriptions do not always necessarily adhere to strict grammatical rules, the use of the indicative present, apart from the otherwise attested aorist in lines 8-17, is noteworthy, as it stresses the recurrence of the provision of grain (*cf.* Kühner *et al.* 1904, 449-450 §567.4).

48 *IG* V 2, 515B, lines 8-10: ὑπέρ τε ἀτοῦ κ[αὶ] τᾶς | [γ]υναικὸς καὶ τᾶν γενεᾶν ἐπαγγείλατο τὸν ναὸν ἐπισκευ[ά]σ[ειν] | παρ᾽ ἀτοῦ.

49 See *IG* V 2, 515B, lines 22-27 and Durie 1984, 140 with n. 20. For line 27 see now Kantiréa 2016, 35. For the importance of the spatial setting of images see Dickenson *this volume*.

50 See Durie 1984, 139-140 and Kantiréa 2016, 38-39 for possible family ties to other persons connected to the sanctuary.

51 *IG* V 2, 515B, lines 25-26: ἁ π]όλις τῶν Μεγαλοπολιτᾶν Ξέναρχον καὶ Νικίππαν καὶ τὰς γενεὰς | [αὐτῶν, εὐ]εργετοῦντας τὰν πόλιν παρὰ πάντα τὸν βίον.

from Epidaurus have shown, heritage mattered. The city, on the other hand, benefitted as well; by rendering praise and honours in advance the city obliged the descendants of Xenarchos to behave like *euergetai* in the time to come. The cult activity associated with the temple could, by the generosity of the benefactors, be maintained in difficult times (Kantirea 2016, 39), and the inscription implies that the city could, in times of need, rely on the provision of food by Xenarchos and his family.

6. Epaminondas of Acraephia

Besides these familial obligations, there are also very explicit references to future benefactors. This is apparent in the case of Epaminondas, who lived in Acraephia in Boeotia under the Julio-Claudian emperors.[52] Epaminondas was honoured for a number of reasons: he paid for sacrifices to Hermes, Hercules and the Augusti, and organized an athletic contest (*IG* VII 2712, lines 21-25). On the same day he offered breakfast not only to residents but also to foreigners and the slaves of citizens (*IG* VII 2712, lines 25-29). Moreover, Epaminondas served as an ambassador for his city in the Panhellenic association in order to present Greek interests to the emperor and other Roman governors (*IG* VII 2712, lines 37-56). An imperial letter of thanksgiving records him as one of the Boeotian ambassadors taking the oath of allegiance to the new emperor Caligula.[53] This means that he not only belonged to the elite of his hometown but also to the elite of Boeotia and Achaea in general. After a thirty-year break he refounded the contest of the Great Ptoia, serving as agonothete, and added the Caesarea to them. This also included annual banquets and breakfasts for a timespan of five years. In the sixth year he organized ancestral processions and an ancestral dance. We are further informed that when the festivities had ended, the citizens spontaneously gathered to honour him. In turn, he again sacrificed to Zeus the Greatest (*IG* VII 2712, lines 55-87).

Above all, he paid more than six thousand *denarii* for the plastering of the great dike, which had apparently suffered over time. This dike was very important as it ensured that the city had enough arable land for the local food production (τοῦ τ[ε] | μεγίστου [κ]αὶ [σ]ώζοντος [ἡμ]ῶν τὴν χώραν χώ[μα]τος).[54]

The inscription ends with the various honours bestowed upon him. Archons, councillors and the demos praised him for his ἐκτενεῖ εὐνοίᾳ ('intense goodwill') (*IG* VII 2712, line 92, all translations from Oliver 1971), as the inscription states. He was awarded a golden crown and a bronze portrait, and obtained a front seat in the theatre. Finally, two bronze or marble portraits of Epaminondas were to be set up, one in the sanctuary of Apollo Ptoios and one in the agora, and the decree should be erected in the same places (*IG* VII 2712, lines 96-106). The inscription explicitly states that future *euergetai* had every reason to expect the same honours for their deeds:

> *So that with these things being so accomplished our city may appear grateful to its benefactors and many may become emulators of his good deeds when the previous good deeds for the city receive recognition.*[55]

Again, the city tries to perpetuate the system of euergetism: by living up to the *euergetes*-recipient expectation, and by commemorating this exchange, the polis promised future benefactors that it would act in the same way.[56]

7. Conclusion

Strategies of remembering played a crucial role in the history of ancient Greece. They were not only an important device in the communication between Greeks and Romans (see Moser, Vanderpool & Scotton *this volume*), but also in the context of polis politics (e.g. Dickenson, Dijkstra, Fouquet, Kuin, Moser *this volume*).

The honorary decrees presented above reflect only a small part of the widespread phenomenon of euergetism. Although we must not forget that coping with shortages was only one aspect for which benefactors have been honoured, it is nevertheless important to see how it was remembered in the context of the decrees. The concept of

---

52 The text follows *IG* VII 2712 with Oliver 1971, 225-236 (ed., tr., comm.). The inscription has in recent times mostly been treated in the context of ritual dynamics: see *e.g.* Chaniotis 2008, 70-85; Graf 2011, 107-110 with older literature.

53 *IG* VII 2711. For the whole dossier see Kantiréa 2007, 178-180. Appendix IB.3.

54 *IG* VII 2712, lines 33-34. See Müller 1995, 459-462 for a critical evaluation of Acraephias economic situation and the restoration of the dike. Although there is no compelling necessity to associate *SEG* 15.330 (line 47: ἐν τῇ τῆς χώρας ἀπωλείᾳ) with a second destruction of the dike (see Kahrstedt 1954, 84-85; Kalcyk 1988, 13), this does not mean that the maintenance of the dike was not an economic obligation. The inscription for Epaminondas (line 34) explicitly affirms the purpose of the dike: [σ]ώζοντος [ἡμ]ῶν τὴν χώραν χώ[μα]τος.

55 *IG* VII 2712, lines 97-100: ἵνα το<ύ>των | οὕτω συντελουμέν<ων> ἡ πόλις ἡμῶν εὐχάριστος φαίνηται πρὸς | τοὺς εὐεργέτας πολλοί τε ζηλ{ηλ}ωταὶ γείνων[τ]αι τῶν ἀγαθῶν | τῶν εἰς τὴν πόλιν μαρτυρουμένων τῶν πρώτων.

56 The hortatory intention is the most obvious way to attract future benefactions, and the main method to anticipate the future for Luraghi 2010, 248-252.

'Eigenzeit' helps to elucidate these strategies of remembrance, that are a vital part of institutionalised euergetism in these cases. It becomes apparent, that the decrees analysed in this article, use language as a tool that is not restricted to retrospective commemoration but that – at least on the level of the text – has a specific importance for the future.

Firstly, the decrees and the honours they describe served as paradigms for solved problems. Although in most cases we do not know how heavily the lack of grain affected individuals, we know that discontent with prices or supply of grain could lead to severe civic unrest. Honouring benefactors as suppliers of (cheap) grain therefore showed a community's capability to deal with these problems, albeit by relying on individual benefactions.

Secondly, the honorary decrees could address future benefactors explicitly by promising to treat them the same way as they had treated past benefactors. The city thereby pledged its social capital in order to benefit from the financial strength of certain individuals.

Thirdly, the language of the decrees suggests that the relationship between benefactor and recipient is perceived as an engagement for a lifetime – and even beyond that. Although the decrees highlight that the honours were granted for past services, they also suggest that the *euergetes*' behaviour should and will continue in the same way. Honorary decrees portray a benefactor whose exemplary behaviour is timeless: in the case of a dead benefactor it is evident that he cannot support his city with new deeds, but that he still can serve as a role model for future benefactors. That is why Kapon is continually well disposed toward the city for all time.[57]

Fourthly, both benefactor and recipient benefited from the inclusion of family members in the reciprocal relationship of *euergesia*.[58] Hereby the benefactor shared the social reputation he gained from his deeds and his lineage with future generations. That is why Dio refers back to his ancestors in front of an angry crowd, and why Xenarchos promises the restoration of the temple in the name of his family too. For the recipients of euergetism the inclusion of family members provided some measure of security. They had already granted certain public honours, so they could expect the benefactors and their family members to help out in times of need, or at least that is the expectation created by the inscriptions.[59] The base in Epidaurus that names four generations of the *gens magna* whose members were omnipresent in the sanctuary made explicit use of family relations to benefit the city.

Although it is often impossible to assess the later behaviour of the benefactors, the inscriptions give insight into how *euergetism* should be perceived, and how the language of the decrees emphasized the aspect of continuity. Seen from this angle, honorary decrees and honorary inscriptions were not only acts of remembering, but also strategies for future actions.

Acknowledgements

This research is part of a project on 'The past as a political resource: Remembering as a strategy in Greece under Roman rule' (TP A02) under the supervision of Dr Muriel Moser within the DFG-funded SFB1095 'Schwächediskurse und Ressourcenregime' at the Goethe University Frankfurt. I would like to thank Janja Soldo, Christian Rollinger and Mills McArthur not only for improving the text in many ways, but also for valuable remarks and discussions. The text has benefited also from the questions and comments from the audience in Athens, and from the editors' remarks.

---

57 This is where the boundary between fiction and actual impact becomes blurred: 'Was als 'Dauer' verstanden und ausgegeben wird […] ist kein bloßes Faktum, sondern ein zu erklärendes Phänomen, und es ist eine der Aufgaben institutioneller Analyse, die 'fiktionale', gleichwohl wirksame und insofern 'reale' Herstellung von Geltung begründender 'Dauer' zu rekonstruieren.' (Rehberg 1998, 387). The same holds true for inscriptions with the adorning epithet αἰώνιος: 'Um kurz zu sein, αἰώνιος ἀγωνοθέτης, ἀγορανόμος, γυμνασίαρχος u. s. w. ist ein Ehrentitel, der dem Stifter selbst zukommt, der durch eine Schenkung die Abhaltung von Agonen, gewisse Erfordernisse der Agoranomie, Gymnasiarchie u. s. w. für alle Zeit sichergestellt oder als ἀριστοπολιτευτής in gleicher Weise für alle Zeit ein nachahmenswerthes Beispiel gegeben hat, daher im Leben und nach dem Tode δι'αἰῶνος als ἀγωνοθέτης u. s. w. ἀριστοπολιτευτής zu betrachten ist.' (Heberdey *et al.* 1896, 154).

58 For the inclusion of other family members see Quaß 1993, 35-37 and for the importance of genealogy see n. 29. Genealogy, whether real or constructed, on the one hand served to stress the ability of family members to act like their predecessor and on the other hand legitimated their future positions (see Rehberg 2004, 16).

---

59 See above n. 27. This becomes very explicit in post-mortem inscriptions for deceased members of famous families, for example in *IPE* I² 52, lines 5-18: ἐπαινούμενός τε ὑπὸ πάντων | καὶ ἐλπιζόμενος πάσας τὰς λειτουργίας ἐκ|[τ]ελέσειν κατὰ τὸ ἀξίωμα τοῦ γένους […] ἡ βουλὴ καὶ ὁ δῆμος στεφα|νοῖ χρυσῷ στεφάνωι Δάδον Τουμ|βάγου παῖδα ἐλπίδων ἀγαθῶν ἀν|τεχόμενον. For further examples see Quaß 1993, 49 n. 149.

References

Adrados, F.R. 1992. *Nueva sintaxis del griego antiguo*, Madrid.

Bekker-Nielsen, T. 2008. *Urban Life and Local Politics in Roman Bithynia. The Small World of Dion Chrysostomos*, Aarhus.

Bentein, K. 2016. *Verbal Periphrasis in Ancient Greek. Have- and Be-Constructions*, Oxford.

Billot, M.-F. 2008. Le temple de Despoina, *Ktema* 33, 135-180.

Blümel, W. 1982. *Die aiolischen Dialekte. Phonologie und Morphologie der inschriftlichen Texte aus generativer Sicht*, Göttingen.

Bourdieu, P. 1983. Ökonomisches Kapital, kulturelles Kapital, soziales Kapital. In: R. Kreckel (ed.), *Soziale Ungleichheiten, Soziale Welt. Sonderband* 2, Göttingen, 183-198.

Box, H. 1933. An Epidaurian Stemma, *JHS* 53, 112-114.

Bresson, A. 2016. *The Making of the Ancient Greek Economy. Institutions, Markets, and Growth in the City-States*, Princeton.

Broadbent, M. 1968. *Studies in Greek Genealogy*, Leiden.

Chaniotis, A. 2008. Konkurrenz und Profilierung von Kultgemeinden im Fest. In: J. Rüpke (ed.), *Festrituale in der römischen Kaiserzeit, Studien und Texte zu Antike und Christentum* 48, Tübingen, 67-87.

Chaniotis, A. 2013. Public Subscriptions and Loans as Social Capital in the Hellenistic City: Reciprocity, Performance, Commemoration. In: P. Martzavou & N. Papazarkadas (eds), *Epigraphical Approaches to the Post-Classical Polis. Fourth Century BC to Second Century AD, Oxford Studies in Ancient Documents*, Oxford, 89-106.

Colpaert, S. 2014. Euergetism and the Gift. In: F. Carlà & M. Gori (eds), *Gift Giving and the 'Embedded' Economy in the Ancient World, Akademie-Konferenzen* 17, Heidelberg, 181-201.

De Souza, P. 1999. *Piracy in the Graeco-Roman World*, Cambridge.

Desideri, P. 1978. *Dione di Prusa. Un Intellettuale Greco Nell'Impero Romano*, Messina.

Dessau, H. 1899. Zum Leben Dios von Prusa, *Hermes* 34, 81-87.

Dietrich, W. 1973. Der periphrastische Verbalaspekt im Griechischen, *Glotta* 51, 188-228.

Dignas, B. 2002. *Economy of the Sacred in Hellenistic and Roman Asia Minor*, Oxford.

Domingo Gygax, M. 2003. Euergetismus und Gabentausch, *Metis* N.S. 1, 181-200.

Domingo Gygax, M. 2006. Les origines de l'évergétisme. Échanges et identités sociales dans la cité grecque, *Metis* 4, 269-295.

Domingo Gygax, M. 2009. Proleptic Honours in Greek Euergetism, *Chiron* 39, 163-191.

Domingo Gygax, M. 2016. *Benefaction and Rewards in the Ancient Greek City. The Origins of Euergetism*, Cambridge.

Durie, E. 1984. Les fonctions sacerdotales au sanctuaire de Despoina à Lykosura – Arcadie, *Horos* 2, 137-147.

Eckert, A. 2016. *Lucius Cornelius Sulla in der antiken Erinnerung. Jener Mörder, der sich Felix nannte*, Berlin.

Erdkamp, P. 2002. A starving Mob has no Respect. Urban Markets and Food Riots in the Roman world, 100 BC – 400 AD. In: L. De Blois & J. Rich (eds), *The Transformation of Economic Life under the Roman Empire, Proceedings of the Second Workshop of the International Network Impact of Empire (Roman Empire, c. 200 B.C.-A.D. 476), Nottingham, July 4-7, 2001, Impact of Empire 2*, Amsterdam, 93-115.

Erdkamp, P. 2005. *The Grain Market in the Roman Empire. A Social, Political and Economic Study*, Cambridge.

Garnsey, P.D.A. 1988. *Famine and Food Supply in the Graeco-Roman World. Responses to Risk and Crisis*, Cambridge.

Garnsey, P.D.A. 1999. *Food and Society in Classical Antiquity*, Cambridge.

Gauthier, P. 1985. *Les Cités Grecques et Leurs Bienfaiteurs*, Athens.

Gehrke, H.-J. 1993. Thisbe in Boiotien. Eine Fallstudie zum Thema 'Griechische Polis und Römisches Imperium', *Klio* 75, 145-154.

Graf, F. 2011. Ritual Restoration and Innovation in the Greek Cities of the Roman Imperium. In: A. Chaniotis (ed.), *Ritual Dynamics in the Ancient Mediterranean. Agency, Emotion, Gender, Representation, HABES* 49, Stuttgart, 105-117.

Griesbach, J. 2014. Jede(r) ist ersetzbar? Zur Wiederverwendung von Statuenbasen im Asklepios-Heiligtum von Epidauros. In: C. Leypold, M. Mohr & C. Russenberger (eds), *Weiter- und Wiederverwendungen von Weihestatuen in griechischen Heiligtümern. Tagung am Archäologischen Institut der Universität Zürich 21.-22. Januar 2011, ZAF* 2, Zürich, 55-69.

Heberdey, R. & A. Wilhelm 1896. Reisen in Kilikien, ausgeführt zwischen 1891 und 1892 im Auftrage der kaiserlichen Akademie der Wissenschaften (Widmung Seiner Durchlaucht des regierenden Fürsten Johann von und zu Liechtenstein), *DenkschrWien* 44, 1-168.

Jones, A.H.M. 1940. *The Greek City From Alexander to Justinian*, Oxford.

Jones, C.P. 1978. *The Roman World of Dio Chrysostom*, Cambridge, MA.

Jost, M. 1985. *Sanctuaires et Cultes d'Arcadie*, Paris.

Kahrstedt, U. 1954. *Das wirtschaftliche Gesicht Griechenlands in der Kaiserzeit. Kleinstadt, Villa und Domäne*, Bern.

Kalcyk, H. 1988. Der Damm von Akraiphia. Landsicherung und Landgewinnung in der Bucht von Akraiphia am Kopaissee in Böotien, Griechenland, *Boreas* 11, 5-14.

Kantiréa, M. 2007. *Les Dieux et Les Dieux Augustes. Le Culte Impérial en Grèce sous les Julio-Claudiens et Les Flaviens. Etudes Épigraphiques et Archéologiques*, Athens.

Kantiréa, M. 2016. Re-Shaping the Sacred Landscape through Benefaction. The Sanctuary of Lykosoura in the Peloponnese. In: M. Melfi & O. Bobou (eds), *Hellenistic Sanctuaries: Between Greece and Rome*, Oxford, 27-39.

Klaffenbach, G. 1957. *Griechische Epigraphik*, Göttingen.

Knoepfler, D. 1999. L'Épigraphie de La Grèce Centro-Méridionale (Eubée, Béotie, Phocide et Pays Voisins, Delphes). Publications Récentes, Documents Inédits, Travaux en Cours. *XI Congresso Internazionale di Epigrafia Greca e Latina. Roma, 18-24 Settembre 1997* Atti 1, Rome, 229-255.

Knoepfler, D. 2006. Bulletin épigraphique. Béotie-Eubée, *RÉG* 119, 652-667.

Kohns, H.P. 1994. Hungersnot. In: *RAC* 16, 828-893.

Kühner, R. & B. Gerth 1904. *Ausführliche Grammatik der griechischen Sprache* 2.2: Satzlehre, Hannover.

Lafond, Y. 2006. *La Mémoire des Cités dans le Péloponnèse d'Époque Romaine (IIe Siècle Avant J.C.-IIIe Siècle Après J.-C.*, Rennes.

Larsen, J.A.O. 1959. Roman Greece. In: F. Tenney (ed.), *An Economic Survey of Ancient Rome* 4, Paterson, 259-498.

Luraghi, N. 2010. The Demos as narrator: Public Honours and the Construction of Future and Past. In: L. Foxhall, H.-J. Gehrke & N. Luraghi (eds), *Intentional History. Spinning Time in Ancient Greece*, Stuttgart, 247-263.

Ma, J. 2013. *Statues and Cities. Honorific Portraits and Civic Identity in the Hellenistic World*, Oxford.

Mackil, E. 2013. *Creating a Common Polity. Religion, Economy, and Politics in the Making of the Greek Koinon*, Berkeley.

Mackil, E. 2014. Creating a Common Polity in Boeotia. In: N. Papazarkadas (ed.), *The Epigraphy and History of Boeotia. New Finds, New Prospects*, Leiden, 45-67.

Mackil, E. 2015. The Economics of Federation in the Ancient World. In: H. Beck & P. Funke (eds), *Federalism in Greek Antiquity*, Cambridge, 487-502.

Mclean, B.H. 2002. *An Introduction to Greek Epigraphy of the Hellenistic and Roman Periods from Alexander the Great to the Reign of Constantine (323 B.C.-A.D. 337)*, Ann Arbor.

Melfi, M. 2007. *I Santuari di Asclepio in Grecia* 1, Rom.

Migeotte, L. 1984. *L'emprunt public dans les cités grecques. Recueil des documents et analyse critique*, Québec.

Moretti, L. 1967. *Iscrizioni Storiche Ellenistiche. Teste critico, traduzione e commento 1*, Florence.

Müller, C. 1995. Epaminondas et les évergètes de la cité d'Akraiphia au Ier siècle de n. ère. In: A.Ch. Christodoulou (ed.), Επετηρίς της Εταιρείας Βοιωτικών Μελετών. Β' Διεθνές Συνέδριο Βοιωτικών Μελετών 2, Athens, 455-467.

Müller, C. 2005. La procédure d'adoption des décrets en Béotie de la fin du IIIᵉ s. av. J.-C. au Iᵉʳ s. apr. J.-C. In: P. Fröhlich & C. Müller (eds), *Citoyenneté et participation a la basse époque hellénistique. Actes de la table ronde des 22 et 23 mai 2004, Paris, Hautes études du monde Gréco-Romain* 35, Genf, 95-119.

Müller, C. 2011. Évergétisme et pratiques financières dans les cités de la Grèce hellénistique, *RÉA* 113, 345-363.

Oliver, J. 1971. Epaminondas of Acraephia, *GRBS* 12, 221-237.

Peek, W. 1969. *Inschriften aus dem Asklepieion von Epidauros*, Berlin.

Quaß, F. 1993. *Die Honoratiorenschicht in den Städten des griechischen Ostens. Untersuchungen zur politischen und sozialen Entwicklung in hellenistischer und römischer Zeit*, Stuttgart.

Raeymaekers, J. 2000. The Grain Hoarders of Aspendus. Philostratus on the Intervention of Apollonius of Tyana (*Vita Apollonii* I 15). In: L. Mooren (ed.), *Politics, Administration and Society in the Hellenistic and Roman World*, Leuven, 275-286.

Rehberg, K.-S. 1998. Die stabilisierende „Fiktionalität' von Präsenz und Dauer. Institutionelle Analyse und historische Forschung. In: R. Blänkner & B. Jussen (eds), *Institutionen und Ereignis. Über historische Praktiken und Vorstellungen gesellschaftlichen Ordnens, Veröffentlichungen des Max-Planck-Instituts für Geschichte* 138, Göttingen, 381-407.

Rehberg, K.-S. 2004. Zur Konstruktion kollektiver 'Lebensläufe'. Eigengeschichte als institutioneller Mechanismus. In: G. Melville & K.-S. Rehberg (eds), *Gründungsmythen Genealogien Memorialzeichen. Beiträge zur institutionellen Konstruktion von Kontinuität*, Köln, 3-18.

Rigsby, K.J. 2010. Aegina and Megara (*IG* IV.2² 750), *CP* 105, 308-313.

Roesch, P. 1965. Notes d'epigraphie béotienne, *RPhil* 39, 252-265.

Rostovtzeff, M. 1998. *Gesellschafts- und Wirtschaftsgeschichte der hellenistischen Welt*, Darmstadt.

Schwyzer, E. & A. Debrunner 1950. *Griechische Grammatik. Auf der Grundlage von Karl Brugmanns griechischer Grammatik 2*: Syntax und Syntaktische Stilistik, München.

Sosin, J.D. 2002. Grain for Andros, *Hermes* 130, 131-145.

Stahl, M. 1978. *Imperiale Herrschaft und provinziale Stadt. Strukturprobleme der römischen Reichsorganisation im 1.-3. Jh. der Kaiserzeit*, Göttingen.

Streeck, W. 2007. Wirtschaft und Moral: Facetten eines unvermeidlichen Themas [Online]. http://hdl.handle.net/10419/41693. [accessed 10 April 2017].

Swain, S. 1996. *Hellenism and Empire. Language, Classicism, and Power in the Greek World AD 50-250*, Oxford.

Thonemann, P. 2008. Review of K. Hallof (ed.) 2007. Inscriptiones Graecae, Vol IV: Inscriptiones Argolidis [Editio altera], Fasc. 2: Inscriptiones Aeginae insulae, Berlin, *CR* 58, 506-507.

Tsiolis, V. 2011. Santuarios de Arcadia y dominio romano. In: J.M. Cortés Copete, E. Muñiz Grijalvo & R. Gordillo Hervás (eds), *Grecia ante los imperos. V Reuníon de historiadores del mundo griego, Spal Monografías* 15, Sevilla, 273-289.

Van Nijf, O.M. 1997. *The Civic World of Professional Associations in the Roman East*, Amsterdam.

Von Arnim, H. 1898. *Leben und Werke des Dion von Prusa*, Berlin.

Von Arnim, H. 1899. Zum Leben Dios von Prusa, *Hermes* 34, 363-379.

Walsh, J.J. 2000. The Disorders of the 170s B.C. and Roman Intervention in the Class Struggle in Greece, *CQ* 50, 300-303.

Wörrle, M. 1995. Vom tugendsamen Jüngling zum 'getreßten' Euergeten. Überlegungen zum Bürgerbild hellenistischer Ehrendekrete. In: M. Wörrle & P. Zanker (eds), *Stadtbild und Bürgerbild im Hellenismus. Kolloquium, München, 24. bis 26. Juni 1993, Vestigia* 47, München, 241-250.

Zuiderhoek, A. 2007. The Ambiguity of Munificence, *Historia* 56, 196-213.

Zuiderhoek, A. 2008. Feeding the Citizens. Municipal Grain Funds and Civic Benefactors in the Roman East. In: R. Alston & O.M. Van Nijf (eds), *Feeding the Ancient Greek City*, Leuven, 159-180.

Zuiderhoek, A. 2009. *The Politics of Munificence in the Roman Empire. Citizens, Elites and Benefactors in Asia Minor*, Cambridge.

Zuiderhoek, A. 2017. *The Ancient City*, Cambridge.

PART IV

Past and Politics in Athens

Anchoring Political Change in Post-Sullan Athens

Inger N.I. Kuin

Abstract

The question whether or not Sulla gave the Athenians a new constitution after sacking the city in 86 BC has plagued generations of ancient historians. This article revisits the relevant source material, a passage in Appian's *Mithridatic Wars* and an inscribed decree from the Athenian agora, from the perspective of political change. Both documents are analysed as examples of how Greeks and Romans adapted to the political transformations of the 1st century BC. This article suggests that a key strategy in facilitating adaptation was to anchor political innovations in (invented) traditions of the past.

Keywords: Sulla, Athens, Roman Empire, political change, anchoring innovation

1. Introduction

From the early 2nd century BC onwards Athens was allied with Rome. Even if the nature and the precise date of the alliance are difficult to determine, it is clear that there was a relationship, and that this relationship was still intact at the beginning of the First Mithridatic War. This war broke out in 89 BC, when the Romans incited king Nicomedes of Bithynia to invade Pontus. The following year Athens elected as hoplite general an Aristotelian philosopher with close ties to Mithridates Eupator, named Athenion, which probably signalled the end of Athens' alliance with Rome. The appointment of Athenion also ended a period of *anarchia*: after Medeius had been eponymous archon for the highly unusual period of three consecutive terms, Athens was briefly without an archon. It is implied in Posidonius' account that the city appealed to the Roman senate for assistance in solving this political impasse, but unfortunately he does not provide any details (Posidon. *BNJ* F 36 5.51). The Athenians, it seems, not wanting to wait any longer for a response from Rome submitted themselves to Athenion instead. In 87 BC, for reasons that are not completely clear to us, Mithridates' general Archelaus replaced Athenion with another Athenian, this one named Aristion. Possibly, Athenion's removal was connected to Athens' failed campaign to Delos during his rule. In the summer of the same year Sulla arrived in Greece. He fought Archelaus in the Piraeus, and Aristion in Athens, and in the winter of 87/86 BC he besieged both the city and the Piraeus from Eleusis. The siege caused the Athenians to suffer a severe famine, until finally Sulla

in: Dijkstra, T.M., I.N.I. Kuin, M. Moser & D. Weidgenannt (eds) 2017. *Strategies of Remembering in Greece under Rome (100 BC - 100 AD)*, Leiden (Sidestone Press).

stormed Athens in March of 86 BC. After capitulating on the Acropolis, Aristion was captured, and later executed.[1]

One consequence of the sack of Athens was, it has often been argued, that Sulla gave the Athenians a new constitution.[2] This idea derived from a brief comment in the 2nd century AD author Appian, and from an inscription that seems to be a record of Sulla's legislative intervention in Athens. Over the past decades, however, the existence of Sulla's laws has repeatedly been questioned because Appian's remark does not actually fit well with the text of the inscription. In this article I revisit the issue of Sulla's 'Athenian constitution' from the perspective of political change: I analyse both documents as examples of how Greeks and Romans adapted to the political transformations of the 1st century BC using the strategy of anchoring. I suggest that the use of this strategy, by which changes and innovations are embedded in (allegedly) older traditions,[3] has contributed to the interpretative problems posed by the sources in question. Before reviewing the possible connection between them, Appian's remark and the inscription of Sulla's 'constitution' are considered independently, as valuable sources in their own right.

The structure of the article is as follows. The second section briefly introduces the central sources: Appian, *Mithridatic Wars* 39 and the inscription *Agora* I 2351. The third section, drawing on Aristotle's *Politics*, explores how change was viewed in ancient political thought, and introduces the concept of anchoring as a possible means of adapting to such change. The fourth and fifth sections are dedicated, respectively, to the Agora inscription in light of the problematic nature of political change in antiquity, and to Appian's comments about Sulla's laws for Athens.

2. The sources for Sulla's 'Athenian constitution'

The 2nd century AD historian Appian, from Alexandria but working in Rome, is a major source for our knowledge of the events of 86 BC. *Mithridatic Wars*, the twelfth book of his now fragmentary *Roman History*, survives in its entirety. At the end of his narrative of Sulla's siege of Athens Appian adds the following comment:

Sulla sentenced to death Aristion and his bodyguard, and all who exercised any authority or who had done anything contrary to the arrangements made for them by the Romans earlier, after the capture of Greece. He pardoned the rest and gave all of them laws, which were similar to what had been determined for them by the Romans before.[4]

The passage raises several questions. What precisely were the arrangements made by the Romans earlier that Appian refers to, and what was their legal status? Which capture of Greece does he mean? What are the laws (*nomoi*) Appian is talking about, and how similar were they to the pre-war 'arrangements'?

The issues raised by Appian's comment are difficult to resolve. To begin with the first question: there is no indication in the evidence available to us that Rome interfered with the constitution of Athens at all before the First Mithridatic War. This means that the 'arrangements' mentioned by Appian here should probably not be understood as a legal system. Instead, the phrase may refer to Athens' alliance with Rome, though the precise date of this treaty is, as mentioned, unknown. 'The capture of Greece' that the passage alludes to can refer just as easily to the conclusion of the Macedonian War in 196 BC as to the end of the Achaean War in 146 BC. This phrase, then, does not help to explain in any way what Appian means by the Romans' earlier 'arrangements.'[5]

The most difficult term from the concluding passage of the siege of Athens is *nomoi*, which I have translated above as 'laws,' though it can also have the weaker meaning of 'customs' (LSJ[9] s.v. *nomos* III). The debate on what these *nomoi* refer to, and on what Sulla precisely imposed on the Athenians in 86 BC, is ongoing. The numerous interpretations that have been proposed can be divided, roughly, into the following groups: a) the *nomoi* refer to peace conditions imposed on Athens by Sulla; b) the *nomoi* refer to a reinstatement of the earlier alliance between Athens and Rome; c) the *nomoi* refer to a constitutional reform for the city, possibly not initiated by Sulla himself; d) the *nomoi* refer to the restoration of constitutional, i.e. non-mo-

---

1 On the status of the second century BC relation between Athens and Rome see Habicht 1997, 212-213; *cf.* Kallet-Marx 1995, 200-201. On Athenion see Posidon. *BNJ* 87 F 36. On Medeius see Kallet-Marx 1995, 206-209; Habicht 1997, 301-304; Verdejo Manchado & Antela-Bernárdez 2013. Habicht (1997, 300-301) sees the election of Athenion as the end of the alliance; Kallet-Marx (1995, 209-211) argues that ties were not severed until Athens' attack on Delos; Antela-Bernárdez (2015) similarly questions Athenion's hostility to Rome.

2 Geagan 1971; Badian 1976; Bugh 2013.

3 On the concept of anchoring see Sluiter 2017, and my discussion below.

4 App. *Mith.* 39: καὶ αὐτῶν ὁ Σύλλας Ἀριστίωνα μὲν καὶ τοὺς ἐκείνῳ δορυφορήσαντας ἢ ἀρχήν τινα ἄρξαντας, ἢ ὁτιοῦν ἄλλο πράξαντας παρ᾽ ἃ πρότερον ἁλούσης τῆς Ἑλλάδος ὑπὸ Ῥωμαίων αὐτοῖς διετέτακτο, ἐκόλασε θανάτῳ, τοῖς δὲ ἄλλοις συνέγνω, καὶ νόμους ἔθηκεν ἅπασιν ἀγχοῦ τῶν πρόσθεν αὐτοῖς ὑπὸ Ῥωμαίων ὁρισθέντων. Throughout translations are my own, unless stated otherwise.

5 On the previous 'arrangements' see Habicht 1997, 315; Antela-Bernárdez 2009, 107-108; Bugh 2013, 114-115; on the ambiguity of the phrase 'the capture of Greece' see Badian 1976, 116; Kallet-Marx 1995, 201.

narchic, rule by Sulla through his defeat of Mithridates Eupator's puppet ruler.[6]

I return to the contested interpretation of Sulla's *nomoi* in Appian below. For now it is worth noting that in spite of the lack of consensus on what the passage in *Mithridatic Wars* means scholars still take it as a given that Sulla did in fact impose a new constitution on the Athenians.[7] The persistence of the view that Appian's remark is clear evidence for Sulla's Athenian constitution is likely connected with the possible epigraphic corroboration of this notion.

In 1971 Daniel Geagan published a newly discovered inscription from the Athenian agora, commonly known as *Agora* I 2351, dating it to 84 BC.[8] He based this date on the preserved first three letters of the deme of the secretary in the third line of the inscription. Geagan understood the inscription as Sulla's 'oligarchic restoration' at Athens, which he would have carried out during his visit to the city in that year. Plutarch, who does not mention any legislative intervention in Athens by him, reports that Sulla visited the city in 84 BC, and that he was initiated in the Eleusinian Mysteries on the occasion.[9] Aside from the date, Geagan based his interpretation on a few phrases that emerge from the highly fragmentary text. In lines six through eight Geagan reconstructed the following:

Demeas the son of Demeas [of Azenia proposed (this decree). After the Athenian people deliberated] *in democracy* [according to the laws (or: in democracy and freedom), as it had been convened by the archons who had been chosen] *by lot and by election, ...*[10]

The significance of these lines lies in the election of the archons by lot and election. This method, writes Geagan, was associated with Solon, and with oligarchic forms of government.[11] The second phrase that Geagan focuses on occurs in lines sixteen through eighteen, which he reconstructs as follows:

[With good fortune the people decided that] *the laws legislated before ... [by the council] of the Areopagus are in force.*[12]

Geagan (1971, 107) comments: 'Sulla (...) would have found in this council a body of experienced men whose sympathy would have belonged to the oligarchy.' The word *demokratia* from line seven Geagan (1971, 108) understands as a reference to the restoration of republican government after the monarchic tyranny of Athenion and Aristion, rather than in connection to democratic-leaning politics.

Only a year after the initial publication of the inscription James Oliver argued, instead, that the decree represents a return from oligarchy to democracy. He dated it to 70 BC, and interprets the decree as a response by the Areopagus to the restoration of the power of the tribunes at Rome, 'to conciliate the common people of Athens by a display of democracy.'[13] Independently Badian also argued that the decree marked a return from oligarchy to democracy, but he dated it to Athenion's rule in 88 BC.[14] Both authors emphasize the appearance of the word *demokratia* in the inscription, arguing, unlike Geagan, that it should be read politically. Oliver later returned to the inscription and proposed several new readings. Additionally, he argued for peripatetic elements in the decree, which fits well with Posidonius' report (*BNJ* 87 F 36) that Athenion was a peripatetic philosopher. Oliver interprets Demeas' decree as a confirmation of peripatetic legislation enacted under Athenion, dating it either to the archonship of Philanthes of 87/86 BC or a bit later.[15]

---

6   The key representatives of each interpretation are: a) Touloumakos 1967, 89n3; Kallet-Marx 1995, 218; Santangelo 2007, 42; b) Antela-Bernárdez 2009; c) Geagan 1971 (by Sulla); Badian 1976 (by Sulla); Bugh 2013 (by Sulla); Bernhardt 1985, 41-42 (not by Sulla); Habicht 1997, 315 (not by Sulla); d) Ferrary 1988, 217-218; Goukowsky 2001, 165.

7   Geagan's 1967 classic *The Athenian Constitution after Sulla* was of great influence; recent examples include Harter-Uibopuu 2008 and Bugh 2013.

8   Geagan 1971. See also *Agora* XVI 333 and SEG nos. 26.120, 30.80, 49.128, 59.131 for this inscription. Geagan 1971 and Oliver 1980 start the line numbers with the first preserved line, referring to the reconstructed opening line as 'a'; *Agora* XVI 333 starts the line numbers with the opening line. I follow the numbering of Geagan and Oliver.

9   Plut. *Sull.* 26; compare *Sull.* 37, where Plutarch writes that Sulla 'wrote a code of laws for their conduct of the city's government' (νόμον ἔγραψεν αὐτοῖς καθ᾽ ὃν πολιτεύσονται) for the inhabitants of Puteoli.

10 *Agora* I 2351, lines 6-8: Δημέας Δημέ[ου Ἀζηνιεὺς(?) εἶπεν· ἐπειδὴ ὁ δῆμος ὁ Ἀθηναίων] | ἐν δημοκρατίαι κ[ατά τε τοὺς νόμους πολιτευόμενος καὶ ὑπὸ ?] | τῶν κλήρωι καὶ χε[ιροτονίαι αἱρεθέντων ἀρχόντων κληθεὶς ?]. Alternatively, Geagan (1971,

104) suggests for line 7 κ[αὶ ἐλευθερίαι instead of κ[ατά τε τοὺς νόμους. Compare also Oliver's (1980) reading for lines 7 and 8: ἐν δημοκρατίαι κ[ατὰ τοὺς παλαιοὺς νόμους καὶ τὰ ἐπιτάγματα] | τῶν κλήρωι καὶ χε[ιροτονίαι ἐκλεγομένων πολιτεύεσθαι βούλεται].

11 Geagan 1971, 104-105, *cf.* Arist. *Ath. Pol.* 8.1.

12 *Agora* I 2351, lines 16-18: ἀ[γαθῆι τύχηι δεδόχθαι τῶι δήμωι] | [τὰ] μὲν προνενομοθετημέν[α ----- ὑπὸ τῆς βουλῆς τῆς] | [ἐν Ἀ] ρείωι Πάγωι κύρια εἶναι.

13 Oliver 1972, 101. For his date Oliver reads Anaflustius for the secretary's deme and thus tribe XI Antiochis; Geagan (1971, 101) read Anakeieus from tribe IX Hippothontis.

14 Badian (1976, 116-117) reads the deme as Anagurasius from tribe I Erechtheis, on the assumption that after Medeius' rule a new secretary cycle had started.

15 Oliver 1980, 199-201. I return to Oliver's peripatetic interpretation below.

I will return to the problematic interpretation of *Agora* I 2351 in section four of this article. For now it is noteworthy that (roughly) the same text has been interpreted alternately as an oligarchic and a democratic restoration. Whether or not the inscription is connected to Sulla, and even if ultimately it cannot be dated with certainty, the decree is worth contemplating in its own right, and should not be dismissed (*contra* Habicht 1997, 321). It is clear that the two existing interpretative models both understand the decree as a witness of a moment of political change. In order to better understand the mixed signals about the nature of this change, oligarchic or democratic, that the inscription appears to send, I now turn to Aristotle's *Politics*. Aristotle explains the risks associated with political change, but also offers a suggestion for avoiding these risks that may explain the mixed messages of our decree. Furthermore, if we should decide to follow Oliver in associating the decree with the peripatetic Athenion, Aristotle will be even more relevant to interpreting this document.

3. Anchoring political change

In ancient Greek political thought stability was a core value. The catastrophic humanitarian consequences of civil war (*stasis*) were deeply engraved in Greek cultural memory, and Athenian democracy was in large part designed to avoid *stasis*. As a consequence the Greeks were in general suspicious of political change. Aristotle's discussion of political change in *Politics* 2 explains this suspicion, while also being attuned to the necessity of change.[16]

Aristotle is prompted to treat the topic of political change in the context of his review of the political thought of Hippodamus of Miletus. Among the ideas of this man, better known as an architect and city planner, was a proposal to have citizens submit political innovations for the city. Those who put forward the best proposals should receive honours; what kind of honours is not made clear. Aristotle believes that Hippodamus' idea is dangerous because it promotes unhealthy competitiveness among citizens, and might lead to political instability. Yet, he uses the proposal as an opportunity for a general discussion of political change. Aristotle starts out with the question 'whether it is harmful or beneficial for the cities to change the ancestral laws if a different law would be better.'[17] The answer, at first, seems clear: surely adopting

a new, better law would further the wellbeing of the city. Aristotle's comparison of doing politics to other crafts (*technai*) supports this line of argument: in medicine and in gymnastic training innovations have led to the advancement of these fields (*Pol.* 1268b34-38). Further, some of the laws of the past are demonstrably worse than the laws of the present. The Hellenes of old, for instance, carried arms and purchased their wives (*Pol.* 1268b40-41).

There are also risks attached to improving the laws, though, and on second thought Aristotle's initial question is actually not so easy to answer. He goes on to present the opposite side of the argument. Even changing the laws for the better might be harmful, because law making is actually quite different from other *technai*:

> [I]t is not the same to change a craft as it is to change a law. The law has no other strength to secure obedience than custom, and this does not come about except through longevity, so that readily changing from the existing laws to other and new laws is to make the power of the law weak.[18]

Laws need to have authority to be effective, while other crafts are effective simply when they deliver the goods. The law's authority is undermined by frequent changes, and those responsible for changing them become accustomed to disobeying the rulers. Aristotle has created a difficult conundrum: the need for changing laws is clear, but if changing the laws weakens them this defeats the purpose of improving them. He concludes his discussion of political change by saying that it should be pursued at a different, more opportune time (*Pol.* 1269a27-28). If he delivered on this promise no text for the continuation of this discussion has been transmitted.

Aristotle ends his discussion on whether or not the laws should be changed in explicit *aporia*: it seems that it ought to be possible to change the laws, but it is not clear that the benefits outweigh the risks. Elsewhere in *Politics*, however, Aristotle presents his own innovative proposal on property, which he thinks should be owned privately but used in common. The way Aristotle introduces his proposal suggests a potential, partial answer to our *aporia*. He connects his plan for property ownership to known practices from elsewhere or from the past, and he explains this approach as follows:

---

16   Van Groningen attributed a general conservatism to the ancient Greeks, including also their political life (1953, 112). D'Angour (2011, 36-40), while arguing against a conservative Greek outlook over-all, maintains Van Groningen's argument for the political realm. The topic of political change in Aristotle will be discussed in greater detail in Kuin forthcoming a.

17   Arist. *Pol.* 1268b26-28: πότερον βλαβερὸν ἢ συμφέρον ταῖς πόλεσι τὸ κινεῖν τοὺς πατρίους νόμους, ἂν ᾖ τις ἄλλος βελτίων.

18   Arist. *Pol.* 1269a19-24: οὐ γὰρ ὅμοιον τὸ κινεῖν τέχνην καὶ νόμον· ὁ γὰρ νόμος ἰσχὺν οὐδεμίαν ἔχει πρὸς τὸ πείθεσθαι παρὰ τὸ ἔθος, τοῦτο δ᾽ οὐ γίνεται εἰ μὴ διὰ χρόνου πλῆθος, ὥστε τὸ ῥᾳδίως μεταβάλλειν ἐκ τῶν ὑπαρχόντων νόμων εἰς ἑτέρους νόμους καινοὺς ἀσθενῆ ποιεῖν ἐστι τὴν τοῦ νόμου δύναμιν.

So similarly we must understand that also other arrangements have been invented many times in our long history, or rather countless times; for probably the necessary things exigency itself teaches, and once those are available it is reasonable that things for refinement and luxury start developing; so that we have to suppose that it works the same way with political institutions. (…) Therefore it is necessary to use existing inventions when adequate, and attempt to investigate what has been passed over.[19]

Aristotle argues that, because the truly necessary political arrangements have already been invented many times over, anyone seeking to improve upon the laws has to investigate and use relevant earlier inventions. This methodology has been dismissed as a proposal 'to bottle afresh (…) old wine' (Lockwood 2015, 83), but the connotation of this phrase is that something that *is not* new is purposely made to *seem new*. This is the opposite of what Aristotle does when he connects his proposals to existing and ancient examples: he makes something that *is* new *seem old*.

In Aristotle's own words his strategy appears as one of economy; all the necessary political arrangements have already been invented, so we should (re)use them. But this is only part of the story. Aristotle's proposal does not just expand old customs to cover extraneous, 'passed over' needs. Rather, the innovation borrows some older elements and incorporates them into a new system. I suggest that this strategy whereby the new is anchored in the old can provide an answer to Aristotle's own conundrum of how to safely accomplish political change. Connecting political innovations to existing or ancient practices helps avoid the risks associated with changing the laws: if the break with older customs and laws seems less radical, citizens no longer feel like they are disobeying the old laws; and if a new law in some respect already appears familiar it is easier to get accustomed to obeying it. Because, as Aristotle says, habituation is vital for the strength of the law, anchoring new laws is not just expedient, but actually *necessary* in order to guarantee the viability and stability of legal systems. I argue that in Aristotle's *Politics* we see both an illustration of the type of problem that the practice of anchoring tries to solve – how to facilitate innovation – and an example of its application. Anchoring changes to

the laws in what is familiar and known, as Aristotle does with his proposal about property ownership, prevents the sudden interruption of the process of habituation.[20]

4. Another look at *Agora* I 2351

Agora I 2351, as discussed, has been interpreted variously as a decree describing a return from a predominantly democratic regime to a predominantly oligarchic regime, or the other way around. The latter interpretation has been favoured by a majority of scholars, with Geagan himself eventually agreeing that it was a possible reading. In what follows I, too, will follow the view that the inscription marks a transition from a predominantly oligarchic regime to a slightly more democratic constitution, or the confirmation of such a transition.[21] Nonetheless, it will be worthwhile to take a closer look at one of the phrases that provoked the opposite interpretation, in order to understand better how the strategic language of the inscription could elicit these diverging views.

For Geagan the mention of the council of the Areopagus in lines sixteen through eighteen initially was an important argument for interpreting the decree as an oligarchic restoration (see above). Oliver departed slightly from Geagan's reading in reconstructing these lines:

[With good fortune the people decided] *that the laws legislated before by the council of the Areopagus* [together with Athenion] *are in force.[22]*

---

19 Arist. *Pol.* 1329b25-36: σχεδὸν μὲν οὖν καὶ τὰ ἄλλα δεῖ νομίζειν εὑρῆσθαι πολλάκις ἐν τῷ πολλῷ χρόνῳ, μᾶλλον δ᾽ ἀπειράκις. τὰ μὲν γὰρ ἀναγκαῖα τὴν χρείαν διδάσκειν εἰκὸς αὐτήν, τὰ δ᾽ εἰς εὐσχημοσύνην καὶ περιουσίαν ὑπαρχόντων ἤδη τούτων εὔλογον λαμβάνειν τὴν αὔξησιν· ὥστε καὶ τὰ περὶ τὰς πολιτείας οἴεσθαι δεῖ τὸν αὐτὸν ἔχειν τρόπον. (…) διὸ δεῖ τοῖς μὲν εὑρημένοις ἱκανῶς χρῆσθαι, τὰ δὲ παραλελειμμένα πειρᾶσθαι ζητεῖν. The connections to known practices are at *Pol.* 1263a30-32, 1263a35-37, and 1329b5-23. For the idea that almost everything has already been discovered see also *Pol.* 1264a2-3.

20 Whether or not Aristotle ultimately condones political change has been debated: Boyer (2008) and Lockwood (2015) argue in favour, Peterson (2011) and Kraut (2002, 352) argue against. The use of the metaphor of anchoring derives from Moscovici's (2008, 104-106) notion that new fields of knowledge are anchored in existing cultural phenomena; on applying the concept of anchoring to antiquity see Sluiter 2017 and Kuin forthcoming b.

21 Geagan on Oliver's reading: Geagan 1979, 375-376. Woodhead (1997, 467-469 = *Agora* XVI 333) follows the text of Oliver, but he is agnostic on the interpretation of the content of the inscription. A major factor in the debate over *Agora* I 2351 has been Meritt's (1977, 188) thesis, now widely accepted, that the cycle for secretary rotation cannot be established from the mid-80s BC onwards; the secretary's deme name in line 3 is now defunct as an argument for dating the inscription, cf. Habicht 1997, 321.

22 *Agora* I 2351, lines 16-18 in the reading of Oliver 1980, 200: ἀ[γαθῆι τύχηι δεδόχθαι τῶι δήμωι] | [τὰ] μὲν προνενομοθετημέν[α σὺν Ἀθηνίωνι(?) ὑπὸ τῆς βουλῆς τῆς] | [ἐν Ἀ]ρείωι Πάγωι κύρια εἶναι. Oliver based his date of the decree after Athenion's rule on the verb προνομοθετέω here, which is rare and otherwise unattested before the first century AD, when it appears in *Milet* I 3, 134 line 17. He argues that if the decree meant to convey that the Areopagus had legislated 'before' in a probouleutic sense one would expect the verb προβουλευώ instead; the inscription is , according to Oliver, a later confirmation of Athenion's democratic reform mentioning the Areopagus (Oliver 1980, 201). Whether *Agora* I 2351 is the decree of Athenion's reform or a decree confirming this reform does not affect my larger argument, and I remain agnostic on this issue.

The only departure in these three lines from Geagan's version is the reconstruction of Athenion's name right before the words 'council of the Areopagus.' Oliver (1980, 200) places a question mark after Athenion's name, noting that though 'the phrase σὺν Ἀθηνίωνι fits the space exactly' the line does not have to be restored like this.[23] The involvement of the Areopagus, however, is beyond doubt. For Geagan (1971, 107) this signalled that the decree was an oligarchic restoration, because the Areopagus was by definition a conservative body, made up probably of magistrates who had served the city before the war.

The Areopagus was Athens' 'old' *boule*, needing the longer name *boule* of the Areopagus (after its meeting place on the Areios pagos, Ares' hill), probably only once Solon had introduced another council (Rhodes 2006). It consisted of former *archontes* and wielded great if poorly defined powers in early Athens, as overseer and enforcer of the laws. Once the other *boule* was instated, however, the Areopagus' position started to gradually decline, culminating in Ephialtes' removing its judicial powers in the early 5th century BC. As a consequence the Areopagus ceased to be politically important over the course of the 5th century. However, starting with Demetrius of Phalerum the Areopagus was granted new powers on several occasions in the Hellenistic period, and in the Roman period the council of the Areopagus once again became very prominent in Athens. The 1st century BC, then, falls into a period of transition in which the status of this archaic Athenian institution was slowly rising again.[24]

Badian and Oliver reconciled the role of the Areopagus in this inscription with their interpretations of the decree as democratic in two different ways. Badian (1976, 117) argued that, after Medeius disappeared, the Areopagus would have been *de facto* in charge of the state; this is why they were included in Athenion's new constitution. According to Oliver (1980, 199-201) the reform that was concluded under Athenion had been initiated much earlier and had been held up by the Areopagus; this might also explain, he suggests, how Medeius justified staying in power for so long. However, even if the Areopagus had been involved at an earlier stage, it seems that Athenion would not necessarily have needed to include them in the phrasing of his reform; perhaps he actively chose to mention the Areopagus with a specific purpose in mind.

I suggest that Athenion may have chosen to include the Areopagus in his reform, because of the reputation of this body as a beacon of stability and tradition. A useful illustration of the 'image' of the Areopagus in Greek thought is Isocrates' encomium *Areopagiticus*. This text shows how this body was already viewed as a symbol of tradition in the early 4th century BC, roughly a century after Ephialtes decimated its powers. Isocrates has a larger argument about the decline, in his view, of Athenian democracy, but he stakes his case on the role of the Areopagus:

> [I]*t is much more just to blame those who directed the city a little before our time* [i.e. instead of the young], *because they led on our youth to this carelessness and destroyed the power of the Areopagus. While this council was still in power, Athens was not rife with lawsuits, or accusations, or tax-levies, or poverty, or war; on the contrary, her citizens lived in accord with each other and at peace with mankind.*[25]

Isocrates presents the Areopagus as a symbol of the 'good old days,' when men were still virtuous and the city of Athens was still properly governed, attributing an unrealistic array of problems to Ephialtes' reforms. He believes that the character of the Athenians would not have deteriorated if the Areopagus had retained its power as overseer of laws and morals. The *Areopagiticus* passage, then, shows clearly that the Areopagus was often associated with the old glory days of Athens.

Athenion employed the powerful positive connotations that this old political body had for the Athenians when he connected his reforms to the council of the Areopagus. He anchored his renewal of Athenian democracy by means of the familiarity and trust evoked by the name of the Areopagus. The second element of the decree that Geagan considered oligarchic was the appointment of offices through lot and election, instead of by lot alone, which was associated with Solon's legislation (line 8, see also above). The inclusion of this phrase, however, can be explained as an anchoring device as well. Claiming or suggesting that one's politics were Solonic was not the prerogative of oligarchic reformers alone (Hansen 1991, 161-177), and Athenion may have chosen to include the phrase 'lot and election' precisely because of its connotations of tradition and archaism.

---

23   Oliver (1980) does not give any parallels for this type of usage of σύν with a proper name in decrees. The attribution of the decree to Athenion's reign, however, does not hinge on the restoration of his name here, as it is corroborated by the content of the text (see below).

24   Fifth century BC decline of Areopagus: Wallace 1974; Hansen 1991, 288-295. New powers in Hellenistic period: Philochorus *BNJ* 328 F 65; Jones 2016. Importance in Roman period: Geagan 1967, 32-61; Rawson 1985.

---

25   Isoc. *Areop.* 50-51: ὥστ᾽ οὐκ ἂν εἰκότως τούτοις ἐπιτιμῴην, ἀλλὰ πολὺ δικαιότερον τοῖς ὀλίγῳ πρὸ ἡμῶν τὴν πόλιν διοικήσασιν. ἐκεῖνοι γὰρ ἦσαν οἱ προτρέψαντες ἐπὶ ταύτας τὰς ὀλιγωρίας καὶ καταλύσαντες τῆς βουλῆς δύναμιν. ἧς ἐπιστατούσης οὐ δικῶν οὐδ᾽ ἐγκλημάτων οὐδ᾽ εἰσφορῶν οὐδὲ πενίας οὐδὲ πολέμων ἡ πόλις ἔγεμεν, ἀλλὰ καὶ πρὸς ἀλλήλους ἡσυχίαν εἶχον καὶ πρὸς τοὺς ἄλλους ἅπαντας εἰρήνην ἦγον. See Konstan 2004 for a recent analysis of the piece as a whole.

Athenion appears to have realized, just like Aristotle, that for the implementation of new laws to be successful it was necessary to embed them in trusted, known institutions. The decree also illustrates the difficulties that the strategy of anchoring can create for ancient historians. By connecting something 'new' with something 'old,' something democratic with something oligarchic, the language of the decree successfully downplays the political changes it enacts. The intended audience of this language were 1st century BC Athenians, but it has complicated the modern interpretation of the text in turn.

As mentioned above, we know from Posidonius that Athenion was a peripatetic philosopher. Oliver (1980) and Antela-Bernárdez (2009) have noted several textual resonances between the text of *Agora* I 2351 and the works of Aristotle and Theophrastus. It is now clear that we can no longer interpret the decree as an oligarchic restoration: the dating provides no support (see n.21), and the repeated emphasis on democracy and sortition (see n.26) argue against it. Yet, the conscious anchoring of the changes in the legacy of the Areopagus, in Solonic language and, if Oliver's text is to be accepted, the mention of a 'shared and moderate *politeia*' show that Athenion was not a radical democrat either.[26] It appears that, inspired by peripatetic political thought, Athens' first Mithridatic ruler gave the Athenians a moderate democratic constitution firmly anchored in the city's civic traditions.

5. Sulla's *nomoi* in Appian

The source that first led scholars to believe that Sulla gave the Athenians a constitution was, as discussed, Appian's account of the Mithridatic Wars. The *nomoi* attributed to Sulla by Appian have been variously interpreted as peace terms, renewal of the alliance, constitutional reform, whether by Sulla or not, and the restoration of republican (i.e. non-monarchic) rule. The difficulties created by the Appian passage can be divided into two sets of problems. On one hand, we need to understand what precisely Appian meant when he represented the post-war intervention as a return to an earlier situation. On the other hand, we need to decide in what way Sulla intervened. The three interpretations that understand the *nomoi* not as laws but as peace terms, alliance renewal, or the restoration of 'republican' rule focus on what Appian says about a return to an earlier situation, stretching the meaning of *nomos*. In these interpretations *nomoi* is understood to describe something that Sulla was indeed responsible for after the siege, and that can to a degree be interpreted as a return to the status quo. So, each of them seems to

provide an attractive solution to this problematic passage. However, if possible it would be preferable to interpret *nomoi* as having its typical meaning of 'laws': in general Appian uses *nomoi* simply to refer to customs or laws. If he meant to refer to peace terms, alliance renewal, or the restoration of 'republican' rule we would have expected him to be more specific.[27]

One way of interpreting *nomoi* as laws while also accepting Appian's claim that these *nomoi* were a return to an earlier situation is to play down Sulla's involvement in the intervention. Habicht (1997, 315), for instance, has argued that 'the constitution in force after 86 was similar to that of the late second century and early part of the first century, up to the overthrow of Medeius in 89 BC.' The similarity is 'the predominance of the oligarchic.' According to Habicht (1997, 316) before the First Mithridatic War power in Athens lay primarily with elected magistrates and the Areopagus; after the war oligarchic elements were given even more weight, since until the 40s BC we only have decrees of the council, none of the popular assembly. He argues that Sulla did not need to intervene because the Athenian elite implemented its own oligarchic restoration after his victory. This is how Appian can say that the post-war arrangements, which he erroneously attributes to Sulla, were a return to the status quo without having to postulate any pre-war Roman intervention in the laws of the Athenians.

An alternative to Habicht's view is the interpretation that Sulla did indeed give the Athenians new laws after his victory, which, however, did not resemble an earlier intervention, because there was no earlier intervention. Badian argues that this is how our passage should be understood. He attributes the erroneous element in Appian's report not to a mistake on the part of the author, but to intentional misrepresentation by Sulla. We must take Appian's comment, he writes, 'not, of course, necessarily as a truthful account of the facts, but as a true reflection of Sulla's chosen image' (Badian 1976, 115). Sulla's chosen image was that of a 'good conservative' in order 'to gain the approval of the Roman aristocracy,' according

---

26 *Agora* I 2351 line 13: κ[ο]ινῆς καὶ [μέσης πολιτείας. Oliver (1980, 200) connects this line to Arist. *Pol.* 1294a41. Mentions of sortition (in Oliver's text): lines 8, 10, 18, 20, 21 and 24.

27 A full analysis of Appian's use of the word *nomos* is unfortunately beyond the scope of this article, and has to the best of my knowledge not yet been carried out. A few examples where *nomoi* clearly means 'laws' are: *Mith.* 94, *B Civ.*1.0.2, 1.1.8. Touloumakos (1967, 89 n.3) influentially argued that in *Mith.* 39 Appian translates the Latin term *leges imponere*, which in Livy typically refers to peace terms, with νόμους ἔθηκεν. Yet, when Appian discusses peace terms elsewhere he does not use νόμους ἔθηκεν, but τὰ προτεινόμενα (*Mith.* 57), or σπένδω (*Mith.* 92). Famerie's (1998) study of Appian's approach towards Latin terminology unfortunately does not discuss our passage, or Appian's use of *nomoi.* He concludes, though, that in general Appian is more likely to use equivalent terms than to translate a Latin phrase into Greek (1998, 208-211); *cf.* Mason's (1974, 16) brief mention of this topic.

to Badian.[28] Presenting his laws for Athens as rooted in a fictitious earlier Roman intervention, then, was part of Sulla's strategy to appear conservative to the Romans back home.

Badian's interpretation is attractive because it is well established that Appian used Sulla's own memoirs.[29] It seems quite likely that Appian's comment on Sulla's Athenian laws indeed goes back to historical Sullan propaganda. If we choose to follow Badian, it is necessary to say something about what *nomoi* Sulla may have given to the city. As pointed out before, Sulla's Athenian constitution used to be seen as a watershed moment, with scholars attributing an apparent ascendance of oligarchic elements in Athenian politics between 86 and the mid-40s BC to Sulla's intervention. Scholars are now more hesitant to trace any specific oligarchic trends in our limited and fragmentary epigraphic evidence, and they are reluctant to attribute such trends, if they did occur, to Sulla.[30] It may not have been necessary for him make any political changes; after the siege the Athenians would have needed no further encouragement to dispose of the city in ways that (they thought) would be to Sulla's liking. Appian himself, however, provides evidence for the possibility that at least one intervention did come directly from Sulla.

In the penultimate chapter of Appian's description of the sack of Athens, just before the chapter cited above, the author tells us what Sulla did after taking the city, while Aristion was still holding out on the Acropolis:

> *The next day Sulla sold the slaves. To those who were free, as many as had not been killed the previous night, and they were very few, he promised to give freedom, though taking away their voting and electing rights because they had fought against him. But he said their offspring would be granted these rights again.[31]*

Sulla decided that any freeborn, male Athenians still in the city after the sack remained free, but lost their voting and electing rights. There is some debate as to how long this disenfranchisement was in place. I follow those who argue that the next generation *did* get their voting rights back: this interpretation represents the sense of the Greek better, and it fits with the existence of decrees, albeit only

from the *boule*, from the decades following the sack.[32] It is clear then that Sulla saw fit to decide about who had the right to participate in the political process in Athens, while also, in a savvy way, rendering the next generation indebted to Rome. Though we cannot know for sure what other arrangements Sulla made, if any, even if the disenfranchisement law was his only intervention this would still be an unprecedented degree of Roman meddling in Athenian politics. Nonetheless, to speak of a Sullan constitution on the basis of this evidence, as so many scholars have done, seems to go too far. It is worth noting that Appian cannot be blamed for this exaggeration: he does not speak of a Sullan *politeia*, merely of Sulla's *nomoi*.

I want to return to Sulla's possible motivations for, on Badian's account, 'lying' about following tradition when he imposed laws, or at least a law, on Athens. Badian envisions the audience of this lie as the Roman aristocracy, for whom Sulla would like to appear as 'a good conservative.' While this was probably part of his motivation, I propose that he had other considerations as well. The primary audience of any intervention in the Athenian laws would be the Athenians themselves. Connecting his *nomoi* with earlier Roman involvement in Athens' laws, even if such involvement were non-existent, would also have appealed to them, and this was likely part of Sulla's strategy.

For Aristotle, as we discussed, political change must be embedded in existing structures in order to be implemented successfully. I used the concept of anchoring to describe how such embedding often makes use of the past, and the same mechanism also helps to explain Sulla's propaganda that his *nomoi* were in line with previous Roman arrangements at Athens. This message served to anchor something new in something allegedly old. Sulla used an 'invented' anchor to affect continuity in the relations between Rome and Athens.[33] But how did he know to do this? It is not necessary to argue that Sulla got this idea directly from Aristotle's *Politics* – even though he was actually well read and highly educated, this would be a difficult argument to make. Sulla could have understood the benefits of embedding political innovation in the past from other Greek and Roman examples. As already mentioned, in Athens there was a strong tradition of claiming 'Solonic'

---

28 Badian 1976, 116; *contra* Baronowski 2011, 145, who thinks Appian was simply mistaken.

29 E.g. App. *B Civ.* 1.105; *cf.* Eckert 2015, 55.

30 Sulla's constitution as defining moment: Bowersock 1965, 106; Geagan 1967. Little or no active meddling by Sulla: Kallet-Marx 1995, 213-218; Habicht 1997, 315-321.

31 App. *Mith.* 38: τῇ δὲ ἑξῆς ὁ Σύλλας τοὺς μὲν δούλους ἀπέδοτο, τοῖς δ᾽ ἐλευθέροις, ὅσοι νυκτὸς ἐπιλαβούσης οὐκ ἔφθασαν ἀναιρεθῆναι, πάμπαν οὖσιν ὀλίγοις, τὴν μὲν ἐλευθερίαν ἔφη διδόναι, ψῆφον δὲ καὶ χειροτονίαν τῶνδε μὲν ὡς οἱ πεπολεμηκότων ἀφαιρεῖσθαι, τοῖς δ᾽ ἐγγόνοις καὶ ταῦτα διδόναι.

32 The interpretation depends on whether one understands, in the last line of the passage, ταῦτα to refer to the disenfranchisement or to the voting and electing rights; the latter possibility is more straightforward. Also, the μὲν…δέ construction suggests a contrast between the generations, pointing towards the same interpretation, *cf.* Kallet-Marx 1995, 212; Goukowsky 2001, 38; White 1912, 309; Eckert 2016, 89; *contra* White 1899, 350; Bugh 2013, 114.

33 This phrase is indebted to Eric Hobsbawm's concept of 'invented traditions', who has shown that traditions need not be authentic to be effective in, for instance, contexts of identity formation, Hobsbawm 1983, 1-14.

Figure 1. Athenian tetradrachm from 84/83 BC with the statues of the tyrant-slayers (ANS.1944.100.24898 American Numismatic Society)

roots for new laws (Hansen 1991, 161-177). At Rome it was of course necessary to align oneself, at least seemingly, with the *mos maiorum*. Sulla likely fashioned the *abdicatio* of his dictatorship as a gesture towards the *mos maiorum* regarding the temporary nature of the office (Eckert 2015, 191, 197).

A well-known Athenian coin illustrates how important historical awareness and the capacity to use the past creatively were to Sulla and the people around him. An Athenian silver tetradrachm dated to 84/83 BC depicts the statues of Harmodius and Aristogeiton. These two sixth century BC Athenian heroes were honoured in the agora as the legendary tyrant-slayers, even though in fact they killed the tyrant's brother (Thuc. 6.54-59). The iconography of the coin connects Sulla's defeat of the Mithridatic 'tyrant' Aristion with Athens' legendary tyrant-slayers for the local Athenian audience. We do not know whether Sulla had any direct influence on the imagery, but it is likely that the mint masters Mentor and Moschion wanted to please him by using it. They knew as well as Sulla how useful the past could be, and placed the violent changes suffered by Athens in the First Mithridatic War in the reassuring context of the city's glorious democratic past. The coin's imagery lets Sulla lay claim to Athens' legacy, making Pontus and Mithridates into tyrannical adversaries. Sulla's capture of the city becomes a continuation of Athens' proud civic tradition.[34]

---

34 On the coin's date and significance see Habicht 1997, 317; De Callatay 1997, 305. Kleinschmidt (2011) connects the coin to the first celebration of the *Sylleia* festival honouring Sulla, which is otherwise only attested for 80/79 BC.

6. Conclusion

I have used the metaphor of anchoring to describe a process where an actor, Sulla or Athenion, connects something new to something (allegedly) old and familiar, with the purpose of making the new more acceptable to a particular audience, in both cases the Athenians. From these examples it might seem that anchoring the new is primarily expedient for the actors who want their innovations to succeed. While this is often the case, Aristotle has shown us that when it comes to innovations to the laws and to political institutions, the situation is more complex. In *Politics* we have seen that the stakes in anchoring political changes are high. Change can be dangerous in large part because it makes people insecure.

The 1st century BC was a period of rapid and often violent change for the Athenians. I suggest that Sulla, with his attempt to convince the Athenians that his intervention in their political system was based on earlier Roman precedent, wanted to alleviate this type of insecurity – even if his ultimate aim of pacifying Greece was self-serving. Likewise, Athenion's renewal of Athenian democracy anchored its proposals in the old decisions of the old Areopagus, in order to suggest stability and continuity. Here, too, expediency of one political group and the interests of the political community at large go hand in hand. Even though we have had to discard the notion of Sulla's 'Athenian constitution,' this vexed topic and the sources connected to it have taught us something about political change in 1st century BC Athens. Sulla and Athenion were well aware of the necessity of embedding political innovations, and, just as earlier generations had done, they turned to the past to do so.

Acknowledgements

I would like to thank Onno van Nijf, the audiences at the Athens conference 'Strategies of Remembrance in Greece under Rome' and the Ancient History Seminar at the Goethe Universität Frankfurt, as well as the editors of this volume for their helpful comments and suggestions. This research has been carried out as part of the OIKOS Anchoring Innovation Research Agenda.

References

D'Angour, A. 2011. *The Greeks and the New: Novelty in Ancient Greek Imagination and Experience*, Cambridge.

Antela-Bernárdez, I.B. 2009. Between Medeios and Mithridates: The Peripatetic Constitution of Athens (*Agora* I 2351), *ZPE* 171, 105-108.

Antela-Bernárdez, I.B. 2015. Athenion of Athens Revisited, *Klio* 97, 59-80.

Badian, E. 1976. Rome, Athens, and Mithridates, *AJAH* 1, 105-128.

Bernhardt, R. 1985. *Polis und römische Herrschaft in der späten Republik (149-31 v. Chr.)*, Berlin.

Baronowski, D.W. 2011. *Polybius and Roman Imperialism*, London.

Bowersock, G.W. 1965. *Augustus and the Greek World*, Oxford.

Boyer, A. 2008. Du nouveau chez les anciens: Remarques a partir d'Hippodamos, *Revue philosophique de la France et de l'étranger* 133, 407-422.

Bugh, G.R. 1992. Athenion and Aristion of Athens, *Phoenix* 46, 108-123.

Bugh, G.R. 2013. Democracy in the Hellenistic World. In: S.L. Ager & R.A. Faber (eds), *Belonging and Isolation in the Hellenistic World*, Toronto, 111-127.

Callatay, F. de. 1997. *L'histoire des guerres mithridatiques vue par les monnaies*, Louvain-la-Neuve.

Eckert, A. 2016. *Lucius Cornelius Sulla in der antiken Erinnerung: Jener Mörder, der sich Felix nannte*, Berlin.

Famerie, E. 1998. *Le latin et le grec d'Appien: Contribution á l'étude du lexique d'un historien grec de Rome*, Genève.

Ferrary, J.L. 1988. *Philhellenisme et imperialisme: Aspects ideologiques de la conquete romaine du monde hellenistique*, Rome.

Geagan, D.J. 1967. *The Athenian Constitution After Sulla*, Princeton.

Geagan, D.J. 1971. Greek Inscriptions: A Law Code of the First Century B.C., *Hesperia* 40, 96-108.

Geagan, D.J. 1979. Roman Athens: Some Aspects of Life and Culture I. 86 BC-267 AD. *ANRW* II.7.1, 371-437.

Goukowsky, P. 2001. *Appien. Histoire romaine / T. VII Livre XII, La guerre de Mithridate*, Paris.

Groningen, B.A. van. 1953. *In the Grip of the Past. Essay on an Aspect of Greek thought*, Leiden.

Habicht, C. 1997. *Athens from Alexander to Antony*, Cambridge, MA [1995].

Hansen, M.H. 1991. *The Athenian Democracy in the Age of Demosthenes: Structure, Principles, and Ideology*, Oxford.

Harter-Uibopuu, K. 2008. Hadrian and the Athenian Oil Law. In: R. Alston & O.M. van Nijf (eds), *Feeding the Ancient Greek City*, Leuven, 128-142.

Hobsbawm, E. 1983. Introduction: Inventing Traditions. In: E. Hobsbawm & T. Ranger (eds), *The Invention of Tradition*, Cambridge and New York, 1-14.

Jones, N.F. 2016. Philochoros of Athens. In: I. Worthington (ed.), *Brill's New Jacoby*, Leiden.

Kallet-Marx, R.M. 1995. *Hegemony to Empire: The Development of the Roman Imperium in the East from 148 to 62 B.C.*, Berkeley.

Kleinschmidt, T. 2011. Die Sylleia und die attischen Tetradrachmen der Münzmeister Eumelos und Theoxenides, *Keraunia* 298, 131-159.

Konstan, D. 2004. Isocrates' 'Republic.' In: T. Poulakos & D. Depew (eds), *Isocrates and Civic Education*, Austin, 107-124.

Kraut, R. 2002. *Aristotle: Political Philosophy*, Oxford and New York.

Kuin, I.N.I. forthcoming a. Competition and Innovation in Aristotle, *Politics* 2. In: C. Pieper & C. Damon (eds), *Eris vs. Aemulatio: Competition in Classical Antiquity*, Leiden.

Kuin, I.N.I. forthcoming b. Rewriting Family History: Strabo and the Mithridatic Wars, *Phoenix*.

Lockwood, T. 2015. Politics II: Political Critique, Political Theorizing, Political Innovation. In: T. Lockwood & T. Samaras (eds), *Aristotle's Politics: A Critical Guide*, Cambridge, 64-83.

Mason, H.J. 1974. *Greek Terms for Roman Institutions: A Lexicon and Analysis. American Studies in Papyrology* 13, Toronto.

Meritt, B.D. 1977. Athenian Archons 347/6-48/7 B.C., *Historia* 26, 161-191.

Moscovici, S. 2008. *Psychoanalysis: Its Image and Its Public*, Cambridge [1961].

Oliver, J.H. 1972. The Solonian Constitution and a Consul of A.D. 149, *GRBS* 13, 99-107.

Oliver, J.H. 1980. A Peripatetic Constitution, *JHS* 100, 199-201.

Peterson, J. 2011. Aristotle's Ridicule of Political Innovation, *Ramify* 2, 119-130.

Rawson, E. 1985. Cicero and the Areopagus, *Athenaeum* 73, 44-67.

Rhodes, P.J. 2006. Areopagus. In: H. Cancik & H. Schneider (eds), *Brill's New Pauly Online*, Leiden. http://dx.doi.org/10.1163/1574-9347_bnp_e133640 Accessed August 16, 2017.

Santangelo, F. 2007. *Sulla, the Elites and the Empire: A Study of Roman Policies in Italy and the Greek East*, Leiden.

Sluiter, I. 2017. Anchoring Innovation: A Classical Research Agenda, *European Review* 25, 20-38.

Touloumakos, J. 1967. Der Einfluss Roms auf die Staatsform der griechischen Stadtstaaten des Festlandes und der Inseln im ersten und zweiten Jhdt. v. Chr., Diss. Universität Göttingen.

Verdejo Manchado, J. & B. Antela-Bernárdez. 2013. Medeios at the Gymnasium, *ZPE* 186, 134-140.

Wallace, R.W. 1974. Ephialtes and the Areopagos, *GRBS* 15, 259-269.

White, H. 1899. *The Roman History of Appian of Alexandria. Vol. 1: The Foreign Wars*, New York and London.

White, H. 1912. *Appian. Roman History Vol. II*, Cambrige, MA.

Woodhead, A.G. 1997. *The Athenian Agora XVI; Inscriptions: The Decrees*, Princeton.

Reused Statues for Roman Friends: The Past as a Political Resource in Roman Athens

Muriel Moser

Abstract

A number of public honorific monuments dedicated by the Athenian demos to Roman politicians between the sack of Sulla and the reign of Nero consisted of old, reused statue monuments. This article explores the history of these statues by looking at the role they played in the relationship between Athens and Rome and in inner-Athenian debates about the management of the public space on the Acropolis, where these reused monuments were located. I hence explore the political strategies that were pursued in this manipulation of the Athenian past. The first part of the article locates the statues in the context of the relation between Athens and Rome. I argue that the Athenian polity used old statue monuments as a means of gaining support and favour from Roman politicians. The second section then considers the reused statues as an expression of the assertion of democratic control over public space.

Keywords: Athens, Roman empire, political resources, honorific statues, Greek polis

1. Introduction

Athens' position was a difficult one in the last decades of the 1st century BC. Financially, the city suffered from the disruptions caused by the sack of Sulla. Her situation was also complex in political terms following the Roman civil wars: the city had supported several Roman generals who had been unable to assert their authority in Rome, including Marc Antony in his battle against Augustus (Tac. *Ann.* 2.55). As a result, it was necessary to secure powerful friends in Rome willing to assist the city with financial and political support. Due to several regime changes, there was also need for political stability and a strong political authority within the city.

The present article discusses one key strategy that was used by Athens in this context: the reuse of old statue monuments. Between the mid-1st century BC and the mid-1st century AD, 21 statue monuments set up in Classical or Hellenistic times on the Athenian Acropolis were being rededicated to foreign benefactors, in particular Roman politi-

in: Dijkstra, T.M., I.N.I. Kuin, M. Moser & D. Weidgenannt (eds) 2017. *Strategies of Remembering in Greece under Rome (100 BC - 100 AD)*, Leiden (Sidestone Press).

cians.[1] Their reuse, which peaked under Augustus, has been interpreted as evidence for the weakness of Athens under Rome or as an attempt to preserve the Greek aspect of her Acropolis.[2] Some of such readings were heavily influenced by a speech by Dio Chrysostom (Dio Chrys. *Or.* 31), who criticizes the cheapening of public honours through the reuse of honorific statues in Roman Rhodes, as well as by an inscription from Roman Lindos (*I.Lindos* II, no. 419) which documents the auction of old statues in the sanctuary. It is also informed by the traditional view of Athens as a weak city under Roman rule engaged in (cultural) resistance against Roman dominance (e.g. Graindor 1927; Day 1942; Touloumakos 1967; Bernhardt 1985, 39-49; Deininger 1971, esp. 242-261; Geagan 1997; Spawforth 2012).

A closer analysis of the material quickly reveals that the reuse cannot be explained only with reference to lack of time, power or financial means: the 21 preserved reused monuments constituted only 13% of the monuments dedicated to Romans on the Acropolis in this period; 87% were new monuments made for the occasion.[3] It also remains to be proven that old statues were better suited to preserve the Greek appearance of the Acropolis than the new monuments, for the latter came in an antiquated, Greek form and hence also emphasized the historical importance of the place.[4] Further, the identity of the Roman senators honoured with such reused statues also strongly calls into question the traditional argument that these were cheap honours (as it is implied by Dio Chrys. *Or.* 31

and Cic. *Att.* 6.1.46 which are often cited in this context). These old statues were rededicated to some of the most influential men in Rome, including the grandfather of Nero and Augustus' son in law.[5] This means that unless we want to concede that the Athenians wanted to jeopardize their relationship with these men by honouring them with cheap, old statues, there must be some grounded explanation to account for the award of old statues to the most powerful senators in Rome.

As I show in what follows, a careful reuse of old statues by the Athenian demos allowed manipulating these survivals of the past as a means to represent new Roman honorands as dynamic, resourceful supporters of Athens. They were hence perfectly suited to function as prestigeous honours to ask for support and favour from influential Roman politicians. The second part of the article proposes to consider the statues in polis culture and society. I argue that the reuse of statues enabled political dynamism in Athens: in the process the Athenian demos asserted its agency in the relationship with Rome, while at the same time also establishing its authority over public space on the memory-charged Acropolis.

2. Old statues for Roman benefactors

Benefactor relationships in Hellenistic cities were a complex matter. In accepting the beneficence of a wealthy elite, cities entered into a social contract with the benefactor. Honorific statues played a key role in this context. Cities often returned the favour with such a statue, which embodied both the gratitude for a past benefaction and the expectation for future beneficence. Honorific statues carried important political messages: they constituted public narratives about the values and expectations of the respective citizenry which communicated unspoken rules as well as expectations of common intentions and action.[6] This matrix was also used for external benefactors, including Roman senators who from the late 2nd century onwards increasingly acted as benefactors in the Greek East (Quass 1984; Tanner 2000; Eilers 2002). By the late 1st century BC, Roman elites had become used to this tradition of receiving honorary statues in return for favours (Tanner 2000 and, for Athens in particular, Corn. Nep. *Att.* 3.1-2 on Atticus' statues in Athens).

While the deliberations of the civic institutions took place orally and were quickly forgotten, the perennial nature of the statue monument and its visual impact had the potential to shape public opinion for a long time. As

---

1   The reused monuments are discussed in detail in Krumeich 2010, 369-385, with photographs and drawings in Keesling 2010 and Krumeich 2010. A new catalogue of the inscriptions of the Roman Acropolis is in preparation, see Krumeich & Witschel (forthcoming). Note that this list excludes the honours to the imperial family (statuary column for Tiberius, *IG* II/III² 3244 with Krumeich 2008, 356, a dynastic statue group for Augustus and three of his successors, *IG* II/III² 3253-3256 and 3892 with Krumeich 2008, 357, as well as two equestrian monuments for Antony and then for Agrippa , *IG* II/III² 4122, and Germanicus, *IG* II/III² 3260, in front of the Propylaea, on which see Krumeich 2008, 362 and Krumeich 2010, 358 with illustrations). Earlier discussions of the monuments include Blanck 1969; Payne 1984; Pérrin-Saminadayar 2007, 131-135; Shear 2006; Ma 2007; Keesling 2007; Krumeich 2008, 2011, 2014a, 2014b; Krumeich & Witschel 2009, 2010 and Lo Monaco 2016. On Augustan Athens, see conveniently Dickenson 2017; Spawforth 2012; Böhme 1995 and Geagan 1979 with references to older literature as well as the classic study by Graindor 1927.

2   E.g. Blanck 1969; Shear 2006; Krumeich & Witschel 2009, 2010; Keesling 2010, 318 (preservation of memory of earlier artists); Krumeich 2008, 2010, 2011, 2014a, 2014b.

3   Krumeich 2014, 71 with pl. 16 d. This proportion accords with evidence from the Lindian Acropolis (on which see Rose 1997, 25,155) and suggests that Dio's statement that in Rhodes most benefactors received reused statues rather than new monuments must be taken with a grain of salt (Dio Chrys. *Or.* 107, 118).

4   Old-fashioned look: Krumeich 2010, 345.

5   *IG* II/III² 4144, L. Domitius Ahenobarbus (*PIR²* D 128) and *IG* I³ 833 + *IG* II/III³ 4147, L. Aemilius Paullus, (*PIR²* A 391).

6   On public honorary statues in Hellenistic cities under Rome, see Van Nijf 2015, 2016; on the strategic wording of the dedicatory inscription see also Luraghi 2010 and Weidgenannt *this volume*.

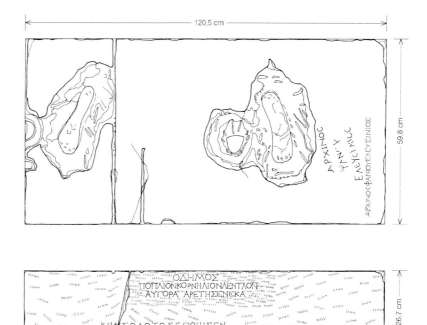

Figure 1. Pedestal of the statue of Archinos/Lentulus (Drawing by Antonia Brauchle & Zoe Spyranti. Source: Krumeich 2010, pl. 54 fig. 2).

a result, statuary portraits of honorific statues were chosen not to offer a truthful representation of the benefactor, but to display the qualities he had shown or which were expected of him (Van Nijf 2015, 341). The shape of the statues hence influenced the way in which their honorands were seen as benefactors.

This raises an important question: what did the Athenians communicate to their Roman honorands in these reused statues? In what follows, I look in detail at three monuments which allow highlighting some of the main characteristics of reused honorific statues on the Athenian Acropolis. There are the monuments of P. Cornelius Lentulus, an influential politician and augur in Rome (Figure 1), L. Valerius Catullus, member of the influential family of the *Valerii Catulii*, some of whom became close supporters of the Julio-Claudian dynasty (Figure 2), and the influential L. Cassius Longinus, a descendant of one of the murderers of Caesar and ancestor of the emperor Caligula (Figures 3 and 4); the monuments of Cn. Acerronius Proculus, C. Aelius Gallus and P. Octavius, all of whom held high office in eastern provinces, are discussed for comparison and contrast.[7] These monuments were reused during the reign of the Julio-Claudian dynasty; both the bases as well as the statues were reused in the process.[8]

What was being communicated through these statues? First, the award of a reused statue was a mark of respect and distinction. It suggested that the Athenians recognized its honorand as a powerful, cultured Roman politician of high standing. These reused statues will have constituted rare, prestigious honours in the eyes of Roman senators

---

7   *PIR*² C 1379; *PIR*¹ V 39; *PIR*² C 502; *PIR*² A 33; *PIR*² A 179; *PIR*² O 19.

8   The lack of any damage to the stones suggests that the original statues remained *in situ* during the reuse, as was the case in other instances of statue reuse in this period (Rhodes: Dio Chrys. *Or.* 31. 47, 154-156, sanctuary of Athena Lindia: *I.Lindos* II no. 419, and Oropos, on which see Petrakos 1997). It is possible that the heads of the statues were exchanged in the process, yet due to the lack of evidence (none of the bronze statues survive), this must remain a hypothesis, see Krumeich 2010, 346-350. The statues may also have undergone restoration, receiving new paint or accessories that fit the new honorand (see Dio Chrys. *Or.* 31. 82), yet there is no evidence for this in Athens. A statement from Cicero, who criticized the reuse of statues (Cic. *Ep. ad Att.* 6.1.46), perhaps rather implies that the statues in Athens were not altered to resemble the new honorand but retained their original shape and appearance.

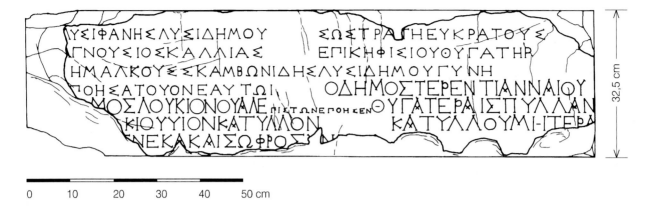

Figure 2. Pedestal of the statues of Lysiphanes and his mother Sostrate/L. Valerius Catullus and his mother Terentia Hispulla (Drawing from Antonia Brauchle & Zoe Spyranti. Source: Krumeich 2010, pl. 67 fig. 21).

(also Shear 2006, 245 and Krumeich 2008, 405-409) due to their shape, quality and age. First, they were a far more impressive sight than the newly made monuments. Their statues were mounted on unusually large and exquisite statue bases which were easily distinguished from the more recent small quadratic bases (Krumeich 2008, 405). Their material was also different: while the more recent statue bases were made of Hymettian or Eleusinian stone, those of many of the older, reused monuments were made of Pentelic marble, which was more sought after as it was used predominantly in Classical time.[9]

The quality of the reused statue was further underlined by the identity of their sculptors, for the reused statues were made by famous artists of the past, whose signatures were carefully preserved on the stones.[10] This is neatly illustrated by the statue of Archinos/Lentulus (*IG* II/III³ 4102 = Krumeich 2010, 374 no. A7, Figure 1). When the inscription for Archinos was chiselled out on the front of the stone, the signature of Kephisodotos, the artist who made the statue it supported, was carefully retained in line 4. The new dedicatory inscription was added in such a way that it stood out as a feature of particular significance, somewhat detached from the content of the new dedication. Another striking example of the preservation of the artist's signature is the dedication for L. Valerius Catullus and his mother Terentia Hispulla (*IG* II/III³ 3850 + 4159 = Krumeich 2010, 382 no. B6, Figure 2). The first line of the inscription for Catullus and the second of that for his mother encircle the signature of Piston, while leaving a noticeable gap to carefully accentuate it.

As a result and as was argued already by Julia Shear, the reuse of old statues allowed the Athenians to honour Romans with 'a bronze 'Old Master portrait'' (Shear 2006, 245). Art from Classical Athens was in high demand among Roman elites at the time (e.g. Plin. *HN* 35,125, 150 and Tac. *Ann.* 54.1; see also evidence discussed in Tanner 2000 and Anguissola 2014), so that the award of an old statue was probably a mark of distinction, even if the respective artists were unknown in Rome (Shear 2006, 245). It suggested that these Roman honorands were connoisseurs of Athenian art. As a result, it is likely that there was competition among Romans for such old statues, as this was sought by one's fellow Roman elites (Shear 2006, 245). Athens had long been recognized as a centre of Greek art and culture by many Romans, who came to the city to study in its schools of philosophy, rhetoric, history and art (e.g. Prop. *Eleg* 3.21); the Athenians were hence perfectly placed to pass judgement on the quality of the Greek sophistication of their Roman friends.

These statues thus had an important antiquarian value. Given the Roman interest in Athenian art and culture, they also carried an important honorific value, in that they could be used as a mark of distinction and culture. However, their honorific value was not restricted to the concerns of students of art. Rather, the reused monuments consciously played with memories of the admired (Classical) past of Athens and its culture, while transporting it into the Roman period. The reuse of old statues for Roman honorands suggested that these could be represented with old statues showing Athenian citizens, thereby implying that the two were in some way compa-

---

9   The new bases measured c. 19 x 63 x 65 cm, while *e.g.* the pedestal for Archinos/Lentulus (Figure 1) measured 26,7 x 120,5 x 59,8 cm and that for Hegelochos/Cassius (Figures 3 and 4) 35 x 64 x 130 cm. The large pedestals of Lentulus (Figure 1) and Cassius (Figure 3 and 4) were made of Pentelic marble. For the measurements and material see the catalogue of Krumeich 2010 and Keesling 2010.

10 Keesling 2007, 156, 2010, 313-331. The preservation of the artist's signature on rededicated statues (even on those cases where the original dedicatory inscription was erased) was common also in Oropos, see Blanck 1969, 71-74, no. B 3-15; Petrakos 1997.

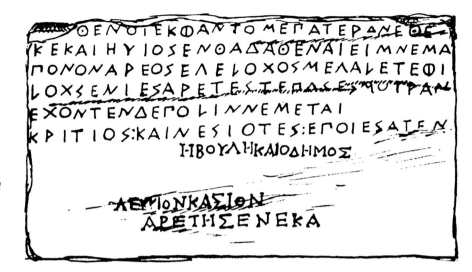

Figure 3. Facsimile of the pedestal of a statue of Hegelochos, reused as a public honorary statue for L. Cassius Longinus (after Rumpf 1964, 142 fig. 5d. Republished in Krumeich 2010, pl. 66 fig. 19).

rable.[11] Further meanings were suggested by the interplay between statue and text. On 18 out of 21 reused statue monuments that have been found on the Acropolis, the old inscriptions were at least partially preserved during the reuse. Only three stones suffered complete erasure of the former inscription (Krumeich 2010, no. A1-3). On another six monuments, the original inscription was erased and replaced by a new inscription, but re-inscribed on another side of the stone (Krumeich 2010, no. A4-11).[12] The statue of Archinos/Lentulus (Figure 1) is a good example of this: as can be seen from the drawing of the stone, the original dedicatory inscription of Archinos was erased and Lentulus' dedication inscribed instead:

ὁ δῆμος | Πόπλιον Κορνήλιον Λέντλον | αὔγορα ἀρετῆς ἕνεκα

The demos (dedicated this) to Publius Cornelius Lentulus, augur, on account of his virtue. (IG II/III² 4102, lines 1-3)

The name of Ἀρχῖνος Φανίου Ἐλευσίνιος, 'Archinos, son of Phanios, from Eleusis', probably part of the earlier dedication, was re-inscribed twice on the upper side of the base (*IG* II/III² 4102, A + B; I return to this in section 3 below). Finally, on the remaining eight or nine monuments, including that of Valerius Catullus (Figure 2) and Lucius Cassius (Figures 3 and 4), the original inscription was preserved in its entirety, on top of the new inscription that was chiselled below the existing inscription (Krumeich 2010, 368-385 no. B1-9).

In most cases, then, the reuse was not undertaken in a furtive manner in Athens (in contrast to Rhodes, so Dio Chrys. *Or.* 31.38-40, 50, 139), but it was highlighted by the preservation of the statue and its old inscriptions. This particular nature of the interplay of image and text, of old and new, invited comparison between the Roman honorand and the Athenian past. The inscriptions on the statue base of the statue of L. Cassius Longinus, a descendant of one of the murderers of Caesar and ancestor of Caligula (PIR² C 502), is a good example of this. Its old inscription is composed of old letters and is set in stoichedon, granting the monument an appearance of age that added to its quality and

---

11   As argued also by Shear 2006, 245. See also the comparison implied in a reused statue monument from Kos, on which Bosnakis 2004 and Ma 2007a, 94-95. *Contra* Krumeich 2008, 361 and 2010, 354-355 who refutes the idea that an analogy or comparison was intended. For the deliberate combination of dedications on reused statues, see also the late-antique examples discussed in Machado 2017, 343-344.

12   On similar re-inscriptions from Oropos, see Ma 2007a.

Figure 4. Reconstruction of the reused statue monument of L. Cassius Longinus (Drawing by Julia Krug-Ochmann. Source: Krumeich 2010, pl. 65 fig. 17).

noteworthiness (Figure 3; see also *IG* I³ 833 + *IG* II/III³ 4147 = Krumeich 2010 no. B4). Perhaps it was even redrawn in red on the occasion of the reuse to heighten its impact.

The arrangement of the statue and the lettering (Figures 3 and 4) invited comparison between Cassius and the Athenian citizen of the Classical period. Cassius seemed interchangeable with him. This was possible also because his name came without any reference to a Roman political office, filiation or, indeed, dating (on which below). As a result, Cassius, like all other Roman benefactors who received such reused statues, merged perfectly into the Athenian past (Shear 2006, 345-346; Krumeich 2010, 367). The manipulation of these survivals of the past as honours to Romans thus made it possible to carry the city's cultural past into a Roman present and to suggest that this was also an Athenian one.[13]

However, it would be wrong to reduce these reused statues to an attempt to honour Roman politicians by inserting them into the Athenian past. As I argue in what follows, the statues also had an important euergetic element: they allowed portraying (would-be) Romans as energetic, godlike benefactors of Athens. They should hence be contextualized within the benefactor relationships between Athens and influential politicians in Rome.

---

13 Shear 2006 and Krumeich 2014a, 80-81; on the Acropolis as a place of Athenian identity, see also Dally 2006; Stefanidou-Tiverriou 2008 and Krumeich & Witschel 2010.

The euergetic aspect was played out in the statues as well as the dedicatory inscriptions of the reused monuments. The new statues showed the honorand in a himation, the traditional Greek dress as was characteristic of Hellenistic honorary statues, which sought to emphasize the civilian, gymnasium-qualities of the represented individuals (Zanker 1995, 254-261; Tanner 2000, 21). By contrast, in many of the older statues there was a great sense of action. As a result, they were better suited to highlight particular qualities that were sought in benefactors: energy, dynamism and unlimited resources.[14] For instance, the monument for the influential senator Cassius Longinus (Figures 3 and 4) we have just examined carried the statue of an idealised man in armour lunging forward (Krumeich 2010, 342-343); it hence insinuated that Cassius had the attitude of an energetic, courageous defender of Athens. Similarly, the statue of Lentulus (Figure 1) represented this senator as a dynamic Greek warrior in heroic nudity with body armour and lance (Krumeich 2010, 334-335), thus presenting Lentulus as a perfect, almost godlike supporter of Athens. Catullus (Figure 2) was shown as a good Athenian citizen (Krumeich 2010, 343) and one that is respectful of his family and ancestors. The emphasis on family relationships – which was played out in the pairing of his statue with that of his mother as well as their dedicatory inscriptions (*IG* II/III³ 4159) – may perhaps be indication of the fact that his family had a long-standing relation with Athens which he was expected to continue.[15] In sum, the statues powerfully expressed Athens' expectation that these Romans would act (again) as dutiful, energetic, almost heroic benefactors of Athens.[16]

The inscriptions were also important in this context. Honorary dedicatory inscriptions became increasingly simplistic in Hellenistic times, yet their grammar as well as the adjectives and honorific attributes used nonetheless functioned as important mirrors of the expectations of the awarding body.[17] It is hence noteworthy that the inscriptions of most of the honorific monuments that were erected between 100 BC and 100 AD on the Athenian Acropolis come without indication of the nature of the benefaction; they justify the honours (only) with vague reference to virtue, ἀρετή, or similar (e.g. *IG* II² 4099 – 4255). As a result, it is not clear what sort of service had been rendered to the city, or, indeed, if a benefac-

tion had ever been effected. Perhaps we are dealing with proleptic honours, that is gifts that were made to wealthy individuals in order to prompt a benefaction.[18] What this means is that at least some of these statues may thus have asked for benefactions rather than acknowledging them; they may not have remembered a Roman benefaction to Athens but have called for a deed that could be remembered in the future. There is another aspect to consider in the case of the reused statues. For while the inscriptions of new honorific monuments often at least included reference to an office, the honorands of the reused statues appear as private individuals in the dedications, without any mention of office. Take for instance the inscription for Lucius Cassius (Figures 3 and 4). This stated only that:

ἡ βουλὴ καὶ ὁ δῆμος | Λεύκιον Κάσιον | ἀρετῆς ἔνεκα

The boule and the demos (dedicated this) to Lucius Cassius on account of his virtue. (IG II/III² 4168)

This lack of reference to any office may reflect an Athenian desire to award honours to the man rather than his office and, thereby, to establish patronage relationships with powerful Roman individuals that rested on personal connections rather than a specific office. I have already mentioned the emphasis on the private in Catullus' statue above (Figure 2). The same holds also for the statue for Cornelius Lentulus (Figure 1). He is one of the two reused statues that come with additional information about their honorand.[19] The office mentioned in the dedication to Lentulus is a public, religious one: he is entitled augur, αὔγορα (*IG* II/III² 4102, line 2). As to why this Roman religious offices was included in the dedicatory inscription in Athens, there are several possible explanations, which are mutually reinforcing. A religious office may have seemed appropriate for the location of the statue, the Athenian Acropolis. Further, the mentioning of the augurship highlighted Athens' recognition of Lentulus' prominent position in Rome.[20] Finally, by including Lentulus' prestigious religious office in their caption of his reused statue, the Athenians could emphasize that he was

---

14   On Greek statues and Roman patrons see generally Tanner 2000.

15   On the reference to generational responsibility as a political strategy in public honours, see also Weidgenannt *this volume*.

16   On the different statue types used on the reused statue bases on the Acropolis, including equestrian and column statues, see Krumeich 2008, 2010, 2011, 2014b. On Romans honoured as Greek heroes, see also Vanderpool & Scotton *this volume*.

17   Heller & Van Nijf 2017b, 9, 13. On Greek honorific inscriptions in general, see McLean 2002, 236-237.

18   On the concept of proleptic honours, see Domingo Gygax 2006, 45-57.

19   The other is that of Cn. Acerronius Proculus, proconsul of Achaea in Claudian or Neronian time, who is called proconsul, ἀνθύπατον (*IG* II/III² 4181), probably he received this honour while being proconsul of Achaea.

20   Lentulus' identity is not clear: he may be P. Cornelius Lentulus Spinther, who belonged to the circle of Caesar's murderers (*PIR*² C 1386), yet is it more likely that the statue was rededicated to his son and namesake, consul in 14 BC (*PIR*² C 1379). Both were prominent augurs in Rome (see Rüpke & Glock 2005, 918 no. 1354 and 915 no. 1344).

a dutiful servant of the gods, thereby suggesting that he could also act as a dutiful benefactor of Athens. In any case, the inclusion of his religious office was a strategic move to emphasize that the Athenians appreciated Lentulus' status in Rome and that they expected that he would act in her interests.

The lack of detail – the absence of any information of the office or the nature of the benefaction – may also have been chosen to highlight the perennial, exemplary nature of the act to assist Athens.[21] It also suggested that even without benefaction, the honorand had the right attitude to Athens. Finally, the simplicity of the dedicatory inscriptions and their civilian aspect were grounded in Greek usage, where emphasis was on the duties of citizens, rather than officials, thus adding to the antiquarian and honorific nature of the monument.

The shape of the reused statues as well as the wording of their dedications hence suitably underlined the qualities sought in benefactors. These old statues presented (potential) Roman friends of Athens as energetic, almost godlike warriors fighting for the well-being of the city, or as dutiful men with respect for familial and religious traditions of Athens. These reused statues employed the Athenian past as a political resource to negotiate Athens' relation with Rome. This was also possible because of Rome's fascination with the Athenian past. Several literary works suggest that Athens' past constituted an important asset in her relation to Rome, in that representatives of Roman power were often reminded of the historical achievements of the city in order to gain their goodwill towards Athens (e.g. Plut. *Sul.* 13.4; Cass. Dio 42.14.2, App. *B Civ* 2.88; Tac. *Ann.* 2.53). In this atmosphere, Roman deeds could also be compared to past Athenian achievements, such as Augustus' successes at Actium, which were compared to the Athenian battle of Salamis (Hölscher 1984 and Newby *this volume*) or Nero's campaigns against the Parthians, which were linked to Athens' battle against the Persians (Spawforth 2012, 132 with reference to *IG* II² 1990).

Our inscriptions contain no clear information about the sort of benefaction that may have been expected of the Roman senators thus approached. Other sources reveal that Romans acted as benefactors in Athens by granting fair loans, financing of building works and giving free grain rations.[22] A hypothesis may be thus ventured on the nature of the benefaction of two related monuments, namely those of C. Aelius Gallus and P. Octavius: both held

office in the grain-rich provinces of Egypt and Cyrenaica, suggesting that their benefaction included the shipment of corn to Athens.[23] However, political favours, such as the reduction of taxation or similar, are also conceivable. Given the lack of detail in the inscriptions of the three monuments discussed above, it is not possible to establish what favours were sought from Lentulus, Catullus and Cassius with these rare, reused statue monuments, yet the political influence of the targeted honorands suggests that Athens expected major favours from these men.

What, then, do these reused statues revealed about the relationship of Athens and Rome under the Julio-Claudian dynasty? They show that rather than being a passive recipient of Roman power, Athens actively managed her relation with Rome. This relationship was not one of resistance. Rather, the Athenians gave great honours to prominent Roman politicians, in view of receiving financial or political support in return. The examined monuments suggest that they targeted not only the imperial family,[24] but also some of the most influential senators in Rome, members of powerful senatorial families who were able to occupy crucial positions under Augustus. In order to attract the attention and goodwill of these men, Athens chose to honour them with outstanding and special monuments like the reused statues examined above which highlighted their education, influence and status. Crucial is the question of agency: as in the case of building projects where agency lay with Athens, not Rome (as argued by Dally 2006; Stefanidou-Tiverriou 2008; Morales 2017, 133; Dickenson 2017, 242-50, 258-64), here, too, the Athenian demos actively approached Roman senators for support and assistance. It appeared in the nominative case, while the Roman honorands were placed in a passive position, the accusative.[25] The granting of honours to external benefactors, while inviting Roman support for the city, thus also allowed reaffirming local autonomy in relation to Rome.[26]

That Athens sought external funding for their city need not reflect financial difficulties. Rather, it reveals that the city continued to draw on foreign capital to finance public amenities, now approaching Roman senators

---

21 I propose to return to the exemplary connotations of these reused statues in a future paper.

22 Loans and corn rations: Corn. Nep. *Att.* 2.4-5. Building works: *e.g.* Plut. *Pomp.* 42.11; Cic. *Att.* 6.2.15; and *IG* II² 3175. On the building works associated with the family of Augustus, see n. 1 and n. 24.

23 Egypt: C. Aelius Gallus, *IG* II/III³ 4117 + 3882 = Krumeich 2010, 375 no. A9; Crete and Cyrenaica: P. Octavius, *IG* I² 859 + *IG* II/III² 4156 = Krumeich 2010, 379 no. B3. I thank Dominic Rathborne for this suggestion. For the role of honorific decrees (to local elites) in times of food shortages, see also Weidgenannt *this volume.*

24 On the involvement of the Augustan dynasty in Athens, see Böhme 1995, 42-75; Hoff 2001; Spawforth 2012, 59-86; Dickenson 2017, 147, 260 n. 259, 242-250, 258-264.

25 Already noted by Veyne 1962; see also Ma 2007, 213-215 and Heller & Van Nijf 2017b, 9.

26 On the relationship of local honours and the imperial system, see now Heller & Van Nijf 2017a.

alongside Hellenistic kings.[27] Still, there is no reason to rule out the possibility that part of the costs of their maintenance, including building projects, were paid by Athens and its local elites.[28]

In sum, Athens rededicated old statues to prominent Roman senators to secure their goodwill and benefactions. Given the careful manner of reuse, the choice of the statues and the wording of their dedications, the reused statues constituted a public honour which allowed putting pressure on Roman politicians to fulfil their potential as friends of Athens. As a result, this use of the past as a political resource allowed stressing the importance of Athenian culture while at the same time proclaiming Athens' interest in attracting Roman support and favour.

3. A polity at work

In the previous section, I have argued that the Athenians re-employed several statue monuments as political resources to attract Roman benefactions to their city. The discussion suggested that rather than being weak, resisting subjects of Rome, the Athenians actively shaped their relationship with Rome. The present section proposes to analyze the reused statues as an expression of the political culture within the Athenian polity, as examples of the manipulation of public space in this period. I argue that their reuse allowed highlighting the authority of the city's democratic institutions over the increasingly politicized public space on the Acropolis also against private initiatives from within Athens.[29]

Honorific statues were the result of a political debate and a vote in the city's assembly.[30] In Dio's Rhodes, the reuse of the statues as honorific monuments was decreed by the people; they sent an archon to choose a suitable statue to be rededicated (Dio Chrys. *Or.* 31.9, 52-53, 71). A few glimpses of the coordinated process this necessitated can also be gained from the sanctuary of Athena Lindia (*I.Lindos* II, no. 419), where the reuse of statues was regulated by decree of the demos. According to these regulations, the magistrates (*epistatai*) had the responsibility of auctioning the new inscriptions, documenting the revenues of the sale of each inscription, in order to submit the sums to the sanctuary. But the Lindians had oversight over them and could ask them to certify the funds procured in this way in its equivalent sum in silver (*I.Lindos* II, no. 419, lines 33-40). The reused monuments

from the Acropolis were very likely the result of the same process. As the dedicatory inscriptions reveal, they were set up following a public decree by the demos (and the boule). There is no information about the selection process, yet it is highly likely that in Athens, too, an official was charged with identifying appropriate objects. Possibly, there even existed a list with appropriate monuments.[31]

Public honours were granted by the demos. Yet in the case of the reused statues from the Athenian Acropolis, the role of the demos needs closer examination. For the statues that were reused had been set up as private dedications; in Roman times they were re-appropriated by the demos as public honours.[32] How was this justified?[33] Dio's speech (Dio Chrys. *Or.* 31) is a useful source in this context, as the question of ownership is one very dear to him. Dio criticizes that in rededicating old honorary statue monuments, the city of Rhodes was appropriating the foreign property (that of the former honorand). Dio goes into this question at length: twenty-three paragraphs of his speech are dedicated to elaborating this topic (31.32-56, 134). Amongst other things, he compares the practice to several common abuses of foreign 'property', such as the abduction of women (31.42) or slaves (31.34, 42). Dio warns his audience that the fact that statues were easily appropriated should not be seen as an excuse: after all, to appropriate other people's statues was as iniquitous a practice as was that of appropriating land, money or houses (31.45). Yet the situation was even more complex. For Dio has to concede that the reused statues were in fact the official property of the city of Rhodes: they were erected on civic ground and listed on the public records of the civic property (31.48). The Rhodians had thus every reason to argue that the statues were their property and that they could use them as they pleased. To defend his position, Dio explained that once the statue had been awarded to a benefactor, it was no longer under the control of the city, but had become the property of the honorand (31.47, 54-56).

The issue of property was thus potentially a problematic one in the context of reused statues. The question thus poses itself: who owned the statues that were reused on the Athenian Acropolis? Given the difficulty of establishing the original location of the statues on the Acropolis with any certainty, it remains unclear whether the reused

---

27 See *e.g.* the shift from Hellenistic to Roman funding in the financing of the refurbishment of the Agora discussed in Dickenson 2017, 242-250, 258-264.

28 Migeotte 1995 discusses the evidence for the Hellenistic period.

29 For private strategies to assert control over public space, see Dickenson and Fouquet *this volume.*

30 On the process of awarding honorific statues in Greek cities, see Tanner 2000; Ma 2013, 72-74 and Van Nijf 2015, 2016.

31 See the papyrus from late-antique Egypt listing columns suitable for reuse with information of their measurements, material and state of preservation (*P.Lond.* III 755), discussed in Machado 2017, 335-336. Such lists may also have existed in Athens.

32 Where it is recorded, the statues were set up as private dedications before being reused as public honours in Roman times, see *e.g. IG* I³ 833, 850, 859, 869, 900. *IG* II/III² 3691, 3823, 3850, 3882, 4323, 4915.

33 On the legal aspects involved in the reuse of statue monuments, see Blanck 1969, 14-25 and Harter-Uibopuu 2013.

statues were erected on the public ground between the individual sanctuaries or within them. If erected on public ground, the Athenian demos may (also) have explained that they were listed in the public property lists and thus at its disposal. But even if the reused statues stood on sanctuary ground, there was in principle also the possibility of reusing them. This is suggested by an inscription from the sanctuary of Athena Lindia, which records that some sanctuaries arranged for themselves to sell the right to have one's name inscribed on existing statues, under the premise that this was not to be removed from its original location without a special decree on the matter (*I.Lindos* II, no. 419, lines 30-44).

The problem of ownership seems to have been interlinked with the treatment of inscription on the reused statue bases. According to Dio's evidence, in Rhodes the former dedications were chiselled out to make room for the new dedication. This disentitled earlier benefactors from the commemoration they had once awarded to them (says Dio Chrys. *Or.* 31.9, 71). The situation that presents itself in Athens is slightly different. As noted above, in most cases the name of the former honorand was deliberately retained (8 or 9 monuments, as in the case of Lucius Cassius, Figures 3 and 4) or partly re-inscribed on the stone (6 monuments, as in the case of Lentulus) (see discussion in Krumeich 2014, 75-79). Significantly, these re-inscriptions were carefully done, as the inscriptions of Archinos reveals (*IG* II/III² 4102 = Krumeich 2010, 373 no. A7, Figure 2). The first re-inscription of Archinos' name, written in three lines and in crude lettering, seems to have been replaced by one in smaller, neater letters running parallel to the right side of the base, possibly replacing the less careful inscription which may have been covered with white paint. This suggests that the quality of the re-inscribed inscription mattered and that it was both deliberate and a matter of concern to at least some of the onlookers.[34] Several explanations present themselves. Dio argues that the reuse of statues could affect the city's relationship with their benefactors, and it seems that he is particularly concerned with local benefactors, who did not receive such prestigious reused honours. His speech reflects the political debates of his time regarding the standing of Greek benefactors in the Roman East more generally (see Jones 1978, 26-33; Platt 2006; Ng 2016), so that the question poses itself whether this may have been a problem also in Athens. Here, too, reused statues

were reserved for foreign benefactors.[35] Yet in Athens only private monuments seem to have been reused, so that local benefactors could not claim to have been dispossessed of their publicly decreed honours. In addition, in the process of reuse the Athenians seem to have retained the name of the original dedicatee, in order to show that they welcomed private donations to the sanctuary, as well as the name of the original honorand, whose deed they deemed worthy of emulation.[36] As a result, as in the case of reused metal objects that were reused in sanctuaries, former honorands and dedicatees were not deprived of the commemoration of their deed.[37] Overall, the issue seems to have been one of memory rather than property: while their monuments could be reused, it was important that the names of the original dedicatees and honorands were not forgotten.

By reusing old statues in this way, the democratic institutions of Athens powerfully asserted their authority over the Acropolis, a place of communal remembering. This is particularly noteworthy because in Hellenistic times, this space was dominated by private, family monuments (Keesling 2007; Krumeich & Witschel 2010, 188-189). In this context, the reference to a reused statue on the old agora in Pausanias (Paus. 1.18.3) is perhaps a reflection of the ability of the demos to exert authority also over this space, as it is also reflected in other (new) buildings on the agora.[38] This suggests that the reuse of private dedications as public honours examined above is a neat example of the 'politicization' or 'officialization' of sacred space', in which the private character of the individual votive offering gave way to public control (Ma 2013, 84). In Athens as elsewhere in Hellenistic cities, public space was not 'simply 'produced' by economic or social forces, but the result of creative acts by a civic community' (Ma 2013, 75). A comparison of this evidence from the material in Rhodes, Oropos and the sanctuary of Athena Lindia reveals that Athens seems to have been particularly notable in this respect. According to Dio, in Rhodes mainly public honours were reused. This may also hold

---

34 But see the irregular arrangement of *IG* II/III² 3442. On *IG* II/III² 4119 + 3691 and *IG* II/III² 4117 + 3882 a (shortened) original text was re-inscribed between the feet of the statue and could be read together with the new dedication on the front side.

35 Only one statue may have been reused for a member of the Athenian elite: *IG* II/III³ 3823 + *IG* II/III³ 3912 = Krumeich 2010, 384 no. B8.

36 This is suggested by the two lines of *IG* II/III³ 3882. Here, the name of the dedicatee as well as the honorand were re-inscribed on the top of the statue base when it was rededicated to Aelius Gallus in Roman times, *IG* II/III³ 4117. This may suggest that in the case of monuments where only one name was retained (such as the monument of Archinos/Lentulus, Figure 1) dedicatee and the honorand were identical. However, due to the difficult source situation, this must remain a hypothesis.

37 See Leypold, Mohr & Russenberger 2014, 13.

38 The monument mentioned in Pausanias has not yet been identified. On the assertion of the authority of democratic control over the Agora in this period, see Dickenson 2017, 317-323.

true for the reused statues of the sanctuary of Oropos; however, here the former inscriptions were often erased, so that there can be no certainty whether they had originally also constituted public honours. That said, the preservation of original inscriptions in the reused private dedication of the people of Troezen (*IG* VII 334) may suggest that the other reused statues, where no inscriptions were preserved, were public honours (Löhr 1993, 207-209, Ma 2007). In the sanctuary of Athena Lindia, the reuse probably concerned primarily private dedications to the goddess, yet only those which came without dedicatory inscriptions (i.e. without indication of the identity or memory of the earlier donor, *I.Lindos* II, lines 30-32). By contrast, the Athenian demos saw fit to reuse private dedications which still carried their inscriptions. This was a powerful expression of the authority of its democratic institutions over public space and potentially private property, and one that was directed not so much at Rome but at private individuals from Athens, who saw their scope of action in public spaces on the Acropolis reduced. In sum, the consideration of the reused statues as an expression of polis politics has revealed the extent to which public spaces had become politicized in Roman Athens, and highlight democratising shifts in the handling of public space and memory in the city as it was played out on the Acropolis.

4. Conclusion

To conclude, this article has argued that the reuse of old statues on the Athenian Acropolis was a deliberate strategy to manage both Athens' relationship to Roman power and inner-Athenian debates about public space. In these monuments the past was remembered in a careful, strategic manner in view of gaining Roman support and favour for the city, in that old statues were awarded as public honours to prominent Roman senators who were expected to act as (potential) benefactors for the city. At the same time, the reuse of private monuments as public honours also powerfully asserted the demos' authority over the Acropolis, a crucial place of Athenian memory and remembering. The reused statues thus highlight the dynamism of local politics in the city of Athens under Roman rule and the importance of strategies of remembering in it.

Acknowledgements

Previous versions of this paper were presented at Groningen, Athens and Frankfurt. I would like to thank my audiences at these occasions as well as Onno van Nijf, Florian Forster and my co-editors for their helpful remarks and suggestions. I am also grateful to Ralf Krumeich for the permission to use his illustrations in this article.

References

Alcock, S. 2002. *Archaeologies of the Greek past. Landscape, Monuments, and Memories*, Cambridge.

Anguissola, A. 2014. Remembering with Greek Masterpieces. Observations on Memory and Roman Copies. In: K. Galinski (ed.), *Memoria Romana: Memory in Rome and Rome in memory*, Ann Arbor, 117-136.

Bernhardt, R. 1985. *Polis und römische Herrschaft in der späten Republik (149-31 v. Chr.)*, Berlin.

Blanck, H. 1969. *Wiederverwendung alter Statuen als Ehrendenkmäler bei Griechen und Römern*, Rom.

Böhme, C. 1995. *Princeps und Polis. Untersuchungen zur Herrschaftsform des Augustus über bedeutende Orte Griechenlands*, München.

Bosnakis, D. 2004. Zwei Dichterinnen aus Kos. Ein neues inschriftliches Zeugnis über das öffentliche Auftreten von Frauen. In: K. Höghammar (ed.), *The Hellenistic polis of Kos*. Uppsala, 99-108.

Dally, O. 2006. Athen in der frühen Kaiserzeit. Ein Werk des Kaisers Augustus? In: G. Emanuele & M. Lombardo (eds), *Atene e l'Occidente. i grandi temi, le premesse, i protagonisti, le forme della comunicazione e dell'interazione, i modi dell'intervento ateniese in Occidente. Atti del Convegno internazionale, Atene, 25-27 maggio 2006*, Athens, 43-53.

Day, J. 1942. *An Economic History of Athens under Roman Domination*, New York.

Deininger, J. 1971. *Der politische Widerstand gegen Rom in Griechenland, 217-86 v. Chr.*, Berlin.

Dickenson, C.P. 2017. *On the Agora. The evolution of a public space in Hellenistic and Roman Greece (323 BC -267 AD)*, Leiden.

Domingo Gygax, M. 2006. *Benefactors and rewards in the ancient city. The origins of euergeticism*, Cambridge.

Eilers, C. 2002. *Roman patrons of Greek cities* Oxford.

Geagan, D.J. 1979. Roman Athens: some aspects of life and culture I. 86 BC – AD 267. *ANRW* 2.7.1, 371-437.

Geagan, D.J. 1997. The Athenian elite: Romanization, Resistance, and the exercise of power. In: M.C. Hoff (ed.), *The Romanization of Athens, The Romanization of Athens. Proceedings of an international conference held at Lincoln, Nebraska (April 1996)*, Oxford, 33-52.

Graindor, P. 1927. *Athènes sous Auguste*, Bruxelles.

Griesbach, J. 2014. Jede(r) ist ersetzbar? Zur Wiederverwendung von Statuenbasen im Asklepios-Heiligtum von Epidauros. In: C. Leypold, M. Mohr & C. Russenberger (eds), *Weiter- und Wiederverwendungen von Weihestatuen in griechischen Heiligtümern. Tagung am*

Archäologischen Institut der Universität Zürich 21./22. Januar 2011, Zürcher archäologische Forschungen 2, Rahden/Westfahlen, 55-69.

Habicht, C. 1995. *Athen: Die Geschichte der Stadt in hellenistischer Zeit*, München.

Harter-Uibopuu, K. 2013. Auf dass Ehren ewig währen. Epigraphische Zeugnisse zum Schutz von Auszeichnungen. In: R. Breitwieser, M. Frass & G. Nightingale (eds), *Calamus. Festschrift für Herbert Graßl zum 65. Geburtstag*, Wiesbaden, 245-260.

Heller, A. & O.M. van Nijf (eds) 2017a. *The Politics of Honour in the Greek Cities of the Roman Empire*, Leiden.

Heller, A. & O.M. van Nijf 2017b, Introduction: Civic Honours, from Classical to Roman Times. In: Heller, A. & O.M. van Nijf (eds), *The Politics of Honour in the Greek Cities of the Roman Empire*, Leiden, 1-27.

Hölscher, T. 1984. Actium und Salamis, *JdI* 99, 187-214.

Hoff, M.C. 1989. Civil disobedience and unrest in Augustan Athens, *Hesperia* 58, 267-276.

Hoff, M.C. 1997. Laceratae Athenae: Sulla's Siege of Athens in 87/6 B.C. and its Aftermath. In: M.C. Hoff & S.E. Rotroff (eds), *The Romanization of Athens. Proceedings of an international conference held at Lincoln, Nebraska (April 1996)*, Oxford, 19-35.

Hoff, M.C. 2001. An equestrian statue of Lucius Caesar in Athens reconsidered. *Archäologischer Anzeiger* 4, 583-599.

Hoff, M.C. 2013. Greece and the Roman Republic: Athens and Corinth from the Late Third Century to the Augustan Era. In: J. DeRose Evans (ed.), *A Companion to the Archaeology of the Roman Republic*, London, 559-577.

I.Lindos II = Blinkenberg, Chr. & K.F. Kinch 1941. *Lindos. Fouilles et recherches 1902 – 1914; Fouilles de l'acropole. 2. Inscriptions publiées en grande partie d'après les copies de K. F. Kinch*, Berlin.

Jones, C.P. 1978. *The Roman world of Dio Chrysostom*, Cambridge, MA.

Keesling, C.M. 2007. Early Hellenistic Portrait Statues on the Athenian Acropolis. Survival, reuse, transformation. In: P. Schultz & R. von den Hoff (eds), *Early Hellenistic Portraiture. Image, style and context*, Cambridge, 141-160.

Keesling, C. M. 2010. The Hellenistic and Roman afterlives of Dedications on the Athenian Akropolis. In: R. Krumeich & Chr. Witschel (eds), *Die Akropolis von Athen im Hellenismus und in der römischen Kaiserzeit*, Wiesbaden, 303-327.

Krumeich, R. 2008. Formen der statuarischen Repräsentation römischer Honoranden auf der Akropolis von Athen im späten Hellenismus und in der frühen Kaiserzeit. In: S. Vlizos (ed.), *Athens During the Roman Period: Recent Discoveries, New Evidence*, Μουσείο Μπενάκη 4, Athen, 353-370.

Krumeich, R. 2010. Vor klassischem Hintergrund. Zum Phänomen der Wiederverwendung älterer Statuen auf der Athener Akropolis als Ehrenstatuen für Römer. In: R. Krumeich & Chr. Witschel (eds), *Die Akropolis von Athen im Hellenismus und in der römischen Kaiserzeit*, Wiesbaden, 329-398.

Krumeich, R. 2011. Vom Krieger zum Konsul. Zwei frühklassische Weihgeschenke auf der Akropolis von Athen und ihre Weiterverwendung in der frühen Kaiserzeit. In: O. Pilz & M. Vonderstein (eds), *Keraunia. Beiträge zu Mythos, Kult und Heiligtum in der Antike*, Berlin, 87-104.

Krumeich, R. 2014a. Denkmäler für die Ewigkeit? Zum Fortbestehen kollektiver und individueller Erinnerung bei wiederverwendeten Statuen auf der Athener Akropolis. In: C. Leypold, M. Mohr & C. Russenberger (eds), *Weiter- und Wiederverwendungen von Weihestatuen in griechischen Heiligtümern. Tagung am Archäologischen Institut der Universität Zürich 21./22. Januar 2011, Zürcher archäologische Forschungen 2*, Rahden/Westfahlen Zürich, 71-86.

Krumeich, R. 2014b. Ehrung Roms und Stolz auf die Polis. Zur Repräsentation römischer Magistrate auf der Akropolis von Athen. In: J. Griesbach (ed.), *Polis und Porträt. Standbilder als Medien der öffentlichen Repräsentation im hellenistischen Osten, Studien zur antiken Stadt 13*, Wiesbaden, 141-153.

Krumeich, R. & C. Witschel 2009. Hellenistische Statuen in ihrem räumlichen Kontext: Das Beispiel der Akropolis und der Agora in Athen. In: A. Matthaei & M. Zimmermann (eds), *Stadtbilder im Hellenismus. Die hellenistische Polis als Lebensform 1*, Berlin, 173-226.

Krumeich, R. & C. Witschel 2010. Die Akropolis als zentrales Heiligtum und Ort athenischer Identitätsbildung. In: R. Krumeich & Chr. Witschel (eds), *Die Akropolis von Athen im Hellenismus und in der römischen Kaiserzeit*, Wiesbaden, 1-53.

Krumeich, R. & C. Witschel (forthcoming). *Katalog der Basen statuarischer Weihgeschenke auf der Athener Akropolis (vom 4. Jh. v. Chr. bis zur Spätantike)*.

Leypold, L., M. Mohr & C. Russenberger 2014. Der Umgang mit älteren Weihestatuen in griechischen Heiligtümern. Eine Einführung. In: L. Leypold, M. Mohr & C. Russenberger (eds), *Weiter- und Wiederverwendungen von Weihestatuen in griechischen Heiligtümern: Tagung am Archäologischen Institut der Universität Zürich 21./22. Januar 2011*, Zürcher archäologische Forschungen 2, Rahden/Westfahlen, 11-19.

Löhr, C. 1993. Die Statuenbasen im Aphiareion von Oropos, *AM* 108, 183-212.

Lo Monaco, A. 2016. Wreaths, shields, and old statues. Roman magistrates in the sanctuaries of Greece. In: M. Melfi & O. Bobou (eds), *Hellenistic sanctuaries between Greece and Rome*, Oxford, 206-227.

Luraghi, N. 2010. The Demos as Narrator: Public Honours and the Construction of Future and Past. In: L. Foxhall, H.-J. Gehrke & N. Luraghi (eds), *Intentional History. Spinning Time in Ancient Greece*, Stuttgart, 247-263.

Ma, J. 2007a. Observations on honorific statues at Oropos (and elsewhere), *ZPE* 160, 89-96.

Ma, J. 2007b. Hellenistic honorific statues and their inscriptions. In: Z. Newby & R. Leader-Newby (eds), *Art and Inscriptions in the Ancient World*, Cambridge, 203-220.

Ma, J. 2013. *Statues and Cities. Honorific Portraits and Civic Identity in the Hellenistic World*, Oxford.

Machado, C. 2017. Dedicated to eternity? The reuse of statue bases in late antique Italy. In: K. Bolle, C. Machado & C. Witschel (eds), *The Epigraphic Cultures of Late Antiquity*, Stuttgart, 323-361.

McLean, B.H. 2002. *An Introduction to Greek Epigraphy of the Hellenistic and Roman Periods from Alexander the Great down to the Reign of Constantine (323 B.C. – A.D. 337)*, Ann Arbor.

Migeotte, L. 1995. Finances et constructions publiques. In: M. Wörrle & P. Zanker (eds.), *Stadtbild und Bürgerbild im Hellenismus*. München, 79-86.

Morales, F.A. 2017. The monument of Roman and Augustus on the Athenian Acropolis. Imperial identities and local traditions. In: W. Vanacker & A. Zuiderhoek (eds), *Imperial identities in the Roman World*, London, 141-161.

Ng, D.Y. 2016. Monuments, Memory, and Status Recognition in Roman Asia Minor. In: K. Galinksi (ed.), *Memory in Ancient Rome and early Christianity*, Oxford, 235-360.

Nijf, O. M. van, 2015. Civic Mirrors: Honorific Inscriptions and the Politics of Prestige. In: A.B. Kuhn (ed.), *Social Status and Prestige in the Graeco-Roman World*, Stuttgart, 233-245.

Nijf, O. M. van, 2016. Monuments, mémoire et éducation civique. Les inscriptions honorifiques commes miroirs civiques. In: S. Benoist, A. Daguet-Gagey & C. Hoët-van Cauwenberghe (eds), *Une mémoire en actes. Espaces, figures et discours dans le monde romain*, Villeneuve d'Ascq, 47-65.

Payne, M. J. 1984. *Aretes heneken. Honors to Romans and Italians in Greece from 260 to 27 BC*, East Lansing, MI.

Petrakos, V.C. 1997. Οἱ ἐπιγραφὲς τοῦ Ὀρωποῦ, Athens.

Platt, V. 2006. 'Honour takes wing': unstable images and anxious orators in the Greek tradition. In: Z. Newby & R. Leader-Newby (eds), *Art and Inscriptions in the Ancient World*, Cambridge, 247-271.

Pérrin-Saminadayar, É. 2007. Visites impériales et visites royales à Athènes au 1er siècle de notre ère: histoire et raison d'un rendez-vous manqué. In: Y. Perrin (ed.), *Neronia VII. Rome, l'Italie et la Grèce. Hellénisme et philhellénisme au premier siècle ap. J.-C.*, Brussels, 126-144.

Quass, F. 1984. Zum Einfluss der römischen Nobilität auf das Honoratiorenregime in den Städten des griechischen Ostens, *Hermes* 112, 199-215.

Rose, C.B. 1997. *Dynastic Commemoration and Imperial Portraiture in the Julio-Claudian Period*, Cambridge.

Rüpke, J. & A. Glock (eds) 2005. *Fasti Sacerdotum. Die Mitglieder der Priesterschaften und das sakrale Funktionspersonal römischer, griechischer, orientalischer und jüdisch-christlicher Kulte in der Stadt Rome vom 300 c. Chr. bis 499 n. Chr. 2. Biographien*, Stuttgart.

Rumpf, A. 1964. Zu den Tyrannenmördern. In E. Homann-Wedeking & B. Segall (eds.) Festschrift Eugen v. Mercklin, Waldsassen, 131-151.

Samons, L.J. 2013. Forms and Forums of Public Speech. In: H. Beck (ed.), *Aux origines de l'Hellenisme. La Crète et la Grèce. Hommage à Henri van Effenterre*, Malden, 267-283.

Shear, J.L. 2006. Reusing statues, rewriting inscriptions and bestowing honours in Roman Athens. In: Z. Newby & R. Leader-Newby (eds), *Art and Inscriptions in the Ancient World*, Cambridge, 221-246.

Spawforth, A.J.S. 2012. *Greece and the Augustan Cultural Revolution*, Cambridge.

Tanner, J. 2000. Portraits, Power, and Patronage in the late Roman Republic, *JRS* 90, 18-50.

Stefanidou-Tiveriou, Th. 2008. Tradition and Romanization in the monumental landscape of Athens. In: S. Blizos (ed.), *Athens during the Roman Period. Recent discoveries, new evidence*, Athens, 11-39.

Touloumakos, J. 1967. *Der Einfluss Roms auf die Staatsform der griechischen Stadtstaaten des Festlandes und der Inseln im ersten und zweiten Jhdt. v. Chr.*, Göttingen.

Veyne, P. 1962. Les honneurs posthumes de Flavia Domitilla et les déducaces grecques et latines, *Latomus* 21, 49-98.

Wörrle, M. 1995. Vom tugendsamen Jüngling zum 'gestressten' Euergeten. Überlegungen zum Bürgerbild hellenistischer Ehrendekrete. In: M. Wörrle & P. Zanker (eds.), *Stadtbild und Bürgerbild im Hellenismus*, München, 241-250.

Zanker, P. 1995. Brüche im Bürgerbild? Zur bürgerlichen Selbstdarstellung in den hellenistischen Städten. In: M. Wörrle & P. Zanker (eds.), *Stadtbild und Bürgerbild im Hellenismus*, München, 251-273.

Strategies of Remembering in Greece under Rome: Some Conclusions

Inger N.I. Kuin and Muriel Moser

As I was on my way back from Asia, sailing from Aegina towards Megara, I began to gaze at the landscape around me. There behind me was Aegina, in front of me Megara, to the right Piraeus, to the left Corinth. Once flourishing towns, now lying low in ruins before one's eyes. I began to think to myself: 'Ah! How can we mortals be indignant if one of us dies or is killed, ephemeral creatures as we are, when the corpses of so many towns lie abandoned in a single spot?' (Cic. Fam. 4.5.4 = SB 248.4; trans. Shackleton Bailey)

Approaching the gulf of Athens on his way back to Rome, Servius Sulpicius pondered the death of cities and men. If so many great cities of Greece suffered from abandonment and decline in the Roman present how could one still be touched by the death of one individual? He wrote to console Cicero about the death of his daughter. However, the impression of death and decay that stuck with Servius Sulpicius was likely coloured, on the one hand, by inflated expectations fostered by an education that focused on a romanticized version of the Greek classical city, and, on the other hand, a feeling of Roman superiority about their eastern conquests (Alcock 1993, 28-29).

The articles assembled in this volume have shown the cities of Roman Greece between 100 BC and 100 AD to be places of great vitality, dynamism, and cultural experimentation. Indeed, there is need to review the traditional discourse of weakness about Roman Greece, a view influenced by descriptions such as that from Sulpicius. Attica and the Peloponnese in this period were characterised by important changes in the urban landscape, building projects, and other transformations of public spaces, which suggests that some forms of financing were available in the cities. Urban rearrangements were often accompanied by cultural changes, for instance when cults were revived or imported, as well as renewals of political institutions and structures. Many of these developments can be traced back to the Hellenistic age, such as shifts in the structuring of urban space (Dickenson 2017) or political culture (Heller & Van Nijf 2017). However, these changes were accelerated by the arrival of a new age, the Roman Empire. At the latest under Augustus the cities of Greece had to adapt to new political realities, the administration of its territory in provinces, as well as the founding of 'new' cities, including the colonies of Corinth and Patras. In this period Roman and Hellenistic traditions converged to shape a diverse but shared cultural and political climate in Roman Greece.

The available sources suggest that in the period we set out to investigate, the 1st century BC and 1st century AD, the communities of Greece were motivated to reflect and draw on their past with particular intensity. Cities were full of old heroes and old

in: Dijkstra, T.M., I.N.I. Kuin, M. Moser & D. Weidgenannt (eds) 2017. *Strategies of Remembering in Greece under Rome (100 BC - 100 AD)*, Leiden (Sidestone Press).

religious cults. Public spaces were charged with political and cultural memory. While the authors of the first article, the members of the Roman Seminar, pointed out that a preoccupation with the past was not restricted to Roman Greece or to our period, this volume has sought to show that the areas of Attica and the Peloponnese stood out in these two centuries because there a heightened local interest in the past was compounded by the fascination with the history of the area on the part of the Roman hegemon.

The contributions in this volume collectively illustrate that the increased Roman involvement in the region of Roman Greece constituted a shared, common experience, and, secondly, that agents in their responses to this experience often utilized the past, indicating that there was indeed a shared element in the reaction to these changes. At the same time, however, the articles show that there were significant local differences in *how* the past was used. These differences concern several factors. For what purpose was the past used? What agents were involved? Which media were used to evoke the past? Which past was mobilized, and in what way? This volume has brought together a set of detailed case studies in order to trace a large-scale trend by investigating its constituent local particularities and specificities.

The purposes of using the past, while generally political in a broad sense of the term, ranged widely, from forging new, shared communities for colonists and natives in Patras and Corinth (Dijkstra, Del Basso), to broadcasting elite distinction in Messene (Fouquet, Dickenson), and encouraging benefactions from Romans in Athens (Moser) or Greeks in Achaea (Weidgenannt). Both in Athens (Newby) and Corinth (Vanderpool & Scotton) competition *with* the past could be used as a way of dealing with the new, local status quo. Finally, the past was used as a means of legitimizing new or renewed institutions and laws in Athens and in the Peloponnese (Eckhardt, Kuin). These examples show that in our period the past was utilized for various societal purposes, but always with an eye to the present or even to the future, for instance in the case of future benefactions or monuments that seek audiences beyond one's own lifetime.

In our case studies the first focus is naturally on the agents, those individuals and groups that we see actively mobilizing the past for such aims as just mentioned, but it is also worthwhile to consider who the intended audience is of strategies of remembering. In many of our examples the agents are individual members or families belonging to the local elites, but several articles show other groups taking the initiative as well: the demos (Moser, Weidgenannt), members of professional organizations (Eckhardt), and, in the case of the colonies, newcomers (including freedmen) carving out a position within the existing social fabric (Dijkstra, Del Basso, Vanderpool & Scotton). In Athens the *ephebes* were particularly active in this regard (Newby, Eckhardt), and even political leaders, Athenian *and* Roman, can be seen participating in efforts to activate the past for purposes in the present (Kuin). The range of social groups involved serves as a useful warning against understanding the usage of the past only, for instance, in the context of elite self-presentation: even in a single city different types of agents mobilized the past in different, sometimes competing ways.

It is more difficult to determine the intended audience of the strategies of remembering under consideration, and in many cases there were actually multiple audiences. When the objective is enticing elite Romans to offer benefactions to Athens by offering them re-inscribed old statues an important audience consists, obviously, of elite Romans, but in this case there was also an Athenian audience, since the demos aimed to assert its power over the public space where these statues stood (Moser). Similarly, the planners of the Julian Basilica in Corinth communicated their knowledge of and control over the Greek past to the native population, while also responding to the Augustan building plan in Rome (Vanderpool & Scotton). The ephebic displays of naval battles activated the memory of Athenian military prowess in order to attract Roman attention, but also served to obtain prestige among Athenian peers (Newby). In Patras imperial agents used the past to appeal to the native population, as did the incoming colonists (Dijkstra). In Messene tombs and statues were carefully positioned within the cityscape to make connections with the past, both for the purpose of competing with one's peers locally, but also to appeal to elite Romans, including even the emperor himself (Fouquet, Dickenson). The breadth of actors and audiences involved in strategies of remembering underscores that the use of the past was understood to be a 'language' that would appeal to Greeks and Romans, to elites and non-elites, and to present and future generations.

With regards to the media that were used within different strategies of remembering there is again great variety. Several articles in this volume were concerned with funerary culture, including the location of tombs (Fouquet) as well as the choice of tomb architecture (Dijkstra). Temple architecture (Vanderpool & Scotton), statuary (Dickenson, Moser), epigraphy (Weidgenannt, Eckhardt), reliefs (Newby, Del Basso), and coins (Kuin) were likewise media that could be used to evoke the past. It is perhaps unsurprising that imagery and language are well suited to establishing connections with the past. Several contributions in this volume emphasize, however, that topographical space could also meaningfully be used to evoke the past and activate memory. Connections between past and present are not restricted to textual or figurative media, but can be embedded in the landscape as well.

Finally, while our phrase 'the past' could suggest that a monolithic, unchanging version of Greek history served as the source for the strategies of remembering investigated in this volume, this was certainly not the case. First of all, the Greek Archaic, Classical *and* recent (Hellenistic) pasts were important – so it was not just the Classical period that mattered. Secondly, events from the mythical, heroic past could be as important as 'historical' events (the distinction, in any case, between the realms of myth and history was of course problematic in antiquity). Thirdly, very specific 'slices' of the past could be activated for specific purposes: historical elements of particular festivals, cults, or professional organizations (Dijkstra, Del Basso, Eckhardt); family history (Weidgenannt, Fouquet); the history of statues (Dickenson, Moser); legal history (Kuin); or military history (Newby). Additionally, while these strategies were aimed at the present, the activity of remembering always shapes the past, through the simple process of selection, through embellishment, through emendation, or, in some cases, even through invention.

The past was a flexible resource in many senses of the word: Greek history was employed not only in relation to the representatives of Roman rule, but also to negotiate power relationships within Greek cities like Athens, Messene and Epidauros, as well as social structures among groups of different cultural backgrounds in the Roman colonies of Corinth and Patras. The Greek past constituted a resource for all sorts of political actors in Roman Greece vis-à-vis many different kinds of audiences. It has become clear that, just as not only the distant past was used, the various pasts in questions were not used only at Athens either: the assembled case studies were spread over a wide geographical area, including traditional Greek cities (Messene) and sanctuaries (Epidauros) as well as Roman colonies (Patras). While the experience of change and the interest in the past is shared among the many communities that were studied in this volume, both problems and reactions to them varied locally and over time. For instance, the period between 90 BC and 30 BC seems to have been challenging for many cities, including Epidauros, Athens, and Corinth, but many were able to pursue important building projects by the late reign of Augustus (Corinth, Messene). Our chosen timeframe allowed for highlighting these transitions, but also for a focus on pre-Hadrianic Roman Greece, a period that has traditionally been underserved in the scholarship. In terms of the political landscape, all cities had to come to terms with the fact that honours and influence could now be won outside the traditional parameters by appeal to Roman authorities. At the same time, the strategic importance of Corinth, whence the Roman province of Achaea was governed, increased, to the detriment of other cities. Together the eleven studies in this collection, by showcasing the richness and diversity of strategies of remembering during the 1st century BC and the 1st century AD, highlight that it is a mistake to characterize this period as one of weakness or passivity. The preoccupation with remembering the past in Roman Greece, far from being a form of dejected escapism, was part of a proactive and strategic response to the changes brought by Roman rule. The tapestry of Greek pasts provided a rich and flexible resource in times of great historical change and transformation.

References

Alcock, S.E. 1993. *Graecia Capta: The Landscapes of Roman Greece*, Cambridge.

Dickenson, C.P. 2017. *On the Agora. The Evolution of a Public Space in Hellenistic and Roman Greece (323 BC-267 AD)*, Leiden.

Heller, A. & O.M. van Nijf (eds) 2017. *The Politics of Honour in the Greek Cities of the Roman Empire*, Leiden.

Index

Acropolis 15, 23, 29, 45, 101, 122, 158, 164, 169-171, 173-175, 177-179
Achaea 13, 15, 24-28, 30, 38-41, 62-63, 72, 98, 113, 134, 145, 150, 158, 175, 184-185
Acraephia 23-24, 74, 145, 150
Actium 38, 51, 57, 88, 102, 176
Aeschines 133
Aegina 74, 76, 183
Aelius Gallus 171, 176, 178
Aemilius Paullus 148, 170
Africa 27-28
agon(es) 15, 57, 63, 85, 97-103, 105, 112, 139, 151
agora 15, 24-25, 39-40, 78, 85, 88, 98, 103, 111-112, 116, 118-122, 125-128, 135-137, 139, 150, 157-161, 163, 165, 177-178
Aianteia 85-86, 89, 93
Ajax 85-87, 93
Ammianus Marcellinus 27
M. Antonius 62, 88, 99, 102, 169-170
Aphrodite 74, 77
Apollo 49, 51, 53-54, 63, 101-102, 128, 148-150
Appian 15, 98, 148, 157-159, 163-164, 176
Arcadia 132, 145
Archaic period 15, 23, 26, 38, 49, 55, 61, 78, 101, 105, 125-126, 162, 185
Areopagus 159, 161-163, 166
arete 60-61, 115, 118, 121-122, 147-148, 173, 175
Argolid 145
Argos 23, 98, 100-102, 111, 116, 118-122
Aristion 157-159, 164-165
Aristotle 77, 144, 158-161, 163-164, 166
armour 57-60, 85, 89, 175
Artemis 37-40, 46, 86, 89, 128-131, 139
artist, artistic 50-51, 62-63, 98, 128-129, 132-134, 170, 172
Asklepios 85-86, 126, 128, 137, 148-149
Assmann, Jan 21-22, 25, 28-29, 84
association 14-15, 44, 46, 71-79, 150
Athena Lindia, sanctuary of 170-171, 177-179
Athenion 157-163, 166
Athens 23, 29, 62, 72, 74-75, 77-79, 83-88, 90, 93-94, 97, 111-112, 126, 132, 134, 136, 144, 151, 157-159, 162-166, 169-179, 183-185
Attica 13, 74, 76-79, 85, 183-184
augur 61, 171, 173, 175
Augustales 46, 73-74, 77

Augustus 27, 29, 37-40, 46, 49-52, 55-63, 72, 87-88, 90, 93, 99, 101-102, 131, 136, 145, 169-170, 176, 183, 185

basilica 15, 26, 49-51, 53-57, 60-63, 136, 184
bath(house) 27, 76, 104, 125, 128
battle 14, 23, 28, 38, 57, 59, 75, 83-88, 91-94, 115-116, 122, 169, 176, 184
Bellerophon 51, 101
benefactor 15, 57, 85, 100, 111-113, 115, 119-122, 125, 136-137, 143, 145-151, 170-171, 174-179
benefaction 15, 62, 137, 145, 146, 150-151, 170, 175-177, 184
Boeotia 23-24, 74, 145-148, 150
Bourdieu, Pierre 112, 121, 145
boule 76-77, 151, 159, 161-162, 164, 175, 177
bouleuterion 24, 26, 98, 121, 128-129
Britain 27-28
burial 15, 23, 25-29, 37, 39-47, 85, 87, 101, 111-113, 115-122, 126, 128-129, 133-135, 139-140, 184

Caesar 26-28, 50-51, 56-57, 60-63, 72, 99-102, 111, 150, 171, 173, 175
Cassandreia 73-74
Cassius Dio 50, 60, 88, 97, 111-112, 176
L. Cassius Longinus 111, 171, 173-176
cemetery 28, 40-47, 51, 133
Chorsiae 146-147
Cicero 37, 98, 170-171, 176, 183
Classical period 15, 23, 25, 38, 42, 49, 51, 56, 61, 63, 71, 76-79, 83-87, 89, 93, 99, 103, 111-112, 115, 117-118, 121-122, 125-126, 133, 162, 169, 172, 174, 183, 185
clementia 51, 59, 61
coin(age) 40, 43, 51, 62-63, 76, 99-101, 113, 165, 184
collegia 71-75, 77
colony, colonist 15, 26, 37-44, 46-47, 49-53, 56, 63, 71, 74, 76-77, 97-105, 183-185
commemoration, commemorate 23-30, 37, 40, 44-47, 77, 83-85, 87-88, 90, 93-94, 125, 135, 137, 140, 150-151, 178
competition(s) 14-15, 23, 40, 46, 90, 92, 98-103, 105, 131, 172, 184
Corinth 15, 23, 26, 37, 40, 44, 49-63, 73-74, 77, 97-105, 126, 136, 183-185
P. Cornelius Lentulus 171-173, 175-176, 178

INDEX 187

L. Cornelius Sulla 14-15, 55, 112, 135-136, 148, 157-160, 163-166, 169
crown 24, 74, 85-86, 90-92, 97, 99-103, 105, 134, 139, 148, 150
cultural memory 21, 28-30, 160, 184
damnatio memoriae 139

Damonikos 129, 131, 140
Damophon 128-129
decree (public) 15, 24, 26, 50, 73, 77, 85-88, 93-94, 98, 129, 143, 145-151, 157, 159-164, 176-178
dedication, dedicate 22-23, 26-27, 29, 39, 50-51, 55, 57, 61, 63, 76, 86-87, 101, 126, 129-130, 133, 136-137, 139-140, 158, 169-170, 172-173, 175-179
Democratia 85, 159
democratic, democracy 23, 78, 112, 125, 159-163, 165-166, 169, 177-179
demos 25, 76, 85, 111, 136-137, 139, 150, 169-170, 173, 175-179, 184
Demosthenes 78
Dio Chrysostom 87, 99, 132, 143-144, 147-149, 151, 170-171, 173, 177-178
dionysiac groups 75-77
Dionysios, son of Aristomenes 132-135, 140
Dionysos 24, 26, 39-40, 74, 76-77, 98, 100
Dioskouroi 56-57
Domitian 40, 90, 137-139, 143
donation 25, 76, 178
Dyme 40, 102

Egypt 26, 28, 46, 72-73, 78, 133-134, 176-177
Eigenzeit 145-146, 151
Eleusis 23, 88, 157, 159, 172-173
elite(s) 14-15, 24-25, 27-29, 37, 42-44, 46-47, 62-63, 73-77, 88, 94, 99-100, 115-118, 121, 125, 129-130, 134-136, 140, 146-148, 150, 163, 170, 172, 176-178, 184
ephebes, ephebeia 14-15, 24, 75, 78, 83-94, 101, 105, 115, 118, 134-135, 139, 184
Ephialtes 162
Ephesos 23-24, 72
Epidaurus 145, 148-151, 185
epistatai 177
eranistai 77-79
euergetism 143, 145-146, 148-151
euergetes, s.v. benefactor
Euripides 75-76
Eurypylos 39-40, 46

family, families 23, 25, 37, 41-42, 44-46, 49, 55, 57, 60, 62-63, 75, 79, 84-85, 88, 93, 102, 113, 115, 118-119, 121, 125, 129-130, 133-137, 139-140, 145-151, 170-171, 175-176, 178, 184-185

festival 14-15, 23-24, 39-40, 76-77, 83, 85-90, 92-93, 97-102, 105, 129, 131-132, 135, 139, 148-149, 165, 185
food 23, 102, 143-145, 147-148, 150, 176
forum 27, 49-56, 59-61, 63, 103
freedmen 46, 49, 51, 62, 77, 99, 101, 184

games, s.v. *agon(es)*
Gaul 26-28
gerousiai 72, 73
grain 143-144, 146-149, 151, 176
grave, s.v. burial
gymnasium 73-74, 76, 85, 88, 97-98, 101, 103-105, 112-113, 115, 118, 125-126, 131-135, 139-140, 175

Hadrian 73, 79, 90, 121, 139, 185
Herakles 50, 78, 91, 128, 133, 150
herm 88, 90, 104
Hermes 133-135, 150
hero 15, 23, 26, 29, 39-40, 49, 51, 55, 60, 79, 85-86, 89, 101, 112-113, 122, 126, 128, 133-136, 140, 165, 175, 183
Herodotus 85-86
heroon 23, 79, 112-122, 126
himation 134, 175
Hippodamus of Miletus 160
honour(s), honorand(s) 15, 23-24, 27, 39-40, 52, 62-63, 85-88, 92, 100-101, 111-113, 115-125, 129, 131-137, 139, 145-151, 160, 165, 170-179, 185
honour(s), proleptic 145, 175

institutions 23-24, 26, 71, 73, 75-78, 85, 88, 98-99, 143, 146, 161-163, 166, 170, 177-179, 183-184
imperial cult 29, 40, 63, 74, 113, 136, 139
inscription, honorary 39, 88, 112, 143, 149, 151, 175
Isis 77
Isocrates 84, 162
Isthmia, Isthmian Games 15, 57, 63, 97-105, 120, 132
Isthmus 87, 97-102

Jupiter Optimus Maximus 77

Kalydon 38-39
Kenchreai 119
Knossos 22
Kos 77, 101, 173
kosmetes 75, 78, 90, 92-93, 134

Laphria, Artemis/Diana 37-40, 46
laws 72-74, 79, 90, 158-166, 184
Lentulus, s.v. P. Cornelius Lentulus

lieu de mémoire 15, 112, 121-122
Lindos, s.v. Athena Lindia, sanctuary of
Livy 71, 98, 148, 163
Lycosura 145, 149

Maenads 75-77
Macedonia 13, 16, 25-27, 72, 74, 76, 85, 115, 158
Mantineia 111, 116, 119
Marathon 25, 75, 84-85, 87, 93
mausoleum 41-42, 44-47, 135
Megara 23-24, 77, 79, 122, 145, 183
Mego 129-131
Melicertes 97, 100-101, 105
Messene 15, 111-115, 118, 121-123, 125-129,
    132-137, 139, 184-185
Minyas 29
Mithridates Eupator 136, 157, 159, 165
mnemonic turn 14, 21, 30
mnemotope 15, 39, 44
monument, honorary 111-112, 146, 169, 175, 177
mortuary practices 14-15, 37-38, 40-42, 44, 46-47
Mounichia 85-86, 89, 91-93
L. Mummius 49-52, 97-98, 100

Nemea(n) 98, 100-101, 105
neoi 72-73, 75
Nero 27, 38, 40, 55, 101, 113, 115, 136-137, 139,
    169-170, 175-176
nudity, heroic 56, 134, 175
nymphaion 120, 136

P. Octavius 171, 176
oikist cult 38-40, 46
oligarchy 85, 159-164
Olympia 29, 61, 98, 100, 129, 136
Orgeones 79
Orchomenos 29
Oropos 132, 171-173, 178-179

Palaemon 77, 100-101, 120
Panathenaea 87, 89, 93, 100
Panhellenic 15, 23, 83-84, 97-103, 105, 150
Patras 15, 26, 37-44, 46, 51, 183-185
Patreus 39-40
Pausanias 23, 26, 37-40, 50, 56, 74, 87, 98-101,
    103-104, 113, 115-118, 120-122, 125-126,
    128-129, 133-135, 137, 139, 148, 178
Peirene, spring of 50-53, 101-102, 105
Pella 25
Peloponnese 13-15, 23, 40, 44, 47, 49, 56, 57,
    111-112, 121, 126, 183-184
Pericles 79
Persian (wars) 14, 23, 60, 75, 83-89, 93, 122, 176
Philippi 26, 73-74, 76-77

Philostratus 84, 99, 144
pietas 61
Piraeus 79, 87, 90-91, 157, 183
Plataea 25, 75, 84
Plato, *com.* 87, *phil.* 77, 84-85, 87
Plutarch 25, 50-51, 61-62, 74, 86-87, 97, 100, 111,
    136, 148, 159, 176
Podares 116-118
polis 15, 23-25, 37-38, 40, 43-44, 84, 97-100, 102,
    125-126, 133, 139-140, 144-150, 169-170, 179
Polybius 97-99
Poseidon 97-98, 100-102
Posidonius 157-159, 163
praktores 78
Preugenes 39-40
priest(ess) 24, 40, 46, 77-79, 102, 129, 131, 137
property, public/private 160-161, 177-179

reciprocity 145-148, 151
Rehberg, Karl-Siegbert 143, 145-146, 151
relief 44, 56, 57-58, 83, 90-93, 115, 184
remembrance, remembering 14-16, 21, 23-30, 37-38,
    46, 61, 71-72, 74-75, 77, 80, 83-84, 99, 101, 105,
    112, 115, 118-119, 122, 125-126, 139-140, 143,
    148, 150-151, 166, 178-179, 184-185
reuse of statues 115, 117, 121, 132, 169-179
Rhodes 77, 136, 170-171, 173, 177-178
romanitas 61

Saithidai 113, 115-116, 118, 135-137, 139
Salamis 15, 60, 75, 83-90, 93-94, 176
Sardinia 28
sanctuary 38, 40, 55, 58, 76, 78-79, 86-87, 93,
    97-98, 101-102, 125-126, 128-129, 148-151,
    170-171, 177-179, 185
sebasteion 128-129, 136
Second Sophistic 21-22, 25
Seleucids 24
senator, Roman 111, 122, 170, 172, 175-177, 179
Sarapis 77
Sikyon 97-98, 101-102, 121
Silvanus 77
social capital 112, 145, 151
Solon(ian) 79, 159, 162-163, 165
Sparta(ns) 39, 51, 56-57, 60, 62, 74, 84, 94, 113,
    118, 122, 126, 134, 145
space, public 51, 62, 88, 111, 125-126, 131, 139-140,
    169-170, 177-179, 183-184
stadium 97-98, 103, 112-113, 115, 131, 135, 139
statue(s) 15, 23-24, 27, 38-40, 44, 49-50, 55-63, 87,
    98, 102-103, 111-112, 115, 117, 121, 125-134,
    146, 148-149, 165, 169-179, 184-185
statue(s), honorific 15, 98, 102-103, 111-112,
    125-126, 129, 169-171, 173, 175, 177

statue base 23, 45, 63, 87, 112, 115, 121, 129-139,
    149, 151, 171-173, 175, 178
stele 41, 43-44, 48, 77-78, 89, 93, 100, 113, 115,
    122, 134
Strabo 16, 98-99, 101-102, 105, 121
Sulla, s.v. L. Cornelius Sulla
synodoi 71, 78-79

temple 15, 23-27, 29, 38-39, 42, 44-46, 49-55, 63,
    74, 102, 113, 116-117, 128, 135, 139, 149-151,
    184
Teos 24, 79
theatre 27-28, 51, 56, 73-74, 103-104, 115-117, 122,
    125-126, 129, 139, 150
Theon 132-134, 140
Thermopylae 84, 122
Thessaloniki 25, 57, 73-74, 76

thiasoi 71, 75-77
Thisbe 147
tomb, s.v. burial
Tyrannicides 14, 111-112, 121, 165
L. Valerius Catullus 171-173, 175-176

victory list 99-102, 104
virtue, s.v. *arete*
Vitruvius 49, 53-54, 103

warrior(s) 60, 85, 175-176

Xenophon 84, 87
xoana 26

Zeus 85-86, 98, 129, 150